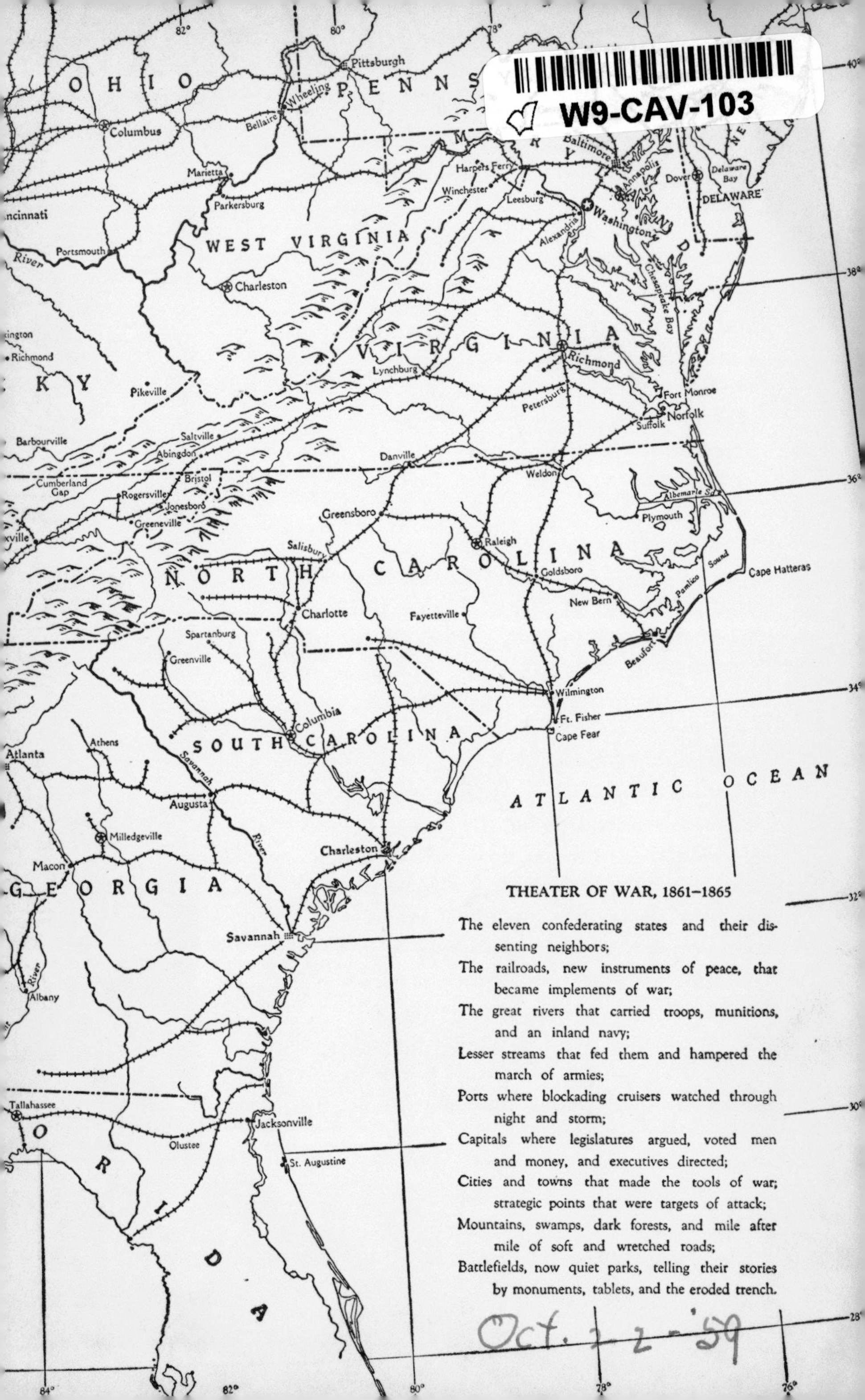
OHIO
PENNS
Pittsburgh
Wheeling
Bellaire
Columbus
Marietta
Parkersburg
Cincinnati
Portsmouth
River
WEST VIRGINIA
Charleston
Harpers Ferry
Winchester
Leesburg
Baltimore
Annapolis
Dover
Delaware Bay
DELAWARE
Washington
Alexandria
Chesapeake Bay
VIRGINIA
Richmond
Lynchburg
Petersburg
Fort Monroe
Norfolk
Suffolk
Danville
Weldon
Albemarle Sd.
Plymouth
K Y
Richmond
Pikeville
Barbourville
Saltville
Abingdon
Bristol
Cumberland Gap
Rogersville
Jonesboro
Greeneville
Greensboro
Salisbury
Raleigh
NORTH CAROLINA
Goldsboro
New Bern
Pamlico Sound
Cape Hatteras
Charlotte
Fayetteville
Beaufort
Spartanburg
Greenville
Wilmington
Ft. Fisher
Cape Fear
Columbia
SOUTH CAROLINA
Athens
Atlanta
Savannah River
Augusta
Milledgeville
Macon
GEORGIA
Charleston
ATLANTIC OCEAN
Savannah
River
Albany
Tallahassee
Olustee
Jacksonville
St. Augustine
FLORIDA
82°
80°
78°
40°
38°
36°
34°
32°
30°
28°
84°
76°
THEATER OF WAR, 1861–1865
The eleven confederating states and their dissenting neighbors;
The railroads, new instruments of peace, that became implements of war;
The great rivers that carried troops, munitions, and an inland navy;
Lesser streams that fed them and hampered the march of armies;
Ports where blockading cruisers watched through night and storm;
Capitals where legislatures argued, voted men and money, and executives directed;
Cities and towns that made the tools of war; strategic points that were targets of attack;
Mountains, swamps, dark forests, and mile after mile of soft and wretched roads;
Battlefields, now quiet parks, telling their stories by monuments, tablets, and the eroded trench.

LINCOLN FINDS A GENERAL

THE MACMILLAN COMPANY
NEW YORK • CHICAGO
DALLAS • ATLANTA • SAN FRANCISCO
LONDON • MANILA
IN CANADA
BRETT-MACMILLAN LTD.
GALT, ONTARIO

Courtesy Library of Congress

MAJOR GENERAL JOHN M. SCHOFIELD

KENNETH P. WILLIAMS

LINCOLN
FINDS A GENERAL

*

A Military Study of the Civil War

WITH MAPS BY CLARK RAY

VOLUME FIVE

Prelude to Chattanooga

NEW YORK

THE MACMILLAN COMPANY

1959

FIRST PRINTING

PRINTED IN THE UNITED STATES OF AMERICA

The Macmillan Company, New York
Brett-Macmillan Ltd., Galt, Ontario

Library of Congress catalog card number: 49-11530

ACKNOWLEDGMENTS

PERMISSION to quote copyrighted material is acknowledged to publishers and authors as follows: Longmans, Green & Co., Inc.—*Grant, Lincoln and the Freedmen* by John Eaton, copyright, 1907, by Longmans, Green & Co., Inc.; James T. White & Co.—*The National Cyclopedia of American Biography,* copyright, 1904, by James T. White & Company; W. W. Norton & Company—*Memoirs of a Volunteer, 1861–1863* by John Beatty, copyright, 1946, by W. W. Norton & Company; Charles Scribner's Sons—*The Ordeal of the Union* by Allan Nevins, copyright, 1947, by Allan Nevins; The Torch Press, Cedar Rapids, Iowa—*Quantrill and the Border Wars* by William Elsey Connelley, copyright, 1910, by William Elsey Connelley; The University of North Carolina Press—*General Jo Shelby, Undefeated Rebel* by Daniel O'Flaherty, copyright, 1954, by The University of North Carolina Press.

The address which appears as one of the endpapers of this volume was delivered by Lincoln to Grant at a ceremony in the White House on March 9, 1864 and is reproduced by kind permission of Major General U. S. Grant III.

PUBLISHER'S PREFACE

THE PROVIDENCE that presides over our affairs does not always arrange them as tidily as we might wish. A year or two more of life could so easily, it seems, be awarded to a statesman or poet or historian who has work to finish and asks only for time in which to do it. The scheme of things is not so ordered, we know, but it does not make it easier to understand.

Kenneth P. Williams died of intestinal cancer in the Bloomington Hospital, Bloomington, Indiana, on September 25, 1958. From the day, late in 1955, when he put the finishing sentence to the manuscript of Volume IV of *Lincoln Finds a General* he had been working steadily on the manuscript of Volume V. During these three years his writing was interrupted by a major operation in the summer of 1957, and he suffered a fatal relapse, which drained his physical vitality but not in any sense his mental vigor, in the early summer of 1958.

As was his habit, the precise habit of a mathematician, after each chapter of Volume V was written, he submitted it to one or two trusted friends, considered their criticisms or suggestions, revised where he felt it necessary, and then added the very full notes which are a feature of his work. It was very rare that he ever returned to a finished chapter to make alterations, unless in the course of later reading he turned up some new fact that he felt was vital. Thus the nine chapters that make up the present volume are exactly as he would have published them had he lived.

In an outline which he dictated only some weeks before his death, he wrote: "As to the first eight chapters a comment seems to be in order. I was a little afraid that the first five chapters, dealing with the Mississippi Valley subsequent to the capture of Vicksburg, were too expanded, being especially concerned about Chapter V where Schofield's difficulties were treated. I was greatly relieved when a friend in November, 1957, expressed special approval of Chapter V. In fact he stated that the first five chapters could be called 'The Unknown War.' This is perhaps an exaggeration, but it is true that even the siege of Port Hudson is frequently passed over hastily, as the comments I make in my notes indicate. The treatment in Chapter IV of the Texas-Mobile question is, as far as I recall, the first adequate analysis of this important matter which is sometimes very inaccurately or inadequately set forth. Likewise Chapters VI and VII fill in months that Rosecrans spent in Murfreesboro that are usually ignored or hastily summarized. When Chapter VIII was reread to me upon my return from the hospital, I did at times wonder whether it was too detailed. Rosecrans's advance to Tullahoma and Manchester is, however, another operation which usually receives no more than a few laudatory sentences."

A few more weeks were left him, after the writing of the outline, in which he was able to compose and finish to his satisfaction Chapter IX, "Chickamauga," which is the concluding chapter in the present volume. Of Chapter IX and what he had planned for the two remaining chapters he wrote:

"I think that there is a chance to make the last of this volume as important and interesting as anything I have previously written. It will include the great battles of Chickamauga and Chattanooga, and the siege of Knoxville, as well as other events leading up to the appointment of Grant as general in chief. Chickamauga had the effect of raising Grant to the command of the Division of the Mississippi, a very important outcome of Rosecrans's defeat. After the Battle of Chattanooga, the next step was a logical one.

"I do not know how full these chapters can be. Chickamauga and Chattanooga should not be slighted, for they were great dramatic events and there has been much argument and disputing about them. However, I have taken so much space in the first eight chapters that a more condensed treatment for the latter ones seems indicated. This would probably be to the good, for it would increase the pace of the narrative and probably its readability."

The personal misgivings which he expressed in the outline were the misgivings which his publishers had come to expect. All of the volumes of *Lincoln Finds a General* follow a certain pattern. Each of them opens with a detailed and leisurely examination of operations, some of which to the reader avid for battles may seem unimportant but which reveal a part of the grand design of the war which the author always had well in mind. These chapters are in a sense the preparation for the climactic battle. In Volumes I and II it is Gettysburg; in Volume III it is Shiloh; in Volume IV, the Vicksburg campaign. In Volume V it is Chickamauga, to be followed by Chattanooga. Against these personal hesitations, that the earlier chapters might be too detailed, was placed the justification that in writing as fully of the Hills of Helena or the capture of Port Hudson he was writing history that had not been adequately covered before.

Of the two remaining chapters, Chapter X, which he had dictated but which was still not, in his own words "a well considered chapter," would have told of Grant's trip to Cairo on orders from Halleck. The summons had been dispatched on October 3 and reached Grant in Vicksburg on October 10. There would have followed Grant's arrival at Chattanooga "wet, dirty and well," his establishing on General "Baldy" Smith's suggestion a supply route, the arrival of Sherman who was now commander of the Department of the Tennessee, the planning for the raising of the siege of Chattanooga, and finally the battle itself. In this chapter the operation which Longstreet conducted against Burnside at Knoxville would have received for the first time the extended treatment that it deserves.

"It seems to me that it was one of the most interesting and instructive campaigns of the war. As Burnside was holding down well toward Chattanooga, Longstreet had hoped that he could inflict severe damage to him before he could get back to Knoxville. There was brilliant maneuvering by both sides in the Federal retirement on the city while heavy efforts were being made to put the place in defensible condition. Even though the treatment is not expanded, it should be possible to have some pages that will do more than limit the operation to Longstreet's failure to carry Port Sanders. In studying this attack I was amazed to find out how careful the preparations were, both for the attack and the defense. For instance, the choice had to be made, as in later days, between a long artillery preparation and a very short one with an effort at surprise. It looks to me as if Burnside had handled everything very well, and Longstreet pays him tribute for his usual gentlemanly character in immediately providing an opportunity for the removal of Longstreet's killed and wounded."

Chapter XI, the concluding chapter, was one on which Kenneth Williams had hoped to expend especial care since he considered it perhaps the most important chapter in the volume. Like Chapter X it had been dictated in outline, and the text is interspersed with many suggestions for possible sources of research. The chapter opens with the arrival of Grant in Washington on March 8, 1864, little more than two months after the November victory of Chattanooga, to receive the next day from the President his commission as Lieutenant General and the command of all the armies of the United States. "In Washington, few, if any, knew that Lieutenant Grant in 1852 had made a hurried trip to the capital to press a claim for the recovery of $1,000 of quartermaster funds that had been stolen from him on duty in Mexico, and for which he had not been reimbursed in spite of the fact that an investigating board had held him guiltless of carelessness. It will be recalled that the young officer found all Government buildings closed because of the funeral of the great Whig leader Henry Clay. Whether recollection of the trip in 1852 flashed through Grant's mind at any time during his journey can only be conjecture, but it would have been strange if he had not reflected on the turn of events which had finally brought him a presidential summons to the capital." A note in the author's handwriting points out that it was not until June 17, 1862, that the President had signed "an act for the relief of Lieutenant Ulysses S. Grant."

Careful comparison would have been made of all the newspaper material that he had had searched and read to him, and an accurate account, using memoirs and histories and the newspapers of the time, would have been written of the unheralded arrival of the quiet and composed general. The simple ceremony in which the President read aloud the paper containing four sentences in which he awarded Grant his commission and Grant's reply would have been given in full. "The President explained to Grant that he wished him to say something that would prevent him from being an object of jealousy to any other generals in the service, and to say something that would put him on good terms with the Army of the Potomac. Grant paid no attention to these requests. Instead he read from a small square of yellow cartridge paper, which he drew from his pocket, the very appropriate and gracious reply:

" 'Mr. President, I accept the commission, with gratitude for the high honor conferred. With the aid of the noble armies that have fought in so many fields for our common country, it will be my earnest endeavor not to disappoint your expectations. I feel the full weight of the responsibilities now devolving on me; and I know that if they are met, it will be due to these armies, and above all to the favor of that Providence which leads both nations and men.' "

But the most important material in the chapter was to have been a detailed analysis of Grant's plans for the final campaign. On March 11 he had started for Nashville to meet and consult with Sherman, and on his return to Washington he took up his headquarters on March 26 at Culpeper Court House a few miles south of Meade's headquarters. "The primary object of his going to Washington was the working out of a system of command for all the armies. He had an entirely new position. He was not replacing Halleck. Halleck had consented to remain as chief of staff in Washington, thus releasing Grant for service in the field. Genius was shown in the decision adopted to have a headquarters in the field and also one in Washington. This fact has not been sufficiently stressed." Grant's detailed instructions to General Butler for his part in the spring campaign would have been set forth. His orders to Hunter, appointed to supersede Sigel in the Kanawha and Shenandoah valleys, would have been examined. The results of his consultations with Sherman would have been noted. Finally, three plans of operation open to him for his own campaign and the reasons for his final decision to turn Lee's right flank would have been fully discussed.

"I stress here [in the outline] the possibilities of this chapter, both from the personal side of Grant's visit to Washington and his reception there, and the later major decisions that he made. The latter are, of course, by far the most important, and are what should receive proper emphasis. None of this will be easy to do."

"An effort would have been made to check the various accounts against one another." Kenneth Williams was a fiercely honest historian; he had visited and carefully examined every battlefield which he described, and he possessed the military training which made the *Official Records* yield their priceless meaning. Nothing aroused him so much as inaccuracy or falsehood when it involved the character of his hero. In an Appendix on Grant's accident in New Orleans on September 4, 1863, which he had not completed to his satisfaction and which for that reason is not included here, he pointed out in the first two pages two serious errors by other historians. Lloyd Lewis in his book on Sherman had written: "Hysteria ran through the North. Telegraph wires sang with fear. Grant was fast in a New Orleans bed, his leg and side swollen from an accident received in the fall of his saddle horse." In actual fact, having consulted the newspaper files for New

York, Washington, and Chicago, Kenneth Williams had established that the newspapers either did not even report the accident, or, if they did, treated it as a minor mishap. Another historian, writing later, had asserted that at the review at Carrollton of the 13th Corps on September 4, Grant was "so bored that he had taken to the bottle again" and suffered "the indignity of falling out of his saddle at the review." But New Orleans newspaper accounts of September 5 and 6, obtained through his friend Colonel H. G. Esden, made it clear that the accident occurred subsequent to the review, on Grant's ride back to New Orleans, and that he did not fall off his horse, but that the beast, terrified at a locomotive whistle, shied and fell on his rider. "Quiet, undemonstrative and reserved though Grant was, this writer believes that he was not 'bored' but deeply touched by the deafening cheers that greeted his and Banks's arrival, by the well drilled regiments of foot and horse, and by the skillfully handled batteries. This was the corps he had commanded before he was given the Army of the Tennessee! The riddled regimental colors that were dipped to him had received their holes in *his* battles; the undipped National colors to which he raised his hand in salute he had often seen on hard marches, or standing steady or advancing under heavy fire." What other historian would have known that regimental colors are dipped to the reviewing officer and that the National colors are to be saluted by him?

Kenneth Williams was never afraid to write a clumsy and tortuous sentence if it was needed to convey exactly what he felt must be said, and he fumed at the unfortunate copy editor who attempted to cut his way through the thicket and thereby in any way altered or diminished his meaning. Nevertheless it must not be lost sight of that he also possessed sober and massive virtues of style. In many passages through the five volumes he rose to the occasion. No one who has read it will ever forget the passage on page 5 of Volume I which describes young Brigadier General Wilson watching his artillery cross the Rapidan:

"As he waited and watched, Wilson . . . probably observed with special interest the handling of the artillery teams, noted whether the lead and swing drivers got their pairs into draft where the pulling was bad, and whether the wheel drivers could make the 'off' horses throw themselves properly into their harness. Guns are grim-looking things, especially in the half-light of dawn as they come up from a river, well handled by skillful drivers, and vanish into shadowy woods. The six two-gun sections with their capable-looking cannoneers must have given the experienced Wilson a feeling of reassurance as he left the river and rode to the head of his column. It was probably well for him that these woods were unfamiliar and did not evoke memories. Though a newcomer to the Army of the Potomac, he had known hard campaigning and bitter fighting in the West, at Vicksburg and Chattanooga, where woods had been as dark and roads as difficult; but his mind was not preyed upon nor dulled by the recollection of past defeat."

This is writing of the highest order, informed by expert military knowledge and colored by imagination. Such passages star the pages of all five volumes, and by themselves redeem them from any charge of excessive detail.

Had he lived it is probable that Kenneth Williams would have carried the scope of the work beyond the day in March, 1864, when "the experienced and modest Grant met Lincoln, also experienced and equally modest," and received from the President his commission as Lieutenant General. His original theme had expanded into a military history of the Federal Armies in the Civil War, as one reviewer of Volume IV has described it, "a major work of scholarship written in the grand style on a grand scale." But this was not his original intention when he began the work. "Lincoln's chief military problem was to find a general equal to the hard task the North faced in the Civil War." This is the first sentence of the Preface to Volume I. He had planned two more volumes which would have covered the last year of the war and included Sherman's campaigns, the Wilderness, Petersburg, and the final "pursuit that had a perfect ending," and had he been granted another two years of life he would have written them.

Yet during these last days on his hospital bed, too weak to write or even to dictate, and in too much pain to be read to, Kenneth Williams must have been satisfied that he had completed his original task. The long search was over. Lincoln had found his General, as Grant had found his Historian.

CONTENTS

ILLUSTRATIONS

MAPS

CHAPTER I

THE HILLS OF HELENA

If both factions, or neither, shall abuse you, you will, probably, be about right. *Lincoln to Schofield*

They hurled regiment after regiment in close column against the works. *Colonel Samuel A. Rice*

AT THE very hour when the men of one of Grant's divisions were forming ranks after dusting off their uniforms and rubbing up their rifles, to march into Vicksburg, the Confederates were making a desperate attack against the defenses that circled Helena. Just one half-hour before the Federal flag was raised above the Vicksburg courthouse, their guns fell silent in failure. This was Independence Day, 1863.

Responsibility for the daring venture, in which casualties were high, must be placed upon Lieutenant General Theophilus A. Holmes, commanding the District of Arkansas, which was part of the large Confederate Trans-Mississippi Department. Holmes had, however, the solace of knowing that such an effort had been approved and urged by Seddon, the Secretary of War. And General Kirby Smith, the commander of the department, actually placed full responsibility upon Seddon because of a letter that the Secretary had written to General Joe Johnston, then collecting the forces with which he was hoping to extricate Pemberton from Vicksburg. The hour was late he well knew, the Secretary wrote, but even if Vicksburg fell, the capture and holding of Helena would "secure a great future advantage to the Confederacy." He ended his letter: "Had I command of communications, this suggestion would be directly addressed and pressed by the

Department. Its policy is so apparent that it is hoped it will be voluntarily embraced and executed."

An extract from Seddon's letter safely crossed the Mississippi and was soon in Kirby Smith's headquarters in distant Shreveport, where, on June 13, Smith's adjutant added a circumspect indorsement addressed to Holmes, whose headquarters were at Little Rock. The department commander could not, the adjutant declared, give actual orders in the case: he did not know the strength of the enemy force at Helena, a strength which was "continually varying." Holmes was handed the problem of decision: "It is, therefore, submitted to Lieutenant-General Holmes to act as circumstances may justify." [1]

Before the reader watches that general make his Helena decision, he should look at the Confederate situation west of the Mississippi, particularly in Holmes's district, for Holmes has been something of a scapegoat.

Kirby Smith could certainly have used more men in the three districts which composed his department—provided they had weapons. But actually he did not have enough arms for the men he had. Vicksburg, as Grant found, had more than enough good rifles for Smith's needy men, but to transfer them safely across the Mississippi had been very difficult after the Federals had gained control of the river between Vicksburg and Port Hudson. Weeks previously, Major General Frank Gardner, commanding at Port Hudson, had issued to his men excellent Enfield rifles and other equipment that Richmond had "distinctly marked for Lieut. Gen. E. Kirby Smith." Called upon to explain, Gardner had said that they could not "be forwarded." [2]

Only half of the 12,000 men with which Hindman had fought the disastrous battle of Prairie Grove against Blunt and Herron in December, 1862, had been in the retreating column that arrived at Little Rock. And they were so tattered, hungry, and low in spirit that they had little combat value. Then came a hard winter which many of the men passed—according to Holmes—"without tents and scarcely with clothing to cover their nakedness." Medical officers blamed the extensive sickness not only on exposure, but also on food —"poor beef and corn-bread being the only diet."

Some of the valiant 6,000 died. Ranks thickened, however, when Holmes issued an order that deserters would not be tried if they were back by February 1. By early March Holmes could write to Jefferson Davis that the morale of Hindman's division was entirely restored, and that if lost arms could be replaced the division would be in excellent condition. Perhaps a greater restorative of spirits even than the coming of spring was the return of Sterling Price from east of the Mississippi, where he has been seen in the battles of Iuka and Corinth. To the many Missourians in the division it was a great tonic again to be under the colorful former governor of their state.

When May ended, Holmes's forces totaled 1,421 officers and 17,712 men present for duty out of a total present of 22,264, and an aggregate present and absent of 34,551. But in mid-June Holmes suffered the loss of John G. Walker's division, which, after its futile blow at Milliken's Bend, was transferred to Major General Richard Taylor's District of Louisiana; along with it there went a brigade that had belonged to Sterling Price. Nor was that all. Kirby Smith took from Holmes a brigade of infantry and one of cavalry—to harass Federal plantations near Lake Providence, "and to annoy, and, if possible destroy their transports." [3]

The name of Holmes's district was deceptive. He was also responsible for Indian Territory, and it was very hard to keep faithful the tribes which were aligned with the Confederacy, especially since the Indian country itself had been so completely exhausted that breadstuffs had had to come from Texas—a haul so long that teams ate half their loads on the way. Holmes's commander in the subdistrict, Brigadier General William Steele, had reported on March 31 that he thought all of the Choctaws were loyal, in addition to part of the Cherokees. But he had discovered a disillusioning trait in his red men: "The disposition to drain all that can be gotten from the public crib exists with the Indian as well as with the white." And a visitor was equally unflattering about Fort Smith, Steele's headquarters town. It was, he said, "a filthy sink of corruption and iniquity, inhabited chiefly by a foul, speculating horde, our enemies at heart, who sell the comforts of life to Confederate soldiers at ten prices." [4]

Before the coming of Kirby Smith in March, the New-York-born Steele—a West Point classmate of Sherman and George Thomas—had regarded himself as a department commander, and inexplicably he soon lapsed into again calling his domain the Department of the Indian Territory. A touch of insubordination showed itself when in May he complained to Adjutant General Cooper that while Holmes had allowed him great latitude, Kirby Smith had withdrawn troops from him in the midst of a campaign, "by orders to my subordinates, without a copy or even a note of explanation." The result, he explained in a letter to Kirby Smith's chief of staff on June 8, had been lamentable. Federal Colonel William A. Phillips had been able to fortify Fort Gibson, near the junction of the Arkansas and Neosho rivers, twenty miles southwest of Tahlequah. According to Steele, that post was a veritable showplace for Unionism, where Colonel Phillips "put his well-clothed and supplied allies in contrast with the poorly clothed and badly equipped Indians who had remained true to the South." [5]

Yet, as June was ending, there were faltering hearts beneath the Federal Indians' finery. The Indians had shown a true devotion to the cause and had made almost superhuman efforts to hold their country, Major General James Blunt, commanding the District of the Frontier, with headquarters at Fort Scott, Kansas, reported to Schofield at St. Louis on June 26. The three regiments in Phillips's command had all been mustered in as infantry, but some of the men in each of them had mounted themselves on their own horses, and the animals which had been lost were worth more than the pay that was due the owners. The earthworks that the Confederates had thrown up across the Arkansas, together with a little ineffective shelling, and the nonarrival of promised white troops, had begun to discourage the Indians, Blunt reported. At the moment there were on the way to Fort Gibson a train of supplies and 1,600 more men, including the First Kansas Colored Volunteers. The accession would, Blunt thought, "inspire confidence in the Indian troops." [6]

A raid across the Arkansas below Fort Gibson that Steele had staged earlier in the month had been met and repelled by such cavalry as Phillips had, an accompanying howitzer being particularly effective in the skirmish of "Greenleaf Prairie." Then, two days before Blunt wrote to Schofield, Steele reported to Kirby Smith that with his Indians, and without artillery support, it would be foolish to attempt to take Fort Gibson. He was accordingly attempting to force Phillips away by cutting off his supplies, "with a good prospect of success." When within a matter of hours a report came about Blunt's supply train, Steele dispatched 1,000 mounted white troops and 600 Indians under Colonel Stand Watie—described by Steele as "above the ordinary mark"—to intercept and capture it.[7]

Matters were shaping for a colorful clash.

Turbulent, guerrilla-infested Missouri was also in Holmes's district. On May 27 he directed that Sterling Price proceed with two of his brigades to the vicinity of Jacksonport, and assume command of all Confederate troops in the vicinity and northward to the Missouri border. Price was also charged with superintending the recruiting service in northern Arkansas and Missouri, from which, it will be

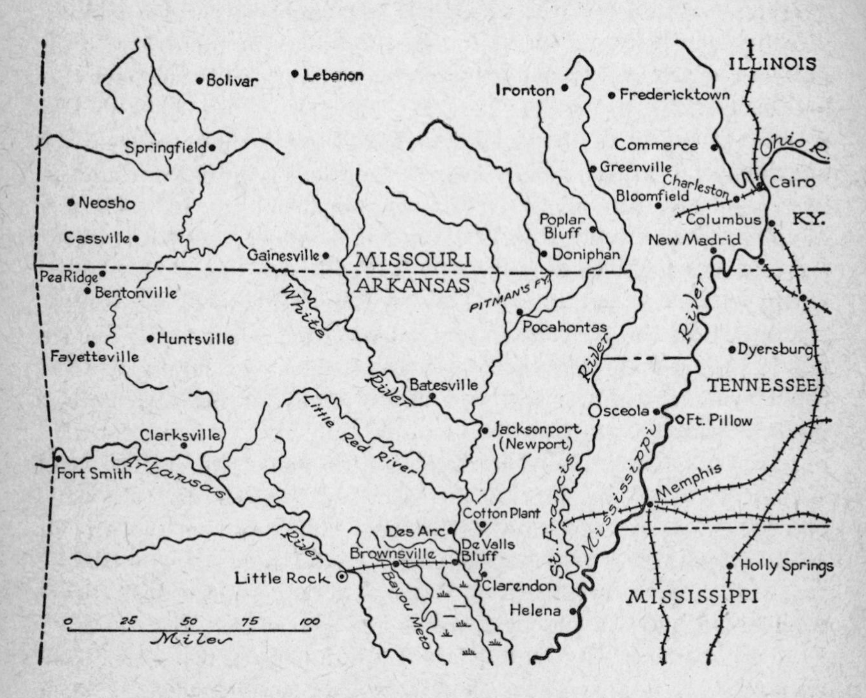

THE MISSOURI-ARKANSAS THEATER

recalled, he had sought in the fall of 1861 to draw 50,000 men to his banners. In Missouri the guerrillas were more than ordinarily vicious, and local conflicts especially deep-rooted and cruel, because of the blood that had been spilled over the question of slavery or freedom in Kansas—which had had so much to do with the effort to break the Union. And Missouri Unionists, on their part, were luxuriating in what Lincoln called "a pestilent factional quarrel." In a letter to Schofield three days after the general had on May 24 assumed command of the Department of the Missouri, the President explained that he had relieved Curtis because Curtis—"perhaps not of choice"—was heading the faction arrayed against the faction of Governor Gamble. Though no stranger to Missouri strife, it was a hard position to which the thirty-one-year-old Schofield—another New Yorker —was assigned, and Lincoln advised, "If both factions, or neither, shall abuse you, you will, probably, be about right. Beware of being assailed by one and praised by the other." [8]

Although Sterling Price was pleased when the Missouri convention, of which he was president, voted negatively on the motion to secede, no one was afterward more ardent in his support of the Confederacy, and his presence just below Missouri's southern border could not but revive the hopes of her hard-core Secessionists, and quicken the activities of every clandestine agent seeking to draw new soldiers from the state. Any idea that Price should strike into the state was discouraged in a letter that Kirby Smith wrote to Holmes at about the time Price arrived at Jacksonport. Smith thought any such move would be unwise unless made with a force strong enough to give reasonable hopes of tenure. He likewise condemned Marmaduke's recent proposal of the use of guerrilla bands; they merely caused, Smith said, "new persecution and misery on our friends there, without advancing the cause one jot or tittle." [9]

In the order in which he assumed command on June 6, Price bade all officers to use diligence in putting their commands in shape for active service, and issued directions with regard to recruiting. Then he launched into a long denunciation of the behavior of the troops that had previously been occupying the area. The defection of his son and two years of marching and fighting had not enfeebled Sterling Price's vocabulary, and he stated that only by strict adherence to the "rules of Christian warfare" was it possible to build a well-disciplined and invincible army that could not only drive the enemy beyond the Confederacy's borders, "but pursue him into his own accursed land." [10]

There was no doubt as to Price's target: Marmaduke. And before the day was ended, that officer had written a long protest against the sweeping character of Price's charges. He did not claim that his men had "done no wrong or perpetrated no outrage" during his April raid into Missouri, but he did assert that he had sought to punish the guilty, and he represented that many of the acts complained about were those of organized bands of deserters and conscripts, as well as of marauders by profession, who had taken advantage of his operations to carry on their depredations.[11]

Marmaduke, however, did not stand well with Holmes, for on

May 22 Holmes had telegraphed Kirby Smith that Marmaduke was not equal to the command of his cavalry division. Then on June 2 he stripped Marmaduke of two of his four brigades, sending them to the region between the lower White River and the Mississippi, leaving Marmaduke in command of a new brigade put together especially for him, and of the brigade of Colonel Joseph Shelby. One of the departing brigades had recently been reported by its commander as being in a state of disaffection verging on mutiny. But the discontent of the Texans of whom it was composed had not arisen from Marmaduke's method of operation; it came from their brigade commander's interfering with them and their companies.[12]

According to the report sent Marmaduke by a captain of an independent company of Missouri Scouts, the Confederacy was suffering because distilleries were flourishing on the border of Arkansas and Missouri. Corn that should have been going to secession horses or to the families of Southern soldiers was being bought at $4 a bushel, to produce liquor that fetched $20 a gallon. But the captain who was so irked at the thought of a bushel of grain putting a neat profit of $60 into the pockets of whisky makers, was an innocent in his knowledge of sin and corruption compared with Colonels George Carter and Colton Greene. Commissary and quartermaster stores were abundant, Carter reported, in the region between the St. Francis and the Mississippi, but he could get nothing except by impressment. Through trade with Memphis the people had developed such an appetite for United States money that they would sell nothing except for Federal greenbacks. Greene wrote of the forage and beef cattle in the rich delta land, but pronounced it a "den of smugglers, negro thieves, deserters, and dealers in counterfeit money." It should, he said, "be thoroughly scourged." [13]

Unionists had immediately sped to Memphis the news that the Confederates were on the march, and on June 11 Hurlbut had it on the wire to Washington. Sterling Price, he said, had left Little Rock a week before with five days' rations and the intention of joining Marmaduke. According to the Federal general, Price's 4,800 men were "badly armed." While a shortage of weapons existed, as we have seen, in Kirby Smith's department, Price's men were to make their bid for Helena with Enfield rifles. Hurlbut doubted Price's statements that he would attack Helena: Prentiss, commanding there, had reported no threat. Instead, Hurlbut thought that Price would go to Jacksonport, and then seek to divert the Federals by a move into southeastern Missouri.[14]

The next day Halleck alerted Schofield, who replied that he believed Price meant to strike some post on the river, probably New Madrid. Being unable to reinforce the small regiment there, Schofield suggested abandonment of the position. The General in Chief's reply was back quickly: "New Madrid in the hands of the enemy would close the river. It must be held." The St. Louis commander was told to take men from Island No. 10, Columbus, and Cairo, and to ask Pennock at Cairo for a gunboat. The same day Schofield requested Governor Gamble to furnish four more regiments of Enrolled Militia for thirty days. And presumably he paid heed to the last sentence of Halleck's message: "Put a reliable officer in command, with orders to hold it [New Madrid] to the last moment." [15]

But it was southward, not northward, that the Confederates were looking covetously, and on June 8 Holmes set out from Little Rock to confer with Sterling Price about the wisdom of an attack on Helena. When the ambulance in which the fifty-eight-year-old general was riding broke down, Holmes turned back. But the mishap could not have seemed prophetic, for a horseman rode on with a message that directed Price to report whether the condition of his troops justified an attempt on Helena. "Fully rested and in excellent spirits," Price said of his men in a reply next day. They numbered only 4,058 —with many on outpost duty—but in the brigade of Texans taken from Marmaduke, and which Price seemed to think would be available, there were 1,170 more. On the other hand, the most reliable information that Marmaduke had been able to obtain put the Federals in Helena at from 4,000 to 5,000. If a movement were conducted rapidly and secretly, and if Holmes brought two additional brigades, Price entertained no doubt that Holmes could "crush the foe" at Helena.[16]

One cannot be certain whether Price's exuberant optimism came in part from having read a long report to Marmaduke that Colonel Carter, commander of the once-angry Texans, had written on June 5; it should have been passed on to him even if it arrived after his excoriation of Marmaduke in his order of June 6. An intelligent lady of Helena had just reached Carter's camp. Not only had she confirmed previous reports; she said of the Federal garrison: "They are exceedingly alarmed, and apprehensive that you and Price will attack them daily." [17]

A sentence in Holmes's reply to Price—dated the 13th—seemed to put an end to a Helena attack: "If there are 4,000 or 5,000 men in Helena, fortified as they are, to take it would cost too much. . . ." It was better, he thought, to send an additional battery to a point below Memphis, "to aid in stopping transports." A letter two days later—Monday, June 15—shows that Helena was still a temptation: Holmes had information that the enemy there was "even less numerous" than Price had said. Actual instructions were a baffling *non sequitur:* "Please make no movement to separate your command until you hear further from me, but have everything in readiness for a move on Missouri." Holmes's record gains consistency if this statement is regarded as a blind soon to be removed, for he ended his letter: "I will probably be with you on Wednesday night." [18]

Before setting out for Jacksonport for the second time on June 16, Holmes telegraphed to Smith—on the 14th according to his report, on the 15th according to the message as given by Smith—"I believe we can take Helena. Please let me attack it." As it will be seen that neither Smith's reply nor the communication from the Secretary of War had been received before Holmes left Little Rock, the Helena decision rests squarely with Holmes. The attack was actually initiated in an order he issued at Jacksonport on June 18, and it is impossible to believe that it did not have the hearty approval of Sterling Price. Yet in a well-known postwar article, Price's former adjutant, able Thomas A. Snead, makes it appear as if Price—who had died in poverty in St. Louis in 1867—had had nothing to do with the decision. Snead, like Price, was a native of Virginia, but instead of migrating to Mexico, as Price did for a short time, he rebuilt his life in New York City, and did so with much distinction. Snead was very critical of Holmes, who did not survive the war, and also of Kirby Smith, who afterward taught mathematics at Altamont. With a home enlivened by five sons and six daughters, Kirby Smith surely had no need to refight the Civil War. Silence seems to have been his answer to Snead's assertion that he was "even feebler than Holmes," a charge Snead drove home by saying that while Smith tried a great deal more than Holmes, he did almost nothing.[19]

Doubtless Holmes did not measure up to the full possibilities of his position, but he is sometimes condemned in an *ex cathedra* manner without adequate examination of his problems.[20] Snead certainly put the Helena case inaccurately when he said that Smith about the middle of June had determined to do something for the relief of Vicksburg, and because the President had frequently suggested an attack on Helena, Smith "ordered Holmes to move from Little Rock for that place." Nothing could have been more foolish, according to Snead, in view of supporting gunboats and the works protecting the 5,000 defenders. Helena, according to Snead, could not have been held for twenty-four hours, even if taken. What he meant when he said that "Price would have done something if he had not been repressed by both Smith and Holmes" is not at all clear. But, in view of his dispatch to Holmes of June 9, it looks as if Price would have done exactly what was done, though he probably would not have ventured to attack Helena without more men than he had in his division at that time.

Back in Little Rock on the 21st, Holmes telegraphed to Price, "I have the sanction of General Smith for our operation, and also a letter from the Secretary of War advising or suggesting it." Even before he left Jacksonport, Holmes had directed Brigadier General L. Marsh Walker to throw an isolating cavalry screen around Helena, and now he ordered that Marmaduke join in the same security work. He also passed on good news about Brigadier General James F. Fagan, whose regiments had been ordered to rendezvous at Clarendon on Friday the 26th, the day Price was scheduled to be at Cotton Plant. Fagan was "ready and in high condition and spirit." [21]

Before the columns got under way, encouraging reports had come from the South. Grant, "badly whipped," and "completely surrounded," had asked for an armistice of three days to bury his dead, but "Johnston replied that he was in command of the boys now, and they had commenced in earnest." The very next day the purveyor of this bright news wrote that Dr. Dunn's son had arrived in Little Rock from Helena. It was common talk there that Grant had been defeated and was hemmed in. Every day the citizens were wishing Price would come "and close in on all below." A watcher on the Mississippi quoted the *St. Louis Republican* as saying that Lee was invading Pennsylvania with a force estimated at 90,000 and that Rebel privateers were making havoc of Federal shipping on the Atlantic.[22]

With such heartening reports of Confederate successes and the assurance of a colonel of outposts to the north that he would put the southward stroke under a blanket of secrecy, the Helena operation got under way. Soon, however, the columns were hit by heavy rains that turned roads into quagmires and made streams impassable. Holmes revealed a good quality in a commander when he wrote to Price: "My dear General: I deeply regret your misfortune. . . ." He neither chided nor pressed, but merely asked about the obstacles with which Price would have to contend, and inquired as to where Marmaduke was, and the time he would probably arrive.[23]

When, after considerable delay because of the rains, the concentration had been completed, and Holmes had established his headquarters five miles from Helena on Friday, July 3, he knew the task ahead was greater even than he had expected. New information indicated that the place was much more difficult of access and more strongly fortified than he had believed. But he went on with his project, and, though his command was a small one, numbering, he says in his report, only 7,646 officers and men, he issued a *written* order.

Fagan, Marmaduke, and Price were respectively given the tasks of taking Hindman, Rightor, and Graveyard hills. The mission assigned to Walker's cavalry is especially interesting because it had an element of maneuver. Walker was to assume a position from which he could resist Federal troops approaching Rightor Hill, and when the hill had been captured he was to "enter the town and act against the enemy as circumstances may justify." [24]

The attack was set for July 4 at daylight—a moment that lacks the precision of a stated hour. More than this, a five-mile night approach-march, over hilly, obstructed roads, to be followed by deployment on difficult terrain, was an invitation to failure.

Because Walker was not assigned an initial attack mission, one might say that he was a sort of reserve. Holmes, however, apparently forgot about him, and later wrote as if Walker should have responded to Marmaduke's call for help. Whether the battle would have gone differently had he done so is very doubtful. But he might not have been mortally wounded two months later in a duel with the resentful Marmaduke.

Helena was a model of alertness. Awareness of danger had come gradually, and Prentiss feared no attack when the gunboat *Bragg* (captured from the Confederates in June, 1862) arrived to strengthen the town about June 22. Along with the *Tyler* and the *Hastings,* she had been sent to the vicinity by Admiral Porter because of reports that had reached him at Vicksburg of a move by Price toward the Mississippi. Upon finding that Prentiss expected no attack, the captain of the *Bragg* decided to leave his assigned station, and went to Memphis to repair machinery. Later he had to write an explanation to an angry admiral.[25]

Intelligence that soon came to Prentiss was better than that which had alerted Porter. Hurlbut sent word on the 24th that Price was at Jacksonport and might drop down the river; his men, however, thought he was going to Missouri. Prentiss already knew that Price was at Jacksonport, he replied three days later, and his latest information indicated that the Confederates would move toward Red River. But three unfriendly cavalry regiments had been making it very difficult to get news.[26]

Although he said that he had less than 4,000 men, of which 600 were cavalry, Prentiss evidently did not request reinforcements; but when indications of an attack multiplied he set to work to strengthen his position. In addition to rifle pits and breastworks, four batteries were erected in commanding positions on the bluffs west of town, which, reading from the north, Prentiss named A, B, C, D. Intervening ravines made it possible for them to concentrate their fire for mutual support; and because they were more remote from the town than Fort Curtis, they covered the roads into Helena. The guns of the four batteries, as well as those of Fort Curtis, were manned by the Thirty-third Missouri Infantry. Since only four companies were needed, the four remaining companies were assigned as sharpshooters—one to Fort Curtis, three to Battery D.[27]

The garrison was chiefly Leonard Ross's division of the Thirteenth Corps, but Ross being absent, the division was under Brigadier General Frederick Salomon, who was first seen in the Federal advance into Indian Territory during the summer of 1862. Of the regiments only the Forty-third Indiana dated from the first months of war; the Twenty-eighth Wisconsin, the Thirty-third and Thirty-fifth Missouri, and the Twenty-ninth, Thirty-third, and Thirty-sixth Iowa were all raised in the late summer and fall of 1862. The Hoosiers had been with Pope at New Madrid and Island No. 10, and all regiments except the Thirty-fifth Missouri had taken part in the Yazoo Pass expedition and the futile operation against Fort Pemberton. Although the infantry had never seen heavy combat, the Third Iowa Battery had been in the Battle of Pea Ridge, and the men of Battery K,

First Missouri Light Artillery, were proud veterans of Fort Donelson and Shiloh.

Supplementing the division, Prentiss had the Second Arkansas colored regiment, an uncertain combat resource since it had not yet been mustered into Federal service. There was also a cavalry brigade composed of the First Indiana and the Fifth Kansas, both the regiments dating back to the summer of 1861—real "old-timers." With its attached battery of four small rifled steel guns, the Indiana regiment had special fire power. While the carbines of its troopers were breechloaders, many of them were unreliable and had been condemned.[28]

Another warning came from Hurlbut, dated July 2. A deserter from Price's army reported that Helena was to be the target if an attack looked safe; otherwise Price would go to Milliken's Bend. According to the man, women were being used as spies, and several of them had started for Helena before Price left Jacksonport. Hurlbut said he could give temporary aid "if necessary." His resources were meager and he had to keep a sharp eye on his rear, for always in his mind there was the possibility of a quick northward move by a part of Joe Johnston's force or by all of it.[29]

For five days Prentiss had had the Helena garrison up and under arms at 2:30 A.M. If he was not actively patrolling at a distance, he at least had reliable scouts and agents, for the night before Hurlbut sent his last warning, Prentiss learned that the Confederates were only fifteen miles away. Realizing now that an attack would soon take place, Prentiss issued an order against a celebration of the Fourth that his regimental commanders had planned.[30]

On July 1 or 2, the *Tyler,* by order of Lieutenant Commander S. Ledyard Phelps, anchored off Helena. Here was truly a veteran of the Western war. She was first seen with Grant at Belmont; then making a dash up the Tennessee after the capture of Fort Henry; then at Fort Donelson, advancing cautiously behind the new ironclads because her sides were frail. Finally, it was the *Tyler*'s guns—and those of the *Lexington*—that did such valiant service at Shiloh. As the word, "The *Tyler* is here," spread among the soldiers, there must have been a lift in spirits and increase of confidence. They were only 4,129 in number, and expected to do battle against several times their number.[31]

The reader should place himself with the pickets on the hilly, heavily wooded and barricaded roads that would be the enemy avenues of approach. Unless hidden by clouds, a nearly full moon gave vision to the sentinels without disturbing their companions sleeping upon their rifles. Their thoughts were such as soldiers' thoughts have always been when expecting the sound of an approaching enemy. Perhaps some sentinel who opened fire that night without bothering to challenge described in a letter home the tension, as distant, scarcely perceptible sounds grew closer and more ominous. If such a letter was written no quotation from it appears in the record. But, colorless though it is, Prentiss's statement is adequate: "On Saturday morning,

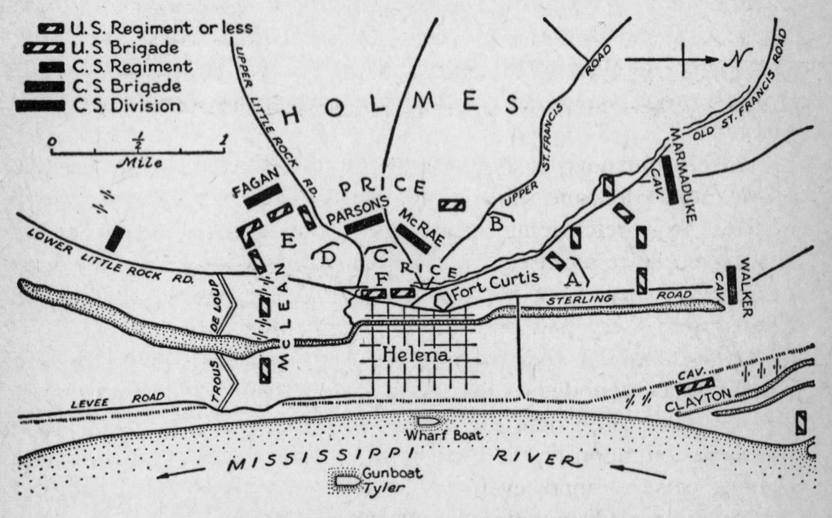

BATTLE OF HELENA—JULY 4, 1863

Prentiss was in over-all Federal command at Helena, and Salomon in temporary charge of two infantry brigades. A, B, C, D are batteries built on commanding positions; there were also infantry intrenchments. Federal regimental positions shown were not all occupied simultaneously; a cavalry regiment counterattacked after the loss of Battery C. The Confederate attack was over hilly and wooded ground; E and F are approximately extreme points reached, where many were captured.

July 4, at 3 o'clock, my pickets were attacked by the enemy's skirmishers." The pickets resisted obstinately, and were not driven back upon the rifle pits and entrenchments until four o'clock, by which time troops were at battle stations. Confirmation of the hour comes from Colonel Samuel A. Rice, commanding the brigade of the Thirty-third

Missouri and the three Iowa regiments that held the Federal center and right. It was four o'clock, Rice wrote, when "the enemy, in heavy force, drove in our pickets, and opened the engagement on batteries A, C, and D." [32]

Iowa infantry, assisted by the cavalry and some excellent gunfire, stopped Marmaduke's attack against Battery A on Rightor Hill. Colonel Thomas Benton, whose Twenty-ninth Iowa was astride the Sterling Road, which was the axis of Marmaduke's advance, said the Southerners came on cheering and exulting, partly shielded from Union rifles by a fog. Recoiling finally before the galling fire that greeted them, they fell back, contesting every inch of ground. Although a day of battle often finds an increase of malingerers, it was not so with the Twenty-ninth, and Colonel Benton noted with pride that quite a number of his officers and men who were sick left their quarters and joined their companies "when the signal gun was fired." [33]

Walker contended in his report that he was engaged in front of Marmaduke's left and said he fulfilled his mission by preventing the Federals from reinforcing Rightor Hill. Two strong efforts to do so, he asserted, were repulsed. Marmaduke certainly could have made no progress on the left of the Twenty-ninth Iowa, for the Thirty-sixth Iowa posted there had practically nothing to do, its colonel saying little more than that they were on the field under arms (one man was killed, none wounded). Inasmuch as the entire Federal cavalry brigade was on the right for part of the time, and the Fifth Kansas was there continuously, there seems to have been ample unused Union strength close at hand, even if Walker had stretched his orders and thrown his two dismounted cavalry regiments into more aggressive action.[34]

With no trouble whatever the troops on the Federal left held back the distracting force that approached from the south, and the Confederate commander told of his inability to attack without being destroyed. A terrific fire from a Federal battery as well as from the *Tyler* broke upon his guns when he tried to use them. On his part, Lieutenant John O'Connell of the Union Missouri battery put it thus: "My entire battery opened fire on their position, and soon had the satisfaction of silencing their guns." He watched the shots carefully and was much pleased with a sergeant and two gunner corporals: their shooting was "splendid." [35]

In the center it was different. There the battle was grim. Prentiss,

Salomon, and Rice all bore testimony to the ferocity of the Confederate attack upon Batteries C and D. Salomon wrote that under cover of a heavy fog which arose about five o'clock, and which hid the batteries from his command post in the fort, the enemy had been able to mass his troops. Rice recorded that they hurled regiment after regiment in close columns against the works. Prentiss, writing now more vividly, reported, "The enemy covered every hill-top, swarmed in every ravine, but seemed to be massing his force particularly against Battery C." Twice they were thrown back; in their third effort they took the battery. But Lieutenant Colonel William H. Heath of the Thirty-third Missouri took pains to say that his cannoneers spiked one gun and carried off all friction primers and priming wires.[36]

It was the Missouri brigade of M. Monroe Parsons, assisted by Dandridge McRae's Arkansans, that captured Battery C, atop Graveyard Hill—the objective assigned to Price. Because of the great difficulty of the road, Parsons's battery had left its pieces behind. The cannoneers marched with the infantry, fully expecting to use the guns of the Unionists. When they found their fellow Missourians had played a practical joke on them, they had to repossess their muskets and fight once more as infantry.[37]

Four assaults against Battery D were repulsed, and after Graveyard Hill had been gained, McRae's brigade tried to aid Fagan in his attempt against the position (assigned to him as Hindman Hill), by maneuvering against its rear. But Federal counterattacks were soon under way, and even before Battery C had fallen, Prentiss had signaled to Lieutenant Commander Prichett of the *Tyler* "to open fire in that direction." The gunboat, which had come up from her early station below the town, responded happily with eight-inch shells, their fuses set at ten and fifteen seconds.[38]

It is obvious that the *Tyler*'s guns were immensely helpful. But Colonel Rice stated that the troops that had been driven from Battery C and the supporting rifle pits had been promptly rallied at the base of the hills and reformed, while Lieutenant Colonel Cyrus Mackey, whose Thirty-third Iowa helped defeat the enemy effort against Battery D, moved six companies to a position 250 yards to the rear of Battery C, where he said they effectively stopped further enemy advance.[39]

There were two large captures of Confederates who had sought sanctuary in ravines from heavy concentrations of artillery and rifle fire. About 250 men of Fagan's brigade, together with 21 officers and a stand of colors, were surrendered by a lieutenant colonel upon the demand of the captain of Battery D. About the same number of men from the Confederate Seventh and Tenth Missouri were captured when the Federal Thirty-fifth Missouri blocked the outlet to a ravine. They gave up, Heath wrote, "by hoisting a white flag, their own sharpshooters upon the ridge at their rear firing from cover upon and cursing them as they marched out prisoners of war." [40]

At some moment while matters were critical in the center, the First Indiana Cavalry was withdrawn from the right, and, dismounted, was used to help check the enemy advance after the loss of Graveyard Hill, when it looked as if the Rebels might enter the town in force. After capturing some hundred Confederates, many of the Union troopers exchanged their poor breech-loading carbines for the reliable muzzle-loading Enfields of their captives. When Salomon ordered the rearmed cavalrymen to recapture Battery C, it was found that two intervening ridges had to be crossed—not only were the ridges heavily wooded, in places they were so steep that the men had to crawl on hands and knees. But the enemy, Colonel Pace found, had already left Battery C, and, forced to retire because the *Tyler* was so active, he re-formed his regiment at the foot of a shaded hill, after an eventful five hours on a very hot day.[41]

It was now 10:30 A.M., and, except for skirmishing, the battle was over.[42]

Prentiss, however, could not be certain that the Confederates had actually written off Helena as an impossibility, and a note he addressed to Hurlbut at 10:30 said they were "evidently preparing for a renewed attack in force." Along with the message Prentiss sent a steamer with about 800 prisoners. Though Prentiss did not know it, the 2,200 men that he had surrendered at Shiloh were a much smaller fraction of Grant's army than his capture of Confederates had been of Holmes's total. While he asked for reinforcements in addition to ammunition, it did not look as if he had fears about his position; he wanted more men so that "the rebel forces in Arkansas" could be punished "in earnest." By midafternoon he was collecting enemy wounded and before night the gunboat *Covington* arrived. When Hurlbut reported the battle to Washington the next day, he dutifully said that Prentiss put the enemy force at 15,000, but added a comment that would be welcomed by the High Command: "I think 9,000 will cover their strength." [43]

Small though his own force was, Hurlbut did not fail to send some men to Helena, and they arrived on the 5th, a day when the Confederates made a cavalry demonstration, which Prentiss, in a message of thanks on the 6th, judged a mere feint to cover a general retirement. He was, he explained, sending out a reconnaissance in force. He understood that the attack against Helena had employed all available Confederates in Arkansas, intelligence that would round out Hurlbut's estimate when passed to Washington.[44]

While Prentiss spoke highly of his officers and men in dispatches to both Hurlbut and Grant, his superiors seem to have awarded him no praise. Toward Prichett, Prentiss was very generous, telling Porter that he could not conceive of a case where promotion was more deserved, and Prichett informed his chief that army officers had said Helena would have been captured by the Confederates had it not been for the *Tyler*. In a note to Secretary Welles, Porter used his commendation to salute the Navy with a literary gem: "I have the honor to enclose you a full report of the late affair at Helena, where the gunboat *Tyler* saved the day and enabled our little band of soldiers to capture a number of the enemy." [45]

The Navy Secretary responded with a fine letter to Prichett that spoke of "successful cooperation with the Army," that alluded pleasingly to "effective management" of the *Tyler*'s guns, that tempered her role as savior of the day with restrictive words, and that ended impeccably: "Accept the Department's congratulations for yourself and the officers and men under your command for your glorious achievement, which adds another to the list of brilliant successes of our Navy and Army on the anniversary of our nation's independence." [46]

Total casualties were 239 for the Federals and 1,590 for the Confederates.[47] More pleasant to contemplate than the great number of Confederates killed or wounded in front of Batteries C and D, or in the deadly ravines, is a scene at the plantation of Allen Polk, five miles west of Helena, where Surgeon W. M. McPheeters of Price's division had established a hospital. After McPheeters had on the 6th declined a Federal offer to have his wounded taken into Helena where they could be given ice and other comforts, Prentiss's medical director appeared the next day with surgeons and an ambulance train. When the offer of the 6th was once more made and once more declined, the Union officer said he would send out ice and other articles which the Confederates lacked. McPheeters compiled a list of needs and wrote to Price, "I must repeat it again that they were exceedingly kind, and I wish to give them full credit for it." [48]

CHAPTER II

ORDEAL AT PORT HUDSON

Fearfully hot here. Several men sunstruck. Bullets whiz like fun. Have ceased firing for awhile, the guns are so hot.

One signalman to another

NEVER HAD the North indulged in such rejoicing as on Tuesday, July 7, 1863. Lee's invasion of Pennsylvania had been turned back in costly defeat at Gettysburg; Philadelphia, Baltimore, *Washington,* were safe. Morning papers carried long stories of the three days of sanguinary battle that had brought deliverance; then at noon came the flash from Cairo. It was one of the capital's great war moments. No recording photograph is needed, even if one were obtainable, to picture staid, white-bearded Gideon Welles, fresh from a Cabinet meeting, rushing back to the White House with the message from Porter that the *V. F. Wilson* had brought 650 miles up the Mississippi.

Elihu Washburne, unshakable defender of Grant when others criticized and defamed him, was sought out and showered with apologies and compliments for his steadfastness and vision. If anyone had the right to announce that he was starting for Vicksburg on the morrow, it was he.

"As soon as the fall of Vicksburg was bulletined here to-day, the whole populace seemed wild with excitement," the Washington reporter for James Gordon Bennett's *New York Herald* telegraphed that night. He emphasized a novelty: "Even the women participated in the excitement, and manifested their appreciation of the recent victories by waving Union flags and handkerchiefs in every direction." But as they gesticulated, the ladies probably kept a sharp eye on where they placed a foot. Washington's streets were notorious, and that very morning a vivid letter to the *National Intelligencer* complained of "gutters filled to overflowing with putridity and filth," which loaded "the atmosphere with exhalations of disease and death."

Hazards, however, were forgotten, and word went out in the afternoon for "a gathering of the Union people of Washington to call upon the President to congratulate him upon the glorious news of the fall of Vicksburg." Assembly was at the National Hotel, whence, headed by the band of the Thirty-fourth Massachusetts, the jubilant marchers proceeded toward the White House, the column swelling as it moved until all available space was filled when the procession reached the mansion.

After patriotic airs had been played, the President spoke. He told the assembly that he was glad to see them and that he thanked Almighty God for the occasion of their call. He mentioned no names as winners of victories; he feared he would overlook someone entitled to be cited. Applause interrupted Lincoln's words, and when he finished the band broke out in the national anthem.

The War Department was the next place of call. Stanton, less chary of names, called for three cheers for General Meade, three for General Grant, three for General Halleck, nine for the Union. They were given lustily as the band joined in.

Less familiar as a speaker to crowds even than Edwin Stanton was Henry Halleck. He gave Grant's score: fifteen battles, fifteen victories. Whenever Grant moved upon the enemy's works it was "to carry them." Then the General in Chief turned prophet: "To-day or to-morrow" Grant would be in Port Hudson.[1]

Not one of the speakers said a word about Prentiss's victory at Helena on the Fourth. The word was not in Washington, though it had reached Chicago and New York. At 9:00 A.M. the *Chicago Tribune*'s special Cairo correspondent telegraphed, "We have good news from Helena by the steamer *Silver Moon,* this morning." The boat had a convincing cargo—prisoners. From them a story of the battle had been secured, including the statement that the attacking Confederates had numbered between 8,000 and 10,000 men. The *Tribune* for July 8 gave the Helena victory precedence even over the news of Vicksburg, which had arrived later. In addition to the account secured from captured men on the *Silver Moon,* there was a Memphis dispatch of the 5th that gave portions of Prentiss's messages of 10:30 A.M. and 3:00 P.M. of the 4th.

On the front pages of the *New York Herald* and *New York Times* for the 8th were short and identical Cairo dispatches that had accurate statements about the fighting at Helena, which, however, made no mention of the *Silver Moon.* But there was a reference to prisoners who asserted that the fighting would be renewed. The dispatch revealed that the assault had been made in three columns, and it also said: "General Prentiss was aware of the contemplated attack and was prepared. He had about four thousand men and was assisted by the gunboat *Tyler.*" Confederates were doubtless only too ready to testify about Prentiss's readiness and the *Tyler*'s destructive shells; but a Union source seems indicated by the statement that Prentiss was confident that he could repel any assault that would be made.

Horace Greeley's *New York Tribune* had a special Cairo correspondent. But "N. C. M." contented himself with writing a letter instead of telegraphing. He had promptly boarded the *Silver Moon,* "and fortunately having a pair of tow pantaloons" he had been "taken for a colonel." Inasmuch as the account of the battle he was giving came from captured Confederates, he considered it "trustworthy," except the statement that they had numbered only between 6,000 and 8,000. To "N. C. M." it was quite inconceivable that they would have dared attack Ben Prentiss with no more men than that; so he put them down at from 10,000 to 15,000 strong.[2]

Why, one must ask, did not some army or naval officer in Cairo telegraph promptly to Washington that there had been a victory at Helena? Officers sometimes grow casual, but the arrival of a boatload of prisoners who admitted defeat was not daily routine. Perhaps officers at Cairo assumed that aboard the *Silver Moon* there was someone with official dispatches for Washington and did not discover their mistake.[3] Thus Washington seemingly went uninformed, and it remained for the afternoon papers of the 8th, the *Evening Star* and the *Daily National Republican,* to make the announcement about Helena. Hurlbut's dispatch to Halleck had by then been received and released. Not until the 9th did readers in the nation's capital see the Cairo dispatch that the *New York Herald* and *New York Times* had carried the day before; then it appeared in both the *Daily Morning Chronicle* and the *National Intelligencer.*

Halleck's prophecy on the night of July 7 had good support in the last sentence of Grant's victory message that arrived from Cairo the next day: "I will send troops to the relief of General Banks, and return the Ninth Corps to General Burnside." Though no time was indicated, one would think from this that the relief of Banks had high priority. An immediate and heavy thrust against Joe Johnston, however, became Grant's absorbing thought on July 4, in addition to important decisions about the captured citadel and the many prisoners, and no troops were hurried southward.

Porter had written to Farragut, who was at Port Hudson, that it was expected that Vicksburg would surrender on the 5th, and on the 4th he signaled to Grant: "I will have a steamer all ready to carry dispatches to General Banks and the fleet below. What time will you wish to send, and will you take up your headquarters in the city at once?" Though Grant wrote to Banks on the 4th from "Near Vicksburg," there was a delay in getting the message started on the 225-mile journey to Port Hudson, for Banks did not receive it until near noon on the 7th. The former Confederate ram *General Sterling Price,* now the Federal gunboat *General Price,* had the honor of carrying Grant's message, and happy Federal soldiers promptly shouted the news to the besieged Confederates.[4]

It was perhaps after the Washington crowd had dispersed on that evening of the 7th that the Confederate commander at Port Hudson, Major General Franklin Gardner, who had stood four places above Grant in the West Point class of 1843, wrote to Banks asking "official assurance" that the Union soldiers had been telling the truth. If Vicksburg had indeed surrendered, Gardner requested "a cessation of hostilities with a view to consider terms for surrendering this position." Though Banks was a fluent talker, he had no desire to engage in argument, and at 1:15 A.M. of July 8 he wrote a message equal to the occasion. The part of Grant's dispatch suitable for enemy eyes was copied, with the assurance that it was "a true extract." But Banks politely declined to consent to a cessation of hostilities to discuss terms of capitulation.

Soon there came from Gardner a note offering surrender; thereupon Banks put an end to firing. The document that was drawn up by three officers from each side, and to which the two commanders affixed approving signatures, specified clearly that the surrender was unqualified, save that the officers and men of the garrison should receive the treatment due to prisoners of war. Private property was to be respected, and the Confederate sick and wounded were to be cared for by the authorities of the United States, "assisted, if desired by either party, by the medical officers of the garrison." There was, however, to be a formal surrender: Confederate troops were to be drawn up in line, with officers in their proper positions.[5]

Just as it has been pleasant to dwell on the scene at the plantation of Allen Polk behind Helena on July 8, so one can pause at Gardner's readiness to accept Banks's word concerning the surrender of Vicksburg. The Confederate general knew how implacable was Banks's feeling toward the South, and that he would forego no military stratagem to gain Port Hudson. But he also was certain that there would be no deceit or trickery in the answer to his note.

Though Banks's Port Hudson campaign does not rival Vicksburg in grandeur, it should not be dismissed as just a sideshow, as has been too frequently done. For the military student the campaign is very instructive, and the part of it between the early stages, previously described briefly, and the capitulation, must be filled in. Great perseverance was required; decisions of much consequence had to be made; logistical problems at times were great. Very dramatically, just in the nick of time, Banks interposed and prevented Gardner from joining Johnston. It is true that the fortress would have been secured with no effort whatever if Banks had tarried just a few days. But there would not then have been the harvest of prisoners, and Banks would not have felt free to join Grant with all his force because there was a very real Confederate threat to the lower Mississippi and to New Orleans, which neither Grant nor Halleck realized.

In his report for 1863, Halleck, after speaking of Farragut's passing the Port Hudson batteries with the *Hartford* and the *Albatross* on March 14, said:

> Had our forces invested Port Hudson at this time, it could have been easily reduced, as its garrison was weak. This would have opened communication by the Mississippi River with General Grant at Vicksburg. But the strength of the place was not then known, and General Banks resumed his operations by the Teche and Atchafalaya.[6]

"Without any just foundation" was the temperate remonstrance that Banks applied to the General in Chief's statement when he finally got around to writing his own report in April, 1865. He based his contention as to the actual strength of Port Hudson in the month of March, 1863, upon information given him by enemy officers, and the records fully support him. No fewer than 15,572 Confederates were at Port Hudson on February 28, 1863; a month later there were 20,388. (What the strength was in mid-March, when Banks made something of a demonstration, is not clear.) Against such a force protected by good earthworks, Banks would have been foolish to contend with the 12,000 to 14,000 men that he could have brought against them.[7] Even to have attempted investment might have been an invitation to disaster.

After Banks had moved his command, except for Augur's force at Baton Rouge, to the watery and treacherous Teche and Atchafalaya region, Pemberton made three levies on Port Hudson. On April 4 he called for Rust's brigade; on May 1 he ordered that Gregg's brigade be sent at once—and rapidly—to Jackson; then on the 4th, after Grant had advanced beyond Port Gibson,* he telegraphed to Gardner, "You must come and bring with you 5,000 infantry." The Vicksburg general specified that Gardner was to bring the brigade of Brigadier General Samuel B. Maxey, Kentucky-born West Pointer of the class of 1856, but to leave that of Brigadier General W. N. R. Beall, another Blue Grass State West Pointer, of the class of '48. Although Gardner had trouble deciphering Pemberton's dispatch, he got under way as soon as possible, only to receive at Osyka (on the railroad to Jackson, just over the Louisiana-Mississippi line), on the 9th, an order to return to Port Hudson with 2,000 men. The position was to be held to the last: the Confederate President had so directed. Retention of Port Hudson "to the last" had not been specifically ordered by Davis. But such was Pemberton's reading of the sentence: "To hold both Vicksburg and Port Hudson is necessary to a connection with Trans-Mississippi." [8]

As Gardner retraced his steps, Maxey continued northward, and nightfall found his little column entering Brookhaven, twenty miles south of Hazlehurst. Attractive Brookhaven had been visited by Grierson a fortnight previously, and he had charged into it almost rudely because he had heard that 500 citizens and conscripts were bent upon resisting him. There was much running and yelling, the Federal raider wrote later; then everything "quieted down into almost a welcome." Grierson destroyed much property in a "large and beautiful camp of instruction" for conscripts, he reported officially, but it was his damage to the railroad and rolling stock that impeded Maxey. Only one engine was at his disposal, Maxey said in a telegram sent

* See map in Volume IV, p. 348, for this and several other places.

at 1:00 A.M. of April 13th to Brigadier John Adams, commanding at Jackson; but he would start shipping out at daylight.[9]

It was on the evening of the 13th that Joe Johnston arrived at Jackson and reported pessimistically to Secretary Seddon that he had come too late. The next day, the day of Grant's capture of the Mississippi capital, Maxey received from Adams—a Tennessee-born Academy classmate—the telegram:

Halt. Don't come any farther. Fall back on your wagons; and don't come any farther up the road. Go in the direction of, or to, Port Hudson. We are evacuating Jackson.

This was all so unexpected that Maxey, who had reached Hazlehurst, thought it possibly a fake dispatch sent by some unprincipled Unionist. So Maxey—who was destined to be a two-term United States senator from Texas in postwar years—unhooked his precious locomotive and sent it cautiously forward with one of his aides (and the railroad superintendent) to learn the truth. The truth came in the form of a handcar with a message from Johnston, bidding Maxey to save his command by marching it to the railroad line east of Jackson, where other Confederate forces were to assemble.[10]

Maxey's brigade was part of the command with which Johnston—with little optimism, it will be recalled—moved up to the Big Black River in early July, only to retire upon learning that Pemberton and all his men were Grant's prisoners and that the Federal flag flew over Vicksburg. It remains a part of the army with which Grant still has to deal. But Grant's classmate Gardner—who would console himself after the war as the owner of a plantation—is safely back in Port Hudson with about a third of the force that he had had when Banks in March decided that the citadel was too strong for him to attack.

Banks's campaign will be picked up at Alexandria, where he has been seen writing a succession of three dispatches to Grant on May 11 and 12, answering Grant's earnest request for cooperation against Vicksburg. Although Banks had had difficulty making up his mind, once he had decided that continuance of the operation against Port Hudson was essential he lost no time. In spite of the fact that units of his command had pursued the Confederates nearly to Natchitoches, and were still northwest of Alexandria, he had one of his divisions on the road to Simmesport on the 14th. The general himself promptly set out for New Orleans, by steamer down the Atchafalaya to Morgan City, and thence by rail to opposite his destination. The 18th found him describing his plans in a letter to Halleck: He would cross the

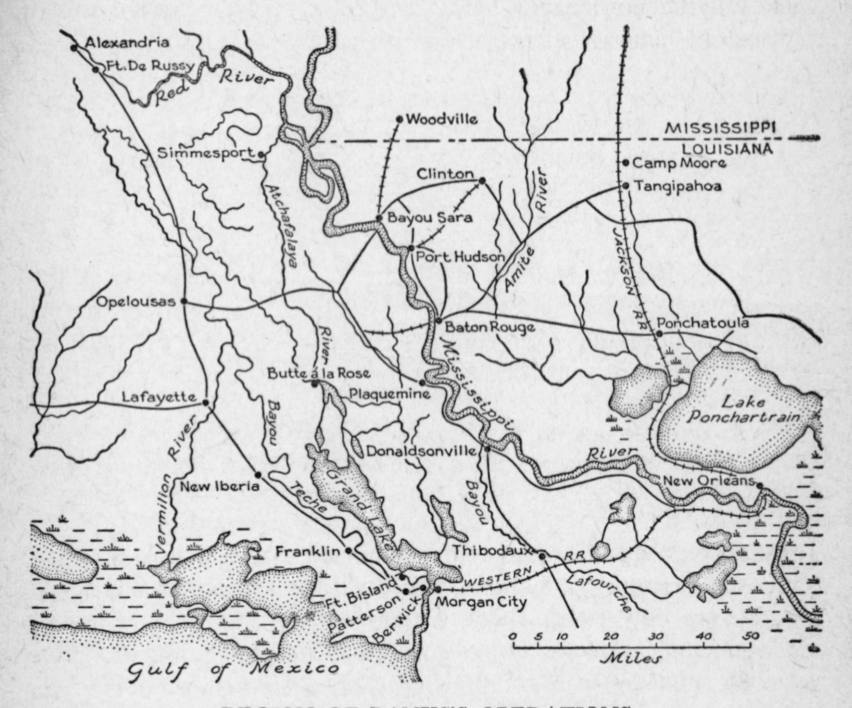

REGION OF BANKS'S OPERATIONS

Mississippi without delay, move on Port Hudson "with the best chances of success, and join Grant immediately after." The past six weeks had, he said, taken a heavy toll of his command—between 3,000 and 4,000 were sick—but the others were in good condition and fine spirit. He would cut the troops in New Orleans to the utmost in order to augment Augur's command, scheduled to move the next day from Baton Rouge toward Port Hudson; Farragut's warships were already lying off that place.[11]

Because of the distance and the infrequency of steamers between New Orleans and New York, Washington was behind in the matter of Banks's activities, nor did the general know what the High Command was thinking. But certainly long before he wrote his own letter on May 18 Banks had received an important one from the General in Chief that should have pleased him. Dated April 3, it gave Halleck's reaction to Banks's roundabout movement, and, as usual, Halleck kept the large issue clearly before his subordinate while fully acknowledging that Banks knew many important things of which he himself was not aware. He wrote:

> Your great object, to be continually in view, must be to connect with General Grant. He has been written to do all in his power to connect with you. It would seem from this distance that the Atchafalaya offers the best means of effecting this object; but you and General Grant can judge best, being on the spot.

Also in this letter Halleck revealed a little of the difficulty of his position. After saying that it had been vainly hoped that more troops could be sent to Banks from Hunter's command in South Carolina, he put his finger on what is frequently the cause of military failure:

> It is unfortunate that the Government, yielding to outside pressure and the impatience of the people, has undertaken too many things at the same time.

Then Halleck bade Banks accept a soldier's role: "But this has been the result of circumstances which neither you nor I could control. We are only responsible for doing our best with the means at our command." Halleck, however, was far from judging matters too narrowly from a soldier's viewpoint; he was both conscious of and sympathetic toward the problems of the President. Having said that he hoped the weather would soon permit some of the armies to move, he concluded: "A successful operation would greatly relieve the Government." [12]

Left in command at New Orleans was William H. Emory, whose blood was that of soldiers. His father had been in the War of 1812, his grandfather in the Revolution. The fifty-two-year-old Emory, now a brigadier of volunteers, had first been a field artilleryman, then had had two years in civil life, then had returned to the army as a lieutenant of topographical engineers, in which capacity he had helped establish the northeastern boundary between the United States and Canada. The Mexican War found Emory with combat troops as a lieutenant colonel of volunteers, and battle action brought him two brevets; after the war, as chief astronomer, he ran the line between

California and Mexico. Early in 1861 he was placed in command of all troops in Indian Territory. Wisely gauging the danger from the widespread insurrectionary movement, Emory evacuated his four posts and, without losing a man, moved to Fort Leavenworth. The small body of regulars he had saved—the only group salvaged out of secession territory—were of importance far beyond their number and became a nucleus of strength in General Nathaniel Lyon's little army. A biographer of Emory, thinking in part at least of Lyon's capture of Camp Jackson at St. Louis, has stated that those men probably prevented the Secessionists from forcing Missouri into rebellion.[13]

Emory—tall and commanding in appearance, called "Bold Emory" at West Point, and twice thanked on the battlefield during the Peninsula campaign—thought Banks had cut the New Orleans garrison below the safety point. In a protesting note he reminded Banks that the population was very "unsettled" because of the enlistment of Negroes, and warned that a raid from Mobile or elsewhere could be disastrous. The great city that Emory had to protect was of inestimable importance, and his query natural: "Could not another brigade be left here?" [14]

Though not revealed to Halleck, there still lurked in Banks's mind the thought that Grant might help him, just as Grant was hoping for aid from Banks. A letter that Lieutenant Colonel Richard B. Irwin, Banks's adjutant, wrote to Banks from opposite Simmesport at 9:00 P.M. on the night of May 17 makes this clear. Irwin had just received a letter from Brigadier General Dwight, whom Banks had evidently chosen as a high-ranking bearer of the second dispatch he wrote to Grant on the 13th. Dwight's letter had been written at 8:30 P.M. on the 16th at Grand Gulf. That was the day when Grant fought and won the decisive battle at Champion's Hill; but the latest Grand Gulf news was that Grant was at Jackson. Irwin said that Dwight *promised* to secure the cooperation desired, but he urged Banks "not to wait for it." As Dwight's letter is missing, that seems to be all there is in the indubitable contemporary record. But in his report two years later Banks stated that Dwight, the commander of a brigade in Cuvier Grover's division, returned with Grant's advice to attack Port Hudson without delay, "and that he would give me 5,000 men, but that I should not wait for them." [15]

Banks must have known that the enemy garrison had been reduced since March, or otherwise he would not have decided to move against the bastion. But how much it had been cut was another matter. Thus he must have been pleased to learn that according to Dwight, information from various sources showed there was but one brigade there, in addition, of course, to personnel for the big guns. But Banks's chief of staff, Brigadier General George L. Andrews, who had been Number One man in the West Point class of 1851, and who had written simultaneously with Irwin, and at greater length, reminded his chief that a Confederate brigade was "by no means a constant quantity"; it might mean 4,000 men, "upward or downward." But on one point Andrews was positive: they should move with all speed to the rear of Port Hudson with the 10,000 men his figures showed they mustered.[16]

Simmes's plantation, where Irwin and Andrews were operating, was bursting with information about the Confederates even in theaters remote from Port Hudson. To Irwin it seemed too pressing to keep until Banks returned to forward it according to military protocol. So, after pronouncing himself "one of the last men in the world to violate official unities," Irwin described some of the intelligence treasures in a long letter of May 10 to Colonel Edward D. Townsend, Acting Adjutant General of the Army, in Washington. One can feel his excitement as he wrote:

> For about a week we have taken every rebel mail intended for Alexandria, the former headquarters of Lieut. Gen. E. Kirby Smith, and the distributing office for Texas and Western Louisiana.

Most of what Irwin set down came from "official sources": an assistant adjutant general in Richmond, who felt himself well esteemed by General Cooper and who had recently taken breakfast with no other than Jefferson Davis, and one of Bragg's inspectors general. Bragg's army was given special attention: its composition, location of its units, and their strengths. Though the information was as of early April, it would be of vast importance to Washington, and the fact that Bragg had been summoned to Richmond would cause speculation. Irwin copied a paragraph from a letter by a clothing manufacturer of Columbus, Georgia, just returned from Richmond with a contract for 50,000 uniforms. For a garment maker, the man had a strange hobby: Confederate ironclads. Two new ones, he said, would soon be finished at Richmond; a large one would be ready in Wilmington in a few weeks; one was being built at Columbus and others were contracted for; more were building at Selma, as well as a seagoing frigate with fifty guns. Two gunboats built at Selma were already at Mobile, "ready to give the enemy a becoming reception."

After reading hundreds of letters, no one at Banks's headquarters, Irwin said, doubted but that the Confederates were concentrating to crush Rosecrans. Neglecting all logistical considerations, and not dreaming of how Grant would act, Irwin expressed the view that the Vicksburg garrison would get past Grant at Jackson and march to Tullahoma. While the Columbus contractor had ended cheeringly, Irwin concluded in a gloomy vein, though he easily was the winner in vividness: "We shall gain Vicksburg and Port Hudson before many days, but if Rosecrans is defeated the fruits of victory will turn to ashes on our tongues." [17]

In miles Banks's target was close to Simmesport. But in between lay not only the great Mississippi, but the tricky Atchafalaya that steals from the Red River and threatens to divert the Mississippi. Troops were to begin to cross the Atchafalaya on the morning of May 18th, but there was only one boat for ferrying. Both Irwin and Andrews called for coal—"hard coal, especially, at once." Then much of the command could go by water directly to Bayou Sara, while the balance marched on roads being reconnoitered to nearly opposite that place. Some boats came—Irwin warned of the falling Atchafalaya—and some coal—Irwin distrusted the quartermaster at Brashear City (Morgan City).[18] Also, Banks himself returned.

The highly competent Andrews, who later taught at West Point as a professor of modern languages for a score of years, must have recognized the distinguished qualities of his chief, and discounted the fact that Banks was not a professionally trained soldier. The characteristics which had made Banks one of the ablest Speakers in the House of Representatives served him well as a commanding general. His decisions as Speaker had been prompt and impartial, and though he served in a period of the bitterest partisanship in our history, no decision he made was overruled. The period during which he occupied the governor's chair in Massachusetts also contributed by giving him administrative training. In connection with his operations in the Shenandoah Valley it was noted in this work that Stonewall Jackson indicated that the North did not appreciate Banks's ability as a soldier, and General Ballard's tribute was quoted: Banks was always willing to fight, and fought well.[19] The closing sentence of Andrews's letter of the 17th was, "I trust you will return speedily." He was not a soldier who would so write merely to flatter his superior or to ingratiate himself, and one must accept his words as indicating that Banks had something of the reassuring presence essential in a commanding general. On his part, the self-educated Banks should have been warmed and steadied by such words from a brilliant chief of staff who had had the benefit of one of the best educations the country then afforded.

Assuredly Banks's first concern on returning to his command was the crossing of the Atchafalaya and the safe landing of his infantry, his guns, and his trains on the east side of the Mississippi. But a long letter that he wrote to Halleck from Simmesport on May 21 said not a word about the progress of his operation. It looked further into the future, and inasmuch as he believed a large part of Louisiana had been potentially won back to the Union, he was thinking of getting the products out of the country, a subject which he had discussed at length in a still longer letter to Halleck written at Opelousas on May 4. In the new letter he noted that the eighty miles of railroad to Morgan City from the east were being managed vigorously, had plenty of business, and were being run for the profit of the government. From Morgan City to Opelousas the extension of the road was graded, bridges were largely built, ties were in place, and nothing was wanting but the iron. In case the portion of the state that he was abandoning as he moved to the Mississippi should be reoccupied, Banks thought the road should be immediately completed either by the government—plenty of labor was available in the Negro regiments—or by private parties, so that there would be good facilities for commerce.[20]

Not every man could have banished from his mind the pressing activities of the moment—in his report Banks said that the Atchafalaya was crossed "with great difficulty"—or the uncertainties that lurked beyond the Mississippi, to write such a letter.

Some of Banks's infantry embarked on steamers; the balance, all the artillery, the cavalry, and the wagon train, after the tedious crossing of the Atchafalaya, made another hot march to Morganza, a ferry point on the right bank of the Mississippi, ten miles above Bayou Sara, but directly west of that place because of a bend in the river. At Bayou Sara there was, Andrews had told Banks in a letter on the 18th, only an enemy picket, and Banks himself landed there with advance units at 2:00 A.M. of the 22nd.[21]

All too often attention is limited to the leading elements in an operation. This is natural, for there it is that "contact" first comes, and that commanders reveal themselves by their appraisals and their deployments, and finally by their actions as the tumult and excitement of battle mounts. While it is only in a retreat that the responsibility of saving a command is likely to fall upon the rear guard, the last troops that take the road in a movement such as Banks was making have heavy responsibilities, and one may be sure that at Alexandria careful thought was given to the selection of the commander of those troops.

The honor fell to Brigadier General Godfrey Weitzel, and he remained at Alexandria until the 17th with his own brigade and Dwight's. On two successive days he had actions northwest of the town. Then on the 19th he sallied out of a camp he had made the day before, to attack some of the pursuers; all the enemy cavalry was following, prisoners and deserters said. This unpleasantness of the 19th was, according to the *Official Records,* only an "affair," but the attack on Weitzel's pickets the next morning gets the rating "skirmish." In the letter in which he reported his arrival at Simmesport, Weitzel told Irwin that he had straightened out a confusion in orders about, of all things, ammunition, and was getting that important commodity sent forward. He was somewhat apprehensive. The Atchafalaya was falling; the enemy might cross and not only attack the trains but even afford the garrison at Port Hudson the opportunity to escape beyond the Mississippi.[22]

On the night of that day, the 23rd, the leading elements that had marched to Morganza began to cross the Mississippi, and a few hours earlier units that had come around by boat were welcomed not far from Bayou Sara by Grierson's famous troopers.[23]

After Grierson's men and mounts had rested from the fourteen days' raid that had begun at La Grange, Tennessee, and ended at Baton Rouge on May 3, Augur had shown no inclination to return them to Grant. Well might any commander wish to keep his hand on such cavalrymen. On May 12 Augur sent Grierson to break rail and telegraph communications between Port Hudson and Clinton, which was done at a point five miles from the fortress. Then Grierson's men spent their time keeping a sharp eye on everything that was going on and studying the enemy position—according to their commander.[24] But troopers being what they are, one can assume that they also did a deal of looking for houses where they could get a home-cooked meal and friendly smiles. Handsome men from Illinois would not quickly forget that, after they had scattered resistance groups in Brookhaven, they had been accorded something like a welcome. When they stood to horse in their camp near Baton Rouge awaiting the command, "Prepare to mount. Mount," they surely did not mind that they were not going upriver to Vicksburg but were headed for country never previously worked by seasoned cavalrymen in natty blue jackets. Though not admitted in any tedious and discreet regimental history or bragged about in any soldier's ill-spelled letter, one may believe that some of Grierson's men were sure they could find planters' daughters who were really not such ardent Rebels as they had always thought themselves.

Augur was not to get his two brigades (the other brigade was that of Weitzel) into position behind Port Hudson without fighting. Warning had come in a dispatch that Colonel N. A. M. Dudley, commander of the second brigade, had written at 8:30 P.M. of the 19th in a bivouac on the road from Baton Rouge to Bayou Sara: "Gardner's pickets have been very impudent for the last three days." Confederate Colonel W. R. Miles, sent to resist Augur, said the fight at Plains Store on May 21 "raged with great fury for nearly an hour"; then, overpowered, he had been forced back. Grierson, whose dismounted troopers supported batteries much of the time, described the engagement as lasting several hours. The cavalryman had only one man slightly wounded, but reported that 20 horses were killed; Augur had a round 100 casualties. As night fell, Colonel John L. Logan, Eleventh Arkansas Infantry, wrote to Gardner that he was advantageously situated in Augur's rear with 300 cavalry and as many mounted infantry; he would keep on the Federal right and "strike as opportunity offered." [25]

It would have been a feather in Gardner's cap and a help to his cause if he could have hurt Augur badly before Banks arrived with troops from across the river. Banks's operation is especially notable because it involved uniting columns in the immediate presence of the enemy, and with a great river to be crossed at the last minute by the major part of his command. Good timing was imperative or the end could have been defeat. In Beal's brigade of Arkansas men and Miles's "legion" and battalions of Louisiana Partisan Rangers, Gardner had a mobile force nearly equal to Augur's.[26] If he had had his entire command in position early on the 21st instead of Miles alone, and had acted with the boldness and vigor demanded by a last chance, he might have dealt Augur a hard blow that would have stopped him. Then uncertainty might have seized the Federal general, at the very time that he was completely out of contact with Banks. He could not have failed to ask himself: Does Banks really have the necessary boats? Will he come? (Weitzel reported transports at Simmesport that were unusable for want of coal.)

Whatever opportunity there was on the 21st for Gardner was gone when Brigadier General Thomas W. Sherman arrived next day with his two-brigade division from New Orleans. This officer was seen briefly in Halleck's advance upon Corinth just a year previously. Since the beginning of 1863 he had been in command of the defenses at New Orleans, but was replaced by Emory, who had been in Banks's advance up the Teche country until poor health had forced him from the field.

Brigadier Sherman was to the left of Augur, over toward the river, he informed Banks on the 23rd. But he had no immediate connection with Augur because of the trackless woods. His "cavalry"—twenty men—had reconnoitered all they could, and he had been repairing bridges on the road to Springfield Landing, which was to be an important base. But, like his horsemen, Sherman's transportation and tools were "very scant." He was nonetheless determined to get ahead, and unless he saw some good reason not to disturb the enemy rifle pits in his front until a general advance, he would take them tomorrow. The old artilleryman craved elbow room.[27]

Sherman took the rifle pits. Elsewhere there was also progress, and at 8:30 A.M. of the 25th Irwin reported to Commodore James F. Palmer, above Port Hudson on the *Hartford,* "Our lines closed in upon Port Hudson yesterday." From the left there was communication with Admiral Farragut, recently back from New Orleans, where he had narrowly missed seeing Banks, and who flew his flag on the *Monongahela.* At Port Hudson the cooperation between army and navy was to be as excellent as at Vicksburg, and at noon on the 25th Irwin described the Federal line for the admiral. Weitzel had arrived that morning, and at last Banks had the four divisions of the Nineteenth Corps together, except for 3,000 men still with the trains, and those holding New Orleans and other essential points.[28]

Lieutenant Stephen M. Eaton, Twelfth Maine, an acting signal officer, put in the record some signalmen's gossip about Weitzel's arrival. Eaton was aboard the *Hartford,* and at 7:30 A.M. he called Bayou Sara and asked where Weitzel was. "Just passed," was the answer. This was not precise enough for Eaton, so he queried, "How long since?" To this he received the reply that Weitzel's brigade was still at Bayou Sara but that the general himself had gone to the

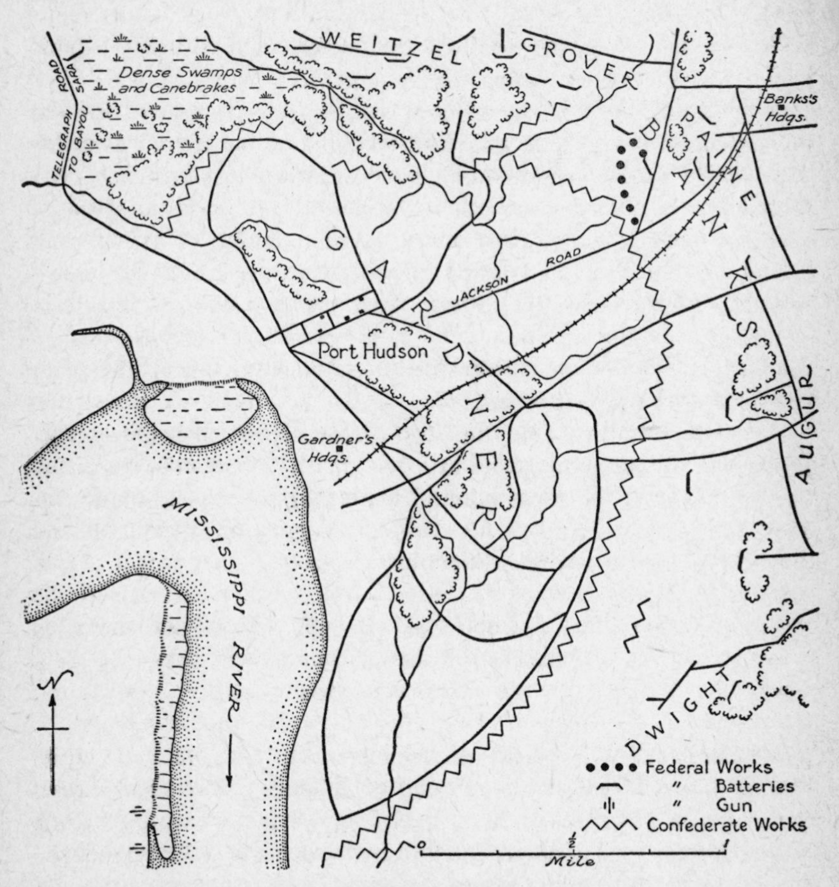

SIEGE OF PORT HUDSON, MAY 27—JULY 9, 1863

Investment took place May 25, and assaults failed May 27 and June 14. Numerous batteries were along the Confederate line, with heavy guns on the river bluff. Five batteries on Dwight's front do not show.

front with an aide at six o'clock. "Who are you?" the curious Eaton made bold to ask. The answer: "Dana. 'Tis very smoky; use large flag. I leave soon with Weitzel's brigade. Hall remains here." The Maine infantryman, whose regiment was with Grover, flashed back: "Would I were with thee! The guns of the army seem to be shelling

Port Hudson." The unsentimental Dana answered: "Too hard on eyes. Cease signaling." Obediently Eaton signed off: "Cease signaling."[29]

"Please let the mortars destroy the enemy's rest at night," Banks asked Farragut when informing him at 1:00 A.M. of May 26th that he would have ninety guns in position by the end of the day and expected to order an attack at daylight on the 27th. According to Irwin the final decision had the concurrence of all of Banks's commanders save one, but just when the decision came is not clear. It was not until midnight that notes carried details to Palmer and Farragut, who were both asked to cease their fire when the army's guns fell silent. The actual attack order had a dangerous looseness, though it hopefully specified that means must be on hand for crossing the ditch in front of the enemy works, and ended bluntly, "Port Hudson must be taken to-morrow."[30]

All ships would be ready to open on notice, or when they judged Banks was "making the grand artillery attack," Farragut wrote back. In simple words the great admiral expressed an artilleryman's constant concern for the fall of his shots on targets near friendly infantry (an admiral is in a way an artilleryman de luxe):

> We will aid you all we can, but I am so anxious about the troops that I fear I will not do as much as I might if I knew exactly where they were; but I will not hurt your men, as that is my whole study.[31]

Weitzel started the attack on the right with his own brigade and that of Dwight. Gardner's covering detachments were forced back, Sandy Creek was crossed, and the advance continued through a dense forest clogged with undergrowth and ravines choked with felled trees. "A gigantic bush-whack," Irwin pronounced the fight in his postwar article. When the retiring Confederates had unmasked their guns, the Federals were hit murderously with grape and canister. But skillful drivers had brought up Union metal, and from commanding positions gunners and cannoneers worthy of the drivers began to beat down the hostile fire, so that the men with deadly rifles could again get forward.

On Weitzel's left Grover had tarried a little; then had taken favorable positions two hundred yards from the objective. There he stopped: from the left there had come no indication of an advance. Weitzel likewise held his attack, while Dwight as a diversion ordered forward the First and Third Louisiana Native Guards, which were on the extreme right. So heavy was the concentration of musketry and artillery fire upon them that they were compelled, after brave efforts and heavy loss, especially by the First, to give up. Irwin justified both Grover and Weitzel, though he stated that it was afterward apparent that if Weitzel had persisted—for a matter merely of minutes, Irwin said—he would probably have broken the Confederate defense, as the attack order contingently bade him do, and been able to take the enemy in reverse.

In front of Augur felled trees covered the open plain; into them enemy riflemen from nearly a mile of works could pour their fire. Only a demonstration had been expected there, mainly to aid Sherman; but it was to be converted into a real attack, if the situation was propitious—according to Irwin's memory. Actually, however, the attack order gave Augur and Sherman identical instructions. According to that document there should have been both artillery fire and the fire of skirmishers upon the left; but Irwin spoke as if there had been a Sunday morning's quiet. His statement that Banks rode to the left, gave Sherman orders to attack, and then, returning to the center at about two o'clock, directed Augur to do likewise, can probably be accepted. At least, Banks wrote to Farragut the next day that there had been a general attack at 2:15. When it ended, the lines on the right were separated by only a few feet; no man, Banks said, could show himself without being shot. On the left, the main force, which in places had gained the ditches in front of the parapets, had fallen back. Skirmishers, however, were clinging to advanced positions.[32]

"We shall hold on to-day, and make examinations with reference to future operations," Banks said to Farragut. In view of the unquestionable strength of Port Hudson, there was not too much exaggeration in his statement that it was the strongest position in the United States. (Two days later he described the difficult approaches in a report to Halleck.) The enemy was stronger than Banks had supposed, but he stated that within three days he could himself increase his force by 5,000 men: there were the 3,000 with the trains that arrived on the 30th, and on the 28th Emory wrote that he was sending two and a half regiments and would the next day send more men called in from Morgan City. More than that, it was not impossible, Banks said, that Grant might help. "We may reasonably expect it," he commented, "if he is fortunate." If the postscript of Banks's letter to Grant on the 28th was written near the day's end, fatigue may partly account for the discouraged tone: "If it is possible, I beg you to send me at least one brigade of 3,000 or 5,000 men. This will be of vital importance to us. We may have to abandon these operations without it." [33]

The bill for that Wednesday was high: 293 killed, 1,545 wounded, 157 missing. Gardner's casualties amounted only to about 235. Sherman lost a leg. Undeterred by the shells that had ominously burst above his head when he was reconnoitering the morning before, the old-fashioned soldier, with his full staff, all mounted, had led the assault of his division.[34]

While arranging for a truce to care for his killed and wounded—which required the passage of a dozen letters between him and Gardner—Banks had also to give some thought to the far side of the Mississippi. Colonel Lew Benedict, located on the important point, called "Faussee Point," was becoming uneasy. A report had reached him that the 500 cavalry that had followed Weitzel from Alexandria were advancing against him; the previous night they were at Morganza. A scant hour before he wrote, midafternoon of the 28th, word had come from a former New Yorker that it was being noised about that Kirby Smith was advancing toward Port Hudson with a large force of infantry and cavalry. Negroes on the way to Bayou Sara on the night of the 27th had been attacked; only a few had escaped. Doubtless the Mississippi grew in width in Benedict's mind, even though he cheered himself by saying the news was probably "compounded of rebel hope, loyal apprehension, and a mixture of guerrilla." He was drawing in his small command. Then, in case of need, he could retreat to the river and the comforting guns of the *Hartford* and the *Albatross*.[35]

Joe Johnston had not heard of the sharp repulse that Gardner had dealt Banks when he wrote briefly to Kirby Smith on the 31st from Canton, Mississippi. Port Hudson, he said, was invested by Banks; Vicksburg by Grant. He was preparing to help Vicksburg, but he could not march to Port Hudson without exposing his little force to destruction. If Smith could save that place, Johnston begged that he do so.[36]

At first sight it looks as if Johnston was culpably slow in ordering Gardner away from Port Hudson. But it is to be recalled that with Banks operating up the Teche country toward Alexandria when

Johnston arrived at Jackson, it did not appear as if Port Hudson were menaced, let alone that a day or two in making up his mind could be fatal. The day of decision was May 19, and the decision was probably caused by Pemberton's misfortunes. At least it was that general's loss of artillery that made it necessary for Gardner to bring all he had, Johnston said, when he ordered him to leave Port Hudson "forthwith" and move toward Jackson.

No move designed for pure deception could have been more effective than Banks's occupation of Alexandria, and Johnston must have had one of the big surprises of the war when he read a letter of the 29th from Colonel Logan, then at Clinton, Louisiana, with 1,200 cavalry and mounted infantry. Logan had sent Johnston's evacuation order through to Gardner; but it was too late; Gardner was completely invested. Not a word had come from that general since the 24th, Logan said, but Gardner had intended to "come out" that night, if possible, and had directed Logan to place his force so as to help. Presumably Gardner had found he could not "cut his way through," or had stayed with hopes of being relieved. And 8,000 to 10,000 men could, according to Logan, drive Banks away and rescue not only the fortress and its garrison, but a region filled with stock and zealous people raising large crops of corn and potatoes for the Southern army.[37]

Quite as he had promised Johnston, Logan made himself a nuisance. So on June 3 Banks sent Grierson, whose cavalry command had been increased to 1,200, to break up Logan's camp. The mission failed, and Logan reported to Johnston that, after a three-hour engagement, he had driven the Federals off. Grierson indicated that he was handicapped because of a shortage of ammunition, and he had in fact only the previous day reported that about half of his command had carbines for which there was no ammunition in the department, and had requested an exchange.

Logan, however, was not to enjoy immunity for his enterprises. Early morning of the 5th saw Grierson once more headed for Clinton, this time with some of the infantry of Halbert Paine's division. Though men collapsed from the excessive heat, the column continued its march and early on the 7th the Federals found that Logan had left Clinton: at their leisure they destroyed military property he had abandoned, as well as the railroad station and a locomotive. On the return trip Grierson added railroad bridges, needlessly it would seem, to the list of demolitions. The dispossessed Logan wrote

Johnston from a camp ten miles from Clinton that he had whipped the Federal cavalry—Grierson reported no action—but could not cope with 4,000 men of all arms. If he expected praise he was disappointed; what he got was something of a reprimand. And it is with regret that one records that Johnston told Logan that he "ought not to be driven back by 4,000 Eastern troops." [38]

At Port Hudson there seems to have been no order for regular approaches such as Grant issued at Vicksburg, and no engineers' reports to match the fine ones of Prime and Comstock. But the numerous reports of signal officers give many interesting messages that flashed back and forth, a feature lacking in the Vicksburg story. "Let the mortars fire on that gun that shot at us last night." "I desire you to fire one of your rifle pieces upon the rebel pivot gun." Such were some of the early calls upon the navy. When Banks on June 6 reported to Farragut about the effectiveness of the mortar fire the night before, the Tennessee-born admiral replied: "I have him under my control. The minute he opens, I silence him. I am glad to know I hurt him." A grateful general answered, "The sextant has arrived. It will be taken care of, and returned safely. . . . Thanks for the hand-grenades." [39]

Three deserters to Dwight's division (Sherman's old command) on June 4 indicated a stiffening spirit on the part of the 6,000 Confederates in the beleaguered works. Citing a sergeant as authority, Dwight wrote, "Sentiment the other day was that we should take the place; now, that we have a small force and cannot."

But preparations for the new assault which Banks had announced on June 2 to Farragut, and which the latter had at once heartily approved, went steadily on, and with knowledge that no help would come from Grant. Following heavy and continuous artillery fire through June 10, an effort was made at three o'clock on the morning of the 11th to get closer to the works, so as to reduce losses when the stroke was made. Some Federals actually worked their way through the abatis and up to the hostile lines, only to be driven back with the loss of several prisoners.

The next day encouragement came when a second trio of deserters to Dwight indicated a fresh deterioration in enemy morale. A Mississippi regiment had actually driven fifty head of cattle out of the works, so as to speed surrender action by Gardner. Everything was in readiness for an assault on the morrow; but it might be delayed a day, Banks informed Farragut. The general was living up to the maxim that the man who makes the decision should not show doubt: "We shall carry the works without fail when we attempt it." [40]

The 13th passed with Banks sending a surrender demand to Gardner, and Gardner replying that duty required him to defend the position. So it was at daylight on the 14th that the assault was made. It was quickly repulsed in spite of the fact that the Federal artillery had mastered enemy guns by a predawn deluge of shells. Dwight's divisional column, which was to penetrate upon the left, where there was located what the Federals called "the citadel," was, Irwin wrote, misdirected by its guides. Augur was only to demonstrate vigorously. But the right, all under Grover, and on which high hopes had been placed, was also quickly stopped. When Irwin was able later to examine a crest that could not be passed, he found it "shaved bald" by the terrific musketry; every blade of grass was "cut down to the roots as by a hoe." [41]

Meagerness of reports makes it impossible to state precisely what was done. The records give the names of about 1,000 officers and men from forty-five regiments who volunteered for the storming parties—the contributions from three regiments was a single officer each, from each of four others, one private. A major commanding the Thirty-eighth Massachusetts said that his regiment, deployed as skirmishers ahead of the storming column on the right, reached the ditch in front of the enemy's works, remained there in a broiling sun awaiting the attackers who never came, and at night received orders to retire. A captain commanding the Thirteenth Connecticut skillfully led his men through a ravine to a height overlooking the coveted enemy line, a mocking twenty to thirty yards away. There his sharpshooters went to work, and as night fell a strong picket took over the captured position. At ten o'clock he was relieved, but whether by fresh troops who were to dig in, or merely to return to his old camp or place in line, is not clear. The dispatch that was promptly sent to Washington with news of the fresh repulse said advanced positions gained in the attack would be held and intrenched "to-night." [42]

Only in the assault on Fort Wagner a month later were more Federals hit by a thousand defending rifles; then the number would be about 630, today it was 460.[43]

Pitiful proof of how close some of the men who struck on that hot June 14 got to the enemy line came from Gardner when he replied to Banks's request the next day to send medical and hospital supplies into the works for his own men and Gardner's, if the latter wished any. He would have the party met, the courteous Confederate commander said, and then told Banks that he had tried to bring in Union wounded close to his breastworks but Banks's sharpshooters had prevented the act of mercy.[44]

Soon a very serious situation confronted the Federal general, largely because of the many regiments whose nine-month enlistment period would terminate in August (a few had ended in May). Troops near the day of their release did not "feel like desperate service," Banks reported to Halleck in a letter of June 18, while those signed up for the war did not "like to lead where others will not follow." Though such sentiments could not in the end defeat him, it was, he stated, a "wholly unexpected defection" which had robbed him of success on the 14th. Even counting the nine-month men, Banks said he had only 14,000 effectives, a small force indeed to press a siege on a seven-mile front.[45]

Quite as if the sickening air was still in his nostrils, Irwin spoke of the stench from the incompletely policed battlefield and the festering ooze exposed by the great fall in the Mississippi. Low water was also hurting the navy, for no longer could ships below and ships above chat easily with each other by means of flags. Messages had to be delayed while they were transmitted across the intervening point, or be relayed by an army station behind the investing lines. Worse than this, the Atchafalaya was now in Confederate hands, and the shallow stream gave them immunity from gunboat attack. Thus the water route to the Morgan City base that had so conveniently bypassed Port Hudson's guns was gone. Palmer's ships were consequently starving for coal. On June 4 he told Banks that he had barely enough for the gunboats "to do their necessary police work up and down the river," and in his dispatch asking Porter to send the hand grenades that Banks wanted, he threw himself on Porter's charity for fuel—which, of course, would have to be floated on barges past the Vicksburg batteries. The ending of the message showed how much sailors, even when cooperating mightily with the army, preferred their own kind to land-bound creatures: "Let me have a line from you when a vessel comes down, for I cannot understand these soldiers' reports." [46]

As he pressed the siege, Banks was to suffer more minor annoyances from Logan and a major loss across the river at the hands of

Richard Taylor, though the loss the latter inflicted was soon partly retrieved by a stiff defeat of a portion of that vigorous general's command.

It was to Logan that Taylor addressed on the 15th a letter detailing an ambitious program. He wrote from Bayou Ferdoche, a little west of the Atchafalaya, and said he was en route to the Mississippi with a brigade of cavalry, two brigades of infantry, and four light batteries. That very night he intended to attack the Federals opposite Port Hudson, establish communications with Gardner, and throw beef cattle across the river to the hungry garrison. He also revealed that "a large cavalry force" of his command would cross the Atchafalaya in the extreme southern part of the state and penetrate to the lower Mississippi. He himself, after rubbing out the Federals from opposite Baton Rouge to Morganza, would move southward to Donaldsonville, where by means of light batteries he hoped to prevent the passage of supplies up the river. Something even more grandiose than this was in Taylor's mind, though perhaps it was only a hope. If means could be devised to cross the river, he would be pleased to throw one or two cavalry brigades across the Mississippi, to strengthen forces there.[47]

Opposite Port Hudson, Taylor accomplished nothing except to give Colonel Clinton H. Sage—Benedict's successor at "Faussee Point"—a good scare. Fearing that his line of supplies would be cut, Sage had retired on the 15th to the protection of the lower fleet, only to receive the next day a sharp reprimand and the order to return to his assigned position, where, Irwin informed him, he could have withstood a vastly superior force. And before the 16th was over Sage was where he belonged, not so chagrined, however, but that he could report that some persons placed the enemy at 500, others at 3,600.[48]

When it became apparent that the enemy had gone southward, Farragut dropped down the river—he had been intending to visit New Orleans anyway—and on the 19th he reported to Banks from Donaldsonville that all the way down he had heard that both that place and Plaquemine were in enemy hands, and that they had 2,000 infantry, 500 cavalry, and guns in great number. All this, he said, he had found to be false. The commander at Donaldsonville felt no uneasiness so long as a gunboat was present; the admiral was leaving one.[49]

But at 2:00 A.M. of the 20th Emory telegraphed to corps headquarters (there was a direct wire) that the captains of two boats just arrived from upriver had said that the Confederates in large force were headed for the Lafourche country. Realizing the importance of the news to Banks, Emory said he had told the captains that they would be hanged if what they had reported proved false. From Irwin there came the prompt direction to leave two companies at Morgan City, and concentrate the balance of his command at Lafourche—where the railway crossed the bayou of the same name. The steamboat captains were surely out of danger when Emory, later in the day, wired Irwin that it had been ascertained that the Confederate column numbered 4,000 men. If a division could move to Donaldsonville and pursue them, they could be captured, he said; but it would have to be done quickly, or Morgan City was lost.[50]

Emory stripped New Orleans to 400 men in order to save Lafourche, and the enemy was repulsed there on the 20th and again on the 21st, a day of drenching rain, before all the reinforcements had arrived. On the 22nd, a day of still more torrential rains, the Fifteenth Maine, just arrived at New Orleans from Pensacola, was pushed forward to Lafourche, even as Emory got the message that the Confederates were for the third time advancing to the attack. "We shall now beat them back," he assured Irwin.[51]

Morgan City was lost. Taylor was at his military best in the operation there, and not far from his literary best when he reported promptly to Kirby Smith on the 23rd:

> We crossed Berwick Bay in skiffs, stormed the forts, drove off the enemy's gunboats, and captured over 1,000 prisoners, ten heavy guns (among them the siege piece I was forced to abandon in my retreat in April), two trains of cars, with engines complete, large numbers of small-arms, ordnance, &c, and thousands of dollars in stores.

His loss, he stated, had been small because he had taken the place with the bayonet, the men having been forbidden to load their rifles; but the real reason for his success had been his totally unexpected attack against water batteries, open toward the rear.[52]

Encouraged doubtless by the brilliant exploit at Morgan City and minor captures as he moved eastward, Confederate Brigadier Alfred Mouton on the 26th ordered Brigadier General Thomas Green to capture the Federal post at Donaldsonville; and after marching all night Green camped at daylight on the 27th some nine miles from his objective. Taylor himself was that day at Alexandria writing at length to Kirby Smith. The commissary and quartermaster haul at Morgan City had been appraised at the tidy figure of $2,000,000. Taylor also made a suggestion: the 5,000 new Enfields and Burnside rifles that were in the booty could be used to arm the regiments kept at Shreveport because unfit for the field. Taylor could in fact equip them completely.[53]

Upon learning of the threat to Donaldsonville, Emory sent some reinforcements and Farragut dispatched another gunboat. While the men and horses of Confederate Brigadier Green's five cavalry regiments and battery were resting, the general himself investigated his target, which had previously been bypassed as too strong by Colonel James P. Major, the officer who had been responsible for the costly attacks at Lafourche. Citizens stated that the Donaldsonville fort contained from 200 to 500 Yankees, and that there were five gunboats (perhaps only one at the time). "Come down and take command," Green continued in a letter to Mouton. "I want you badly." Not knowing Mouton's views, he wished to take no steps conflicting with his superior's desires. Green himself believed the fort could be rendered "nugatory" by taking a position below it; an act which might induce the Yankees to come out for an open-field fight. "Come down as soon as you can," was his final plea to the former United States senator, onetime governor of Louisiana, and president of the convention which had voted secession for the state.[54]

In spite of what he had written, Green decided to attack Donaldsonville with two enveloping columns of dismounted cavalry during the early morning hours when darkness seemed to promise immunity from naval guns. (Perhaps it was the hateful name of the fort—"Fort Butler"—that riled him beyond restraint.) The carefully devised plan was explained to officers, and guides were furnished; but a picket fired upon one of the columns before it had reached its attack position. Thereupon guns in the fort opened; then from the river came a deadly fire. The *Princess Royal* had been alerted at 12:30 by a red light in the fort. Steaming slowly, "ship clear and ready for action," she opened her guns on the woods around the fort and beyond when a second light flashed fifteen minutes after the first.[55]

The attackers succeeded in entering the stockade between the levee and the river, but were halted by a ditch that no one had thought to tell Green was there, and which his men had no means to cross. Thereupon a most unconventional fight started. According to Green's report: "Our men here used brick bats upon the heads of the enemy, who returned the same." Without intermission the strange contest raged between the defenders—500 or 600, Green claimed—and the assaulting parties of 800, until dawn, when he withdrew. Whence came the supply of missiles, Green did not explain, but he did say that he must have saved 100 men by having an officer bearing a flag of truce order them away from a little shelter they had found near the fort—an act hardly in accord with the best of usage.[56]

From both New Orleans and Baton Rouge small reinforcements were hastened to Donaldsonville in answer to the plea in the victory message of its commander: "I want more men. I must have more men." The next day Emory pronounced the action "a brilliant affair," with heavy casualties to the enemy: 100 killed, 120 captured, number of wounded unknown. The reinforcements which he had previously sent were actually still aboard a transport at the time of the battle, and the costly repulse was dealt the enemy by 225 men, including convalescents, of the Twenty-eighth Maine, under Major Joseph D. Bullen, who had had only 9 killed and 15 wounded.[57]

Many of the enemy fatalities were unquestionably caused by the guns of the *Princess Royal* and the *Winona,* already on the way to Donaldsonville from above, which had heard the *Princess Royal* and had arrived ready for action. At 3:30 her four guns joined the battle with shell and shrapnel. At 5:40, an hour after quiet had fallen on the river, the *Kineo* arrived from below, with men at quarters; noon had barely passed when the *Monongahela* came up the river and joined the fleet; then the *Genesee* arrived from above. In the evening, the now impressive flotilla shelled the woods beyond the town, an act they repeated the next day. The *Winona,* upon dropping down the river a short distance, saw Confederates in force upon the left bank. She "beat to quarters" and dispersed them; on returning upstream she sent a boat to shore and arrested two men "charged with being accessory in cutting the United States telegraph wires." [58]

Such was the defense of the town that Weitzel had occupied on October 25, 1862, without opposition.[59]

But Emory knew that his troubles were not over, and he may have thought that the stroke against Donaldsonville was merely a diversion, with New Orleans the real objective of the force he put at 9,000 men.

An effort to raise a brigade of "unconditional" Unionist citizens in New Orleans soon proved a failure. Emory's call to Banks, "Something must be done for this city, and that quickly," got through before the wire was cut at 5:00 A.M. on the 29th, but not a reply. The next day Emory reported directly to Halleck: "The enemy's object is evidently to raise the siege of Port Hudson by attacking New Orleans." The land force in the city, and in the extensive works about it, was, he said, less than a brigade. Upward of a week would be needed for the message to be in Washington. Probably it was carried by the steamer that bore 500 Confederate prisoners, guarded by 100 convalescent officers and men. They were not safe in New Orleans, Emory explained in a message to General Dix; at Baton Rouge they would be even less secure.[60]

"We only want three days more here," had been the much too optimistic ending of a telegram that Banks sent to Emory on June 25. Five days previously Palmer had written to Porter that Banks was preparing for a more vigorous assault; though it was to be made with picked men and volunteers, the sailor thought it would meet the same fate as the previous two, which he had heard had been badly managed. Perhaps some of the commodore's gloom came from the fact that he had "neither coal nor provisions." But there were also army officers who were discouraged, and on the 26th Dwight placed two lieutenant colonels in arrest—with a circle of a quarter-mile radius as a roaming area—for speaking discouragingly of the prospects. He exhorted: "The soldiers are cautioned not to listen to the voices of alarmists afflicted with diseased imaginations." [61]

Except for work on the regular approaches which were now being dug, and some artillery firing by the Confederates during a morning fog,[62] June 27 seems to have been uneventful, so one can turn to Washington, where Halleck was writing an important letter which Banks probably did not receive until matters were finished at Port Hudson.

After having written approvingly to Banks on April 3 concerning the Atchafalaya as a route for uniting his force with that of Grant, the General in Chief was much surprised when he read in the papers that Banks was at Alexandria, and Grant at Jackson. "This may be well enough so far," he said, "but these operations are too eccentric to be pursued." Banks should join his force as quickly as possible to that of Grant, lest the enemy concentrate against Grant and crush him. It devolved upon Banks to prevent this; Halleck had no more troops to send to Grant, or to Burnside and Rosecrans, both of whom were calling "loudly" for them. When Banks, upon turning back eastward, went to Port Hudson, Halleck, who had again learned of the move from the newspapers, thought it was a mistake. In answer to Halleck's criticism, which was evidently approved by both Stanton and Lincoln, Banks wrote a lengthy explanation on June 18, dwelling upon the fact that New Orleans would be in danger if he took the bulk of his force to Vicksburg, while if he left enough below to keep New Orleans out of peril, he could not carry to Grant more troops than Gardner would be able to add to Johnston.

In his reply, Halleck first directed himself to the part of Banks's letter that attributed the failure of the assault of the 14th to the "unexpected defection" of men whose enlistment period was drawing to a close. Defection on the field of battle Halleck pronounced a criminal offense. The remedy for such action was artillery placed in the rear, loaded with grape and canister, "in the hands of reliable men, with orders to fire at the first moment of disaffection." A knowledge of such orders would, he said, probably prevent any wavering; if not, one punishment would suffice. Banks would be fully sustained in any measures he thought necessary to enforce discipline.[63]

That question disposed of, Halleck said, "The reasons given by you for moving to Port Hudson are satisfactory." When he read Emory's letter, he could see that danger to New Orleans was a reality.

Thirty deserters came into Banks's lines on the 29th; those arriving in the afternoon had had a meatless dinner, and reported that they had been told that in the future the only meat would be that of mules. Perhaps it was one of the thirty who favored the Federal commander with a copy of the June 28 issue of the *Port Hudson Herald,* which stated that an officer had entered the beleaguered place with dispatches from Johnston. The sheet also carried an order by Gardner saying he would hold the place to the last extremity; Johnston would soon relieve Vicksburg; then he would send help to Port Hudson.

On Grover's front the sap had been pushed to within thirteen feet of the ditch, and that night Dwight was to attempt to enter the hostile works with an élite storming party of about 850 men selected from the entire force, led by Colonel H. W. Birge of the Thirteenth Connecticut.[64]

The effort was not made, though when or why it was called off is not clear. Artillery fire was stepped up. "Fearfully hot here. Several men sunstruck. Bullets whiz like fun. Have ceased firing for awhile, the guns are so hot. Will profit by your directions afterward," was a message that flashed near noon of July 1 from a battery to an observer across the river. The next day the observer signaled, "Howitzer's shell goes 6 feet over the gun every shot; last was too high; little too high again. Can't they, or won't they, depress that gun?" The answer was, "Won't, I guess." Then: "Was that shot any better, and that?" To this eager and touching inquiry the unhappy observer had to reply: "Both and forever too high." [65]

The day saw Dwight writing a mortifying indorsement on a dispatch from the colonel commanding at Springfield Landing, reporting a successful attack that the ubiquitous and enterprising Logan had made about 8:30 A.M. upon Banks's supply base. The stroke had fallen heavily on some Negro troops who had retreated, allowing extensive stores to be burned. "Our troops did not behave well," Dwight wrote. "The officers refused to volunteer to bring a dispatch to the headquarters of the commanding general."

Irwin had to devote the 3rd to making an investigation and writing a long report to Banks. He attributed the surprise entirely to the lack of fidelity of well-posted pickets who had allowed themselves to be approached without firing a shot. While he was at the landing, a crowd of contrabands, seeing a party of Federals approaching from the direction whence the raiders had come the day before, raised the cry, "The Rebs is coming," whereupon "a terror-stricken mass of men, women, and children, with loud cries" rushed toward the river, to be stopped by the bayonets of the Sixteenth New Hampshire. Two Negroes eluded the bayonets, rushed into the river, and were drowned.[66]

The Fourth came and went with Emory writing to Farragut that the enemy, estimated by returning Federal parolees at 13,000, with numerous guns, was slowly but steadily advancing upon New Orleans, making strong fortifications at all the passes. To Emory—a soldier who had been in tight spots before—a decision seemed imperative, and he said, "It is a choice between Port Hudson and New Orleans." To Halleck he also wrote. From Morgan City, Taylor wrote to Kirby Smith that upon returning to Thibodeaux in the evening he hoped for more news from New Orleans. He might, he said, "establish important relations there, so as to justify a *coup*." If any opportunity offered, he would, he promised, throw himself into the city and try to hold it, leaving his communications to take care of themselves. Already he had "a powerful artillery" on the river between Banks and his base. So high did Taylor's spirits rise on this Independence Day, when Vicksburg was surrendering and Holmes was being badly beaten at

Helena, that he ended his letter: "I beg leave to add, with great respect, that if all the forces in Arkansas were thrown upon Helena, and firmly established there, with adequate artillery, more could be done to relieve Vicksburg than by any other move on this side of the river." Taylor could be visionary at times, but he was well advised when he inserted the word *adequate* into his appraisal.[67]

The next day brought a letter to Farragut from Porter. It was expected that Vicksburg would surrender on the 5th; pride kept the Confederates from giving up until after the Fourth. A heavy rain that night prevented much work upon approaches at Port Hudson, but Banks's engineer could still report on the 6th notable accomplishments during the preceding daylight hours: the left cavalier was finished and occupied; the right one was nearly completed, but was being constantly injured by a hostile 24-pounder. "Both on the right and left we are now engaged in pushing mines to blow up the parapet, and the enemy is clearly counter-mining," Banks said in a letter to Halleck. "The column of stormers is fully organized and ready." [68]

Colonel W. R. Miles, holding the right of the Confederate line, terminated a dispatch to Gardner's adjutant, protesting depletion of his force:

> Let me be understood; I will hold my line as long as a man stands up; but in justice to the men, who are worked and fought without rest day or night, I earnestly request that enough be left with me to give them an occasional respite of a day.

On the 7th the faithful Miles reported heavy fire from Federal batteries on both sides of the river, while sharpshooters in swarms hailed bullets on his line. There had been a lot of vociferous yelling by the Federals, the colonel said, and there had been a salute-like firing with shotted guns; later in the day the fleet had also broken out in a salute. Some "of them" had hallooed over that Vicksburg had fallen on the 4th. But it was Miles's impression that "fictitious good news" had been given the Union men to raise their spirits, perhaps to stimulate them to make a charge the next morning. "We will be prepared for them should they do so," was the last sentence of Miles's last dispatch.[69]

Perhaps no one but a commander who has held a position such as Gardner held can realize how deeply he was stirred by Miles's assurance of the constancy of the hungry men in gray. But his decision to write to Banks for confirmation of the surrender of Vicksburg and his own capitulation have never been challenged for correctness.

Banks's chief of staff, George Andrews, had the honor of leading the column that marched into the Confederate works early on July 9 to receive the formal surrender. Already, however, on the afternoon of the 8th, a mercy train of wagons filled with rations had moved into the town. Behind Andrews came Colonel Birge and the picked stormers, then two regiments from each division, with bands playing, then two batteries. At the end marched the sailors who had manned the battery of 9-inch Dahlgrens, accustomed now to dust and mud and other inconveniences of land.

"By General Banks's order, General Gardner's sword was returned to him in the presence of his men in recognition of the heroic defense —a worthy act, well merited." So wrote a soldier upon whom hard work and much responsibility had fallen throughout the campaign, Banks's adjutant, Richard Irwin.[70]

In Jackson, Joe Johnston was telegraphing to Jefferson Davis an answer to the message the President had sent on learning of the capitulation of Vicksburg. The message revealed a lingering hope that Port Hudson might be saved, and complained because Johnston had kept silent about his plans with regard to that position. Now on the 9th Davis would read Logan's dispatch about his triumph at Springfield Landing, which Johnston forwarded as he set out from Jackson on the 3rd to see what he could do for Pemberton. The news of the disaster at Vicksburg and the reply had sped through quickly. The one that told of Logan's stroke for some reason had loitered on the way. It may well have renewed the hope in Richmond that the force that had been unable to rescue Vicksburg might salvage Port Hudson, on the very day, perhaps at the very hour, that a man from the U.S.S. *Richmond* raised the Federal flag above the place as a battery thundered in salute.[71]

A MONTH OF MOPPING UP

> The feeling is very strong here in favor of your generals.
>
> *Halleck to Grant*
>
> To send small bodies of cavalry to be put at isolated posts is to give them to the enemy. *Hurlbut to Asboth*

BANKS WAS certainly under no lingering influence of congressional habits when he chose 7:00 A.M. as the time for his occupying column to march into Port Hudson. And three hours before that militarily midmorning moment, Weitzel was to report with his brigade at Augur's headquarters—with two days' rations in haversacks, three more in wagons, and a full supply of ammunition—to be the advance of a move to dislodge batteries harassing Federal steamers below Donaldsonville. No fewer than eighteen guns had been emplaced by Brigadier General Thomas Green, the Texas cavalry general, after the failure of his attack on Fort Butler. And, on the very day that Banks began procedures to dislodge them, Emory was writing to Commodore Henry W. Morris that the enemy expected that New Orleans—within whose confines there were from 12,000 to 15,000 paroled Confederates—would rise as soon as the river was cut below as it already was above.[1]

When Green saw ten transports crowded with troops arrive at Donaldsonville on the 11th, with several following the next day, he lost no time in withdrawing his guns and Colonel James P. Major's brigade of supporting cavalry to Bayou Lafourche, which taps the Mississippi just north of Donaldsonville. Major's four regiments of some 800 effectives with supporting guns took position on the east (descending) side of the bayou, while the three regiments of Green's brigade, which had been keeping an eye on events at Donaldsonville, located themselves, along with a section of guns, on the opposite bank, just across from Major's command. There had been, Green wrote, warm skirmishing for several days between his troops and the Federals on both sides of the Lafourche.[2]

Of the Federal actions in the engagement at Koch's plantation, near Donaldsonville, on July 13, little that is commendatory can be said. Former infantryman Grover (West Point, 1850) was a few months senior as a brigadier general to former engineer officer Weitzel (West Point, 1855), who was commanding the part of Augur's division that was present. Certainly Grover had received instructions from Banks, but precisely what they were is not in the record. In the report that he wrote, Grover did not say whether or not he knew that the Confederate batteries had been withdrawn, or whether or not he had begun a serious advance up the sides of Bayou Lafourche or had merely taken advanced positions pending the securing of information. Weitzel wrote no report at all, though the commander of one of his brigades, the Colonel Dudley who was seen in Augur's advance on Port Hudson from Baton Rouge, submitted one that tells something about the mortifying action.

At 3:00 A.M. of the 13th, Dudley, who had advanced a short distance down the right (west) bank of the bayou the day before with three regiments and two gun sections, had his command under arms, and the enemy attack that he expected struck his skirmishers about 4:30. After some hours of action and maneuvering, the Confederates appeared to be enveloping Dudley's right flank, and he asked for help. Without delay the brigade of Colonel Charles J. Paine arrived and took up a support position.

While Dudley was engaged, an attack was also made upon the brigade of Colonel Joseph S. Morgan, of Grover's division, which had advanced down the left bank of the bayou. Although Dudley had arranged for coordination with these troops by means of flags, an enfilading fire from the left into his command soon showed that Morgan had retired, and Dudley fell back—in perfect order, he said—upon the line which Paine had formed. Then it was—some time well into the afternoon—that Weitzel arrived on the field, and directed a retirement to the bivouac near Donaldsonville. Where Grover was is the big mystery of the day. In his report he said, "Colonel Morgan behaved badly," and backed this up by submitting charges against him. The court that tried the colonel ordered that he be cashiered from the service for misbehavior in the face of the enemy and drunkenness on duty. Banks, however, set the proceedings aside; the evidence, he said, was "too conflicting and unsatisfactory." In a little more than three months Morgan was back on duty.[3]

Green stated that he remained in the vicinity for two days and departed only when he received orders to move toward the Gulf, the Federals remaining meanwhile in and around the fort, apparently with no demonstrations of unfriendliness. In an indorsement Taylor again commended the brigadier who had ended his report, "The victory completely paralyzed the enemy in our rear, and enabled us to move from the La Fourche after the fall of Vicksburg without molestation."

Although the clash of arms had been anything but glorious for the Federals, an important position on the west bank of the Mississippi had been made secure, and the promptness with which Banks had acted is not to be forgotten in the record of that general.

But even before troops had left Port Hudson for Donaldsonville, Grant had Sherman on the march to drive Joe Johnston eastward, and the army he furnished his subordinate had much power. In addition to the Thirteenth and Fifteenth corps (the former under Ord, the latter under Steele), Sherman's force contained the two-division Ninth Corps, although Grant had told Halleck in his victory message of the 4th that he would return Parke's men to Burnside.[4]

On the 4th Sherman reported that three bridges would be built the next day over the Big Black. He expected Ord and Steele some time on the 5th; the following day he would cross and advance on Bolton. The plight of the inhabitants of the region between the Big Black and the Federal lines was disturbing him. All the crops had been destroyed and the cattle eaten, and Sherman had been promising the destitute that if Grant could find a locomotive he would run cars out to the river and make that a depot (actually the Vicksburg harvest included five undamaged locomotives and some cars). For himself Sherman asked for but one thing: maps. But he had to repress a longing: "I feel an intense curiosity to see Vicksburg and its people, but recognize the importance of my present task, and think of nothing else." Of course, every soldier in Grant's army would have liked to get into Vicksburg, and Ord terminated a dispatch about the status of his command for the eastward march: "Am of opinion many men broke by the guards and went into town." Perhaps it would have been better to say that guards had looked the other way. Sherman himself said to Grant, "Surely will I not punish any soldier for being 'unco happy' this glorious anniversary of the birth of a nation, whose sire and father was a Washington." [5]

Even McPherson—who was to stay at Vicksburg and supervise the prisoners and their paroling—indulged in rhetoric uncommon for a former engineer officer. Perhaps he thought he must keep up with Sherman or emulate John Logan and Frank Blair, whose congressional eloquence was well known. But he kept to good, simple words when he suggested to Logan that the Forty-fifth Illinois be at the head of the column that marched into Vicksburg: it had borne the brunt of battle more often than any other regiment in his command, and always with distinction. And Grant used ungilded sentences even when answering Sherman: "The enemy will march outside their works, stack arms, and return inside as prisoners. No troops, except those specified in special orders, will enter the city for the present." [6]

It may be that Francis Herron—whom Dana pronounced something of a dandy as well as a tight disciplinarian—displayed a fresh white handkerchief on the Fourth; though it was not until the next day that he congratulated Porter on his part "in reducing the Sebastopol of rebellion," and heaped praise on the Navy men who had served the heavy guns that Porter had lent him for the left of the Union line. Herron, whose division was charged with collecting everything in its front and keeping it for the army ordnance officer, got a warning from Grant: "None of the colors are to be taken by any individual; they are all to be sent to Washington." [7]

The 6th saw Sherman in position to start, but reporting that the troops were "somewhat disordered by Vicksburg, Fourth of July, and the terrible heat and dust." He had in fact written on the 4th to Osterhaus, whose division was at the destroyed railroad bridge over the Big Black, that he feared "the dust, heat, and drought quite as much as the enemy." Apparently rains of flash-flood proportions had fallen higher up in the state, for while Sherman suffered from the dust he had also to contend with a sudden four-foot rise in the Big Black. The surge of water had interrupted the throwing of bridges and had made fording impossible. Nonetheless, Sherman planned to cross that day and be at Clinton by the 9th; by then he expected to "know the purposes of the enemy, and act accordingly." [8]

Rear attack—the great lesson of Grant's campaign—dominated Sherman's thinking when he prepared his march order. If one of the three columns encountered the enemy in force, the commanders of the other two corps were to direct their march so "as to reach the field of battle to the rear and flank of the enemy." From Bolton, Sherman sent Grant on the 7th some news that was out of date, but must have been of interest anyway, because it lifted the veil of uncertainty that had hung over Johnston during the weeks of siege and particularly during the culminating days when it was known that he was moving toward Vicksburg with the intent to rescue Pemberton. Johnston had intended crossing the Big Black on the 4th and 5th with 400 wagons; word of the capitulation had turned him around. One division of his army had been opposite Birdsong's Ferry; with it Johnston had been personally present. Three divisions had been opposite Messinger's Ford, and one opposite Bridgeport. All columns had pontoon trains. The entire country was marked with Confederate encampments, especially at Bolton, from which Breckinridge had retreated with his division only at midnight of the 6th.[9]

The midday temperatures being what they were, Sherman marched at night—with men jostling each other in the dark and dust. Forenoon of the 10th saw his three columns arriving before Jackson, Ord on the south, Steele in the center, Parke to the north. Corps commanders were at once ordered to gain ground to the front without sacrificing too many lives, and all officers were told of the importance of procuring water near the camps—this on the day that Johnston was thinking want of water would force Sherman to assault without delay. Ord and Parke were directed to send detachments as far as Pearl River to secure favorable points from which to attack. Ord was also to send cavalry for demolition work on the railroad to the south, and Colonel Cyrus Bussey—chief of cavalry—was to dispatch all available horsemen to Canton for similar employment.

Like hungry vultures, guerrillas had kept eager eyes on Sherman's columns; three wagons bringing in forage had been pounced upon and burned.[10]

Reconnaissance quickly revealed that Jackson had been the center of much activity since Sherman had interrupted his demolitions in May to hasten westward to join Grant as he closed on Vicksburg. On both flanks the entrenchments had been extended to Pearl River; they had also been much strengthened. Johnston's entire army appeared to be behind them, and though Sherman said on the 11th that he had kept his artillery quiet, the Confederates had not been hesitant to open theirs—mostly fieldpieces, but also "some heavy rifled 6 inch guns." Cars had been running over the repaired railroads to the south and north, but east of the town the river bridge had not been completed, and both passengers and freight had to be unloaded and transferred to horse-drawn vehicles. In the vicinity of the Federal camps, all houses had been vacated; Sherman interpreted this as meaning strong resistance was intended.[11]

The previously unresponsive Union guns awakened at 7:00 A.M. on the 12th for an hour's cannonade. As was their wont, Sherman's 20-pounder Parrotts used too much ammunition, and he made haste to ask Grant to send him 20,000 more rounds for them; he also asked

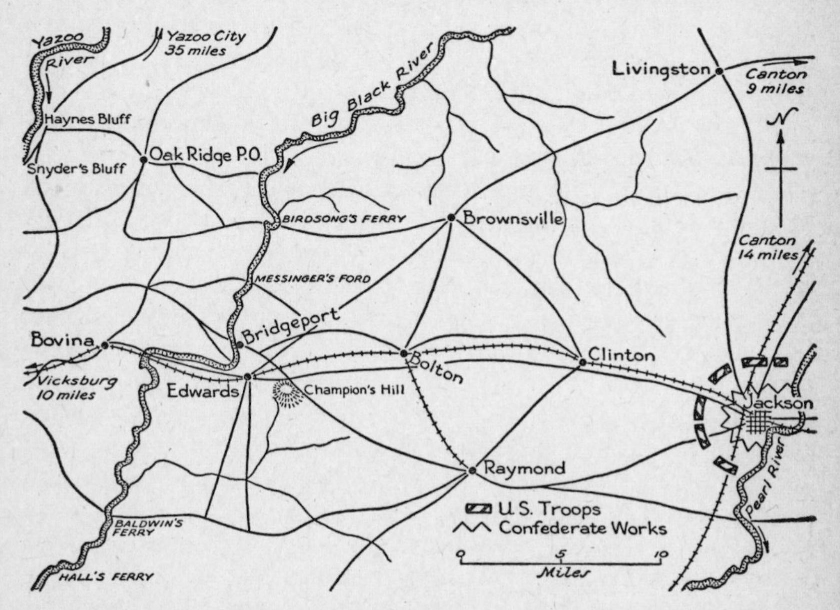

REGION BETWEEN VICKSBURG AND JACKSON, MISSISSIPPI

to have ready for his call—or to send if that seemed best—6,000 6-pounder shells and 1,000,000 musket cartridges, "assorted"—thus revealing the presence of shoulder arms of different calibers and types. If he but had plenty of rifle ammunition Sherman could, he said, "make the town pretty hot to live in." [12]

As the investing lines were pushed closer they were also extended to reach the river on both flanks. Losses were small, except that

Lauman's division, working in an area obscured by trees and bushes, got too close to hostile parapets and was hit by a cruel cross fire from guns and rifles. Ord promptly relieved him, and Sherman sustained Ord, though he probably did not know how warmly Ord had praised Lauman at the Hatchie the preceding October. From a scout there came word that within the hostile lines, against which a steady fire was being maintained, there were four—not five—divisions of infantry, numbering 19,000 men, and that 10,000 more men were expected. But the effectiveness of the 19,000 was doubled or even trebled by their entrenchments, and Sherman had no intention of assaulting. Here, as there had not been at Vicksburg, were flanks that could be turned, and on the 15th Sherman told Grant that if Johnston tarried a day or two, he would so threaten his rear that Johnston would be compelled to come out and fight. On a small scale he was already coming out and fighting, and Ord reported that four sorties in his front were quickly contained and the enemy driven back to shelter.[13]

Sherman naturally hoped he could detect signs of a pending evacuation—a stroke properly timed could then play havoc—but little could be seen because of the enveloping smoke from campfires and burning railroad ties. As night fell on the 15th it must have been maddening to Sherman as he studied the hostile position with his glasses. Of only one thing could he be sure: the heavy guns still glowered from their emplacements.[14]

When morning came, Johnston was still there, and soon the report came that enemy cavalry had crossed Pearl River to the north. "Be vigilant," was the injunction that Sherman sent to the commanding officer at Clinton. John McArthur—whose two brigades seem to have been something of a reserve—was hurried back, and when the hostile cavalry struck—1,500 strong according to Sherman—they were repulsed. Sherman bade Parke to "get everything ready for a good cannonading to-night," and promised to send ammunition as soon as it arrived. After darkness had closed in, the sound of wagons could be heard in Jackson, mingled, however, until midnight, with the noise of picks and shovels, as if the works were being strengthened. When the lines were pushed forward early on the 17th, empty works were found. Johnston had conducted the first of the skillful withdrawals which have done much to give him a good and firm place among generals. But it must be said that Ord wrote ruefully in his report that if they had been able to march with a full supply of ammunition, or if the train afterward sent forward had arrived in time, greater damage would have been done the Confederates in their withdrawal.[15]

In prompt orders to his corps commanders Sherman stated that the weather was too hot and the country too destitute of water to attempt to follow Johnston toward Meridian and Selma. Such a move, he said, would have to be deferred until October. But he wanted to do everything possible to give the Federals the advantage when a campaign opened against Mobile and Alabama. To this end Ord was directed to break up the railroad "absolutely and effectually" for ten miles south of Jackson, while Parke did the same to the north. From Grant there came the statement that he did not favor marching the men too much; but he still was loath not to have Johnston followed by cavalry, believing that trains might be destroyed and desertions encouraged. Decisions, however, were left to his subordinate. At first Grant considered holding Jackson with one corps; then before the 17th had ended, he telegraphed to Sherman, "You can return slowly to Black River." [16]

Men from Potter's division of Parke's corps had reached the statehouse first and raised the Federal flag for the second time above the Mississippi capital. But all entering columns were withdrawn when occupation of the city was turned over to Blair's division. Fire had spread from storehouses that Johnston had ignited, and the new damage, added to what the Federals had done on their May visit, caused Sherman to call the place "one mass of charred ruins"—though actually many fine buildings were undamaged. The Confederate commander had not waited until he marched out to apply the match. During the siege he had burned many handsome dwellings outside and near his line of defenses to improve his field of fire and deny them to Sherman. Now, as he retreated, he not only destroyed bridges but brought into the war something seemingly new. He mined the road, and a Jackson citizen was severely wounded by one of these weapons, while a Union soldier was killed and two others injured by a second.[17]

On the 19th Sherman wrote to Porter, "Last night, at the Governor's mansion, in Jackson, we had a beautiful supper and union of the generals of this army, and I assure you the 'Army and Navy forever' was sung with a full and hearty chorus." He remained until the 24th, by which time the three brigades of the Fifteenth Corps which had gone to Brandon, thirteen miles to the east, had finished their destruction of three miles of track, and the other extensive demolitions that Sherman prescribed had been carried out. While the siege was in progress Sherman had written to Grant that the absolute stripping of the country by his foraging parties to a distance of fifteen miles was terrible to contemplate. Then he rationalized: "It is the scourge of war, to which ambitious men have appealed, rather than the judgment of learned and pure tribunals which our forefathers had provided for supposed wrongs and injuries." [18]

When Sherman marched away he sought to lessen the suffering of the innocent. Hospitals received supplies, and to a responsible committee there was given enough hard bread, flour, pork, and bacon to sustain five hundred people for thirty days. To a committee at Clinton fifteen thousand rations were presented, after they had signed a pledge that none of it would be converted "to the use of the troops of the so-called Confederates states." [19]

Though there had been no hard battle, and casualties had numbered only 1,122,[20] the experience of commanding an army of three corps had been invaluable to Sherman. His orders were careful and clear and his almost daily dispatches to Grant once more reveal his admirable trait of keeping his superior constantly well posted. The lessons learned at Vicksburg had been reflected, he commented in his report, in "the sagacity and skill" with which his troops had thrown up their works in front of Jackson.

As Parke ended his report about the Jackson operation, the excessive heat, the choking dust, and the great scarcity of water seemed to haunt him like an awful dream. Not many of his men had been killed; not many had been wounded; not many had been captured. But each one of them had been tried to the utmost. When one reads what this fine Eastern soldier wrote, and Sherman's statement to McArthur on the 12th, "Nothing troubles me but water," and to Grant on the same day, "I fear the weather is too hot for me to march to Grenada," [21] one cannot but be irked at the harsh criticism of Halleck for not marching from Corinth to Vicksburg in the summer of 1862. That summer, it has been seen, was also one of excessive dryness in Mississippi, and Halleck's men were not the seasoned veterans that Sherman had in 1863; and Sherman's supply line was a trivial problem compared with what Halleck would have had.

The night when Johnston marched away after considerable clatter, to leave Sherman to gaze the next morning at empty works, was only four days later than the crossing by Lee in a downpour of rain into

Virginia over the swollen Potomac in the face of Meade's army. Lee's escape was soon known everywhere in the North, where it caused heartache, and at no place more than in the White House. Stunned by the shock, the slow-arriving news about Johnston's marching eastward from the Pearl quite unhindered may have seemed a minor disappointment. Any discerning analyst, who knew the conditions in Mississippi, could, however, have seen that there was a great difference. Lee had been isolated from his haven of safety by a raging river, and had had to improvise the bridges on which he crossed after some abatement of the flood. The works with which he had protected his bridgehead were mostly constructed after his arrival at Williamsport, using the time that Meade's leisurely pursuit had given him. Meade had had plenty of cavalry which he could have thrown across the river at Harpers Ferry to hold the southern bank of the Potomac opposite Lee's precarious position and prevent the throwing of bridges.

As early as July 14 Sherman had provisionally, at least, decided to let Johnston go, for on that day he said in a message to Rawlins: "I think we are doing well out here, but won't brag till Johnston clears out and stops shooting his big rifle guns at us. If he moves across Pearl River and makes good speed, I will let him go." This intention he probably neglected to communicate to Johnston when on that day, under a flag of truce, he sent the Confederate general copies of Northern newspapers of the 7th and 8th, which, of course, were bursting with the Gettysburg story and what then looked like a splendid prospect of destroying Lee's army. Considering that sleep must have been a little difficult under the best conditions on those hot Mississippi nights, Sherman showed himself unsparing in waging war upon his adversary's mind, the finest of all targets at which to strike. He thought, he said to Rawlins, that the papers he had sent, together with the gunfire he had arranged for that night, would disturb Johnston's "slumbers."

Just as Grant had not held against Sherman his failure in front of Vicksburg in the closing days of 1862, and had quickly forgotten how vigorously his outspoken subordinate had opposed his bold move to a point below Vicksburg and Sherman's entreaties to halt operations after he had crossed the Mississippi until supplies could be brought up, so now apparently he did not think that Sherman had been slothful or negligent in his operations against Johnston. Still, Grant must have been greatly disappointed—as Lincoln was over Lee's escape—for on the 11th he had closed a dispatch to Sherman by saying he hoped to hear of Sherman's "giving Johnston a good thrashing and driving him beyond Pearl River, with the loss of artillery, transportation, and munitions of war."

Two weeks to the day before Sherman on July 25 recrossed the Big Black and went into nearby camps, with headquarters at Parson Fox's, Pemberton's paroled men marched out of Vicksburg and headed eastward. Sherman had kept an eye on them and reported to Grant on the 13th that the column was headed for Brandon by way of Raymond. A captain sent to apprise Johnston of Pemberton's itinerary was denied permission to enter Jackson, and Sherman seemed impenitent at having broken up the ferries over Pearl River so that Pemberton would have to cross as best he could.[22]

The Confederate government was very eager to get data about the number of men who were being paroled so as to begin arrangements for their exchange. Pemberton, of course, could have furnished it rather promptly, but on the 6th McPherson informed him that Grant had said that he could not permit a courier to be sent that day with dispatches "to your Government." He would, however, "do so as soon as the public interests will admit"—a way of putting the matter that for all its delicacy had a barb. Apparently nothing was allowed to go to Richmond, and there is error in the heading "Vicksburg, Miss., July 10, 1863," of the message that Pemberton sent to Jefferson Davis that began, "The great and apparently intentional delay in paroling the garrison made it necessary to leave General [Martin L.] Smith behind to complete the rolls." The rolls had been sent for, Pemberton said, but they could not be obtained in less than five days. The message must have been sent at some time after Pemberton's departure from Vicksburg on the 11th.[23]

For his insinuation that there had been purposeful delay in carrying out the paroling, some consideration should perhaps be shown. The Confederate general had been in a decidedly uncomfortable position, both with regard to his own command and to the Richmond authorities, and the long, hot days had not been conducive to an unruffled mind. Grant was eager to get the captured men paroled and marched away as soon as possible, so as to proceed with other matters and to save rations and forage. The order of July 5 that turned the paroling over to McPherson enjoined "all possible dispatch," and directed that every available printing press be requisitioned to make the necessary blanks. Two days later the printers were rapidly supplying the needed forms, and eleven officers with an adequate force of clerks were doing "all that mortal men can do," an assistant provost marshal informed Grant's adjutant. If the work took longer than had been expected it was because there was more to be done than had been anticipated, and because of the determination to do it well.[24] While Pemberton had held Vicksburg much longer than Grant had expected that he could, he also had the distinction of providing a clerical problem for whose measurement there was no yardstick of previous experience.

Before departing, Pemberton had had a final favor to ask of Grant. His copies of the notes that gave the conditions of surrender had, "by mistake," been sent out in his trunk. As he wished General Smith to have copies of these documents, he had the "honor to request" that Grant furnish Smith copies. He managed to make the request without expressing a word of regret over his own negligence.[25]

It was a low-spirited column which Pemberton led over the road the day Sherman was settling down in front of Jackson. "Many of the men are leaving for their homes without authority," he said in a dispatch sent on the 15th to Johnston from Raymond. Two days later he telegraphed to Davis from Brandon, earnestly recommending that he be allowed to furlough his army for thirty days. If that were done, the army could, he said, be brought together again; otherwise not. A dispatch from Davis showed no enthusiasm for the furlough idea. In Richmond, he said, they were anxiously waiting for the number of each grade who had been paroled. Then, after an immediate exchange, those who were fit could serve their country in its hour of sorest need. Hopefully Davis was praying "for their better fortune on another field." [26]

"Hour of sorest need" assuredly had reference to Gettysburg as well as Vicksburg, about which (and about Helena and Port Hudson too) Grant's men had surely informed their prisoners—charitably, of course, so as to lessen their chagrin. And Joe Johnston's troops must likewise have known about Port Hudson and Gettysburg when they marched from Jackson. To them the news of the defeat in far-off Pennsylvania must have been a shock, for in an address to his men on July 9, Johnston had sought to raise morale by saying, "The telegraph has already announced a glorious victory over the foe, won by your noble comrades of the Virginia Army on Federal soil," and asked them "to emulate the proud example of your brothers in the east." [27]

As he toiled over the hot road, another telegram from Davis reached

Pemberton. The President still resisted furloughing the men: they must, he said, realize the pressing nature of the Confederacy's condition; thirty days could be important to its future. Pemberton himself, Davis said, as well as the other generals whose names had gone forward, had already "been discharged" from their parole; they were to enter duty at once. There was little consolation for Davis in Pemberton's reply. Misled by their officers, his men, he said, were insisting on going home. In spite of all that he could do—he noted that he had no arms—those from west of the Mississippi and from the state of Mississippi had already "deserted"; as they neared their homes, Georgians, Alabamians, and Tennesseans would do the same. In what remained with him there was only a hard core of 1,600 Missourians who would go wherever Davis wished. Under such circumstances, the President could do nothing but yield: accordingly Pemberton on the 18th offered his men a furlough of thirty days. When the period was over they were to reassemble in Alabama at Demopolis (where the railroad from Meridian to Selma crossed the Big Warrior and the Tombigbee); there they would be rearmed and otherwise re-equipped.[28]

Charges and countercharges were to be made by the exchange agents and commissioners of the North and South over the question of Pemberton's paroled men, with higher officials joining the dispute. Each side claimed that the other had been violating the Dix-Hill cartel; each side claimed that it was doing only what the other had already done. For months the dispute dragged on, with the Federal authorities asserting that many Northern men who were being offered in exchange had never been properly paroled. In their arguments and denunciations they could certainly have made excellent use of a dispatch that Seddon sent to Pemberton on July 18. The War Secretary requested a list of men who were deemed "reliable" as well as a list of the sick and wounded who would not be available for early service. Candidly, if not wisely, he explained: "We shall not have enough captured men of the enemy to discharge all our men [from their paroles], and it is important to make selection of the most serviceable."[29]

While no question was raised by the Confederates about Grant's action with the great Vicksburg capture—though the Richmond exchange agent was embarrassed by not receiving accurate rolls from Pemberton—it was otherwise with the some 6,000 men whom Banks paroled at Port Hudson and sent to Mobile for release. August had

Courtesy Library of Congress

MAJOR GENERAL ETHAN A. HITCHCOCK

barely begun when a Confederate agent in Demopolis wrote to Johnston's adjutant, "In regard to the Port Hudson prisoners, I have in consultation with Lieutenant-General Pemberton, General Stevenson, and Commissioner Watts, decided their paroles to be illegal, as they were not properly paroled." His, of course, was not the final voice in the matter, and the major reported that Gardner's men were demanding the same privilege accorded their Vicksburg comrades. It would have been hard to convince them that the little slips they carried were not legal, and before long some of them were on furlough even beyond the Mississippi.[30]

Five days after the enemy major made his pronouncement, Banks was reading a letter from Halleck that must have given him a shock: the General in Chief feared the Confederates would not consider his paroles as according with the Dix-Hill cartel. In the reply that Banks made haste to write, he protested that his action had been in strict conformity with that document; and Gardner had approved the place of delivering the parolees and everything else connected with the matter, over his signature. More than this: "The prisoners insisted upon having each a copy of his parole, that they might not be compelled to enter service again until they were exchanged." Before Banks's letter arrived Halleck had seen in Richmond papers statements that the Port Hudson paroling did not harmonize with the cartel. While the alleged flaw had not been pointed out, Halleck supposed, he said in replying, that it was the one he had pointed out in his previous letter, and which he drove home in clearer terms than before:

> As General Gardner after becoming a prisoner of war did not command in the field, he was no longer a commanding officer and could not bind his Government. Had the agreement been made by him before his unconditional surrender, it would have clearly been within the terms of the cartel.[31]

In contrast, the patroling of prisoners was part of the terms that Pemberton had accepted while still commander of the Vicksburg garrison.

By the middle of September, Halleck was writing to Grant quite as if the paroling that Banks had done was perfectly proper, and Major General E. A. Hitchcock, the Federal Commissioner of Exchanges, evidently did not think much of the point Halleck had raised with Banks—if indeed he knew about it. In his report for the year, the elderly and scholarly general strongly asserted that Banks's agreement with Gardner to parole and deliver the Port Hudson men at Mobile was justified by the cartel, and he roundly denounced the Confederate agent for stating in a letter in a Richmond paper that the troops so delivered were under no obligation to observe their paroles.[32]

As checkers were calling Pemberton's rolls on the roads leading out of Vicksburg, there was also activity on the waterfront: Grant was sending Herron on an expedition up the Yazoo River. Morning had found that general's infantry aboard transports about to depart for Port Hudson. Then almost simultaneously with the word of Banks's success there arrived a report that Joe Johnston had directed that all the Negroes in the vicinity of Yazoo City should be set to work fortifying that place. "This we cannot permit," Grant said in a note that assigned Herron a new mission.[33]

The Yazoo was up—six feet, according to General Washburn, Grant informed Porter. But that stream also had the habit of falling rapidly, and Herron transferred his command to boats of lighter draft, using the delay to embark a battery which Grant told him to take if there was time. Not until nearly noon on the 12th did Herron get under way with his fleet of some five transports convoyed by the 14-gun *Baron De Kalb* and two 6-gun tinclads. Lieutenant Commander John C. Walker, on the *De Kalb's* bridge, had had experience with the tricky Yazoo, but Herron, acquainted though he was with the difficulty of dragging guns over Arkansas mountains in wintertime, was getting his first experience of combined operations. Soon he would learn that when aboard even an armored gunboat one must be prepared for surprises.

A citizen living twenty-five miles below Yazoo City sent word of the expedition to Lieutenant Colonel William B. Creasman, of the Twenty-ninth North Carolina Infantry, who commanded at Yazoo City. Thus warned, Creasman by nightfall had his regiment in prepared redoubts and rifle pits, with the guns of his light battery covering the road from Vicksburg. Men from the Confederate Navy under Captain Isaac N. Brown—who will be remembered as the commander of the *Arkansas*—took their battle stations near the heavy ordnance that bore upon the river. But Creasman knew it was a time to take precautions, so he loaded his baggage and cooking vessels and sent the wagons out of town.

When Herron tied up a mile and a half below his target near noon of the 13th, the *De Kalb* continued upstream to reconnoiter. The narrow, winding river kept Walker from using much of his formidable gun power, and after throwing some thirty shells and receiving the fire of six hostile pieces, he dropped back—driven away in the Confederate reports. In the meantime Herron had landed his cavalry—twenty-five men whom he had picked up at Haynes Bluff—on the west bank of the river, with the mission of obtaining information and, if possible, preventing the escape of boats reported to be at Yazoo City.

Herron was not too long on patience, and receiving no report from his horsemen, he debarked three regiments on the east bank and marched on the enemy works. A damaged bridge over an unfordable stream was soon encountered, and by the time it had been repaired and the march resumed, Creasman had departed. The regiment that Herron sent in pursuit picked up a few prisoners and a little equipment before returning; but in the Yazoo City works undamaged heavy ordnance was found, and in addition Captain Robert Voigt's company of Waul's Texas Legion was captured. The captain had refused to obey Creasman's evacuation order, and Brown acidly wrote that if Voigt had been captured it was because he wished to be.[34]

The twenty-five cavalrymen well earned their day's pay. They captured a picket boat seven miles above the town, and compelled the burning of five one-time luxury steamers that were still high up the Yazoo. Four other steamers escaped, the sole survivors, according to a correspondent of the *Atlanta Appeal*, of "the splendid fleet which sought refuge in the Yazoo River."

While the discouraged Atlanta journalist said that the day had closed "the history of another strongly defended river," Brown had a little substantial consolation: the *De Kalb* had been sent to the bottom by two of his mines (torpedoes, he called them). With Herron and an aide aboard she was steaming slowly up the river when, at 7:30 P.M., as she was abreast of the navy yard where the *Arkansas* had been built, one mine tore out her bow and another ripped her stern. Though she sank in about fifteen minutes, all her small arms and many other things were saved. Her crew, many of whom were badly bruised but none seriously injured, was no more than aboard the *Kenwood* when a third mine exploded near her port bow. The next day Walker took one gun off the *De Kalb* and before long had salvaged her entire armament.

In reporting the next day the loss of his once-proud gunboat, Porter managed to tell a characteristic story. As a usual thing, he informed Welles, Negroes and deserters gave helpful information about torpedoes; but they had not this time. Furthermore, when Brown had once sought to plant mines, the people of Yazoo City had threatened to hang him. Thus, though a lookout had been kept for them, none had really been expected. In the future Porter promised more caution, for, "While a rebel flag floats anywhere, the gunboats must follow it up." [35]

On the morning of the 16th Herron received an order to proceed to the Big Black and protect Sherman's flank and rear. As no transportation whatever had been brought, wagons had to be impressed, but by twelve o'clock he was on the road with seven regiments and his battery. Midafternoon of the next day found part of his command at Canton, but completely exhausted. Upon learning on the 18th that Johnston had evacuated Jackson, Herron returned to Yazoo City. With more "borrowed" wagons, he hauled in 2,000 bales of cotton from the surrounding country. When they had been loaded on his transports, together with 800 secession horses and mules, and, in addition, mattresses, sheets, towels, pillows, and blankets, from the steamers, in sufficient amounts to equip a 450-bed hospital, Herron sailed for Vicksburg. Every man that he had brought up the Yazoo he took back, but many were sick. Sick also was Yazoo City; its guns were gone; its works were blown up "entirely."

As far back as Herron had seen, the country was full of corn, beef, hogs, and sheep. And hidden in the woods and valleys were great stores of cotton; not less than 50,000 bales, he wagered, could be gathered in from the community. Confederate Captain Brown's happiness over the success of his mines was tempered by sad thoughts of the accumulation of cotton. In a letter on the 17th urging that all west of the Big Black should be burned, he said, "If the cotton is left for the enemy it will more than pay their expenses in taking Vicksburg." [36]

A tale to rival Herron's report of fabulous stores of cotton came from Natchez, where Brigadier General Thomas E. G. Ransom debarked his brigade of McArthur's division of McPherson's corps on

July 13. Grant of course knew that it was principally at Natchez that the Confederates were sending supplies across the Mississippi, and he even seems to have had a conception of the magnitude of the commerce. Named after the Natchez Indians, who had massacred the garrison of the first fort the French had built upon the bluff in 1716 to protect their warehouses, the banners not only of France, but of Britain and of Spain had floated above the town before the flag of the United States was raised in 1798. For Natchez, Jefferson Davis had a special warmth of feeling, for it had been the girlhood home of his second wife, Varina Howell, and the "Briars" where she had lived was still one of the many extremely impressive mansions of the community. Natchez was also the site of "Monmouth," the estate of New-York-born John Anthony Quitman, a prominent major general in the War with Mexico, and afterward a governor of Mississippi, dead since 1858, but in his closing years very bitter toward the North. In addition to its Catholic cathedral, the town was well known for its Protestant churches and for the Jefferson Military College founded in 1802 six miles from the city. The first cottonseed mill in the country was built at Natchez in 1842, and many of the wealthy planters whose plantations were in the Delta region or across the river in Louisiana had great homes there. Citizens of the town during the years 1817–1821 had the pride that comes from being residents of a state capital, and in subsequent years they doubtless regarded Jackson—not laid out until nineteen years after Natchez had received a city's charter—as a mere upstart village unenriched by culture and tradition.

Those who lived upon the bluff could, however, take no pride in the reputation of "Natchez Under the Hill," where the famous Natchez Trace that came from Nashville ended on the Mississippi. No place on all the Western waters was of more ill repute for its heavy concentration of vice and iniquity. In the brothels, the grog shops, and the gambling dens of this other Natchez, life was cheap, and the river gave a convenient depository for the body of a hapless pleasure seeker or gambler into whom a knife had been thrust or a bullet fired.

More than a year of war had passed before the Federal flag was seen from Natchez. Then on the afternoon of May 12, 1862, the U.S.S. *Iroquois* and four smaller craft dropped their anchors off the town. The little flotilla was under command of Commander James S. Palmer, who on the 9th had restored the United States flag to its old place above the arsenal at Baton Rouge. In informing the mayor of Baton Rouge that he was leaving no occupying force, but that the flag must not be molested, Palmer had said, "War is a sad calamity, and often inflicts severer wounds than those upon the sensibilities." The letter which Palmer sent ashore addressed to the mayor of Natchez was refused by a Confederate lieutenant who was at the wharf with nine men: the cutter bearing it was not flying a white flag. When a party of seamen and marines with two howitzers arrived without much delay, they were met by two members of the common council and proffered the mayor's apologies. Palmer's officer was received by the mayor not only courteously but with a touch of kindness, and the mayor stated that the Confederate flag had never been displayed officially in Natchez. If Palmer chose to hoist that of the United States, the authorities would, the mayor promised, do all they could to protect it; but they hoped they would not be responsible for acts of an excited populace. Whereupon Palmer proceeded up the river without bothering Natchez any further.[37]

When Beauregard learned of what had taken place, he wrote—on May 25, while engaged in preliminaries to the evacuation of Corinth to Halleck's army—warmly commending the lieutenant who had refused Palmer's letter, and strongly denouncing the Natchez authorities. Today he might have called them "collaborators"; actually he pronounced their conduct "ill-becoming Southerners fighting for their homes and independence." Nor did he stop there. He contrasted their quailing before an insidious foe with the bright examples of patriotism and love of principle of the people in Missouri and Virginia. In neither of those states had the enemy ever entered a city of importance without being received "with scorn and abhorrence." [38]

But the Mississippi flowed quietly on, and in the hot summer months the people on the hill and the people below saw many vessels flying the Federal flag pass their city. They saw Farragut's fleet twice ascend the river to attack Vicksburg; they saw the transports carrying the brigade of Brigadier General Thomas Williams go upstream to make the land assault that was called off because of the strength of the position. Jubilation must have been great when the fleet and the transports returned southward after the project had been abandoned in late July, 1862. Soon, however, there came the news of Williams's sharp defeat of Breckinridge at Baton Rouge on August 5, and the destruction of the well-loved and renowned *Arkansas* the next day. A little more than a month after that the

Essex, which had been responsible for the blowing up of the Confederate ram by her own commander, came to anchor off Natchez. Her commander, William D. Porter, of whom much has already been heard, wrote thus about the visit:

> At Natchez a boat's crew from the *Essex* were sent ashore to procure some ice for my sick, when they were wantonly attacked by over 200 armed citizens, wounding the officer in command and killing and wounding 5 seamen. I immediately opened fire on the lower town and set a considerable number of the houses (from whence they were firing on us) on fire. After bombarding the place for an hour the mayor unconditionally surrendered the city.[39]

What the comment of the recuperating Beauregard was when he learned of what had taken place can only be surmised. But the denizens of the lower town surely knew and freely used Porter's nickname—"Dirty Bill." And the refined inhabitants of the great mansions on the bluff may have thought the social outcasts below the hill had been treated more roughly than they deserved for merely shooting Yankees.

The officer who ten months later arrived with an occupying force in Natchez was one of Grant's old and well-tested commanders. As lieutenant colonel and commander of the Eleventh Illinois, Ransom, a Vermont-born civil engineer before the war, was severely wounded at Fort Donelson. But he was again at the head of his regiment at Shiloh. He had been at Champion's Hill, though not engaged, the brigade which he then commanded being attached to McClernand's corps, and his name had gone to Washington in a telegram that Dana sent shortly before the surrender of Vicksburg: in front of his rifle pits one of the mines was being dug.[40]

So swift were Ransom's moves after debarking in midafternoon that twenty Confederate officers and men were captured before they could escape, and a large quantity of mail was seized. Promptly the mayor and council met him at the courthouse and received Grant's instructions as to their behavior to pass on to the citizens. Very important information was soon in Ransom's possession: only a few days previously 150 wagons with ordnance stores for Kirby Smith had been ferried to the west bank, and a large number of cattle that had come from beyond the river were still not far to the east. Having not a single cavalryman, Ransom was at a disadvantage; but by three o'clock the next morning two hundred infantrymen were astride impressed horses and setting forth, some to the west, some to the east.

The converted foot soldiers were repaid for their loss of sleep, and thrills usually reserved for cavalrymen atoned for saddle chafings. Those who had crossed into Louisiana overtook the rear guard of the ordnance train, destroyed 268,000 rounds of artillery ammunition, and brought back 312 new Austrian rifles with much ammunition, together with a lieutenant and an order he was carrying. Most of the train had, however, gone too far for safe pursuit by a small, improvised force. The expedition to the east came upon a drove of 5,000 Texas beef cattle only four miles away. The small Confederate cavalry guard fled, and the animals were driven back and were soon being loaded on steamers, some going up the river, and some to Port Hudson.

Ransom was proud of his Illinois and Wisconsin regiments, and on the 16th he wrote:

> My troops have worked hard—frequently forty-eight hours on duty—and have behaved admirably. Hardly a case of pillaging, or even of disrespectful treatment of a citizen, has occurred, and the people constantly express their gratitude and happy disappointment in their treatment.[41]

That Ransom's thoughts turned to Grierson was quite natural, and on the 14th his aide wrote to the fine cavalryman, "If you could manage in any way to get a troop here, you would be doing very great service, almost inestimable service." Ransom wished to have at least one hundred troopers make the return trip on one of the transports that was taking cattle to Banks, and his aide said, "it is of the last importance that you should have a command here soon." There was no working behind Banks's back, for the letter was to be shown to him, and it ended, "Don't do anything to cripple his movements." At the moment Banks was at New Orleans, but a dispatch from his acting chief of staff informed Grant that a battalion of Grierson's cavalry was embarking—it was the 16th—on the *Planet* and that the rest would probably follow the next day on the *Imperial,* one of the two steamers that had brought the cattle whose arrival was pronounced "most opportune and acceptable." [42]

Ransom's old Eleventh Illinois was sent to reinforce him, and McPherson directed, "When you have collected all the cattle, stores, ammunition, lumber, &c., which you can get, you will report to this post with your command." In acknowledging on the 20th—at 3:00 A.M.—receipt of the instructions, Ransom said he could get several thousand more beef cattle intended for Joe Johnston, and much cotton, if he had a battalion of cavalry to give protection against Logan, who was reported scouting the country. In closing, the engineer in Ransom came out: "Please send me some tracing cloth. I wish to preserve some maps of this country." Four days later Ransom was pleading for fifty wagons and harness; then, with conscripted mules, he could haul in cotton from near Hamburg that belonged, not to citizens, but to the C.S.A. His mounted infantry was just back from a two-day scout, and their sharp eyes—aided perhaps by information from Unionists—had turned up 207,000 rounds of rifle ammunition and some for artillery hidden in a ravine. It was indeed an interesting country. And Ransom had a novel item: "There was a large public meeting at Hamburg (twenty miles east of Natchez) on the 22d, to consider the question of abandoning the Confederacy. I have not heard the result of it." [43]

Grant's pride in the Army of the Tennessee matched the affection that Ransom had for his brigade. If at times his men showed a lack of disciplined military behavior, there was a compensatory quality, and he had said in his report:

> It is a striking feature, so far as my observation goes, of the present volunteer army of the United States, that there is nothing which men are called upon to do, mechanical or professional, that accomplished adepts cannot be found for the duty required in almost every regiment.[44]

Though the most responsible assignment since the surrender had been given to the professionally trained McPherson and Sherman, the volunteers Herron and Ransom had carried out missions with an energy and a finish that could not have been exceeded by many regulars. Both knew how to use the resources of their commands, and both held their men under discipline that would have been envied by Sherman—perhaps because as civilian soldiers they were closer to the men in the ranks.

On the day that Ransom reported about the Hamburg meeting, Grant was writing to Lincoln at length, respectfully but urgently recommending the promotion of Sherman and McPherson to brigadier generalcies in the regular army. The letter was the result of a strong suggestion that Halleck had made in one to Grant on the 11th—a friendly letter in which the General in Chief sent his kindest regards to his old friends in Grant's army and said that he was utterly tired of the political hell that was Washington. Meade, recently made a brigadier general in the regular army, seemed to be the right man in the right place—the first who had ever fought the Army of the Potomac well. Hooker had been more than a failure—had he been continued in command, he would have lost both the army and the Capital. But the main point to the letter had to do with the remaining vacancy in the rank of brigadier general in the regular army, and Halleck hoped three more openings would be caused by the retirement of Harney, Anderson, and Cooke.

Prominent candidates for positions in the regular army were, Halleck explained, Sherman, McPherson, Thomas, Sedgwick, and Hancock. His own idea was that Sherman and McPherson had rendered the greatest service and should come first. "State their services pretty fully, and mention the battles they have been in under your command," Halleck said after suggesting that Grant write to the President if he agreed with the views in the letter. Then he added, "The feeling is very strong here in [favor of] your generals." That Grant agreed heartily with Halleck need hardly be said, and there was nothing perfunctory in the story of his two leading subordinates that he unfolded to the President. In view of McPherson's death on the field of battle, one sentence stands out: "his corps, the advance always under his immediate eye, were the pioneers in the advance from Port Gibson to Hankinson's Ferry." With Halleck's own view of where outstanding military merit lay, supported by such testimony as Grant gave, the result was inevitable. Sherman was made a regular brigadier from July 4—thus ranked by Meade by a single day—and McPherson received the next appointment, with a commission dating from August 1, the day of Harney's retirement.[45]

A few days later Grant recommended to the Adjutant General of the Army the promotion of a number of his officers for distinguished service in the Vicksburg campaign. None of the four brigadiers was given the second star that Grant requested; in spite of Halleck's efforts, all openings had been "gobbled up" before the arrival of Grant's recommendations. But promotion was awarded the eight colonels that he asked to be made brigadier generals. A single lieutenant colonel was included with the eight—Rawlins. His was the promotion that Grant said he would particularly like, and considering the fact that Rawlins had never commanded troops, Grant made the surprisingly strong statement, "I can safely say that he would make a good Corps Commander." [46]

In an uncommon way Grant had on July 20 expressed his high opinion of another of his volunteers, already a major general—Logan. Before the start of the final Vicksburg campaign, a leave of absence had been sent to Logan because of his impaired health; but it had been declined—well, or not well, Logan would not be absent at such a time. Now Grant *ordered* him to Illinois, to recuperate and then return. Grant was losing another able Illinois soldier—Major General Richard Oglesby. He had been with Grant in early Cairo days, had led a brigade at Fort Donelson while still a colonel, and had been seriously wounded at Corinth. No longer fit for hard field service, he had been commanding the left wing of Hurlbut's corps, but early in July his resignation was accepted.[47] He would be a stanch war governor in Illinois a year later and finally a senator during Reconstruction days.

Throughout July there was continued important and excellent service from Hurlbut at Memphis—seen a little in connection with Helena. Dodge at Corinth was sending him intelligence obtained by his efficient scouts, which was forwarded to both Grant and Halleck, while the troops under Dodge (who succeeded to the command of the left wing of the Sixteenth Corps) had a major responsibility in protecting northern Mississippi and western Tennessee; from that region the Confederates were seeking to draw supplies and recruits, while doing all they could to harass Union forces. Most of the troops with which the Federals had to contend were irregulars—guerrilla bands, or at best Partisan Rangers.

On July 7 a mounted command of about 750 men and a battery of mountain howitzers caught up near Iuka with Confederates who the previous afternoon had tried to drive off a large drove of cattle from the vicinity of Corinth. After a brisk action in which the Federals had twenty casualties, the enemy retired toward the fastnesses along Bear Creek,* though—according to estimates given Federal commander Colonel Florence Cornyn of the Tenth Missouri—they numbered from 1,500 to 2,000 men and had a battery. Three days later some Confederates were driven out of Bolivar, and Dodge reported that

* See maps in Volume IV, pp. 158 and 220, for Bear Creek and Tennessee towns mentioned in the remainder of this chapter.

Newsom, Biffle, and J. A. Forrest were all raising regiments in the vicinity, while Richardson was said to be on the Hatchie in the vicinity of Denmark.[48] Biffle and Richardson already had extensive records as troublemakers.

Although there were some West Tennessee Federal regiments, that part of the state was in the large as strongly Secessionist as East Tennessee was Unionist. On his famous raid against Grant's communications the previous December, N. B. Forrest was received with affection and given much aid. His first move after crossing the Tennessee and driving away a Federal force at Lexington had been against Jackson, where Grant for several weeks had had his headquarters before beginning his overland operation against Vicksburg. After a skirmish on the 19th a few miles from Jackson, Forrest reconsidered, and moved on Trenton and Humboldt, where there were little more than token Federal forces. Riding with Forrest at that time was a four-man battalion under Colonel Jacob B. Biffle.[49]

But now at last, in mid-July of 1863, Jackson, Tennessee, had its sharp skirmish, even while Sherman was trying to make Jackson, Mississippi, "pretty hot to live in." And Jacob Biffle was a main actor, though not a word about his dashing part at the head of 800 men is found in a report by himself or any other officer on his side. Those who were trying to wrest West Tennessee from Federal hands at this time seem to have put little if anything on paper about their exploits, a fact that gives color to the belief that they had a distinctly irregular tinge.

Colonel Edward Hatch of the Second Iowa Cavalry, who has previously appeared in the pursuit of Van Dorn after Holly Springs, and who must by now have been about as familiar with the region as a native, was in command of the Federals. At the head of 360 Michigan cavalrymen, 300 from Iowa, and 200 West Tennesseans, with 300 Illinois infantry and some Michigan guns giving a hard core to his command, Hatch closed on Jackson on the 13th. The engagement which he described in detail was exciting, marked by much maneuvering in which success swung quickly back and forth. There was street fighting, with firing from windows, and with Confederates pouring in destructive volleys from behind a barricade into two fleeing companies of their own, mistaken in the smoke and dust for Yankees. The conflict ended in a complete victory for Hatch, and he pursued the enemy on several roads for ten miles, returning because of night. Then, his men having come upon thirty barrels of whisky, Hatch had as much trouble saving the town as he had had in "whipping" the enemy. The Maine-born colonel, who did not seem to miss anything, gave a salute to feminine Secessionists: "The women of Jackson, previous to our attack, carried ammunition for the enemy in a very gallant manner under fire." [50]

While the Jackson contest was at a dramatic stage, Biffle had arrived from the north, where three days previously he had completely surprised a Federal cavalry outpost of about a hundred men at Union City. The incident greatly mortified Hurlbut, and he said so in a dispatch of the 14th to Brigadier General Asboth, who, with headquarters at Columbus, Kentucky, was in command of the district. Asboth, it may be recalled, had previously been the recipient of a rather stinging reprimand from Halleck, and now Hurlbut laid out for him some sound military doctrine, more pleasingly expressed than one usually finds it: "To send small bodies of cavalry to be put at isolated posts is to give them away to the enemy. You have certain posts to hold which are impregnable to any irregular force. Confine yourself to this, and when you move your cavalry move them in force." The ending glittered as a maxim for any soldier: "Only constant activity saves my line." [51]

When some ten days later Grierson was back again at Memphis, Hurlbut must have been pleased indeed, and he lost no time in making Grierson chief of cavalry of the Sixteenth Corps. The bad news traveled rapidly, and the Confederate commander at Grenada, Brigadier General James R. Chalmers, promptly ordered much of his force—largely Partisan Rangers and guerrillas—back to Panola (near present Batesville).[52] Four days later—on August 1—Grant issued a long order regulating matters in the parts of Kentucky and Tennessee west of the Tennessee River, and the portion of Mississippi west of the Mississippi Central Railroad. Members of legally organized Confederate companies would, if captured, be treated as prisoners of war, but it would be different with those who belonged to irregular bodies, as well as with Confederate agents hunting deserters, or attempting to enforce conscription.[53]

Already Dodge had instructed Colonel August Mersy, commander of one of his brigades: "Any band of rebels or single person caught interfering with the railroad or telegraph, in any way, who are not regularly in the Confederate service, shoot on the spot. I don't want any prisoners of that kind." [54]

Once in camp at Parson Fox's "with fine shade and plenty of

water," the urge to write again seized Sherman. The personal and official thanks which he had given to the officers and men in the order of July 19 that turned them westward were not enough, and a long address to them on the 27th began: "When in progress of the war, time and opportunity present a favorable occasion, we should pause to reflect upon the past." Three days later, in a note to Parke, Sherman's conscience was still hurting. Neither orally nor with his pen had he—he feared—given adequate expression to his feeling for Parke and his veterans of many Eastern fields, then under orders from Grant to return to Cincinnati. So Sherman tried again:

> Be kind enough to assure all of my hearty respect. When you see Burnside, give him my love. Tell him for me that we are armed against all the enemies to law and Government; that we fire upon the secessionist of the South, the autocrat of the North, and the anarchist everywhere. If another Vallandigham arises, let him be banished to that land from which there is no appeal on earth. Our Government must govern, and not be ruled by every agitator of the hour.[55]

A gala reception and great honors would be given the men of the Ninth Corps when they disembarked. Of the great army which had opened the mighty river, they were the only body of men whom the people of the North for many months would see marching beneath proud banners.

But the great moment of Parke's men was when they stood at parade and listened to Grant's farewell order that briefly recited in unembellished language what they had done. Eyes could well have been a little moist as soldiers heard fall from the lips of officers who had led them well, Grant's concluding words: "Major-General Parke will cause the different regiments and batteries of his command to inscribe upon their banners and guidons 'Vicksburg' and 'Jackson.' "[56]

CHAPTER IV

MOBILE *vs.* TEXAS, THE GRENADA RAID, AND THE LETTER OF THE MONTH

The truth is, general, the war is not so near its end as you seem to suppose.

Halleck to Hurlbut

It should be our policy now to make as favorable an impression upon the people of the state as possible.

Grant to Sherman

WHEN GRANT issued his order of August 1 seeking to restore tranquillity to western Mississippi, Rosecrans had been away from Murfreesboro for over a month. His skillful advance had caused Bragg to surrender the well-prepared positions centered about Tullahoma, which he had held throughout the winter and spring, and the Confederate army was now in Georgia, Bragg's headquarters having been at Chattanooga for about three weeks. In the valley of the Mississippi there would be no other great battle and no other crucial campaign during the remainder of the war. And as there was, for the most part, nothing but minor maneuvering by the Army of the Potomac during the summer and fall of 1863, interest in the North tended to center on Rosecrans's Army of the Cumberland. Ahead of it was the most sanguinary battle in the West of the whole war, and the brilliant Confederate victory on the field of Chickamauga would raise Southern spirits, badly depressed by Gettysburg, Vicksburg, and Port Hudson, and force the North to realize that the contest was by no means won.

Because the battle is the payoff, and gives the suspense and the great but tragic drama to war, the reader seeking only excitement may desire to leave the Mississippi and move to Rosecrans's headquarters, when late in June, after his six-month sojourn in Murfreesboro, immune to all prodding, he at last set forth. But by flitting from great battle to great battle one does not learn the full story of the war and of its chief figures—to say nothing of the lesser commanders or of the men in the ranks. The great decisions in the tumult of conflict, upon which the outcome hinges, have to be made swiftly; and what leads to them cannot always be recaptured. While orders were sometimes written, battle orders in the Civil War were largely oral—and they still are. Try as one may, one can only vaguely picture a general in battle unless the general's character is revealed through messages in the approach of battle or in its aftermath, or in the planning of his campaign and in his dealings with superiors and subordinates. And unless one knows about the minor campaigns and operations that were a necessary basis for the great campaigns, or a consequence of them, and about the marches, the railroad and river movements, and about the way in which the all-important problems of supply were handled, and knows something about the information of the enemy upon which decisions were based, one's knowledge of the war is pitifully circumscribed. It is also in their behavior in their camps, upon the march, and in the minor operations, quite as well as in the excitement of great battles, that soldiers reveal themselves. And it is in some minor operation that a lower commander usually has the chance to reveal his military character—his ability to make decisions, to act quickly and resolutely, and to control his men.

Thus, merely because the Army of the Cumberland both literally and figuratively occupies the center of the stage, we cannot now trace its advance up to the moment, take position at Rosecrans's headquarters in Winchester, Tennessee, look into the future with him, and then accompany him in his bold and able move across the Tennessee, and through rough mountain passes into the valley beyond where catastrophe awaits him.

Before we join Rosecrans, we shall watch Grant throw converging cavalry columns against Grenada to destroy a concentration of locomotives and cars massed there by the Confederates for safety's sake. With Sherman's withdrawal from Jackson, the Rebels would wish to put their rolling stock back in operation hauling troops and supplies, at the same time that the whistles of the trains cheered faltering civilians. As Grant's troopers ride to their target, the general will try to make them models of good behavior so as to stimulate the Union feeling of whose existence he has learned in many ways. Grant also writes a very revealing off-the-record letter to Charles Dana.

Beyond the Mississippi, Federal troops are to enter not only Fort Smith but Little Rock. It is well over a year since Curtis first set out from the northeastern corner of the state with Little Rock as a seemingly possible objective, to halt—largely because of logistical considerations—at Helena. While the campaign that finally won the state capital was marked by no great battle, it was distinctive in many ways, and the war had few moves bolder than the one on the final day when Frederick Steele threw half of his small command across the Arkansas River in the face of an enemy about his own size, strengthened by difficult terrain. In the last of August news is to come from Kansas of an outrage that incensed the North as few things did. In the middle of September, as the people intently watch Rosecrans's hazardous progress, they have also read not only of the bitter guerrilla warfare in Missouri, but of the exasperating conflict there of the two irreconcilable factions of Unionists, one of which sent a huge delegation to Washington to secure Schofield's removal. They have also to read and argue about Lincoln's proclamation suspending the writ of habeas corpus.

Before these matters are dealt with, consideration will be given to a question regarding the future operations of parts of Grant's and Banks's forces, which had engaged the Federal High Command and those two generals even while events described in the last chapter were transpiring. Because there has been considerable misunderstanding about it, a somewhat detailed explanation is required. The reader will note the delay in Federal communications, and he should keep in mind the advantage the Confederates had from the speed with which telegrams could pass between Johnston, Bragg, and the Richmond authorities. If Washington had been connected by reliable wires with Vicksburg and New Orleans, and Grant had had circuits to Port Hudson, Helena, and Memphis, the Federal command problem would have been simpler.

The question begins with Banks's letter of July 8 giving Grant the good news of Port Hudson's capitulation. After driving away the troublesome hostile guns below Donaldsonville, he "earnestly" desired to move into Texas, which he pronounced denuded of Confederate troops. The operation which he contemplated would not, he thought, take more than two months. But it would require more force than he had, and he wanted Grant to furnish 10,000 to 12,000 men. Doubtless it was his experience with the nine-month men that led him to comment, "I want Western men." In his answer on July 11th—in which he spoke of having had Herron on transports ready to go to Port Hudson—Grant seemed to imply approval of Banks's Texas idea, for he said it would give him great pleasure to help after Sherman's return, which he thought would be in less than a week—provided he did not receive other directions from Washington. There would even seem to have been some enthusiasm for Banks's proposal in Grant's statement that he could spare "an army corps of as good troops as ever trod American soil," which he strengthened by adding: "No better are found on any other." Grant had telegraphed to Washington the substance of Banks's request and the reason for it. (And in regard to the men, he specifically asked, "Shall I send them?") In addition, he had forwarded Banks's actual dispatch to Cairo by Colonel Riggin. Thus Banks was soon aware that the Washington authorities knew of his eager proposal to conduct an operation in Texas.[1]

Encouraged by Grant's reply, Banks seemingly clung to the Texas idea after he went to New Orleans, where he soon heard that the nine-month men were continuing to make trouble at Port Hudson. They would think of nothing but going home, and a company of mutineers was being shipped down the river for confinement at hard labor on Ship Island for the duration of the war, if the general approved. In a letter to Grant on the 18th Banks said that his own men at Donaldsonville were too disabled by the recent campaign to do more than prevent the 8,000 Confederates in the Lafourche district from reaching the Mississippi. He looked eagerly for the corps that Grant had spoken of sending; it would be of "infinite assistance." Although not actually named, Texas was surely the target he had in mind.

Then Banks set down a new idea and a new task for Grant. Banks confidently believed, and he said the Rebels expected, that Joe Johnston would fall back on Mobile. After saying, "The capture of Mobile is of importance second only to the opening of the Mississippi"—a statement that could well have been taken from Halleck's instructions of the previous November—Banks expressed the hope that Grant would have Johnston followed southward. He himself could give some aid, both by land and by sea, in case Mobile should be Grant's destination. "No pains," he added, "should be spared to effect its reduction." [2]

Before Banks's letter had arrived, Grant may well have read a short telegram from Halleck that seemed to dispose of Banks's Texas aspirations. Dated 8:00 P.M., July 15, it read:

> No expedition to Texas will be undertaken at present. First clean out Mississippi, Arkansas, and Louisiana. I have written fully to you and to General Banks by mail.[3]

This looks much like the decision of the General in Chief alone, without the intrusion of the President from a high-policy standpoint because of foreign relations that were soon to dominate the issue.

The letter to Grant of which Halleck spoke reveals how desirous the latter was to start further operations without delay. It carried the date July 11—the day when John Hay recorded that Lincoln was in buoyant spirits, believing that Meade, in spite of his delays to date, would still make an end of the Confederate army defeated at Gettysburg. All that had come from Grant to date was his short victory message of the 4th; the General in Chief was eagerly waiting for more information from him; he was likewise "exceedingly anxious" about Banks, from whom he had not had a word since June 29. Basing his thought on the assumption that Johnston had been driven away and that Port Hudson had been captured, Halleck said: "What is to be done with the forces available for the field? This is an important question, which should be carefully considered." Knowing that it was the desire of the Administration to get seceded states back into the Union, and that the President must set the war aims, Halleck said: "If the organized rebel forces could be driven from Arkansas and Louisiana, these States would immediately be restored to the Union. Texas would follow, almost of its own accord." [4]

Here was optimism rivaling Lincoln's momentary high spirits. But Halleck gave no orders; he merely expressed views for Grant to consider. Circumstances could easily require a different course from that described: Joe Johnston, for instance, might be so reinforced as to require all of Grant's force to oppose him.

In bringing forward Mobile as an objective, Banks had been anticipated by a full six days by Sherman. The place should be attacked, Sherman had said in a message to Grant on July 12 (after acknowledging receipt of the news of Banks's Port Hudson success, and Prentiss's at Helena); once Mobile was taken, a move on Selma, Alabama, would be possible. But Sherman wanted no Mobile assignment with the army with which he was then investing Jackson. The move against the place should, he said, be from New Orleans. Grant's first mention of Mobile to Halleck appears to have been in a dispatch of July 18, the very day that Banks was giving it high priority in his letter to Grant, and certainly subsequent to Grant's reading of Sherman's dispatch. After reporting that Johnston had evacuated Jackson and that Pemberton's parolees were deserting, and describing the success of Herron up the Yazoo and of Ransom at Natchez, Grant said, "It seems to me now that Mobile should be captured, the expedition starting from some point on Lake Ponchartrain." But Grant gave no indication that he could assist in a Mobile operation. In fact, his thoughts were directed elsewhere. Schofield, who had aided Grant at Vicksburg, had, in a letter congratulating Grant upon his success, asked for reciprocity, and Grant, after noting that there was much sickness in his command, said to Halleck, "I will co-operate as soon as possible with General Schofield, so as to give him the line of the Arkansas." [5]

Grant's message closed with the query whether he should retain or send the Ninth Corps back to Burnside. The reply that Halleck wrote at 11:30 A.M. on July 22 should be seen in full:

> Yours of the 15th and 18th just received. Should Johnston escape and join Bragg, the Ninth Corps must be sent to Rosecrans by the quickest route. If not, it may be used elsewhere. Before attempting Mobile I think it will be best to clean up a little. Johnston should be disposed of; also Price, Marmaduke, &c, so as to hold the line of the Arkansas River. This will enable us to withdraw troops from Missouri, Vicksburg, and Port Hudson, remodeled so as to be tenable by small garrisons; also assist General Banks in cleaning out Western Louisiana. When these things are accomplished there will be a large available force to operate either on Mobile or Texas. The navy is not ready for co-operation. Should Fort Sumter fall, ironclads can be sent to assist at Mobile. Please send copy to General Banks.[6]

This by no means closed the door to an operation against Mobile, except possibly for the present; in fact, the dispatch has more the tone of a discussion of possible operations than of a hard-and-fast directive. In view of Halleck's telegram to Grant on the 15th, indicating that Texas would not be an immediate objective, the mention of that state is significant. The Mobile-Texas question was being weighed in Washington, and a letter that Halleck wrote to Banks two days later indicates that a decision had been made. After stating that Banks's operations—following a cleanup in the Teche and Atchafalaya regions—must depend "very much upon the condition of affairs," he said:

> Texas and Mobile will present themselves to your attention. The navy is very anxious for an attack upon the latter place, but I think Texas much the most important. It is possible that Johnston will fall back toward Mobile, but I think he will unite with Bragg.

Banks was directed to make preparations for an expedition into Texas, and it was indicated that Grant could probably send him assistance.[7]

When taken in connection with later statements to both Banks and Grant, Halleck's expressed preference for Texas over Mobile constitutes something of an enigma. Uncertainties in the puzzling question doubtless come in part from conferences and decisions in Washington of which there is no written record.

Six days after his first Mobile recommendation, Grant, in an uncommonly long letter, written promptly upon receipt of Halleck's letter of the 11th, again pressed for Mobile. Now he implied that he could furnish troops; but how many, he did not say. His command was "entirely unfit" for any present duty requiring long marching; yet, "by selecting," any pressing duty could be done. Though he still favored a move on Mobile from Lake Ponchartrain, he added a significant comment: "I have not studied this matter, however, it being out of my department."[8]

On July 30 Banks urged Mobile as the next target even more strongly than Grant had on the 24th. The captor of Port Hudson has been seen, in his letter to Grant on the 18th, still apparently eyeing Texas. He was looking both ways when he said in a letter five days later to Halleck: "The possession of Mobile and the occupation of Texas would quiet the whole Southwest, and every effort should be made to accomplish this. Its importance can hardly be overestimated." But all thought of Texas had left him by the 30th, as well as the belief that Johnston would move to Mobile. He painted matters in his department in a very rosy tint—the Confederates were retiring toward Shreveport; Morgan City had been reoccupied; New Orleans was calm (in his letter of the 23rd he had said it was never healthier at that season)—and he urged a move against Mobile by 20,000 to 25,000 men. But the loss of twenty-two regiments of nine-month men had left him with only 12,000 effectives; thus the force to take Mobile must come from Grant. Banks, however, had given up the thought of an overland move from Mississippi. Because of their need of rest, the Western troops could not make long or rapid marches; and the operation that he outlined involved a landing on the Gulf Coast and a short march against the land works protecting Mobile, which the 5,000 Confederates reportedly at the place were then "industriously engaged" in strengthening.[9]

Banks may have come to a decision to talk to Grant immediately after he had written this letter; he certainly must have soon been on his way to Vicksburg, where he arrived at 9:00 A.M. of August 1. In a letter he wrote to Halleck from that place he said he "understood" that a movement against Mobile met with Grant's approval, to which he added the interesting qualifying words, "if it be consistent with the general plans of the Government, upon which condition only I urge it." He mentioned the tempting possibility that if the "rebel government" lost Mobile, it had no outlet to the Gulf except Galveston. Warming to the project that he now thoroughly endorsed, he concluded that the Mobile operation "need not last more than thirty days"; thus it could scarcely interfere with any other movements east or west.[10]

When he read Banks's prediction of thirty days, Halleck might well have recalled that Banks had never expected that it would take him as long as it did to capture Port Hudson, but had written to him on May 18—while his command was at Simmesport and he himself was in New Orleans—as if he would soon be successful there, and would then join Grant. Although Banks's estimate might have had Grant's concurrence, Halleck also knew that Grant had taken longer at Vicksburg than he had anticipated. There had been optimism about the ill-fated Yazoo Pass expedition when Grant said on February 15 that the gunboats were within six miles of the Coldwater River, and the naval commander expressed no fear that they would reach it "and the Yazoo." [11] The General in Chief must have remembered that Grant had believed that his assault of May 22 would succeed, and that, when the siege had begun, he had not expected Pemberton to hold out as long as he did. Time estimates for a recommended operation are matters a superior must always be careful about in his own planning of coordination with other projects.

Grant himself, however, indulged in no time prediction in the telegram he sent on the same day to Halleck. After stating that everything indicated the withdrawal of Kirby Smith's troops to Natchitoches and Shreveport, he said merely: "Mobile can be taken from the Gulf Department, with only one or two gunboats to protect the debarkation. I can send the necessary force." (Would that force have been the 20,000 to 25,000 that Banks stipulated in his letter of July 30?) The telegraph line out of Memphis being still out of order because of saboteurs, the dispatch went to Cairo, where it was not put on the wire until August 8. At least it had the important effect of causing Lincoln to reveal in a message to Grant the next day that it had been his authoritative voice that had caused the decision to go against Mobile:

> I see by a dispatch of yours that you incline quite strongly toward an expedition against Mobile. This would appear tempting to me also, were it not that, in view of recent events in Mexico, I am greatly impressed with the importance of re-establishing the national authority in Western Texas as soon as possible. I am not making an order, however; that I leave, for the present at least, to the General-in-Chief. . . .[12]

In spite of the last sentence, it is idle to say that the President had merely expressed views to Halleck which the General in Chief had been completely free to accept or reject. It would in fact be hard to imagine a case in which it was more properly the function of the government to direct where military forces should be used.[13] Whether Lincoln and Seward were unduly alarmed over the possibility of foreign intervention in the summer of 1863—after the Confederate defeat at Gettysburg and their loss of Vicksburg and Port Hudson—is quite beside the point. But what Lincoln meant by the words "I am not making an order" is a little hard to see. Actually, he was not entirely up to date; three days previously Halleck had telegraphed Grant to send a special messenger to Banks with the dispatch:

> There are important reasons why our flag should be restored to some part of Texas with the least possible delay. Do this by land, at Galveston, at Indianola, or at any other point you may deem preferable. If by sea, Admiral Farragut will co-operate. There are reasons why the movement should be as prompt as possible.

In the covering sentence Grant was directed to give all possible assistance in the execution of the order. But before the arrival of this dispatch, Grant had—on August 7—received a directive to send to Banks a corps of from 10,000 to 12,000 men.[14]

Lincoln's and Halleck's statements differed in important details. The President thought the flag must go up in western Texas; the General in Chief virtually said that any place in the state would do. What was behind the order of August 6 that went to Banks through Grant, with a copy mailed directly to New Orleans, Halleck explained in a letter to Banks on the 10th. Recalling that the order left Banks entirely free to select any point in Texas for occupation, Halleck said it had been sent at the explicit direction of the Secretary of War. As Halleck understood it, the order "was of a diplomatic rather than of a military character, and resulted from some European complications, or, more properly speaking, was intended to prevent such complications." After stating that he did not think either Galveston or Indianola was the proper point of attack, Halleck drew aside the veil still further:

> If it be necessary, as urged by Mr. Seward, that the flag be restored to some one point in Texas, that can be best and most safely effected by a combined military and naval movement up Red River to Alexandria, Natchitoches, or Shreveport, and the military occupation of Northern Texas. This would be merely carrying out the plans proposed by you at the beginning of the campaign, and, in my opinion, far superior in its military character to the occupation of Galveston or Indianola. Nevertheless, your choice is left unrestricted.

By an operation such as Halleck described, Banks would, he said, keep in contact with his own base, while separating "two points of the Rebel Confederacy," and thus cutting off supplies and reinforcements from Texas. On the other hand, the occupation of Galveston or Indianola would divide Banks's troops and enable the enemy to concentrate all his forces upon either of those points or on New Orleans. In closing, the General in Chief again stressed that complete freedom of decision remained with Banks; he was "writing simply as a suggestion and not as a military instruction." [15]

Occupied as he was with reading a great number of letters and telegrams, it is not strange that Halleck sometimes forgot an item that had been reported, or failed to recall what he himself had said in a hastily written dispatch. When he dwelt on the military virtues of the Red River route, Halleck had forgotten that the great drought in the Southwest had eliminated that important stream as an available avenue of entry into Louisiana. But no harm was to result, precisely because Banks had been left with freedom of choice, and, being in the theater, was in no danger of overlooking a virtually dried-up river.

Halleck's letter could hardly have started on its long ocean trip before he received Banks's letter of July 30 from New Orleans and the one Banks sent two days later after his hurried trip to talk to Grant. In reply the General in Chief said: "I fully appreciate the importance of the operation proposed by you in these dispatches, but there are reasons other than military why those heretofore directed should be undertaken first. On this matter we have no choice, but must carry out the views of the Government." [16]

In Banks's general report, written two years later, is the statement: "After the surrender of Port Hudson, I joined with General Grant in recommending an immediate movement against the city of Mobile." Candor would have required that he at least admit that he had initially urged the Texas operation that he later condemned. Grant, on the other hand, speaks in his *Memoirs* as if the decision against Mobile had been entirely Halleck's, mitigating his criticism by saying that he was well aware that the President was anxious to get a foothold in Texas.[17] From this, one would hardly suspect that Lincoln had taken the trouble to telegraph to Grant and explain why he was not at the time in favor of an attack on Mobile.

Surprisingly, in Nicolay and Hay's discussion of Texas *vs.* Mobile, not one word is said about Grant's having urged a move on Mobile—in spite of the fact that it was Grant who would have furnished the troops. Nor does Halleck emerge as the person who had persuaded Lincoln to adopt the Texas move—as one might think from his statement to Banks that Texas was more important in his judgment than Mobile. It was Secretary Seward, as the General in Chief confirmed in his letter to Banks, who had caused the selection of Texas as the next target, because of concern over Napoleon III's plan to establish an empire south of the Rio Grande.[18] Although we do not know what Halleck may have said to the President, we do know that Lincoln read Grant's dispatch to Halleck of August 1 urging a Mobile operation; and we must believe that he gave careful thought to it. But he rejected the proposal and telegraphed his highly regarded commander gently and considerately.

Very fortunately, a long letter that Grant wrote to Halleck on August 11 reveals his thoughts and plans when the summer of 1863 was well advanced. After stating that he had taken great pleasure in notifying Sherman and McPherson of their appointments to brigadierships in the regular army, and commenting upon their high qualifications, Grant said, "I feel under many obligations to you, general, for the interest you have ever taken in my welfare and that of the army I have the honor to command. I will do the best I know how to satisfy you that your confidence has not been misplaced." Then, having explained that, though the letter was intended to be private, he would mention some matters that were at least semiofficial, he continued, "I have no doubt movements here seem slow since the fall of Vicksburg; but this could not possibly be helped." The capture of Port Hudson had, he said, put a great demand on him for transportation; he was only then getting off the last of the 9th Corps, while the movement of the 13th to New Orleans was just beginning.

In some detail Grant told of expeditions that he would make—as soon as transports could be had—into Louisiana from both Natchez and the Lake Providence region. Inasmuch as he proposed to advance as far as Monroe, he thought his move would not only force back upon Shreveport the few troops that Kirby Smith had left to annoy plantations between the Quachita and Red rivers, but that, once at Shreveport, they would remain there (presumably even after Grant withdrew). This wishful thinking was strange in view of Grant's experience with the persistence and resiliency of the enemy. In the letter there was a paragraph which, because of Grant's generally careful judgment and temperate pronouncements, must have made quite an impression at Washington:

> This State and Louisiana would be more easily governed now than Kentucky or Missouri if armed rebels from other States could be kept out. In fact the people are ready to accept anything. The troops from these States, too, will desert and return as soon as they find that they cannot be hunted down. I am informed that movements are being made through many parts of Mississippi to unite the people in an effort to bring the State into the Union. I receive letters and delegations on this subject myself, and believe the people are sincere.

A pronouncement of this sort can have influence on superiors after its writer has forgotten that he has made it. Actually, the peace feeling among citizens of Mississippi was, Grant indicated in his *Memoirs,* ephemeral, and "soon subsided."

Grant's habitual sanguine outlook may have been stimulated by the fact that he no longer feared that a large part of his army might be fated for a spell of sickness; its health was better than there had been "any reason to hope for," and physically his troops were ready for another campaign. But he still had worn-out guns. The worst of these, some of which had fired 3,000 shells, had been replaced by captured pieces, and requisitions for others had been made.[19]

Just what does all this show? Merely this: on August 22, the day of the arrival of Grant's letter, the Washington High Command could feel that Grant was planning operations across the river that he believed were important, and that he agreed that there was a possibility of bringing these states back into the Union. More than this, in Grant's long letter Washington found no mention of Mobile.

At about the time the Texas expedition was starting, Halleck should have received a letter from Banks indicating that he saw great virtue in the operation entirely apart from the reason given him for its precedence over Mobile. Under date of August 26 he wrote:

> Independent of any political or diplomatic considerations, Texas presents an arena as important as any portion of the country. . . . The rebellion in Louisiana is kept alive only by Texas.

The occupation of Galveston, the capture or dispersion of a considerable part of the enemy Texas troops, and the destruction of steamers in the central rivers were listed as essentials for crippling the rebellion in Texas beyond recovery.[20]

What were the actual facts about the vulnerability of the important port that as late as August 1 Grant and Banks urged as the next target; and what in general were the Confederates doing during these hot and desperate months?

A warning to look to the safety of Mobile had come to Johnston in a message that Brigadier W. H. Jackson wrote at Brandon at 10:00 P.M. on July 18. Jackson, watching carefully the operations of the force that Sherman had sent to tear up railroad track east of Pearl River, wrote, "Prisoners report that enemy will endeavor to take Mobile at once." Far away in Chattanooga, Braxton Bragg was looking solicitously in the same direction; in a telegram to Johnston he said, "The loss of Mississippi involved Mobile; that virtually includes the productive part of Alabama." Believing that Rosecrans could not advance for six weeks, Bragg offered his command to Johnston to use as he saw fit. Aroused by such warnings, Johnston on the 19th queried Major General Dabney Maury as to the Mobile situation. Maury's reply of the 20th was anything but cheering. His force amounted to only 2,000 infantry, 600 cavalry, and 10 field guns. This he pronounced "utterly insufficient"; he should have 15,000 additional men and four more batteries.[21] Such an appraisal—which looks as if Maury were thinking of a full complement of men for all the Mobile works—could not do otherwise than make Johnston resolve to visit the place himself.

A trip to the Gulf city soon became feasible, both because Johnston had been reduced to a department commander, with no further responsibility for Bragg, and because Lieutenant General Hardee had recently reported to him for duty. In the telegram that he sent from Mobile to Secretary Seddon on July 29, Johnston said not one word about the Mobile defenses. Instead he struck hard at the ineffective use of Confederate manpower: "Many conscripts keep out of service on plea of being in militia, under authority of War Department. The militia won't serve." His remedy, of course, was the revocation of the order; then conscripts would have to go to the army.[22]

Back the next day in Morton (thirty-five miles east of Jackson), Johnston once more wired to Seddon, in answer to a telegram that had come to Hardee during his absence. If Bragg were threatened, he would lend him his entire force—infantry and artillery numbered a little less than 20,000—except two brigades which he would hold out for Mobile. Johnston denied the accuracy of a telegram Hardee had sent that most of Grant's army had left Vicksburg and that the Yankees were hinting that they were going to Tennessee and to Mobile. From news just in, it seemed that nothing was clear as to Federal intentions. New information three days later made Johnston think that Grant's army would be used in Virginia and Tennessee "until the mild season." But it looked as if the general himself would summer in Vicksburg: his informant had said, "Mrs. Grant has just arrived."[23]

A telegram from Richmond on July 31 assured Maury that his needs were being considered: a full report was requested. Before long a staff officer was eastward bound, and on August 8 Maury telegraphed to Adjutant General Cooper not to send him troops for the present. A letter of the same day was hopeful. Prisoners returning from several points stated that Grant and Banks would not operate against Mobile until fall. Maury was using the time in defensive preparations; labor, which until recently had been withheld, was coming in freely; he hoped for ammunition sufficient for a six-month siege; subsistence stores were being received "plentifully." In concluding, Maury begged Cooper not to think that he wanted troops withdrawn prematurely from other places in order to defend Mobile.[24]

While Banks wrote that Mobile could be taken in a month, Grant in his *Memoirs* speaks of the possibility of capturing important points "without bloodshed." Since his next sentence refers to Mobile,[25] it looks as if he thought that the important seaport would have been yielded with little if any contest. This seems quite improbable. The right and left of the entrenchments rested on streams, so that a flank or rear attack would not have been a simple matter. Mobile had defensive possibilities. Nor is it to be forgotten that in the region there were two masters of defense: William Hardee and Joseph Johnston.

To Sherman it looked as if Johnston's failure to depart from the region came from something akin to perverseness. He could not imagine, he said in a letter to Grant on August 6, why Johnston should remain at Morton, to which place he had actually returned after having gone thirty miles beyond. Johnston hated to give up Mississippi, Sherman's informant had said. While there was a touch of injury in Sherman's statement that "rascals" in Wirt Adams's cavalry had eaten "our bread," he took solace in the thought that citizens of Jackson, for whom he had left it, had protested. Two days after Sherman's lament, Johnston sent Brigadier W. N. Jackson across the Pearl, to occupy both sides of the railroad to Vicksburg, with orders to reach out to Grand Gulf with a strong reconnoitering party and "as far as may be safe to Natchez." He was exhorted to give confidence to the inhabitants, burn cotton, and "awe unruly negroes." Johnston could think also of ways to combat Union sentiment. On the 9th—two days before Grant was writing so hopefully about Mississippi sentiment—he directed Chalmers at Grenada to arrest all persons in his district who were "openly advocating the policy of reconstruction." [26]

Everywhere throughout the South an effort was being made to fill the army with reluctant men and those out of service because of flaws in the Confederate conscription law or faults in its administration. To the Army itself Davis on August 1 addressed a fervent proclamation. The Washington Government was duly vilified; the men there would not "make peace lest they be hurled from their seats of power" (a charge that looks as if Davis believed the prevailing sentiment in the North was to see the war through). The specter of slavery and subjugation and the utter ruin of themselves, their families, and their country were held before the Southern soldiers. The heavy defeats of the summer were labeled "temporary reverses," and the army was told, "The victory is within your grasp." Wives, mothers, sisters, and daughters of the Confederacy were appealed to: They should not, Davis said, shelter from the disgrace of having deserted a duty anyone who owed service in the field.[27]

It is hardly likely that the Davis pronouncement caused dismay in the White House, and before long Lincoln received Hurlbut's verdict that it was "a cry of despair, not courage." This harmonized with what the Charleston-born Union general had said in an unofficial letter of July 10 tendering his resignation: "I believe the war as war is practically over. I think most of the seceded States will, as States, offer to return." Unless he soon got back to his office, Hurlbut had fears of being "but a fourth-rate lawyer." [28]

Letters of appeal to remain at his post came to Hurlbut from both Halleck and Lincoln. The tone of Hurlbut's letters had made a favorable impression on the General in Chief, who had seen both the official resignation and the private communication to the President that had been brought from the West by Charles Dana. "We all must make sacrifices for our country," Halleck reminded Hurlbut in a letter of July 30. Then, with vision into the future, and almost as if he had read a draft of the Davis proclamation, he wrote:

> The truth is, general, the war is not so near its end as you seem to suppose. The enemy will now make a desperate effort to repair his losses. He will force into his ranks every man capable of bearing arms. His fellow traitors and copperhead coadjutors in the North will do all in their power to help him by opposing the draft, which is the only possible means of supplying the loss of our forces by the expiration of those enlisted for nine months and two years.

After saying that the enemies of the Administration made themselves the enemies of the country, and that they would ruin the latter for the sake of defeating the former, and that, though it would take time, the draft would be enforced, Halleck bluntly said, "Under these circumstances we cannot consent to dispense with your services."

How matters looked from Halleck's difficult position, Hurlbut could see from the last paragraph of the General in Chief's letter, which should have left him with a feeling of reward as well as renewed determination:

> General officers who obey orders, who perform their duties faithfully, who do not quarrel with those temporarily placed over them, who neither protect thieves nor steal themselves, are not so numerous that we can well spare one, who, like you, has faithfully, honestly, and ably performed every duty. The President and Secretary of War are both anxious you should remain in service.

When Lincoln himself wrote to Hurlbut on the 31st, he had far more in mind than the general's good service and the loss he would be. After asking Hurlbut to reconsider his resignation, he launched into the subject of emancipation, thus giving the Western general with whom he felt especially closely acquainted an accurate view of his own thinking about one of the hardest questions of that year. His proclamation of January 1 applied to Arkansas, and Lincoln thought it valid in law, and that it would be upheld by the courts; nor did he have any intention of retracting or repudiating it. "Those who shall have tasted actual freedom I believe can never be slaves or quasi slaves again," he said. In places not covered by the proclamation, gradual emancipation "would be better for both white and black"; but Lincoln disliked the recently adopted Missouri Plan because its application was postponed seven years. "It should begin at once," he stated, "giving the new-born a vested interest in freedom which could not be taken away." Fully appreciating the importance of the communication from the President with which he had been favored, and knowing that it should be before Grant as a guide for his actions, Hurlbut wrote in his letter to Grant withdrawing his tender of resignation: "I will send to you by next mail a copy of the President's letter, which contains his views on questions of great importance."

Though much shorter, the letter that Hurlbut wrote on August 11 in answer to Lincoln's concluding appeal, "Write me again," is reminiscent of the report he had made about his visit to Charleston in March, 1861, as a special emissary for the newly inaugurated President. The rank and file of the Southern army Hurlbut portrayed as having awakened to the fact that they were not fighting their own battle, "but the battle of the officers, the politicians, and the plantation class." This, he recalled, accorded with a prediction he had made a year since. In northern Alabama "heavy bodies of deserters, with their arms," were actually holding the mountains and defying conscription. An overwhelming majority of the people of Tennessee were represented by Hurlbut as ready to repeal the Act of Secession, establish a fair system of emancipation, and go back into the Union. As to Mississippi, the Emancipation Proclamation and the arming of Negroes were bugbears there. At the very moment, Hurlbut had "an application from some fifty men of mark and position in Mississippi, asking if they may hold a meeting to consider the possibilities of recognition by the United States." Arkansas, which Hurlbut said would soon be relieved from Price and Holmes by the expedition then on foot, would readily come back into the Union. It was, he pointed out, "not a plantation country, but one of small holders." [29]

With such an outlook, it would appear as if Hurlbut may have brushed aside what Halleck had said as the views of a gloomy pessimist, or a man out of personal touch with important aspects of the question. But when he consented to stay in service, he could hardly have supposed that it would be for nearly two more years.

On August 11, the day he wrote to Lincoln, Hurlbut gave the order that set in motion his part of the cavalry raid that Grant had directed should be made against Grenada and its great accumulation of locomotives and cars. When he told Sherman to start a column on the 10th with that objective, Grant had said the rolling stock should be taken to Memphis, "if possible." All the way from Mississippi to Richmond Confederate officials were also looking longingly at the equipment; and on July 29 the superintendents of the Mississippi Central, and the New Orleans, Jackson and Great Northern had written to Johnston that they thought eight hundred men could in thirty days repair track and rebuild bridges so that the cars and engines could be taken to the Alabama River. Then, on the very day that Grant gave Sherman his final instructions, the Confederate chief of engineers queried Johnston by wire if he could not "rebuild temporarily and promptly the bridge over Pearl River" at Jackson.

Though Grant's words, "If it will do any good," suggest that he did not have too much faith in the efficacy of the admonitions he prescribed for the conduct of the troopers on their march, Sherman at least nodded enthusiastically at the statement: "It should be our policy now to make as favorable impression upon the people of the State as possible." It would, Sherman replied from the comfort of Parson Fox's, give him "excessive pleasure" to instruct the cavalary as Grant had directed; the policy set down met every wish of his heart.

The $4,000,000 worth of equipment from various roads had naturally been giving great anxiety to the ailing Chalmers, its custodian, especially since he had learned of the return of Grierson to Memphis. On the very day—August 4—that Grant sent Sherman a warning order about the desired operation, Chalmers—who two weeks previously had proposed a fantastic Confederate expedition into Missouri and back to Tennessee by way of Illinois and Kentucky—was issuing a circular stating that it was probable that the Federals would soon attempt a raid into the Grenada region. Men enough there were, he stated, in the district to repel any attack, and he appealed to all categories: those liable to conscription, those absent from the ranks (with the promise that he would recommend a full pardon for all absent without leave who returned), and finally all men and boys able to handle a gun. A frightful picture was set before them as the alternative: "The blazing towns, the desolate farms, the plundered citizens, the outraged women who mark the path of the enemy wherever they have gone, warn you what to expect if they are allowed to succeed here."

Hurlbut seems not to have given instructions about decorous conduct to Colonel Mizner, now chief of cavalry of the left wing of the Sixteenth Corps, who was to furnish the column striking from the north. But he directed Mizner to send fifty engineers to rebuild bridges if practicable or help with the wrecking if the equipment could not be saved, and he reminded him: "Wheels and axles are difficult to get in the South." Over the telegraph line from La Grange there flashed to Hurlbut on the 19th a report from Mizner. The 1,500 men of the two brigades (united en route) under Lieutenant Colonel Jesse L. Phillips, Ninth Illinois Infantry (mounted), had reached Grenada on the 17th, and had wrecked and burned 57 locomotives, upward of 400 cars, depot buildings, machine shops, blacksmith shops, as well as commissary and ordnance supplies. Among the cars there were, according to Major Datus Coon, not only coaches, but "sleeping cars."

The ride down had been through oppressive heat, and a terrific electric storm had struck one of the brigades at night. As the column neared Grenada there was some skirmishing, and smoke in the distance announced that the bridges over the Yalobusha were being burned. When four regiments of Chalmers's command were discovered behind entrenchments on the south bank of that stream, supported by three guns, Phillips ordered the brigade of Major Coon, Second Iowa Cavalry, to pin down the enemy at the upper ford, while Lieutenant Colonel Martin Wallace, Fourth Illinois Cavalry, led his brigade to the lower ford. Wallace had no more than crossed than the opposition to Coon, who had put two 12-pounders in action, melted away. Then, as the enemy retired to the southeast, Coon crossed with two hundred men, and Grenada for the first time was entered by Yankees, Wallace having already been recalled to the north bank. Immediately Coon began the destruction of the engines and cars, "so closely packed as to make a small town of themselves."

When the work of destruction was almost completed, Colonel Edward F. Winslow, Fourth Iowa Cavalry, arrived with the eight hundred men of the three regiments that Sherman had sent. Believing that the railroad from Grenada to Memphis would be found to have been repaired, Sherman had given Winslow an unqualified order not to destroy rolling stock, and Phillips wrote that Winslow, the senior officer, even tried to stop what was being done at Grenada. When, because of a destroyed bridge, Winslow had found himself unable to bring forward seventeen locomotives and one hundred cars that he had captured twenty miles below Grenada, he merely abandoned them. Fearing that some of W. H. Jackson's cavalry would interpose to prevent his return southward, Winslow used a permissive statement in his orders and rode on to Memphis to get a boat trip home, while the units in the northern column returned to their proper stations.

Winslow reported that the inhabitants along his line of march were "kindly, firmly, and fairly treated"; the careful Phillips attached to his report a provost marshal's receipt for $8,641.50 Confederate funds, and $3.38 specie, most of it a contribution by Chalmers's captured quartermaster. While the hard money could barely have made a jingle in Phillips's pocket, his column returned impressively augmented by several hundred Negroes—brought back "in accordance with instructions"—several hundred horses and mules, and forty prisoners.

From a point twenty miles east of Grenada, Chalmers wired to Johnston on the 18th one of the most accurate reports in the war of an enemy force: 1,700 from the North, 800 from the South. But the exhortations in his circular had not given constancy to his Mississippians: one brigade "in falling back to Grenada dwindled from 1,700 to 700." It was far too soon to expect that Chalmers would have a list of violated homes, and he merely said, "Enemy burned some bridges and trestles, and a large fire was seen in Grenada last night." [30] Four hundred cars should indeed have made quite an illumination, and doubtless Joe Johnston thought that the rolling stock was too delicate and sorrowful a subject for Chalmers explicitly to mention.

The amazingly persistent Rebels poked about in the rubbish heaps, and Hurlbut was saddened when he learned that they were carting away the precious locomotive driving wheels. The next time, he ruefully wrote to Rawlins, instructions must be given to crack off their flanges.[31] Association with Abe Lincoln had given an uncompromising cast to the Charlestonian's Unionism. One cannot even imagine what Jeff Davis might have said about him when at his best.

Although many important letters were written in August, 1863, the unofficial letter that Grant wrote to Dana on the 5th was, in many ways, the letter of the month.

After leaving Vicksburg with little more than a good look at the battered town, Dana stopped at Helena, and got a picture of Prentiss's fine fight there that must have been listened to with interest by those in Washington. Following a call at Memphis, where he pocketed Hurlbut's letter of resignation to Lincoln, the Assistant Secretary of War proceeded to Cairo. Why he did not continue directly to the Capital is not exactly clear. Perhaps he wanted to complete a written record of his trip West, and thought that Cairo, though unattractive, was more conducive to writing than Washington. Where the originals of the lengthy letters that he wrote to Stanton on July 12 and 13 are it would be good to know—merely reading them in the great journalist's handwriting would give a sense of freshness. And where his retained copies are is also not clear; all there are at present are the versions of the letters in Dana's well-known book published thirty-six years after they were written. Whether or not Dana edited them, or gave the world precisely what he wrote in Cairo, is a natural question that cannot be answered.

While the dispatches that Dana sent to Stanton during his three months with Grant's army gave occasional and revealing appraisals of officers, the Cairo letters were devoted entirely to an analysis of Grant's subordinates down to brigade commanders, and to his staff officers. The latter did not fare so well, and Stanton may have had in mind Dana's pen picture, when he eyed Rawlins, who had just arrived with Grant's Vicksburg report, at the Cabinet meeting of July 31, and listened to see if Rawlins was as unkind to the English language in speech as Dana had said he was in writing.[32] (Rawlins could not have done too badly, for Welles was generous to him on the day he virtually consigned Seward and Halleck to the scrap heap, where Stanton had long since been cast.)

When Dana arrived at Washington there was a highly critical feeling toward Meade because of Lee's escape across the Potomac River after Gettysburg in spite of the delay caused by high water. Only a few days previously Lincoln had written him the letter he left unsigned and unsent, a letter that was devastating for all the mildness of its words: Meade had had Lee within his "easy grasp"; had he "closed upon him" the war would have been ended; now it was to be "prolonged indefinitely." The letter that Dana wrote to Grant on July 22 must have been something of a surprise after Halleck's recent commendatory statement about Meade (which, however, rather contrasted him with Hooker). As Dana's letter is unavailable in any form, its contents must be judged entirely from what Grant wrote in reply on August 5:

> Gen. Halleck and yourself were both very right in supposing that it would cause me more sadness than satisfaction to be ordered to the command of the Army of the Potomac. Here I know the officers and men and what each Gen. is capable of as a separate commander. There I would have all to learn. Here I know the geography of the country and its resources. There it would be a new study. Besides more or less dissatisfaction would necessarily be produced by importing a General to Command an Army already well supplied with those who have grown up, and been promoted, with it.

Surely military literature does not have many better expressions of how the problem of higher command appears to an experienced and successful general, possessed not only of great ability, but of high character and a rare absence of narrow, personal ambition. After giving some news, particularly about the Thirteenth Corps as it now was under Ord, Grant wrote in a way that shows that there had been at least a tentative decision to replace Meade as commander of the Army of the Potomac, although he had been given less than a month's trial and had turned Lee back at Gettysburg: "I feel very grateful to you for your timely intercession in saving me from going to the Army of the Potomac. While I would disobey no order I should beg very hard to be excused before accepting that command." [33]

After having thus revealed what had been considered in the innermost councils at Washington, Grant, in ending his letter, drew aside the curtain and gave a glimpse into his own headquarters: "It is about time for the mail to close and I must do the same thing. I intended writing much more when I commenced but have been interrupted every thirty seconds and forget what I intended saying." That the departure of a steamer would not be delayed for a personal letter from the department commander to an Assistant Secretary of War probably did not seem strange to Dana; nor did the picture of intense application. With Rawlins away, and a meager and not too competent staff, Grant was giving personal attention—as he always had done—to a multitude of important matters.

Banks's sudden call for twenty-two boats, as well as for coal, rations, forage, and other supplies, had changed Vicksburg into almost an advanced base for Port Hudson. Everything called for, Grant had furnished to the best of his ability, with inconvenience to himself no doubt. Porter had sought to help by recommending that the Marine Brigade, which had seven fine steamers, be transferred to Grant's command, but not until the end of August did Washington order the transfer. Porter was unquestionably eager to get rid of the Marine Brigade both because of lack of discipline among the men and because of his own unhappy relations with their commander, Brigadier General Alfred W. Ellet; the record is complicated by a September 20 statement by the admiral to Welles that the brigade had been actively employed ever since the fall of Vicksburg in the transportation of troops.[34] Such, however, was the shortage of boats that Grant had had to authorize the furloughing of paroled Confederates who had returned to Vicksburg, because he could not ship them to the Northern prisons which they preferred to the prospect of exchange and more marches and more battlefields.[35]

The improved health of his command, mentioned by Grant in his letter to Halleck six days later, had already manifested itself, and the general told Dana that his army was "in very good trim for another campaign." But he said nothing that indicated that anything had been done to replace his worn-out guns; the brass-rifled pieces he pronounced "entirely used up."

However much business pressed, one may be sure that Grant's headquarters were the same friendly place which trembling Chaplain John Eaton had entered the preceding November at La Grange; and that it was the same cordial commander who had hailed Eaton when in June he had brought to Vicksburg his report to Rawlins about his contraband problem, which Grant had insisted upon having read to him. It was the same general who had then sat down and written a letter for Eaton to carry to the President of the United States, a letter that ended with a deft but softly worded suggestion that there should be some action in Washington. And now the same general thanked Dana and Halleck for having interceded to *prevent* Washington action, and did so partly out of habitual consideration for brother officers.

Grant had set Eaton at ease, in a circle where shoulders probably carried no lesser insignia than eagles, by a remark with an amusing touch. The letter to Dana, besides important military sentences, contained one priceless for its humor. Grant was hoping for the return of Adjutant General Thomas because, since the departure of Brigadier General John P. Hawkins, there was no one with the Negro troops who could organize them effectively.[36] Colonel Isaac F. Shephard had proved entirely unfit; and a Colonel Wood, whom Grant thought was next in rank, was currently absent without leave, coincidentally with much cotton and several thousand dollars' worth of furniture from houses of government lessees. Though it probably was hotter in Vicksburg than in Washington, Dana may have wished he was back when he read the comment: "Wood is a preacher."

CHAPTER V

VICTORIES AND TRIBULATIONS FOR JOHN SCHOFIELD

I regret to find you denouncing so many persons as liars, scoundrels, fools, thieves, and persecutors of yourself.

Lincoln to Blunt

I think you will not have just cause to complain of my action.

Lincoln to Schofield

WELL BEFORE the start of the operation—hastily thrown together and with an ambiguous over-all command—that aimed at securing central Arkansas and the long-coveted state capital, James Blunt had crossed the Arkansas River at Fort Gibson and had fought and won a sharp battle with some of the forces of General William Steele. And ten days before Federal columns triumphantly entered Little Rock, close on the heels of Price's rapidly departing veterans, Blunt's troops had marched into Fort Smith. Rough and seamy though the place was, Holmes had on February 17 said in a letter to Marmaduke, "If they take Fort Smith, the Indian country is gone." [1]

Steele had held high hopes of intercepting the essential train of supplies that Blunt has been seen sending to Colonel Phillips at Fort Gibson in late June, and his best Indian commander, Colonel Stand Watie, did attack the train. But troops that Brigadier General William L. Cabell was supposed to send by way of Fayetteville, and others that Brigadier Douglas H. Cooper was to furnish, failed to make a rendezvous. As a result, Watie's blow was ineffective. A touch of skepticism about the tardy commanders seemed to lurk in Steele's mind when he later wrote that their failure was "officially ascribed to high waters intersecting their line of march." Skepticism was justified, for in January Colonel Phillips had written to Curtis that a prominent captain on Cooper's staff was an influential member of the Union League in western Texas, and that there were numerous members of the league in some of the Confederate regiments.[2] Because of the miscarriage of Steele's plans, much-needed supplies had reached Fort Gibson as well as the reinforcements whose nonappearance had caused signs of faltering among the Federal Indians.

On July 11 Blunt himself reached the post, after probably picking up on the way a dispatch that Colonel Phillips had written on the 7th, in which he said: "I have had for some time the utmost difficulty in getting information from the enemy over the river. My spies were taken or killed, and many of my expedients failed." Phillips had, however, opened some new leads, and he had just sent back over the river a lady who had brought him dispatches in her bonnet slits. She had been sent over by Cooper to get information for him, armed with a little coffee and a bottle of whisky. The coveted articles had been furnished the lady by Phillips as an incentive to Cooper "to keep up the channel of communications." [3]

Inasmuch as Phillips did not mention it in his letter, it must have been subsequently that word came that on the 17th, 3,000 men under Cabell would join the 6,000 that Cooper was believed to have in camp twenty-five miles south of the river. The combined force would then strike the Federal fort. Though Blunt apparently accepted the enemy figures, which were exaggerated, he decided to attack Cooper before Cabell arrived, and he immediately began building boats to cross the badly swollen river. Starting at midnight of the 15th, he moved up the river a short distance with 250 cavalrymen and forded or swam the stream, his four guns being taken over in a boat. The pleasure of capturing enemy pickets entrenched across from Fort Gibson was denied him, for they had circumspectly departed upon learning of his crossing. Two days were used in getting his command over the Arkansas, but at 10:00 P.M. of the 16th, Blunt—who, it may be recalled, had made a hard night march to strike the enemy at old Fort Wayne the previous October—started southward with something under 3,000 men, mostly Indians and Negroes, and twelve guns.

As day was breaking, an enemy detachment was encountered, which Blunt's cavalry drove back upon their main line, deployed for

Courtesy Library of Congress

MAJOR GENERAL FREDERICK STEELE

a mile and a half across the road to Texas. After allowing his weary men to rest for two hours behind a sheltering ridge, eating the while from the cold, cooked rations in their haversacks, Blunt moved forward in two carefully arranged columns, which were rapidly thrown into a line of battle covered with skirmishers a quarter of a mile from the enemy. Within a few minutes the engagement spread to the whole force, which advanced steadily into the edge of the timber where the Confederates were awaiting them. After fighting that was "unremitting and terrific for two hours" the enemy's center was broken, and they retreated in something of a rout. But some cool-headed men took time to kindle the supplies amassed by the long haul from Texas in buildings two miles south of the battlefield. For five miles Blunt pursued, stopping only when the cavalry mounts were exhausted, and artillery horses could no longer draw their guns. Though at four o'clock Cabell's force appeared, and Blunt's ammunition was running low, he bivouacked where he was, ready if need be to fight again next morning. But when day came—July 18—it was found that the enemy had retired to the south of the Canadian River.

Blunt praised all units of his multicolored force, but especially the First Kansas Colored Infantry. He had, he said, never seen their coolness and bravery exceeded; "they were in the hottest of the fight, and opposed to Texas troops twice their number, whom they completely routed." In the postscript of his letter to Schofield detailing his success, he designated the engagement the "Battle of Honey Springs," in honor, as it were, of General Cooper whose headquarters had been at that choice spot, close to the battlefield. In a report some months later, Steele tartly commented upon the fact that Cooper had done nothing to strengthen his position, and he added that the best portion of Cabell's brigade and all his artillery were within hearing of the battle. On July 11 Steele had written that he did not think the Federals would attempt anything without reinforcements in addition to those that had recently arrived with the train, and on the 22nd he wrote that Blunt had displayed at Honey Springs "a larger force than he was supposed to be able to move." [4] Aggressive boldness had paid off.

Blunt thought the moment auspicious for striking those he considered enemies in his rear, and on the day he described the battle to Schofield—July 26—he also wrote a "private" and resentful letter to Secretary Stanton, captioned, "In the Field, Fort Blunt." The victorious general's ill temper derived in part from Schofield's charge that there had been irregularities in Blunt's administration of the Department of Kansas, recently reduced to a district of Schofield's Department of the Missouri, and in part from Blunt's having wanted to give orders to the quartermaster at Fort Leavenworth, over whom, as commander of the District of the Frontier, he had no authority whatever. "Baser traitors" did "not exist in Jeff Davis' dominion" than the Fort Leavenworth quartermaster and commissary, Blunt asserted; "two greater thieves" did not live than the governor of Kansas and the Superintendent of Indian Affairs. These men knew he was on their track; thus they wanted to get rid of him. Of his own merits Blunt entertained no doubt. With clumsy irony he doubted that Schofield was guilty of any such "irregularities" as he himself had committed: his move to the Arkansas River the winter before (in consort with Herron), and the recent occasion when, astride a mule, he had in five days covered with three members of his staff the 180 miles from Fort Scott to Fort Gibson, and had then crossed the river and made the night march and the attack on 6,000 of the enemy in a chosen position.

A letter to Stanton was not enough. Five days later, Blunt reiterated his complaints to Lincoln and emphasized his exploits. The Secretary seems to have made no reply; perhaps the President said, "Leave Blunt to me." "Your military position looks critical," he said in a letter on August 8, "but did anybody force you into it? Have you been ordered to confront and fight 10,000 men with 3,000 men?" Blunt got more than questions. He got a sentence that recorded faults of character that greatly lessened his value: "I regret to find you denouncing so many persons as liars, scoundrels, fools, thieves, and persecutors of yourself." [5]

His own illness, and the exposure of his position, as well as distance from his supplies, had caused Blunt to return to his fort before he wrote his letters, while Steele on his part personally rallied his defeated troops and reinforced them at Honey Springs. Steele had, he reported on July 29, some 2,500 white troops and 4,000 Indians. Blunt's total he put at 5,000, of whom 2,000 were white; the Federal Indians were better officered and better armed than his own. The next day Blunt reported to Schofield that he had not over 3,000 men for duty, while Steele had 9,000; deserters and Union refugees reported that 4,000 Texans with four guns were marching to join his opponent. Though it was Steele's intention to attack—and that had indeed been his purpose—Blunt said he preferred that role himself, but he could make no movement until another train arrived with ordnance supplies. Soon Steele's Arkansas troops began deserting "nightly by tens and fifties"; powder from Texas turned into paste when exposed to the air; the expected Texans were diverted; and on August 9 Steele wrote that he would be doing well if he avoided disaster. But by the 14th Blunt was also wavering. Hearing that Colonel William F. Cloud had been sent from Springfield to Fayetteville with the Second Kansas Infantry and four guns, he summoned him to his aid. "A battle is pending," he declared, "and will be fought within a few days with heavy odds against me." [6]

"To-day I have a burning fever again, and the prospect looks as though I might be quite sick," Blunt, who had once been an Ohio doctor, wrote on the 19th to his adjutant back at Fort Scott. With the mercury at 90°, his horses were giving out, and what with the flies and the tough grass, his mules could not be worked. But there was good news. Steele had fallen back; he had sent his own family away from Fort Smith; and the indications were that all Secessionists were moving as far south as the Red River. When Colonel Cloud arrived with his Kansans and he himself had sufficiently recovered, Blunt hoped to renew his campaign.[7] This he did on the evening of August 22.

No real opposition was encountered; Steele with Cooper and Stand Watie obliged by retiring toward the Red River, while Cabell retreated in the direction of Fort Smith. On the evening of the 26th, Union cavalry and guns that had followed the southern column came upon a rear guard trying to remove stores from the little town of Perryville. After taking the place, Blunt burned it because nearly every building contained Confederate stores. Part of his force he then sent back to Fort Gibson, while he proceeded with the balance to Fort Smith, which was found deserted on September 1; but Cloud, who pursued the departing enemy, had something of a skirmish at the Devil's Back Bone sixteen miles to the southeast. Placed in command of Fort Smith by the ailing Blunt, Cloud reported that the Choctaws, who had been abandoned by Cooper, were much disgusted, and were disposed to lay down their arms and return to treaty relations. He also said:

> My office has been constantly thronged by Mountain "Feds," deserters from the rebel army, who deliver themselves up, and citizens from the country, to the distance of 80 miles, who come in with joyful

countenances and cheering words, to assume the relation of citizens of the United States.[8]

Nine days before Blunt entered Fort Smith, Federal Major General Frederick Steele, commanding the column advancing on Little Rock, was writing to Hurlbut from De Valls Bluff,* "The sick list is frightful." One brigade was commanded by a lieutenant colonel, two colonels having given up in the last three days. Out of a total of 12,000 men, over a thousand were reported as unfit for duty. It was the poorest command Steele had ever seen, except for the cavalry.[9]

The cavalry—a division of three brigades and three batteries, numbering something under 6,000 men—was Schofield's contribution to the operation. A Virginian was riding at their head, John W. Davidson, who had graduated from West Point in 1845 and who was a major in the Second United States Cavalry when made a brigadier general on February 3, 1863. Starting from Bloomfield, Missouri, he had arrived on August 8 at Clarendon, where Steele joined him on the 17th with two infantry divisions of two brigades each, two small cavalry regiments, and four batteries from Helena. The only general officer in the column was Steele himself (Colonel Samuel A. Rice, commanding one of the divisions, would soon become a brigadier general), just as Davidson was the only cavalry officer wearing stars. There had been much sickness at Helena, as at Vicksburg and Memphis (Hurlbut ordered a dose of strong bitters for everyone), and Steele had left well-filled hospitals. Prentiss, unhappy because he was not given command of the expedition into the interior, had tendered his resignation. "I think it should be accepted," Hurlbut wrote to Grant on August 8. "He thinks himself undervalued, and in all such cases it is well to relieve the army and make way for men who are not plagued in that way." [10]

That Steele and some of Grant's Vicksburg men were able to march from Helena for Little Rock when they did stemmed from an erroneous report that Schofield had made to Halleck. To the request in his letter to Grant of July 8 for aid in securing the line of the Arkansas, Grant had replied sympathetically but rather discouragingly. When Sherman's siege of Jackson would end, Grant could not say; and having sent Herron up the Yazoo with two brigades, and Ransom

* In addition to the end map, see map, p. 5, for the Little Rock operation.

to Natchez with one, he had only three remaining at Vicksburg. But two days before Grant had written to Schofield, "I can give you nothing definite of future operations yet," Davidson had reported to Schofield that Price had crossed the White River at Jacksonport and was moving to attack him at Bloomfield with 12,000 infantry and 7,000 cavalry. Davidson seemed unalarmed: "Rebels are fully aware of the nature and strength of this command," he wrote. "We are all right." The next day Schofield put the report on the wire to Halleck, and, not being able to reinforce Davidson without leaving depots unguarded, he queried, "Cannot troops be sent up White River immediately?" A similar dispatch to Grant ended, "You can capture all of Price's infantry and artillery." Halleck's thoughts ran in the same direction in telegrams on the 15th to Hurlbut, Prentiss, and Grant; and a message informing Schofield that troops had been ordered to get in Price's rear ended, "If properly resisted in Missouri by General Davidson, he must either disperse or surrender." [11]

By the time Halleck's dispatch reached Grant on the 21st, Sherman was on his leisurely return from Jackson, and Grant informed Halleck (the message cleared Cairo on the 26th) that he was sending a division to Helena "to move after General Price." It was the sum total of troops he had who were not worn out with fatigue, but he would later send others to Helena "to release that entire garrison to go after Price." [12]

Just when it was discovered that both Davidson and Schofield had been completely deceived by a captured lieutenant from a Confederate regiment is not clear. But on July 28 Hurlbut informed Halleck and Schofield that 6,000 men would be sent from Helena for the White River expedition to get in the rear of Price. Grant had told him to organize the operation. From Halleck he asked explicit directions, and to him he said, "I shall look to Schofield for cavalry." To Schofield he wrote, "I dread the results of a march through that desolated country at this season, especially as I have no certain knowledge where Price's force is to be found." The misconception had vanished by the last day of the month, when Hurlbut informed Steele, who was then at Helena organizing the expedition, that he had heard from Davidson, now at Wittsburg, Arkansas (on the St. Francis River, about due west of Memphis), that the Confederates had divided. No one but Marmaduke was at Jacksonport; Price with the remainder of the force had gone to Little Rock which he was fortifying (Price had been at Des Arc, not Jacksonport). As Hurlbut did not put

Price's force at over 6,000, while Davidson had 5,000 horsemen and Steele could march with a like number of infantry and four batteries, he said (forgetful of conditions which shortly before had filled him with dread), "The union of the two forces will give you a command competent to crush out the entire rebel force in Arkansas." [13]

Thus it transpired that an operation originally meant to destroy the troublesome Price in a pincer operation was changed into one in which Davidson and Steele were to unite at Clarendon for a move against Little Rock. Under the circumstances it was not strange that there was some confusion as to whether Schofield or Hurlbut was the officer directing Steele. After Halleck had telegraphed to Grant that responsibility lay with Schofield, and Hurlbut in perplexity had appealed to Grant, the latter gave one of his characteristic commonsense solutions:

> The troops with Steele are in Schofield's department, and will be subject to his orders, according to General Halleck's dispatch; but being nearer Steele than the headquarters of the department in which he is serving, any aid you can give him it is advisable that you should give, whether it is men or supplies he may require.[14]

Even before he completed crossing the White River, the healthy men with whom Steele had marched from Helena began to sicken with "fevers, and chills and fever." To find a more salubrious base, he moved up to De Valls Bluff, his sick and supplies going by boat. In the high plateau region there were considerable beef and corn, and the shortage of lumber to build hospitals and shelter for provisions was made up largely by tearing down vacant buildings, the Union cause being especially helped by a commodious church, where secession doctrines had been "extensively promulgated." Inasmuch as Steele could count on four feet of water in the river, there would be no trouble about supplies, but the general complained about the four gunboats present: one was "unfit for service," and the other three were "out of repair." They had reached Clarendon the day after Davidson, and in an apparently hale and hearty condition, for he had put some troops aboard and sent them up the Little Red River, where they captured two good steamers and destroyed the pontoon bridge by which "the ubiquitous Marmaduke" who kept "Missouri in a fright" had just crossed to the south side of the stream. The expedition also brought back word that no other than Davidson's old classmate Kirby Smith was personally in Little Rock. Actually he was in Shreveport, but the belief that the Confederates would make a maximum effort to save Little Rock, and the precarious state of his own command, had no doubt been responsible for Steele's saying to Hurlbut in his letter of August 23, "If you do not send re-enforcements, I shall very likely meet with disaster." [15]

While moving up to the bluff, Steele had Davidson develop the situation to the west, and on August 25 the Federal horse came upon the cavalry of Walker and Marmaduke at Brownsville (present Lonoke). After a short action the enemy was dislodged and driven westward for nine miles, leaving in Davidson's hands a brigade commander who, one may be sure, was entertained with questions and invited to be as talkative as he wished. The resistance had not been stubborn, although Sterling Price, who had on July 23 assumed command of Holmes's district because of that general's illness, stated in his report that on August 25 he had ordered Walker to take position with his cavalry and Marmaduke's on Bayou Meto and hold on as long as possible. After reconnoitering the next day, Davidson attacked about noon on the 27th—"in greatly superior numbers and considerable spirit"—according to his fellow-Virginian Price. The ground being unfavorable for the use of his entire force, Davidson (who prided himself on the fact that his command had been trained as dragoons, and thus were well prepared for fighting on foot) used one dismounted brigade, as well as the battalion of infantry he had as artillery support, and some guns, to push the enemy successively from two positions and back into an entrenched camp three-fourths of a mile east of the bayou. After a sharp action they were once more driven, this time across the stream, a bold dash by the First Iowa Cavalry in the face of artillery and sharpshooter fire failing to save the bridge that the retiring enemy had lighted. Then for an hour and a half battery pounded battery, and skirmishers showed their petulance with their rifles, to close the engagement in which Davidson had forty-five casualties (twenty-eight in the First Iowa).

On the following days reconnaissances were pushed to the left, and a wounded prisoner taken on the 30th gave detailed information about the enemy order in battle, confirmed, Davidson reported, "to a greater or less degree," by citizens, spies, and deserters. On the 30th a reinforcing infantry brigade from Helena crossed the White at Clarendon, and on September 1 Steele started his infantry toward Brownsville, and the next day completed his concentration there, the base at De Valls Bluff being left largely to the protection of convalescents.[16]

The day he started for Brownsville, Steele put Schofield in the picture with a hasty note: The enemy had collected everything in front of Little Rock. There was good reason to believe that Kirby Smith was concentrating at the Arkansas capital everything in the Department of the Trans-Mississippi. Frequently he had been heard to say that if he could not hold Little Rock, he could not hold Texas. Price was entrenched three miles north of the capital; the position was covered by a heavily timbered swamp; he was supposed to have about 14,000 men. Steele's total present-for-duty strength was considerably less than 12,000; but he was finding more water on the route than he had anticipated—"such as it was." [17]

Washington was eager to have this stroke against a state capital meet with success. With the Ninth Corps returned to Burnside and a strong corps sent by Grant to Banks, and Missouri already stripped of troops, the General in Chief faced a rather difficult possibility when he read Schofield's dispatch:

> General Steele thinks Kirby Smith's force is marching up to Little Rock to join Price. General Hurlbut says if General Rosecrans can clear the valley of the Tennessee and unite with a force from Corinth, to drive back Johnston, he can spare 5,000 more men for General Steele. If Steele's information is correct, he will probably want more force than he now has.

Already Halleck had sounded out Pope, whose headquarters were now in Milwaukee, about a possible surplus of troops in the Department of the Northwest, and when word came of the success of Brigadier General Henry H. Sibley's campaign against the Sioux, Halleck lost no time in telegraphing to Pope, "Any troops you can possibly spare should be sent to Helena to reenforce General Steele." In a letter which followed, he wrote: "If the rebels can be driven out of Arkansas, the guerrillas in Missouri will be comparatively quiet. They are always expecting that Price will come to their assistance." [18]

Should Steele move by the right flank or the left? Prudence favored the left flank, as giving security to communications, but Steele did not decide until he had pinned down Walker and Marmaduke with his infantry, and Davidson had investigated possibilities on the right, and found them poor. So on September 6—while Walker was being "rubbed out" by Marmaduke's angry pistol—Steele struck for the

Arkansas below Price's right, reaching it the next day. Davidson, whose writing shows that, though a general, he must have been an agreeable officer to ride beside even on a hot summer day in Arkansas, had cleared the route by some sharp skirmishing. The 8th and 9th were used in reconnaissance, sniping more or less good-naturedly at the enemy across the river, repairing roads back to Bayou Meto, and bringing up the fresh crop of 700 sick and the supply train, which had all been left at Brownsville under the guard of an infantry brigade and one of cavalry. "I had now definitely determined upon a plan of attack," Steele wrote in his report.[19]

The boldness of Steele's plan marks him as a good general. He would throw Davidson to the south of the river and have him advance up that side as the infantry moved against the Confederate works on the north bank. While some of Stonewall Jackson's moves have been praised until they are known to even a casual student of the war, the brilliance and boldness of Steele's performance in treacherous terrain and against an able and alerted enemy have attracted little attention.

An important figure in the defense lines against which Steele directed his infantry was an officer seen in the opening incident of the war in the West—Brigadier General Daniel M. Frost. It was this West Point graduate who commanded the Missouri troops at Camp Jackson, St. Louis, when energetic Nathaniel Lyon captured the camp and its personnel on May 10, 1861, with the unknown U. S. Grant an approving observer on the march out and return to the arsenal. Until summoned to Little Rock by Price, Frost had been at the quiet little town of Pine Bluff, where he had been in command of Confederate defenses on the lower Arkansas, from time to time reading the letters and enjoying the packages sent to him from St. Louis by his wife, "a wealthy, influential woman," who the Federal provost marshal thought should, along with some others, be "sent through the lines to join their husbands and sons." Price had put Frost in command of his own old division, largely Missourians, which included practically all the infantry defending the Arkansas capital. His troops, Price said in his report, barely added up to 8,000 men, but he stated that they were "in excellent condition, full of enthusiasm, and eager to meet the enemy." To ensure freedom of movement if matters went badly, three pontoons had been thrown over the river, and Price's report makes it clear that he would have been very pleased if Steele had moved directly to attack his fortified line.[20]

The bold plan required careful preparation, especially on the part of Davidson. On the night of the 9th arrangements down to minute details were made for the crossing of the cavalry brigades of Colonels Merrill and Glover, while that of Ritter, supported by a battery, demonstrated four miles below at a ford held strongly by the enemy. As day was dawning a pontoon bridge was begun at a point where a double bend of the river made a salient which advantageously placed Federal batteries could deluge with metal. Twenty guns beat into quick silence enemy pieces that opened on the bridge. Promptly a brigade of infantry crossed the bridge and pushed a short distance to cover the passage of the vulnerable horsemen. By eleven o'clock Merrill and Glover were over the river, Merrill, seemingly impatient, having crossed with permission by a ford that he had found. At the ford below, Ritter's battery set fire to an enemy fort made of cotton bales, manned by men of Walker's division, now under Colonel Archibald S. Dobbin. Though little damage was done by Confederate shells and bullets, four artillerymen fell victims to the cruel sun. His diversionary task completed, Ritter and his guns moved upstream and crossed the bridge.[21]

In the advance up the right (south) bank of the river, Glover led, while an officer and a trooper carrying a guidon rode close to the river, to mark the progress of the column for General Steele, who led the infantry on the other bank—with some guns well forward. The first opposition that developed—precisely at noon, according to Glover—was disposed of by the aggressive action of his leading units—a matter of mere habit, Glover said. But it was a different story when the column reached the Bayou Fourche, which emptied into the Arkansas five miles below Little Rock. There the road divided, the right-hand road, after it crossed the bayou, running through a dense forest of standing and fallen timber, while the left road led through cornfields and, after following a short northward stretch of the bayou, crossed it after the stream turned westward. Not far beyond this crossing point the two roads reunited. Before Davidson had made his crossing, Dobbin had moved upstream and joined Marmaduke to give battle to Davidson in the tangled forest and from behind the levee along the bayou near where the western road crossed it.

Glover continued up the right-hand road into the forest, only to have his leading units ambushed. Casualties were fairly heavy in personnel; in addition, two howitzers were lost. Merrill, who took the other road, found difficulty because of lack of knowledge of the terrain, and there was poor coordination at the bayou; as a result some of Merrill's men were hit by Glover's fire. But the dismounted troopers were aggressive, and guns across the river pounded the Confed-

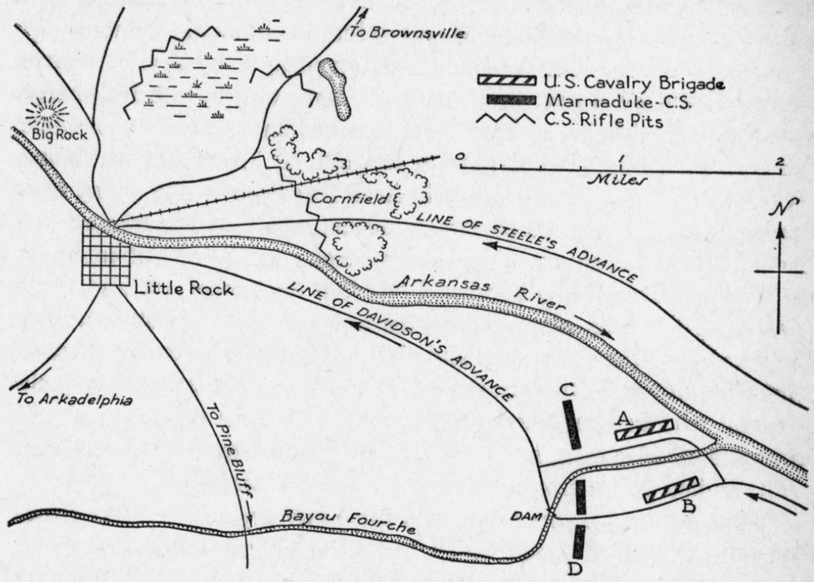

THE CAPTURE OF LITTLE ROCK, SEPTEMBER 10, 1863

Glover's brigade, A, advanced into a heavily timbered region; the road followed by Merrill, B, ran through a cornfield. Steele used guns in his infantry column north of the river to help break resistance to Glover. Price's infantry C, D, was initially in the intrenchments north of the river.

erates in flank and rear. A battery commander, whose nearest previous battle contact had been in the pursuit of Forrest the previous December, told with relish how he was engaged for three hours, firing 314 rounds, which completely broke up "the enemy's line of battle twice, producing disorder, and the tallest kind of skedaddling."

Columns of smoke rising from Little Rock told Steele that the position north of the river had been abandoned and that the bridges were being burned. That was cheering, but heavy dust clouds above the road leading southward from the city were disturbing. They might indicate a concentration to destroy Davidson. To the cavalryman there went an order to withdraw, in case he were heavily attacked, to a position along the river, where his horses could be protected by a high bank, and where batteries across the river could protect his flanks, while infantry was sent through a ford to his assistance. No such maneuver was, however, being made by Price, and he was, in fact, in full retreat. When informed of the crossing below, the Confederate commander had replied, Steele later learned, that "the Yankees were not going to entrap him like they did Pemberton."

After Davidson had resumed his advance, Glover and Merrill were relieved by Ritter, who ended the operation by a brisk charge into Little Rock with an Iowa regiment and one from Illinois, while his own First Missouri followed in support. At 7:00 P.M. the capital of Arkansas was formally surrendered to Davidson by the acting civil authorities. The old United States arsenal was found uninjured, together with some stores, all of which Steele said Price had intended to blow up. Things had happened fast that September 10, and Price was eager to be on his way with his force which probably outnumbered Steele, whose baggage and sick had been left heavily guarded when he moved to the attack. When, three days later, the Virginia Federal who had marched so far and handled his division so well, congratulated his men, he said, with feeling that obviously went deep, "The United States arsenal, uninjured, is repossessed." [22]

It was not long before Steele and some infantry arrived after crossing the river on a bridge which had been only partially destroyed. Also saved were two locomotives that would be useful in bringing supplies over the uninjured railroad from De Valls Bluff; but nothing could be done for the six blazing steamers, except to gaze at them ruefully. In view of the fatigue of the command, Steele attempted nothing that night in the way of pursuit of the column that had taken the road to Arkadelphia. The next morning at six o'clock a strong cavalry column with plenty of guns, all under Merrill, set out. Much abandoned equipment marked the path of the defeated force and "fagged-out soldiers" were continually brought in by Merrill's advance guard and flankers. Though the road was broad and good, it led through broken country abounding with positions where a very small force could easily compel a time-consuming deployment by a large one, and the lack of side roads made it impossible for Merrill to strike the enemy's main body or cut off his rear guard. After pursuing for two days with some minor skirmishing, he returned to Little Rock.[23]

Steele felt that Merrill's pursuit had not been as vigorous as he had expected it to be, and said so in a direct report to Halleck.

Basing his view on the large amount of strong Union sentiment in Arkansas which he himself had seen, and whose existence had also been communicated to him by Colonel Cloud at Fort Smith, he concluded, "With 6,000 more infantry, I think I could drive Smith and Price into Mexico." Had he said "Texas" the claim would have been more plausible, but considering the 860 hot, dry miles between Little Rock and the Rio Grande, it must be put down as an exaggeration, and the General in Chief probably so regarded it.

Nothing, however, can take from Steele the credit for a fine operation. In the early days of September, while Grant was in New Orleans, McPherson had put together a division to reinforce Steele, but Hurlbut, upon learning of the capture of Little Rock, had halted it at Helena. Steele could hardly have organized himself in the captured town before a letter from Hurlbut informed him that Grant had withdrawn the division which—with his fine strategic sense—he had sent to Monroe, Louisiana, where, though intended largely to protect plantations in the region opposite Vicksburg, it was also a deterrent to the reinforcing of Price from the south. People who had promptly committed themselves to the Federal Government soon became alarmed over the report that Price and Kirby Smith had reunited forces and would try to retake Little Rock, but, as will be seen later, this was not what Price attempted.[24] Instead he sent Shelby on a raid deep into Missouri.

The Navy had not forgotten Steele. On the day of the capture of Little Rock, Lieutenant Commander Phelps, now heading the Sixth and Seventh divisions, Mississippi Squadron, wrote to the general from De Valls Bluff, reporting that he had brought up additional gunboats. Phelps knew that Steele had reached the Arkansas River, and had Phelps been able to find a "conveyance" he would have driven over to see him, but he gave a sailor's explanation for any apparent lack of fraternal feeling: "Horseback riding for such a distance is rather too much for the uninitiated." [25]

Had Phelps not listened to the voice of prudence, his course through the woods of Arkansas would have merited historic markers.

Hurlbut, on his part, on the day that Steele took Little Rock was still worrying about the ambiguity in command. To Grant he wrote: "Schofield does not give any orders, and General Halleck telegraphs me as if I were responsible. I do nothing but advise Steele, and leave him to his own devices, which, after all, I fancy, is the best way." [26]

On July 7, but certainly before the Vicksburg news reached Washington at lunchtime, Halleck wrote Schofield a letter with a sentence that vividly portrayed the atmosphere in which the High Command operated: "So long as we gain success, the interference of politicians in military matters can be resisted, but on the first disaster they press upon us like a pack of hungry wolves." There was, according to the General in Chief, no danger "at present" that there would be a change in the organization of Schofield's department. The promptness with which Schofield had sent men to Grant had given great satisfaction in Washington, and Halleck stated that for over a year he had been laboring to prevent commanders from holding back troops to guard unimportant points not in the theater of active operations. Such points, if lost, could, he continued, be recovered "after a decisive success in the true strategic position." Applying the idea to Schofield's department, he said that roving bands might do harm on the southern border of Missouri, a matter of little consequence, however, if the Mississippi and Arkansas rivers could be opened. Local authorities would complain, Halleck concluded, but in a few months they would see the wisdom of sending the Missouri troops south.[27]

Schofield of course received the Vicksburg news that day, and at 10:30 P.M. he queried Halleck by wire whether, in view of Grant's victory, it would be necessary to send the two additional regiments that were already aboard steamers. Though the records give no answering telegram, the letter that Schofield wrote to Halleck on the 10th, in reply to Halleck's of the 7th, suggests strongly that the two regiments were still at St. Louis.[28]

Schofield would soon have to draw on the credit of good opinion that he had with the President, and do so even more extensively near the end of August. Already he had worked directly and harmoniously with Lincoln upon the most thorny of all questions. On June 20 he had made bold to ask whether he could, directly or indirectly, pledge Lincoln's support to the protection of slavery in Missouri during any temporary period preceding emancipation that might be decided upon by the state convention then in session. The prompt reply fell short of what Schofield had requested; Lincoln did not wish to make a pledge of affirmative support of even temporary slavery. But he thought, he said, that that was not actually the real issue; he believed that what was wanted was a policy of no interference by Federal troops in temporarily reserved legal rights in slaves during the progress toward freedom. This, the President said, was his desire. The most the department commander got was the authorization to act in accord with what Lincoln was writing, while giving regard to military necessities. In view of the denunciation of Schofield that soon took place, the ending of Lincoln's letter is significant: "Although this letter will become public at some time, it is not intended to be made so now." [29]

Certainly Lincoln could have had no desire for the publication of the letter he had written to Schofield on May 27 explaining why he had removed Curtis, and exhorting the new department commander to maintain a neutral position between the two bitter Missouri factions of Unionists. But upon returning to St. Louis after a short absence, Schofield found that the letter had appeared in the strong Unionist *Missouri Democrat*. Naturally, he had regarded the letter as "official and confidential," and his immediate concern was how William McKee, editor of the offending paper, had come by it, though he doubtless understood why a journalist would delight in displaying to the public a letter so frank and so deft as the one the President had written. Had it been obtained surreptitiously from his own headquarters, or had a copy sent by Lincoln to Curtis been slipped by one of that general's supporters to an eager, sensation-hungry reporter? One of the proprietors of the *Democrat* promptly responded to a note from Schofield to come to see him. He, however, knew nothing of the circumstances of publication, beyond that McKee had been responsible. A verbal request to McKee carried by the proprietor failed to bring the editor to see Schofield. A note to McKee by one of Schofield's staff officers who was a friend of McKee's also failed. Then the editor was brought in by the provost marshal. Although McKee declared that a copy of the letter had not come from Schofield's headquarters, he refused to tell how he had come by it—more than to claim that it had been "honestly." When McKee requested ten days' time to consider answering further, Schofield suspected that he merely wanted the chance to appeal for presidential protection. While the request was granted, McKee did not leave headquarters without giving his parole to return.

Of course, a telegram was speedily on the wire to Lincoln from a congressional friend of the editor. It stated that McKee's arrest was "unkind, unjust, against the spirit of your instructions, and an insult to the supporters of the Union and the Government." A longer dispatch to Stanton gave sufficient details for Lincoln to reply the same day (July 13) with some understanding. He did not think that the publication of the letter without permission was justified; but he did not consider it as of sufficient consequence for an arrest. Yet, inasmuch as there had been a parole, the arrest had been merely nominal, Lincoln pointed out, and he queried, "Cannot this small matter be dropped on both sides without further difficulty?" But the telegram that Lincoln sent to Schofield could not have been anything but disturbing, for he said, "I fear this loses you the middle position I desired you to occupy," and having stated that he did not know which of two letters it was that had been printed, he ended, "Please spare me the trouble this is likely to bring."

Perhaps it was the necessity of writing Lincoln a long explanation of his side of the McKee matter that caused Schofield to weigh less carefully than he otherwise would Davidson's report about Price, for it was on this same day that he reported to Halleck that Price was definitely moving to attack Davidson at Bloomfield. But the general was far from being unable to defend himself, and, in addition to relating the facts, he assumed the offensive by saying that he thought that misrepresentations had been made to the President, precisely to make it appear that he had departed from that "middle position" which Lincoln wanted him to occupy. Also, if it were true that a copy of the letter had been sent to Curtis, this would at least raise a doubt as to "infidelity" at his own headquarters, as he had thought at first, and he would overlook everything and "pardon the offender without knowing who he may be." Apparently Lincoln never gave Schofield the small bit of information he wanted, and he seemed a little ill-humored on July 15 when he wired another St. Louisian, probably also a protester of the purely nominal arrest, "The *effect* on political position of McKee's arrest will not be relieved any by its not having been made with that *purpose*." [30]

Could it be that the man who usually grasped things so broadly did not see that it was important for Schofield to know whether there was an untrustworthy officer on his staff? (Schofield can surely be pardoned for wanting something more than McKee's statement.)

A tour around Missouri shows familiar faces, and in considering Schofield's problems one should know the subordinates upon whom he was depending to keep his volcano under control with the use of a diminished number of regular regiments and the militia units that he told Halleck were "nearly worthless, except when the danger is apparent." A new duty had recently been placed upon all district and post commanders, that of furnishing guards when called upon to enable United States provost marshals to discharge their duties in carrying out the draft, which, as previously related, caused bloody and destructive riots in New York City in mid-July.[31]

Brigadier General Thomas A. Davies commanded the District of Rolla, with headquarters in the town that had been an important railhead and base since the first summer of the war. Davies has been seen bearing a heavy part in the Battle of Corinth, and then at Columbus, Kentucky, where he showed a touch of panic during Forrest's raid into West Tennessee. On July 20 Brigadier General Clinton B. Fisk issued an order taking over the District of Southeastern Missouri, with headquarters at Pilot Knob, near Ironton, where Grant began to display aggressive resourcefulness in August, 1861. Fisk was first seen mildly enjoying the alarm of Davies, whom he had reinforced at Columbus, and greatly pleased with the thought of having his headquarters in the house once occupied by General Leonidas Polk, the one-time bishop. Then he was observed going down the Mississippi, hopeful of fame, which, however, had not come, for he had been stopped at Helena. Fisk had been something of a flatterer of Curtis, and one wonders a little about his attitude toward Schofield. Commanding the Central District of the state, with headquarters at Jefferson City, where Grant had also spent a part of August, 1861, was Brigadier General Egbert B. Brown, whose conspicuous bravery during Marmaduke's unsuccessful attack upon Springfield in January had won the praise even of the enemy.[32]

The Springfield commander now is Brigadier General John McNeil, who deserves more than the previous short reference to his defeat of Joseph C. Porter's extensive irregular force at Kirksville on August 5, 1862. Among the prisoners captured on that occasion, fifteen were found who had sworn not to take up arms against the United States or the Provisional Government of Missouri. Tried without delay by a drumhead court-martial, they were sentenced to be shot, and McNeil, then a colonel of a Missouri militia regiment, having approved the sentence, it was carried out.[33]

In the order by which McNeil took over command of the District of Southwestern Missouri on July 15, he promised that he would protect those who at the "outbreak of this wicked rebellion" had faltered in their duty, but who now would give *active* support to the Government of the United States, quite "as though they had never erred." It was his earnest desire, he also stated, to return the government of his district to the normal courts and civil authorities. Grimness as well as leniency was, however, in the order. It was McNeil's intention to "pursue, with untiring vigilance, all guerilla bands, marauders, and bushwhackers, and when taken" they would be "summarily dealt with." Recruiting officers or other persons claiming connection with the army of the "so-called Southern Confederacy" would, if arrested within the bounds of his district, be treated as spies of the enemy.[34] Probably McNeil thought spelling out what all this implied would be superfluous.

An officer not even mentioned before, Brigadier General Odon Guitar, commanded the District of North Missouri, comprising the entire part of the state north of the Missouri River. More than any other officer, he made it clear in an order issued at his Macon headquarters on July 12, six days after his appointment, that the state's terrible affliction did not come solely from bands seeking to aid the South:

> The assassins, incendiaries, brigands, and marauders who infest this district, whether claiming to be rebel soldiery or acting under the guise of loyalty, are equally the enemies of peace, order, and good government; no just discrimination can be made between them. Any seeming antagonism in motives by which they claim to be actuated is utterly contradicted by the harmony and consistency of their villainous practices. These men must be brought to justice—driven from the district or exterminated —together with all who sympathize with or aid them in their hellish work.[35]

The district commander against whom there will soon be hurled denunciations of cruelty and inhumanity that echo even to this day is Brigadier General Thomas Ewing, Jr., another of the foster brothers and brothers-in-law of Sherman. Ewing has the specially troublesome District of the Border, where hate and outrage have roots going back for six full years prior to the war. The district contains all of Kansas north of the 38th parallel of latitude and the two tiers of western Missouri counties, six and a fraction in number, lying between that line and the Missouri River.[36] While the parallel was elusive as a dividing line (McNeil's and Blunt's districts lay below it), there were sound military reasons for having the smoldering border region under a single control, though many residents of the two states did not relish the official association.

Several times during the summer reports reached Ewing at his headquarters in Kansas City, Missouri, that guerrillas were assembling in large numbers in the border counties. They actually threatened, alternately, Lexington, Independence, and other Missouri towns, and scouts and spies brought reports that it was the intention of the guerrillas to sack and destroy various towns in Kansas. In the latter places Ewing placed garrisons and issued arms and rations to local volunteer companies. Toward the last of July a reliable source reported a threatened raid on Lawrence, the town so strongly connected with the efforts that had finally made Kansas a free state. In May, 1856, this little town of several hundred people had been badly damaged by a disgraceful proslavery force composed largely of Missourians, and its name was well known throughout the country. Now, when warned of a second threat, Ewing diverted to Lawrence an infantry company en route from Fort Riley, Kansas, and for more than a week it remained there, not departing until after the guerrillas had been dispersed by a force sent against them.[37]

But the guerrillas would soon begin to reassemble under the leadership of a man with whom burning, looting, and murdering had become an overpowering passion—William C. Quantrill. This human fiend, born in Ohio in 1837, had taught school in his native state, and in Indiana, Illinois, and Kansas, before turning murderer and border ruffian at Lawrence under the alias of Charley Hart. He had already become an outlaw when in December, 1860, he treacherously betrayed and entrapped a band he had accompanied into Missouri. There he remained, resuming his proper name, covering up his past more or less successfully, and organizing forays against his former associates in Kansas. "The notorious Quantrill and his gang of robbers" is the style in which he makes his entry in the *Official Records*. The date was February 3, 1862, and a captain of the Seventh Missouri was reporting that Quantrill would not leave the vicinity of Independence (ten miles east of Kansas City) unless chastised and driven out. Families of Union men were coming into town and asking for escorts to bring in their goods and chattels, which the captain had been furnishing. Then, on March 19, it was reported from Leavenworth that "the rebel Quantrill had with his band" crossed into Kansas, murdered several citizens, and carried away considerable booty.[38]

Apparently in mid-August, 1862—just after he had given crucial help in the capture of Independence on the 11th—the Confederate

Government adopted Quantrill, and commissioned him a captain of a company of 150 men and three lieutenants. As fall came, and thickets that had been his hiding places lost protective leaves, and as Western Missouri Secessionists showed signs of uneasiness, Quantrill went down into Arkansas, leaving only small squads in Missouri. When he reached Fort Smith, his force was attached to the command of Jo Shelby, but the outlaw himself set out for Richmond to try to talk himself into a colonelcy of Partisan Rangers. Uncertainty shrouds Quantrill's reception, but it is to the credit of the Confederate authorities that no such commission seems to have been given him, though he purchased a colonel's uniform and had himself photographed in it.[39]

A dispatch from Warrensburg (fifty miles southeast of Kansas City) on January 19, 1863, brought the news that Quantrill's band was back and had mustered from two hundred to five hundred men. Thereafter his name appeared in many messages, but during the summer he left the operations of his men to subordinates, while he planned the Lawrence raid and revealed the secrets of a bandit's life in the brush to Kate Clarke, the girl he had kidnaped and turned into a sympathetic mistress.[40]

Of few events in the war are the details known with such minuteness as they are of Quantrill's march and his bloody hours at Lawrence. The hard-core band of guerrillas that started on the morning of August 19 from a point some twenty miles south of Lexington proceeded cautiously, well spread out, with scouts reporting every hour. In addition to Quantrill, there were other well-known killers, notably Frank James, the Youngers, George Todd, and Bloody Bill Anderson, and the band was increased when Colonel John D. Holt and a party of 104 Confederate recruits were encountered. It seemed a good opportunity to christen the new men, and Holt went along as third in command. With a force raised to not less than 450 men by other accretions, Quantrill halted for a while at a point ten miles beyond the state line, to resume his march near sundown of August 20. After the setting moon had brought heavy darkness on the woods and prairies, guides were impressed at farmhouses. When one became useless, he was shot. In a distance of eight miles, no fewer than ten men were thus wantonly murdered. Yet in spite of his precautions, Quantrill's march had not only been observed but his objective divined. Heroic efforts were made to warn Lawrence, where a half-hour or so would have made it possible for five hundred citizens to assemble with good arms from a well-stocked arsenal. But, as Connelly has put it, "Fate stopped them all."[41]

At sunrise Quantrill struck a completely unsuspecting town. For several hours his men burned, looted, and murdered, though some felt revulsion and held back from the killing, or even were instrumental in saving lives. One hesitates to mention that property was destroyed to the value of a million and a half dollars, when one thinks of the women of Lawrence that day with their dead and wounded, on porches, in yards, in gutters, and in the streets—183 men and boys.[42]

Though Quantrill had cunningly eluded border guards, word of his passing into Kansas had spread to the posts of various small cavalry detachments, and they were in pursuit. Ewing himself was at Leavenworth, but at 1:00 A.M. of the 21st his chief of staff, Major P. B. Plumb, rode out of Kansas City with fifty men. After catching up with two other detachments numbering about two hundred, Plumb at 10:30 A.M. was six miles southeast of Lawrence, only to see from burning farmhouses that Quantrill was in retreat. The band was overtaken, and it was then discovered that some fifty to one hundred citizens with Senator Jim Lane (seen previously as commander of a Kansas brigade), one of those who had escaped from Lawrence with his life, was already boldly following. By now the Federal horses, mostly young and untoughened, were nearly exhausted by sixty-five miles of marching with neither food nor rest. Quantrill, on the other hand, had remounted many of his force on stolen animals, and a rear guard of disciplined men on good horses effectively delayed the pursuers. However, at Paola he almost ran into a trap formed by citizens and a small garrison. After deploying a battle line a few miles north of the town as darkness was falling, Quantrill turned northeastward into the night. Precious hours passed while search was made for his trail; but when it was found the pursuit was resumed, new detachments joining en route, among them a small one from Leavenworth headed by Ewing himself. The time that Quantrill had gained enabled him, however, to reach a region favorable for concealment, and there his force broke up, many men leaving their horses and seeking safety on foot from the merciless troopers who continued to search them out. Upward of three hundred horses had been abandoned before the raiders disintegrated as a body, many of the animals bearing on their backs goods and money stolen at Lawrence. Nor did all the men reach safety by any means; Ewing put the number killed at not fewer than a hundred. "No prisoners have been taken, and none will be," he telegraphed to Schofield.[43]

Men as well as animals suffered terribly as they pushed the band of booty-laden murderers. An Ohio lieutenant, riding beside Ewing, fell dead of sunstroke as he dismounted to rest.

Lane was nearly as prompt and vigorous in pursuit of Schofield as he had been of Quantrill. On the 25th he joined a congressman in telegraphing to Lincoln that there would probably be a collision between outraged Kansans and the military. The telegram continued, "The imbecility and incapacity of Schofield is [*sic*] most deplorable. Our people unanimously demand the removal of Schofield, whose policy has opened Kansas to invasion and butchery." The White House reply was chilly: "Notice of your *demand* for the removal of General Schofield is hereby acknowledged." To Schofield the President sent a copy of the telegram he had received, omitting the names of the senders. That Lincoln was not being stampeded Schofield could easily see from the sentence: "The severe blow they have received naturally enough makes them intemperate even without there being any just cause for blame." Even the injunction with which the message closed was gently expressed: "Please do your utmost to give them future security and to punish their invaders." [44]

After reading two long letters from St. Louis, Lincoln thought it not improbable that retaliation for the Lawrence crime would lead to indiscriminate slaughter on the Kansas-Missouri border. He would be obliged, he wrote in an endorsement on one of the letters, if the General in Chief could make a suggestion to Schofield. But Ewing, who was denounced by one of the St. Louis writers as a mere Kansas politician, had already taken the matter in hand. The threatened crossing of the Missouri at Leavenworth for a raid into Platte County, Missouri, would, he said in a dispatch to Schofield on the 28th, be prevented. The message ended: "You may rely on my doing everything to prevent a collision with citizens of Kansas; but if one must occur, my soldiers will do their duty." [45]

Matching the means Ewing meant to employ to protect Missourians from reprisals was the broad and stern measure he adopted to protect Kansas from another outrage. But it merely extended a plan that he had often discussed with Schofield, and which Schofield wrote he had not only decided upon but had commenced to execute before the Lawrence massacre: the removal from the Missouri border counties of all families known to have given aid to guerrillas. Such persons, and some neutralists, made up the bulk of the population remaining, outspoken Unionists having moved away to save their lives. It was with a mind made up that Ewing rode back to Kansas City on the 24th, after leaving troops still searching the brush for Quantrill's men, and he immediately issued his often-criticized General Order 11, that, with certain exceptions, allowed residents of the border counties fifteen days to leave his district.[46]

Washington knew the order would raise a furor, and a telegram from Halleck to Schofield inquiring whether he had approved or disapproved it reached the department commander on the evening of the day the order was sent, not at headquarters, but at Leavenworth, where Schofield had seen Governor Carney of Kansas and Senator Lane. Quite naturally the governor was making demands for the security of Kansas and the punishment of Quantrill's men; and in view of Lane's past record it was equally natural that he was using the Lawrence attack for a contemplated move into Missouri. Though Lane told Schofield that the expedition would be solely for the purpose of recovering property and punishing the guilty, Schofield well knew what would happen. He felt too that the offer to put the expedition under his direction was only a crafty way of getting him blamed for the inevitable consequences. From Kansas City, Schofield telegraphed to Halleck the next day—September 3—that he would not permit such a column to enter Missouri, adding that Lane had told him he would appeal to the President. While Schofield did not think he would be compelled to meet an invading column with force, he believed a dispatch from the President or the Secretary of War to Lane would help in preventing a collision. But the meeting on the 8th at Paola, where a great throng was supposed to organize the "invasion," had taken place in the rain with nothing more than the passage of resolutions by the few hundred present, before Halleck telegraphed Lincoln's response: the President declined to intervene unless Lane actually appealed against Schofield's order.[47]

After spending several days in the region affected by Ewing's order, talking with people "of all shades of politics" who were affected by it, Schofield was fully satisfied that the measure was "wise and necessary." Though he pronounced it very harsh, he also said it was humane. The milder policy of removing only aiders and abettors of guerrillas he saw was not only impractical, but was one that would put in jeopardy the lives of all who were left, for it would be presumed that they had informed on the friends of guerrillas who had been moved out.[48] Men who had killed in Lawrence without any grievance to redress, but only for the pleasure it gave them, would be happy if they could exterminate those who were responsible for their finding empty houses where they had once been welcomed, sheltered, fed, and furnished with information about Federal garrisons and patrols.

From St. Louis, Schofield telegraphed to Halleck on the 11th that he had approved Ewing's order after two important modifications. Destruction of crops would not be carried out, and loyal people would be allowed to return as soon as they could do so with safety. Three days later, in a formal report, he amplified: "Persons who come to the military posts and claim protection as loyal citizens are not turned away without perfectly satisfactory evidence of disloyalty. It is the first opportunity which those people have had since the war began of openly proclaiming their attachment to the Union, without fear of rebel vengeance." [49] Anyone who is less touched by that picture than by the thought of the friends of guerrillas and neutralists being forced from their homes might recall the deportation of Unionists from East Tennessee. None of them had helped prepare the way for anything that even resembled the horror of Lawrence.

On the very day—September 15—that Schofield was telegraphing to Halleck that the radical papers were seeking to create dissatisfaction among militia units newly called out, Steele was authorizing Union men in three Arkansas counties to organize for the protection of themselves, their families, and their property; McNeil was writing to Schofield from Springfield, "Cruelty to the bushwhacker will be mercy to the loyal and peaceful citizen"; and Lincoln was issuing a proclamation suspending the writ of habeas corpus. The question, which had caused bitter debate early in the war, whether it was the President or Congress that had the power to suspend the cherished right, had been settled by a congressional Act approved on March 3. The authority which he now unquestionably possessed Lincoln used largely because of resistance to the draft. His proclamation made it impossible for anyone in the military or the naval service, or anyone amenable to military law or to the Rules and Articles of War, to obtain a writ that would free him from custody. Nor—and this was very important—could a person secure a writ if he had been arrested for resisting the draft, "or for any offence against the military or naval service." [50]

Broad as was the explicit coverage of Lincoln's proclamation, Schofield found it expedient to issue an order on September 17 in which he held that the suspension of the writ of habeas corpus applied to all militia units that he had called or would call into active service. The President's action had indeed been timely for the Missouri commander, for the 16th had seen members of the militia seek writs because they had been illegally "restrained of liberty." Schofield, after some very hard days, had additional cause for satisfaction. The news of Steele's capture of Little Rock was in. Although Pope had apparently not replied to Schofield's query as to when regiments from the north would arrive, he had informed Halleck on the 16th that three regiments would start as soon as possible, with a full complement of wagons and mules, a fourth following by October 1. Ewing reported from Kansas City on the 16th that Quantrill's main camp had been surprised; although only two of his men had been killed, forty horses had been captured, as well as a great amount of clothing, provisions, arms, and ammunition. Successful pursuit had been impossible because the guerrillas, after firing one brave volley, had disappeared into the brush. Reports from Fort Scott stated that many men were returning from the Rebel armies; while eleven deserters from Marmaduke had given themselves up, most of those coming north were joining guerrilla bands. To Ewing it looked as if another raid might be in preparation, or perhaps an attack upon one of the posts. When on the 18th Ewing queried Schofield whether some captured guerrillas should be selected as a retaliation for three Missouri militiamen who had been taken from a steamboat and shot, Schofield hesitated at reprisals *per se,* but said in a prompt reply, "I think it much better to condemn and execute the guerrillas for their own acts." [51]

On the same day that Schofield thus endorsed the extreme penalty for guerrillas, he meted out stern punishment to men of the Eleventh Provisional Regiment of Enrolled Missouri Militia. This brand of militia, as distinct from the State Militia, was one of the main causes of the radicals' bitter criticism of conservative Governor Gamble. They saw something illegal in the organization, and they broke out in denunciation when Gamble, who had refused to let Curtis have any control over the Enrolled Militia, promptly put it under the orders of Schofield. In radical minds this act apparently made Schofield almost a friend of slavery, for gradual emancipation had been part of Gamble's program, and was one of the points of cleavage between the two bitterly quarreling Missouri Union factions. When Schofield called out two St. Louis regiments of the Provisional Enrolled Militia to send to New Madrid to replace the Twenty-fifth Missouri, which was under orders to reinforce Steele, radical politicians and papers made bold to suggest resistance. Some of the men promptly mutinied. Having taken over the boat on which they were embarked, they brought it ashore and then dispersed. Very brief, however, was the sanctuary which they found in their homes, for the provost guard of Brigadier General William K. Strong, commander of the District of St. Louis, soon began gathering them in. Confinement in the military prison to await trial by a general court-martial was the order Schofield issued for the leading mutineers. Other participants in the uprising were sent to Rolla to be put "at hard labor, under a strong guard, on the block-houses and other fortifications now being erected at that point." [52]

No commanding general could relish inflicting such punishment upon men who had been the dupes of editors that he considered worse than reprehensible. On the same day Schofield was able to give some thought to matters more congenial than the vexing state of things near his headquarters. In a long letter to Halleck he discussed the further prosecution of the campaign in Arkansas. He wanted the anomalous command arrangements there to be straightened out; no harm had, however, he thought, been done up to the present, and probably what had been done had been unavoidable. But he said, "I see no better arrangement that can now be made than to restore all of Arkansas to this department." Turning to the Missouri situation, he said that the habit of waging guerrilla warfare had become such a passion with the Western people that he apprehended more trouble in the future from that source than actual enemy armies had given in the past. Finally, he sounded a note that would have caused some radicals to suffer almost unto death. The guerrilla evil, Schofield stated, was aggravated by the fact that loyal people would not permit recanting Rebels to return and live among them; thus such men were forced to remain in bands for self-protection, as many of them would also do for the purpose of plunder.[53]

Unionists were not suffering solely from bands of guerrillas: on this same September 18th, men of the Sixth Missouri Cavalry, while pursuing guerrillas, committed outrageous excesses in the vicinity of Sikeston, twenty miles east of Bloomfield. In their pursuit they were successful, and within a few days Brigadier Clinton B. Fisk would report that his forces had killed over one hundred guerrillas and captured fifty. With understandable satisfaction he stated that "the notorious Jeff. Thompson and staff," captured in late August, were being sent forward for safe confinement. The man whose name was to be perpetuated in Fisk University had other interesting and hopeful things to report. He had been encouraging the people to re-establish their schools, reopen their churches, and cultivate fraternal and social feelings instead of running to him with complaints of their neighborhood quarrels. And he was obtaining results; two seminary buildings that had been serving as stables and barracks had been reconverted to their original purpose; more than thirty common schools had been opened.[54]

In his order of the 17th Schofield not unnaturally sought to curb as many of his afflictions as possible. In addition to stating that the President's proclamation would be regarded as applying to militia, he said that martial law would thereafter be rigidly enforced throughout his department against all persons who should in any manner encourage mutiny, insubordination, or disorderly conduct, or try to create disaffection among troops. He went even further than this and invited new denunciations when he suggested that he meant to control the press if it indulged in falsehoods or misrepresentations calculated to embarrass or weaken military authorities. More than a week passed before Schofield received from Halleck a written statement of the President's approval of his order. But though Lincoln was standing behind his department commander, the General in Chief uttered words of caution about the execution of the order, especially its provisions with regard to the press. "Anything," he said, "that has the appearance of persecution or oppression will incite public sympathy in favor of the culprit and against you." Probably as well as anyone Halleck described the Missouri situation as it appeared in Washington: "Neither faction in Missouri is really friendly to the President and his administration, but each one is striving to destroy the other, regardless of other consequences. In their mutual hatred they seem to have lost all sense of the perils of the country and all sentiments of national patriotism."[55]

Even before Halleck's words of caution had been received, Schofield had issued an order that should have been reassuring to reasonable men—of which not too many seem to have been left in Missouri. An election was soon to be held in the state, and the department commander issued a strong order that sought to protect the polls and lawful assemblages of persons seeking to express their will by their ballots. Any officer, soldier, or civilian who sought to intimidate a qualified voter from the exercise of his voting right was to be punished by a court-martial or by a military commission.[56]

As September ended, word of the difficulties still abounding in the turbulent state continued to flow to Washington. To Lincoln it was reported that Union men were being driven from northwestern Missouri into asylum in Kansas. Schofield appealed to Ewing for the facts; Ewing appealed to his subordinates. Before long General Guitar was telegraphing to Schofield that he had "no hesitation in pronouncing the whole thing an infamous falsehood, gotten up to aid the radical delegation at Washington in their revolutionary scheme." The next day—October 2—he reported more at length: "This is but part of the preconcerted scheme to carry the day at Washington. The lie told, of course, will be persisted in. If Lane, Jennison, and company are to determine who are loyal men in Missouri, you and I, of course, would be driven from the ranks." He gave the assurance that no Rebel had been or would be armed, and no law-abiding, peaceable citizen would be driven out. But he promised also that men who burned houses over the heads of helpless women and children and outraged innocent and unprotected girls would be "exterminated, if found, though they die shouting for the Union." In passing the result of his investigation to Lincoln, Schofield named the leader of the group who had manufactured the report sent to Washington—a man Lincoln had once pardoned at Gamble's request, but who was now engaged in efforts to overthrow the state government. "It is," said the general, "a base attempt of my enemies to influence your action." [57]

Even while he was thinking of the western part of Missouri, and of the radical delegation under Lane that had journeyed to Washington to get him ousted from command, Schofield had to give thought on this October 2 to what was happening on the Arkansas River. From Fayetteville a telegram had come the preceding day saying that a force reported to be Jo Shelby's had camped the night before near Huntsville; Missouri was named as its destination. As the four-deep column had passed their houses, loyal women had counted: 1,260 men in all, 900 armed, three guns—two of brass, one of iron. "Look out for them," the reporting colonel warned. "The women report a large number of them in Federal uniforms." To Frederick Steele at Little Rock, Schofield sped a telegram by way of Cairo.[58]

The morning of the same day saw Lincoln appealing to Schofield not to increase his difficulties. Acting on a report of inspectors who had investigated both Ewing's district and Blunt's, Schofield had wired to Halleck on October 1 that he intended to replace Blunt by McNeil. From the President there came the dispatch, "If possible, you better allow me to get through with a certain matter here before adding to the difficulties of it." "Meantime," the President added, "supply me the particulars of Major-General Blunt's case." The denunciatory letter that Blunt had sent to Lincoln on July 31 would hardly help him; nor would Blunt's answer then on the way to Lincoln's critical reply.[59]

The delegation of radicals to which Guitar referred had arrived in Washington on September 27—seventy strong. Two days were spent in preparing an address—"artfully phrased," Nicolay and Hay say—as well as in recruiting and making preparations generally for an impressive appearance at the White House. The President's secretaries tell how Lane arranged what he styled "his little army" about three walls of the East Room on September 30. Never did Lincoln, in the minds of his eminent biographers, appear to a greater advantage than during the two long hours devoted to the reading of the delegation's memorandum and the resulting desultory conversation. He would have to study the document before replying, Lincoln said, and he promised, "No painful memories of the past and no hopes for the future, personal to myself, shall hamper my judgment." Yet he did on the spot analyze to some extent and in a masterful way the charges against Schofield. Weighing heavily in Schofield's favor had been the wholeheartedness and promptness with which he had sent help to Grant at Vicksburg. As to Schofield's order of the 17th, the President had, he stated, given his approval to it *after* the *Missouri Democrat* had done so. This observation brought from a slow-witted member of the delegation the comment, "We thought then it was to be used against the other side." To this Lincoln made the response: "Certainly you did. Your ideas of justice seem to depend on the application of it." [60]

The President's formal reply to the delegation on October 5 was one of the great documents of the war. Knowing that Schofield must be discharging his heavy duties with uneasy thoughts, Lincoln had wired to him at noon the day before: "I think you will not have just cause to complain of my action." [61]

The General in Chief gave some enlightenment to Schofield. On a very busy day, the day when Lincoln wrote his reply to the delegation, and General Robert Allen—efficient quartermaster in St. Louis—was writing to Halleck about the alarming destruction of steamboats by fire, and in perplexity asking, "What would you advise?" Halleck wrote to Schofield:

> I have not heard the President say anything about the representatives of the mammoth committee, but I don't think they did you much harm. They have the support of the ultra-radicals, but not of the leading men in the Cabinet. The whole thing is regarded as a political attack on the President, and your name is used merely as a cloak to strike at him.[62]

From his own five months in St. Louis, Halleck no doubt was acquainted with some of the "mammoth committee." Certain among them would seem to have desired nothing more—at least ostensibly—than the replacement of Schofield by "General Butler or some other suitable man." But Schofield, as well as Guitar, well knew that there were actual "revolutionists" in Missouri who aimed at the violent overthrow of the provisional state government, the first act on their program being to seize Gamble and Schofield and lock them up. The preceding year men had been so indiscreet as to approach General Frank Blair with their scheme. While refusing to divulge names, Blair had warned Schofield. And now, with the state still inflamed, some of the conspirators had so lost their heads that they tried to tamper with the guard at Schofield's residence in the St. Louis suburbs, hoping to spread disaffection among his troops. Again the general learned what was afoot.[63]

Halleck in his letter of October 5 once more gave counsel to Schofield. The abuse Schofield was receiving was probably no worse than was being meted out to himself by several prominent papers that he named. Then the General in Chief added: "The only ground upon which I would stop a newspaper is that of giving aid and comfort to the enemy by publishing information, inciting desertions, mutiny, riot, etc. And even in such cases I would avoid all appearance of any personal grievance, as would be charged in this case. Such gross abuse seldom does much harm."

Untried though Schofield still is as a commander in heavy battle—at Wilson's Creek, it will be recalled, he had been Lyon's adjutant—he has gone through some hard months of testing. He has shown that he is not only an officer who will obey orders wholeheartedly, but one who will pay heed to the wishes of superiors, and listen to the advice of older men.

On Wednesday, August 26, the weather was surely as oppressive in Memphis as it was at Brownsville, where Davidson's cavalry was operating against the horsemen of Walker and Marmaduke, or in western Missouri where Ewing's men were still searching the brush for Quantrill's guerrillas, or in southeastern Missouri where Fisk had just captured troublemaker Jeff Thompson and was gleefully saying that he meant "to keep the border too hot for the rascals." But in spite of temperature it was a gala day in Memphis. The conqueror of Vicksburg was in town. Whether Hurlbut would have still declared that Memphis possessed more iniquity than any place since Sodom, or whether he and Brigadier James Veatch, local commander, had given it a little respectability, cannot be said. But without doubt the provost marshal and his men, as well as the garrison, got uncompromising instructions to make everything look its best during the first visit of the department commander since his departure in late January to conduct operations against the mighty stronghold four hundred river miles down the Mississippi.

Only five days previously the *New York Tribune* correspondent at Vicksburg had been pining for the "glorious days," when "it seemed as if everything was going to happen at once, and we reveled in a luxury of events." There was not at the moment, he stated, any real scarcity of items, but there was "a certain gentleman up town—he with the whiskers and a slouched hat, surnamed Grant—that humps his shoulders and says 'No' to any such thing as transmitting army news." Disobedience of orders, the reporter continued, was sure to be followed by punishment; so he saw fit to be obedient.[64]

But Greeley's Memphis correspondent used a fearless pen in describing the first great entertainment and banquet of the many that were to be given in Grant's honor—with no great pleasure to himself. Flags and pictures decorated the reception room at the famous Gayoso House, while the tables in the dining room were "spread with a sumptuous repast," and in front of Grant's place there was a pyramid inscribed with the names of his battles, beginning with Belmont. To the two hundred guests at the tables S. F. Hallman gave the toast, "Your Grant and my Grant." Following loud cheers and calls for Grant, the general rose and made a long speech for him—two sentences. In the first he thanked the enthusiastic diners for their kindness; in the second he promised to do all he could for their prosperity. Revelry continued and amid deafening applause the letter in which Grant had accepted the celebration was read. He would not, he had said, want to refuse "for considerations of personal convenience," to acknowledge anywhere or in any form the existence of sentiments which he had so long and so ardently desired to see maintained in the department.[65]

The 28th saw Grant back at Vicksburg telegraphing briefly to Sherman at Parson Fox's about troops for Steele and the disquieting news concerning Vicksburg parolees. Southern papers had been contending for the right of setting aside their pledges not to serve until properly exchanged. The one of Grant's two messages that referred to Sherman's dealings with the paroled Confederate General Stephen D. Lee terminated, "I have no doubt but what your action will be just right." The answer the wire quickly brought from Sherman began, "Glad you are back." [66]

But Grant did not remain long. A trip to New Orleans had apparently been inspired by Banks's visit to Vicksburg; that it must have been discussed by the two generals is obvious. The short telegram Grant sent to the General in Chief on August 1—the day Banks was at Vicksburg—as to taking Mobile with troops that he could furnish, ended, "With your leave, I would like to visit New Orleans, particularly if the movement against Mobile is authorized." Lincoln answered the proposal with regard to Mobile in the telegram whose importance was stressed in the last chapter. Halleck, on his part, telegraphed on the same day—August 9—to Cairo for transmission by boat: "There is no objection to your visiting New Orleans, leaving an officer in Vicksburg to receive and carry out any orders that are sent from Washington." [67]

Unfortunately, Grant had forgotten about Halleck's dispatch when writing his *Memoirs,* and he there states that Halleck "refused" his request, a word the reader must take as meaning that an actually negative reply had come from the General in Chief. (Badeau in his work on Grant states that the requested leave "was not granted," which could mean that Grant's request had merely been ignored.) To the inaccurate statement, which by itself was damaging to Halleck, Grant added the lethal sentences, "So far as my experience with General Halleck went it was very much easier for him to refuse a favor than to grant one. But I did not regard this as a favor. It was simply in line of duty, though out of my department." [68]

Grant saved himself from appearing to have disobeyed an explicit order—which would have been completely out of character—by speaking two pages later of an order to cooperate with Banks, with the clear indication that it was this directive that caused him to visit New Orleans. Actually, however, Halleck's direction for Grant to confer freely with Banks was made in his letter of August 22, and it is by no means certain that it had reached Grant before the latter began a letter to Halleck on the 30th: "I shall start this evening on a short trip to New Orleans, remaining there but a day or two. General Banks is not yet off, and I am desirous of seeing him before he starts to learn his plans and see how I may help him." [69] This looks like nothing more than the natural expression of one of Grant's most distinguishing and laudatory characteristics: a readiness and eagerness to help any other commander in every way possible.

Though Grant did not mention it, Adjutant General Thomas, then in Vicksburg to organize Negro regiments, accompanied him down the river. An accident caused by the running away of a very spirited horse that Banks had furnished Grant for reviewing troops was to detain him for an extra ten days. New Orleans papers, in describing the accident, prove beyond doubt that it occurred while Grant was *returning* to the city *after* the review, and they speak of his horse running into a carriage before falling with its rider. But it has been said that Grant fell from, or was thrown by, his horse *at* the review.

Officially, Rawlins reported in accordance with New Orleans papers when he said in a letter on September 17 to Halleck's adjutant: "General Grant has returned from New Orleans, and although unable to walk from the effects of injuries received while there by the falling of his horse, his general health is good and he is able for duty." Fortunately, on the same day Sherman was indulging his love of writing by a many-page letter to Halleck about Reconstruction, and the letter must have been sufficient to keep Grant's mind occupied for some time in reading, digesting, and pondering about the hard problem. In a dictated letter to Halleck on the 19th, in which he stated that he was not in full agreement with Sherman, Grant said he was still flat on his back, but would try to perform his duties, though he found them fatiguing, and he hoped soon to be able to take the field at any time he might be called upon. But knowledge that Grant was back at his headquarters did not have to await the slow coming of the Vicksburg messages by way of Cairo. On the 19th a quartermaster captain put on the wire to Halleck a telegram Grant had given him to forward upon arrival in New York. Written on Saturday the 12th, it said, "I will leave for Vicksburg on Monday. Am improving rapidly, but not yet able to leave my room." [70]

On a flag-of-truce boat out of Cairo, in a hotel in that town, at Fort Donelson, at Shiloh, at Satartia, and astride a horse at New Orleans—at all these places it has been charged that Grant was drunk. There is still the chance that a lover of the sensational may add to the fable the claim that at the Memphis banquet Grant imbibed so heavily that when called upon for a speech, he rose unsteadily and could stand only long enough to utter two incoherent sentences before collapsing.

CHAPTER VI

STONES RIVER AFTERMATH

> Their numerous cavalry goads and worries me, but I will try to be equal to them. *Rosecrans to Halleck*

IF THE reader is to follow the full sweep of the War he must now turn back to the beginning of the year 1863, place himself at Rosecrans's headquarters in Murfreesboro, and from there follow the sequence of events, none of them large in themselves, which are the inevitable prelude to Chickamauga. There will be raids, reconnaissances, and skirmishes, and a long and occasionally acrid correspondence between Rosecrans and Halleck.

Rosecrans could well have been proud of his high place in the class that graduated from West Point in 1842—the year ahead of Grant. Unlike his fellow Buckeye, he had come from a family which, although established here since pre-Revolutionary days, was in straitened circumstances; and to stand Number Five among fifty-six, many of whom had previously enjoyed superior educational advantages, was necessarily the result of ability and diligence. The years 1843–1847 saw Rosecrans engaged as an instructor at the Academy and in work on fortifications, and he missed the Mexican War—the valuable training period for many officers, both regulars and volunteers, in marching and supply as well as in combat. Curiously, the army lost both Grant and Rosecrans by resignation in the same month and year—April, 1845. But unlike Grant who, after his unrewarding years near and in St. Louis, had resorted to a position in his father's store at Galena, Illinois, Rosecrans, by the outbreak of the Civil War, had become a successful entrepreneur in Cincinnati.

The Queen City was certainly awarded a questionable number of high appointments when a major generalcy in the regular Army, dating from May 14, 1861, was bestowed upon McClellan, and a brigadiership in the Regulars was given to Rosecrans two days later. Officers who had stood as high as or higher than these at West Point, who had marched hard and fought gallantly in Mexico, and who had remained in the service could well have been surprised and displeased at such a proceeding. Fortunately for Rosecrans and for the Administration which had chosen him for distinction with no sufficiently discernible reason, he soon flashed forth before the country by a real achievement during McClellan's brief campaign in western Virginia. Prominent in that campaign, it may be recalled, there was yet a third high-standing West Point graduate, Thomas A. Morris, Number Four in the thirty-six-man class of 1836, and a distinguished builder of railroads after his retirement from the Army. But Morris had received no Federal commission; he had merely been chosen by Governor Morton, of Indiana, as the brigadier assigned to the state in Lincoln's original call for 75,000 militia.

After Morris had set the pattern of success by the capture of Philippi on June 3, 1861, only to be later ill used and cast aside, McClellan and Rosecrans won the greater victory at Rich Mountain * on July 11 at the head of six infantry regiments, some dragoons, and a battery. It was Rosecrans, as previously noted in the account of that engagement, who had proposed a bold turning movement and had then led four regiments and seventy-five horsemen through rain and over exceedingly difficult terrain. The victory to the Federal standards caused a considerable retirement by the enemy and was largely responsible for Lincoln's calling McClellan to Washington after the disheartening defeat at Bull Run. While McClellan's conduct, when carefully examined, reveals the caution, hesitation, and fear that he later constantly revealed when in higher command, Rosecrans's record sustains careful scrutiny. Though the newspapers naturally stressed McClellan's role as the over-all commander in West Virginia—and unfortunately hailed him as the "Young Napoleon"—it is to their credit that they did not overlook Rosecrans's feat. Nor could it have escaped the attention of Thomas Jonathan Jackson, at the moment not overly occupied with his brigade in the vicinity of Winchester. According to Henderson, Jackson's one ambition had been to be selected as the instrument for blocking the Federal advance

* For Philippi and Rich Mountain see map, p. 107, Vol. I.

under McClellan—a former classmate—into the mountain region where he had been born and reared.[1] While this wish was denied him, he must have noted and remembered the early demonstration by an enemy commander of the effectiveness of a wide-circling flank or rear attack. Rich Mountain multiplied many times gives Chancellorsville.

Rosecrans's operations in western Virginia after McClellan's departure have not been described; but it has been remarked, in connection with his assignment to the Corinth theater in May, 1862, that they had been "notable." When Kentucky-born John Pope—Rosecrans's classmate, but twelve satisfying places below him—was called to the East in July, Rosecrans became commander of the Army of the Mississippi.[2] Elevation to army command was certainly gratifying, though it is entirely probable that Rosecrans did not relish subordination to Grant, commander of the District of West Tennessee since Halleck's call to high command in Washington soon after Pope's departure. Grant's capture of Fort Donelson the preceding February was a far greater accomplishment than anything done by Rosecrans, but the criticism and libelous defamation that were circulated against Grant after Shiloh may have influenced Rosecrans, and he may have had an exaggerated idea of the role played in the battle by the Army of the Ohio, commanded by that third Ohioan—Buell—who had graduated from the Academy just a year ahead of him.

The good standing that Rosecrans had with the public grew with the battles of Iuka and Corinth, and in the brief interval between them Halleck had said, when answering an unofficial letter, "You have my entire confidence, and if it is possible I will give you a separate command." Before even a month had passed, Rosecrans was on his way north to take over from Buell the command of the Army of the Ohio soon after bloody Perryville. Yet it is possible that in spite of Rosecrans's successes, Lincoln, even at that time, might have written to him—as he later did in the masterpiece to Hooker—that there were things about him with which he was not entirely satisfied. A telegram Rosecrans had sent to Lincoln resulted in Halleck's branding Rosecrans's delay in leaving Corinth "very reprehensible." The harshness of those words was not mitigated by the remainder of the sentence of the previously quoted dispatch: Halleck had been directed to inform Rosecrans that unless he immediately obeyed the orders sent to him, he would not receive the command to which he had been summoned.[3]

Unlike Rich Mountain, Iuka and Corinth, as the reader may recall, do not bear close examination. What were merely defeats for the Confederates could have been catastrophes if, at Iuka, Rosecrans had not withdrawn his cavalry from the road by which Sterling Price escaped and which Rosecrans had told Grant he would hold; and if, at Corinth, Rosecrans had made full use of the knowledge that Grant had had a force seize the road by which Van Dorn and Price had advanced and by which they sought to retire. It is not just a matter of pointing out errors: all generals make mistakes. The question is whether Rosecrans had that essential honesty of character which would make him frankly and objectively analyze what he had done. (As Rosecrans disappears as a field commander, the reader will certainly want to appraise him.) About Corinth more should be recalled. After the fighting had ended, Rosecrans denounced a division, a quarter of whose men had been killed or wounded, as a "set of cowards." What is more ominous for the future, he gave two ambiguous battle orders. At Stones River, Rosecrans had shown himself personally brave, but he must have intruded beyond all reason upon the province of subordinates; or Crittenden, who commanded the crucial left, would hardly have said under oath, "I have heard him censured by commanders because they said they could not turn their backs on their commands without his ordering portions of them away." [4]

Gratitude for a victory when gloom weighed heavily on the North because of the defeat at Fredericksburg, followed shortly by Van Dorn's destruction of Grant's Holly Springs base, and then in the early days of 1863 the news of Sherman's failure at Vicksburg, caused the righting of an injustice to Rosecrans, which he had not borne without complaint. His long-delayed promotion to a major generalcy of volunteers the preceding September had still left him subordinate to men he had previously outranked and who had not to their credit accomplishments to match his. A War Department ruling had prevented full justice being done him at the time; but not long after the battle near Murfreesboro an appreciative Secretary of War telegraphed, "The date of your commission shall be attended to, and arranged to suit you as nearly as possible." [5]

Only a few days previously Stanton had telegraphed to Rosecrans that Captain James St. C. Morton, efficient commander of Rosecrans's newly organized engineer brigade, which had been thrown into combat with resulting casualties, would, in accordance with the general's request, be jumped to the rank of brigadier of volunteers, and that McCook, Thomas, and Crittenden, commanders respectively of the segments of the old Fourteenth Corps, awkwardly called "Right Wing," "Center," and "Left Wing," would be made corps commanders, with proper designations for their units, exactly as Rosecrans wished. Then the Secretary added, "There is nothing you can ask within my power to grant to yourself or your heroic command that will not be cheerfully given." [6]

The telegram about adjusting Rosecrans's relative rank as a major general showed that Stanton had not been activated by a mere fleeting impulse, and it must have brought much satisfaction to the general in his room in a fine old Murfreesboro home. Rosecrans would have been even happier if he could have read a long telegram that John Dix—then at Fort Monroe—had sent to Lincoln, with quotations from the *Richmond Examiner,* which was in such ill humor over the reports from Tennessee that it commented:

> So far the news has come in what may be called the classical style of the Southwest. When the Southern army fights a battle, we first hear that it has gained one of the most stupendous victories on record; that regiments from Mississippi, Texas, Louisiana, Arkansas, &c., have exhibited an irresistible and superhuman valor unknown in history this side of Sparta and Rome. As for the generals, they usually get all their clothes shot off, and replace them with a suit of glory. The enemy, of course, is simply annihilated. Next day more dispatches come, still very good, but not quite as good as the first. The telegrams of the third day are invariably such as to make a mist, a muddle, and a fog of the whole affair.[7]

Unhappily by the time that Rosecrans knew that the date of his commission would be so adjusted that he would be the actual senior of his principal subordinates, the enemy was not behaving in what, in view of their recent defeat and retirement, may have seemed the proper manner.

Very commendably, Rosecrans had not made haste to ride into Murfreesboro after it became known that the enemy had retreated on the night of January 3. There was plenty for him to do at his battle headquarters near the pike to Nashville, and some hours of rest were due him.

His telegram to Halleck on the 4th not only said that the day had been spent in distributing ammunition but also that the pursuit had been started with the center, the two leading brigades having arrived at the *west* side of Stones River "this evening." "We shall occupy the town and push the pursuit to-morrow with the center," the Federal general announced; and quite in accordance with that statement, an order went to George Thomas to prepare his command to pursue the enemy, with 7:00 A.M. set down as starting time.[8]

Jeremiah Boyle in Louisville, Horatio Wright in Cincinnati, Halleck in Washington were doing all they could for the general who by a narrow margin had won a crucial battle. On the afternoon of the 3rd Wright directed Boyle to relieve the garrison at Bowling Green so that it would go to Rosecrans. But, his mind reverting to the damage done to the Louisville and Nashville Railroad by Morgan's recent raid, he was not sure that he should detach more men to Rosecrans unless the latter was in pressing need. To Halleck, Wright telegraphed that, his force being mostly infantry, he could do little but hold important points. He wanted authority to mount 3,000 infantry, purchasing their equipment if necessary. With a mounted force to operate against future raiders, he thought he could protect Kentucky and spare more than 3,000 infantrymen for Rosecrans.[9] (A very minor dispatch in the operations being studied, it nevertheless warrants a fine mark for the military acumen of Wright, who, throughout Rosecrans's campaign, had been playing a very difficult and important part, in which many another general would have failed because of inability properly to appraise his own needs in a delicate situation relative to those of another commander with an aggressive role.)

One can well believe that wires were more than busy that day, and restrained exasperation may lurk in the sentence with which Halleck began a message to Wright on the 4th: "Your telegram of yesterday was twenty-four hours in reaching me." Action, however, had been swift; the chief of ordnance would send equipment from Pittsburgh; but the Secretary of War had authorized purchase, if Wright deemed it necessary. To cut red tape, Wright was to communicate directly with the Pittsburgh Arsenal and with General Ripley in Washington. Halleck's broad grasp of necessities revealed itself in another dispatch to Wright: "Do you hear anything about General Rosecrans' supplies? If re-enforcements should be sent to him, could they be supplied in the present condition of the Cumberland River?" —a point such as many critics overlook when expatiating on what someone should have done.[10]

The next day—January 5—when the busy General in Chief was telegraphing Rosecrans, "Artillery will be immediately attended to.

I have barely time to add my congratulations to you and your army on your success," Wright was replying reassuringly to the query about supplies, and Thomas was reporting to Rosecrans that he had occupied Murfreesboro with Negley's and Rousseau's divisions. Troopers of Stanley's cavalry division were following the enemy on the roads to Shelbyville and Manchester.

While there had not been a real pursuit by the center, Thomas, upon hearing from cavalryman Colonel Zahm that he was engaging the enemy rear guard upon the Shelbyville Pike, had ordered an infantry brigade and a battery to his support. Negley on his part had ordered Spears's brigade of East Tennesseans, recently attached to him, out on the Manchester Pike. After night had fallen, Thomas knew that Spears had returned, but not until one of his regiments had charged and compelled the retirement for "a short distance" of a considerable body of dismounted hostile cavalry. Actually, both of Thomas's divisions were—according to his dispatch to Rosecrans—out of rations. And he had found other pressing matters to attend to, doubtless unsuspected by Rosecrans the night before: a large number of Federal wounded suffering for medicines, dressings, and care, as well as the enemy sick and wounded who had been left in inadequately equipped hospitals.[11]

In view of the ration situation, Rosecrans's statement about pushing the pursuit had been ill advised. It could not only have misled a superior, but it might have been released to an always news-hungry press, thus leading the public to unwarranted hopes. Actually, Rosecrans did not have a good body of fresh troops provided with the rations needed to press a retiring enemy effectively, though it may be recalled that Spears's brigade had not really been used in the recent battle. (While pursuers should not so stuff their stomachs as to become sluggish, they should not have to neglect them completely.) In the victory message that he sent to Stanton from Murfreesboro at 4:30 A.M. of the 5th, Rosecrans had more cautiously said, "We shall press them as rapidly as our means of traveling [soldiers' legs principally] and subsistence will permit." But the next day his tendency to be flippant reappeared in a dispatch to Wright: "I now wish to push them to the wall," an announcement qualified by the statement that pursuit would be "heavy work."[12] "Pursuit" was, however, no longer the correct word; any operation now would be merely an advance against an enemy who had successfully disengaged himself and retired to a position from which he had advanced only a few weeks previously. And soon even the idea of following was abandoned, as Rosecrans became absorbed in calling for reinforcements, particularly cavalry, and in concern over his communications.

Rosecrans's communications certainly required thought. Looking forward to the opening of the railroad from Louisville to Nashville, the general had a telegram sent on January 5 to Brigadier General E. A. Paine at Gallatin. (Morgan's burning of the linings of the tunnel near that place the previous July, together with the shrunken Cumberland, had, it will be recalled, combined to cut off supplies to Buell, and had thrown him largely upon the resources of the country, a

THE MURFREESBORO REGION

means of supply he disliked because it was not only harmful to discipline but also contrary to the policy toward Southerners in which he believed.) Paine was directed to have abatis constructed, with ground so cleared as to give a good field of fire. "If attacked, let the enemy come close before firing," he was told at the same time that he was instructed to pass similar instructions along the railroad with the order for all commanders to be constantly on the alert against surprise.[13]

Prompt advance would seem to have left Rosecrans's mind by

the night of January 8, when he said in a telegram to Wright, "Infantry re-enforcements will be needed as our line extends, and anything you can spare will be well placed here." Two days later a lady dropped in on the general and reported that the Confederates had returned to Shelbyville (after having retreated beyond that place) and were "talking of making an advance." Noon saw a courier riding to McCook, upon whose command Bragg's blow had fallen so heavily early on December 31, telling him of the fair visitor at headquarters and directing him to send at once a brigade to reconnoiter. One can only conjecture whether it was the lady of Shelbyville—a town where Union sentiment was strong—who was responsible for a note to Stanley that there was "good reason to believe that General Wheeler, with about 1,000 cavalry" had left Shelbyville "for the purpose of coming in and cutting the railroad." [14] In view of the mischief that Wheeler had done in Rosecrans's rear during the recent battle, here indeed was a possibility for him seriously to consider.

The next day—Sunday, the 11th—appears to have been critical in Rosecrans's thinking. In a dispatch to Halleck at an unnamed hour, he said he was hurrying up ammunition and supplies, and hoped the railroad would be open by Tuesday night. (Whether he meant from Louisville to Nashville, or from Nashville to Murfreesboro, is not clear.) The enemy was reported to be preparing to defend the line of Duck River. To this he added a statement indicating that considerable information had arrived since the Shelbyville lady had passed the word which had caused a brigade to start marching. In spite of the Duck River report, "the signs" were that the Confederates would move to Chattanooga, unless assistance came from Virginia. This could have been mystifying to the High Command, especially since Rosecrans followed with an assertion which, if true—though it was not—would have given support to the Duck River report: "They fought us with equal, if not superior, numbers." [15]

An order by Bragg removes all doubt that Rosecrans was not wanting for intelligence. According to Bragg, information was being given to the Federals daily by persons permitted to pass his lines "on various and frivolous pretexts"—which in turn shows that Bragg was not lacking for reports from Murfreesboro, outstanding for rugged Secession spirit. To check the evil, the Confederate general ordered that no one be allowed to pass infantry outposts except on passes granted by his own headquarters.[16]

Late visitors at Murfreesboro headquarters on January 11 may have accounted for a second dispatch that Rosecrans sent to Halleck when midnight was close at hand. Basing his opinion on the state of "public 'secesh' feeling," as well as upon the "interests and necessities of the rebels," he said they would strip every place they could to reinforce Bragg, and assume the offensive at an early day. Here was a little intrusion on the province of the High Command, though it was not delivered in the offensive manner Rosecrans sometimes used. Nor was the sentence that followed: "I think, therefore, the more speedily you send forces this way the better for the public service." Had Rosecrans laid down his pencil there, it would look as if he had been thinking merely of holding the important part of middle Tennessee already in possession of the Union. Perhaps, however, it was a fleeting recollection of his statements about pursuit, perhaps it was merely the changeable quality of his mind, that caused him to add: "We ought to hold the Tennessee River with a force adequate to cover the country south of Duck River, and cover that flank from [with] cavalry, of which they have four to our one." [17]

In spite of doubt as to Confederate intentions, Rosecrans should have slept well—in a room that may have been too attractive with a bed too comfortable for the best interests of the Union—if he had received, as he should have, a telegram that Stanley wrote at 8:15 P.M. at Gallatin. A large "scout" that the cavalryman had had made that day between the Murfreesboro and the Nolensville pikes had brought word that three hundred of the enemy were three miles south of Franklin, and that they were the advance of Forrest's command, returning from his raid west of the Tennessee upon Grant's communications. This was hardly cheering news, nor was the information: "Guerrillas are collecting at Charlotte to fire on the boats." There was comfort, however, in Stanley's concluding sentence: "I have a scheme to fix them." [18]

With mounting reports that an enemy column of 3,000 to 4,000 cavalry, with a little infantry and some guns, was moving northward from Franklin, Rosecrans on January 12 sent an expedition of two brigades under Colonel C. D. Wagner westward from Murfreesboro. If Wagner, upon arriving at Triune, where Wheeler was reported to have been, thought there had been a union of the two forces, and that the real objective was the river *below* Nashville, then he was to march for Franklin, so as to be on the hostile flank and rear. Brigadier General Robert B. Mitchell, still in command at Nashville,

Wagner was informed, was preparing to move against the enemy with eight or ten regiments and some of Stanley's cavalry. To Colonel William Lowe, at Fort Henry, there went a sharp warning: Forrest would come out and try to interrupt river transportation.[19]

In spite of countermeasures that seem to have been well taken, it looks as though the unexpected turn of events had shaken, if it had not unhinged, Rosecrans. The next day—January 13—he telegraphed to Halleck that there was no longer any doubt that Longstreet was expected with reinforcements from Virginia for Bragg. While Lee's lieutenant had been nearer to the bottom of the West Point class of 1842 than Rosecrans had been to the top, Rosecrans did not discount him. The large enemy cavalry force was, he said to the General in Chief, constantly annoying him, Forrest and Wheeler being momentarily headed to attack his river transportation. In yet another message to Halleck that same day, Rosecrans reported that the enemy had retraced his steps and was occupying Duck River from Shelbyville to Wartrace. Gloomily he said: "Their numerous cavalry goads and worries me, but I will try and be equal to them. Look out for reenforcements." [20]

Though in actual fact Forrest was at Columbia refitting from his operation west of the Tennessee—which had been in friendly territory, for the most part conducted in a rather leisurely way, with no strong enemy cavalry force opposing him—Rosecrans believed Forrest was with Wheeler. Knowledge of the actual situation on his right would have been disturbing enough. But, according to a dispatch from Gallatin, the mischievous Morgan, with a thousand men, was on the left, after having spent the night at McMinnville. The outlook, however, brightened when a dispatch arrived from Mitchell. A brigade he was expecting from Gallatin would be sent in Stanley's wake; Stanley, now fifteen miles behind the enemy on the Charlotte road, wanted to know how far he should pursue. Said Rosecrans in reply: "Let the two forces combine and pitch into them, if they can, with all fury. They may whip the life out of them." [21]

Probably it was after he had indulged in the pleasant thought that Stanley might do some really harmful whipping that Rosecrans received melancholy messages from Mitchell that showed only too clearly that the cavalryman's "scheme" for "fixing" the guerrillas had not matured, to say the least. The steamer *Charter,* loaded principally with commissary stores, had been burned the night before by

Wheeler, five miles above Harpeth Shoals, midway between Nashville and Clarksville. Stanley had reported the enemy as having two full batteries and 4,500 men. (His planned countermeasures had certainly not contemplated a force like that.) The Rebels, Mitchell informed Rosecrans, were burning everything on the river; at least four freight boats in addition to the *Charter* had been destroyed; and insult had been added to injury by the capture and burning of the gunboat *Sidell*.

After two locomotives had exasperatingly "given out," the last regiments of Harlan's brigade had finally arrived from Gallatin and would that night march out the Charlotte Pike. The ending of one Mitchell telegram was emphatic: "Damn the railroad, say I!" Preserving equanimity as hours pass and expected troops do not appear when the need is great is a severe test for any commander. In another telegram Mitchell turned to Shakespeare: "There is 'something rotten in Denmark' with the management of the railroad." [22]

The day after the river was ablaze, a gunner from the *Sidell* arrived in Nashville, in a wagon or astride a horse perhaps, though he may have been a sturdy infantryman accustomed to marching. Disaster, he stated, had come because the *Sidell*'s pilot had left the wheel; the gun crews had been so anxious to punish the Confederates on the high riverbank that they had knocked a side out of the boat with blasts from her own pieces. Later, Admiral Porter explained to the inquiring Secretary Welles that he understood that the *Sidell* was merely an old ferryboat with a fieldpiece aboard, adding a comment that did him little credit: "The army undertakes sometimes to get up an impromptu navy, which generally ends by getting them into difficulty." [23]

An ugly scene had occurred during Wheeler's triumph at Harpeth Shoals on January 13. After the *Hastings,* bearing Federal sick and wounded, had received musketry fire and artillery shells, in spite of the hospital flag she flew, she was brought to against a steamer stopped two hours previously. The chaplain of an Ohio regiment, who at the request of the boat's captain had taken charge, wrote in his official report that she was immediately boarded by "a gang of drunken rebels, under command of Colonel [W. B.] Wade"—the officer who rode at the head of the Eighth Confederate Cavalry, a *regular* regiment in the brigade which Wheeler had commanded before being made Bragg's chief of cavalry, and which still went under his name. Continuing, Chaplain Maxwell Gaddis wrote, the opening sentence being a frequent sort of exaggeration:

Then followed a scene of plunder and theft never before witnessed. They robbed soldiers and passengers indiscriminately; took from your wounded soldiers their blankets, rations, medicines, and in many instances their clothing; robbed the officers of their side-arms, overcoats, hats, &c.; the boat of all her freight, stores, and money, and her officers of their personal property. I demanded of Colonel Wade some explanation of this inhuman course. He, being so drunk, only made me an idiotic reply.

An appeal to Wheeler's adjutant, an old acquaintance of Gaddis's, brought no help; "he was powerless, from the fact that the whole gang was drunk." Nonetheless, the adjutant reported to Wheeler and received authorization to parole the *Hastings* on condition that she carry no more supplies for the Federal Government. After the injured on two other steamers had been transferred to the *Hastings,* the Confederates discovered that her wounded were lying on bales of cotton, which was contraband to them. (It was dubious procedure to fly a hospital flag above such an item, even if the bales were being used exclusively as beds.) When Gaddis refused to obey Wade's order to remove the now almost naked wounded men to a muddy cornfield, in gathering darkness and falling snow, so that the cotton could be burned, a report was again made to Wheeler, and his humanity caused him to order that the *Hastings* be allowed to proceed upon her way, after Gaddis had promised either to have the cotton burned at Louisville, or to return himself as a prisoner of war. This indeed was well, or otherwise there would have been a still more shocking contrast between the scene at the shoals and at Murfreesboro, where four days previously an order by Rosecrans had read: "To insure proper care of the Confederate sick and wounded within our lines, Surgeon Avent, C. S. Army, is appointed medical director for them. . . . Needful supplies will be issued on requisitions sanctioned or submitted by Surgeon Avent, and approved by authority of the medical director of this army." [24]

Wheeler, in spite of what he did do, does not appear too well. Gaddis's charge of drunkenness on the part of Wade and his officers is supported by the report of the surgeon of an Indiana regiment who had charge of the Union sick and wounded, and of rolls bearing their names. Officially he wrote: "The Confederate officers, being intoxicated and getting rapidly more so, took the lists, names, and plunder, and hurried off, in spite of my protest and demand for copies." The paper, signed by Wheeler's adjutant, about the paroling of the 212 Federals, which was all that Surgeon Luther Waterman received, closed with the statement that they were not to do "anything prejudicial to the interests of the Confederate States until they are duly exchanged according to the cartel." [25] Since City Point and Vicksburg were the only places that the cartel authorized for exchange of prisoners, or *paroling,* unless commanders of *armies* otherwise agreed, there was a touch of irony in this.

Wheeler appears not to have written an account of his actions of that day, but what he told Bragg must have been gratifying, for four days later a telegram to Cooper ended, "I ask his promotion as a just reward to distinguished merit." Soon Wheeler was a major general, and four months later the Confederate Congress passed a resolution tendering thanks to him, his officers, and his men—including, of course, Wade and his command, who, Wheeler's most recent biographer says, "seem to have been ruthless in their attacks on the steamers." In his report to Adjutant General Alonzo Thomas, Rosecrans charged "inhuman violations of the rules of civilized warfare." [26] While such words were used so often by both sides as to make them something of a formality, they seem justified in the present case; though it should be carefully noted that there was no charge that lives had been taken.

And what about the expedition that Rosecrans had sent out under Wagner, with orders which, as things developed, should have taken them to Franklin and the rear and flank of the Confederates who had struck the river? The road-and-battle-toughened men of Wagner's own brigade, and Colonel Charles Harker's, the latter now under Colonel Abel D. Streight, together with some essential cavalrymen—700 of them under Captain Elmer Otis—headed for Triune at 2:00 A.M. of the 13th, to camp for the night on the road to Nolensville. Having received reports that Wheeler had moved toward Nashville and that he had been joined by Forrest and 1,000 men (which was not true), making a total of 3,000 men and seven guns, Wagner was on the point of starting on the morning of the 14th for Brentwood, when a new order came from Rosecrans. Under his latest instructions, Wagner sent two regiments toward the Wilkinson Pike, which came into Murfreesboro from a westward direction, and with the balance of his force marched on Eagleville, fourteen miles southward on the road to Shelbyville. Thence he was to turn seven miles eastward to Versailles, to join two brigades there and at Salem, and "move with the whole force to strike the enemy"—not the enemy detachment, however, that was dealing a blow to Rosecrans's communications, but a covering force in front of the main Confederate line to the south.

"Fruits" were gathered—twelve or fifteen hostile cavalrymen and their mounts near Eagleville, and a hundred or so horses and mules that favorably impressed quartermasters on the expedition. A mill that was to be left untouched if it were not aiding the enemy army was found harboring much meal "ready to send to the rebels"; so it was burned. A hard storm had rendered movement impossible except on a macadamized road and since the only such road led back to camp, Wagner turned thither on the 15th, soon to be met by another order from Rosecrans to do exactly that. It was Wagner's opinion that, had it not been for the storm, he could have struck a hard blow on the 15th at Fosterville. Everything would have depended on whether Colonel Elmer Otis and his cavalry could have cut off the enemy cavalry at Fosterville—nothing else was there—and held them for a fire fight with, or prompt surrender to, Wagner's sturdy infantry.

Just how sturdy the men with rifles were, one learns from a statement in Wagner's report to Brigadier General Milo Hascall, who was seen playing an important part in the terrific fighting on Rosecrans's left on December 31: "The officers, particularly the mounted ones, did not suffer so much, yet, I am sorry to say, some of them complained more than those who waded water knee-deep; the men, when they came to a vast pond or creek, raised a shout or song and plunged in."

The horses and mules that the bright-eyed quartermasters brought back far exceeded in rarity and in value the infantrymen's shoes cut to pieces by the new stones upon the pike. Before his own brigade could march again, Wagner would require seven hundred pairs; doubtless, he said, the other brigade needed just as many.[27]

As the laments of farmers who suffered because of the loss of animals doubtless echoed and reechoed in postwar years, one can well mention a general order that Bragg wrote just a week before Wagner reported on his expedition.

He had perceived, Bragg said, with surprise and pain, that some of his troops had been engaged in the indiscriminate destruction of fences and houses, "devastating a fair and fruitful country, on the productions of which our salvation depends." Harsh things have been said of Braxton Bragg, but one thanks his candor for the sentence: "Fields of growing wheat have been left without fences, and property, which even a rapacious enemy had respected, has been needlessly destroyed." [28]

"We shall fight him again at every hazard if he advances, and harass him daily if he does not," Bragg had written in a long letter of January 11 to Joe Johnston,[29] who was then at Jackson, Mississippi. The testing of the first part of the resolve would wait for the hot summer months, but the last portion of the promise had been punctually initiated. In striking at Rosecrans's communications, Bragg —perhaps more than he realized—was carrying the war against that most desirable of targets, his enemy's mind. While Rosecrans's denunciation of what had occurred aboard the *Hastings* was well justified, it cannot be said that that painful scene was responsible for any general weakening of his resolution or for a change in plans. The alteration of Wagner's mission was, so far as one can see, merely an instance of habitual indecision and lack of steadfastness of purpose—remindful of Rosecrans's withdrawal of cavalry from the Iuka-Fulton road, in spite of his word to his superior.

June would be nearing its end before Rosecrans actually marched from his camps "to push the enemy to the wall"; thus his entire stay at Murfreesboro cannot be traced with anything like the detail given to the first important days. But before these months are sketched in, his reaction to the blow against the Cumberland, where water was once more flowing in great abundance, should be seen.

The statement in his midnight telegram to Halleck on January 11 about the enemy cavalry having a four-to-one advantage over his was casually tacked to another sentence, and might have been regarded as a figurative exaggeration of a tired man at the end of a busy day. But a telegram that the general sent to Stanton on January 14 made the claim a major one, for the message began: "The rebel cavalry, which outnumbers ours four to one, is doing great mischief to us. They go in such masses that only a strong force can handle them." After describing the loss of transports the day before, Rosecrans said that he must immediately have some light-draft transports with bullet-proof boilers and pilothouses; they were a necessity because he had not force enough to cover the country by which the enemy could approach the Cumberland. "Please authorize them at once," he said. The dispatch ended with another "must": "I must have horses and saddles to mount some infantry, and have asked authority to buy the horses and saddles for 5,000." [30]

The assertion that Bragg's cavalry exceeded Rosecrans's four to one may have brought to Stanton the unhappy recollection of some of McClellan's reports as to enemy numbers. The actual situation is revealed by inspection of strength returns. That of Rosecrans for January 10 gives his cavalry division a present-for-duty strength of 4,974 out of an aggregate present of 5,656, and a present-and-absent total of 9,146 (up 1,159 from his last return). How many additional cavalrymen were scattered through divisions or were unattached is not clear, but the total may well have been 1,500. Ten days later the figures for Bragg's cavalry (the brigades of Morgan, Wharton, Wheeler, Forrest, and Buford) were 9,348 present for duty, 11,057 present, and 15,480 present and absent, with only an additional 240 set down as belonging to the corps of Polk and Hardee.[31]

The amazing thing is that Rosecrans had very accurate knowledge about the hostile mounted arm, and that he betrayed himself in a telegram to Quartermaster General Montgomery Meigs the very day after he had made the untruthful statement to Stanton. After increasing his request for horses for mounting infantry to 8,000, he indulged in a little of his too frequent boasting. With more mounted men and the pack mules he was expecting, he would do more than "smash up" the hostile cavalry; he would gather in all the horses in the country. In concluding, he gave the figure that so effectively condemns him: "At present the rebels have 10,000 to 12,000 cavalry, and have things their own way." [32]

Rosecrans's figure for enemy horsemen, combined with what he had said to both Halleck and Stanton, implies that in the Army of the Cumberland there were at most 3,000 cavalry. Both the Secretary and the Quartermaster General knew that this was false, and both also knew that the revolving rifles that had been sent to Rosecrans had, by increasing its fire power, made his cavalry more effective without cluttering the roads with longer columns. Rosecrans was acting unintelligently if he assumed that there would be no comparing of his different dispatches. As one of the very best criminal lawyers of the day, Stanton was a good cross-examiner; Montgomery Meigs, fifth in the forty-nine-man Academy class of 1836, had an excellent head upon his shoulders. Playing trickily or deceitfully with the Secretary of War is a very serious offense, and the removal of Rosecrans would have been justified on the basis that he was unreliable. While the relief of a general after an important success is a delicate matter, there were impressive cases in the Civil War where it was done, and there have been others since.[33] But in mid-January, 1863, Rosecrans was securely in the saddle—even though 5,000 of his infantry were not. Not only had he won a great battle at a moment of extreme crisis; Stanton had also promised "cheerfully" to give him anything in his power.

Unless Rosecrans thought that he should be entirely free to write his own ticket—and it looks as though he did—he should have been pleased at the response to his calls. Halleck had wired to Rosecrans on the 7th that he had heard that Rosecrans proposed to send Kentucky cavalry back to that state. Retain them, said Halleck; Kentucky would be supplied from other sources. The 14th saw much attention in Washington to the calls for horses and equipment. (Rosecrans had also wired to Halleck: "I must have cavalry or mounted infantry. Had I horses and saddles I could mount infantry.") Strangely enough it had been Governor Morton of Indiana who had first written to Meigs before the beginning of the year about buying horses so that Rosecrans could mount infantry. At that time Meigs knew nothing (nor perhaps did Morton) of the law of 1850 authorizing the mounting of infantry in a public emergency. Of course, no law would have been required to hoist reluctant foot soldiers onto horses (that have to be fed, watered, and groomed) which had spontaneously walked into the Union lines, or which had taken a fancy to a neat-looking column of Bluecoats and gaily followed them back to camp. *Buying* horses for foot soldiers was something different, but the 14th saw the now enlightened Meigs writing in some perplexity to Stanton: "As the General in Chief informs me that Rosecrans has called for 5,000 saddles, it is presumed that he will want 5,000 horses. So large a number it will require some time to collect and forward to him, especially as the Department is largely in debt." The distressing thought of a depleted treasury was passed on to Rosecrans by Halleck, and the General in Chief raised the question of Rosecrans's partially supplying himself from the country. Meigs too suggested that the general do some seizing of horses, and a few days later pointedly asked, "Are there any horses left in the country for Forrest to seize?" Taking the hint, Rosecrans replied that there were some for Forrest to "steal"; but if his men could get the start he meant to "steal them ourselves." "Unofficially," the practice was already under way, the quartermaster's department, however, "unfortunately" being the chief sufferer so far. Even before this exchange of dispatches Rosecrans had received Meigs's assurance of 2,000 horses from Indianapolis, of which half were already on hand; contributions could also probably be made by the Louisville quartermaster and Colonel Robert Allen at St. Louis.[34]

Equal promptness was given the matter of protected steamers, but difficulty soon developed. After Stanton had wired in the waning afternoon of the 15th, "Orders have been given to provide transports, such as you desire, as fast as they can be procured," the Secretary was informed by Meigs that the use of plating for the steamers would, according to the Navy Department, result in delaying the completion of armored gunboats. To Rosecrans the Quartermaster General wrote, "The Navy employs all the workmen, buys all the iron, and all the boats fit to be made into armored light-draught gunboats." Undaunted by a previous facetious rebuff that Rosecrans had given him, Meigs suggested cargo—bales of hay, sacks of grain, or earth—as a cheaper, quicker, and equally efficient means as plating to give protection to steamers, except to the upper parts of pilothouses, for which five-eighths-inch iron might possibly be obtained. But transports, Meigs said, could not contend with forces such as those led by Forrest. Only gunboats could carry transports safely through.[35]

The first appeal to Cairo for naval help was an unhappy approach. It was written by Major Calvin Goddard, Rosecrans's chief of staff, who at times affected the lofty tone his chief too often used. Fleet Captain Pennock at Cairo was irked at even a suggestion of an *order* from the Army, and in his reply he reminded Major Goddard that on the preceding October 1 the gunboats had been transferred from the War to the Navy Department. (It will be recalled that though the Navy Department had operated the gunboats from the start, they had been built by War Department funds. It was not until the transfer that sailors could walk the decks with a pleasant feeling of proprietary security.) Their commander, Admiral Porter, Pennock explained, was acting "exclusively" under orders from the Navy Department. "This department is his, not mine," he added, and, as if fearful there might be surviving misconceptions, "I am acting under his orders, and am ordered to report only to him and to the Navy Department." Nevertheless, the sailor gave some information: at Cairo there were three light-draft gunboats; but on one there was smallpox; a second had weak steam power; the third was under orders to join Porter down the Mississippi. He would, Pennock said, send Goddard's communication to Porter by the "first opportunity." Such hope as Murfreesboro could get for prompt naval aid had to be extracted from the concluding words of the Fleet Captain's message: "Previous to the admiral's leaving he sent up the Cumberland and Tennessee rivers all the force he has to spare, and directed their commanders to cooperate with the army."

Copies of the two telegrams were sent to Washington, and on the 24th Welles said in a letter to Pennock—after referring to a dispatch from Rosecrans and his prompt answering message of the 13th—"It was in accordance with this reply, doubtless, that you were addressed, and although the request for cooperation was not in such terms as more thought would have dictated, yet your answer was not such as the Department desired."

But previous to this—on January 19—Welles had telegraphed to Pennock that Rosecrans desired naval protection for steamers, and he had queried, "Can you not send vessels for the purpose?" Spurred by this, and doubtless by some unexceptionable telegrams from the general, Pennock on the 24th wired to Rosecrans that the *Silver Lake* was leaving for the Cumberland, though with a short crew; the heavy-gunned veteran *Lexington* would leave the next night. This would give five gunboats in the river, and Pennock promised, "Will do all I can to assist you." A short reply began, "I am greatly obliged." [36]

How hard the convoy problem was Lieutenant Le Roy Fitch revealed in a telegram to Pennock from Fort Donelson on the 27th: "The channel of the river is so narrow. Have in this convoy up some thirty boats, all in single file, which makes a long line to be convoyed with only three boats." "No gunboats arrived yet," Mitchell telegraphed to Rosecrans that night from Nashville, adding hopefully that four were expected. But the *Lexington,* so often mentioned in this story, had been up as far as the shoals, quite unhurt by shells that had struck her. The enemy, Mitchell said, had been driven away. "Matters are quiet here," Colonel S. D. Bruce, seen previously at Bowling Green, telegraphed on the same day from Clarksville. He was keeping strong pickets on the north side of the Cumberland at the shoals. Across the river enemy cavalry were in view; reportedly they were 5,000 strong and had eight guns.[37]

Men, horses, saddles, protected steamers, and—most legitimately—gunboats to bring convoys through were not the complete list of items for which Rosecrans pleaded. On January 15 he telegraphed to Stanton, "If you cannot add to my numerical strength, please make a great effort to send me 5,000 revolving rifles." Each such weapon would, he said, add an additional man to his strength; for the service he contemplated, they would "add two men for each gun." Though there was truth in this, it was something that Rosecrans would forget; and it is remindful of his assurance that Stanley, if given to him, would double the strength of his cavalry without expense. But the busy Secretary may not have recalled the message to Halleck in which Rosecrans had asked for Stanley, and four and a half hours later he replied, "All the revolving rifles that are manufactured in this country have been sent you, and more will be sent as fast as they can be procured." [38]

Recovering, as he had been on the 14th, from Wheeler's blow of the day before, Rosecrans may have been depressed by the opening sentence of a telegram from Halleck: "I have no troops to send you, except from General Wright's command." Robbing Peter to pay Paul never seemed to worry Rosecrans, so long as he was Paul; and Halleck, after saying that Wright had been repeatedly directed to send all the force he could spare, cut red tape by directing, "Communicate with him on the subject." The General in Chief did not, however, let the matter rest; and the next day he showed his firm grasp of what was taking place, as well as his effective use of language, in a telegram to Wright: "It is believed that the quiet of Kentucky can be best secured by the certain defeat of Bragg's army." After telling Wright to send all available troops to Rosecrans, he enjoined: "Do not paralyze our forces by keeping them so scattered as to be of little use. Murfreesboro is the most important point for both Kentucky and Tennessee." (This was three days after Halleck had sent Grant, then at Memphis, the telegram that read: "You are hereby authorized to relieve General McClernand from command of the expedition against Vicksburg, giving it to the next in rank or taking it yourself.") [39]

Enough has been seen of Wright—Number Two man in the West Point class of 1841—to know that he would carry out both the spirit and the letter of Halleck's dispatch. A heartening telegram was soon on the way to Rosecrans, while others sped to Boyle at Louisville and

Gordon Granger at Lexington, outlining the message from Washington, and directing that troops be detached for Rosecrans. Naturally, Wright had apprehensions, and he said to Granger, "This is the principle; but unless Rosecrans acts promptly, we run great risk of Kentucky being overrun." "Answer and come up to-morrow," he said in conclusion. "Acknowledge and answer. Snowing," was the termination of the telegram to Boyle. A dispatch to Rosecrans on the 17th, replying to a query as to the route by which he would send reinforcements, ended, "Will telegraph you as to route, and more fully after seeing Granger, who can't get here on account of snow, which blocks up everything, and may delay movement some days." [40]

One may well wonder what Lincoln was thinking and doing during these days, about the Department of the Cumberland. He was, one may be sure, keeping well posted, at the same time that he was apprehensive lest there be delay in Murfreesboro as there had been in Nashville. But he kept hands off. Of course, the President was also thinking of questions not purely military; and on January 10 he queried Andrew Johnson, military governor of Tennessee, as to his "opinion of the effects of the late battles about Murfreesborough upon the prospects of Tennessee." The answering dispatch of the next day began:

> The battle of Murfreesborough has inspired much confidence with Union men of the ultimate success of the Government, and has greatly discouraged rebels, but increased their bitterness. If the rebel army could be expelled from the State, and Union sentiment developed without fear or restraint, I still think Tennessee will be brought back into the Union by decided majority of popular vote.

While that was encouraging, the next sentence showed that a difficult task lay ahead: "Eastern portion of the State must be redeemed before confidence can be inspired with the mass of the people that the Government has the power to assert and maintain its authority in Tennessee," a sentence that one should read with the recollection that Johnson did not have a detached view about East Tennessee—it was his home, and the plight of Unionists there had been his major concern.

Johnson thought that it had been an act of wisdom not to include Tennessee among the states where slaves had been emancipated by

Courtesy Library of Congress

MAJOR GENERAL HORATIO G. WRIGHT

the President's New Year's Day proclamation. Those who had been denouncing such a step as unjust and unwise had been disarmed, Johnson said. But he did not like the way things were being run in Nashville. The so-called detective police, under charge of persons wholly incompetent, if not corrupt in the grossest sense of the term, was, he said, causing much ill feeling, "and doing us great harm." [41]

While Johnson had slipped in his plea for the region of his birth in a reply to a message from the President, the other great protagonist of East Tennessee, Horace Maynard, had without any such pretext struck almost viciously at Halleck because of imagined neglect of the district. The success of Carter's raid had been the spark that caused him to explode. He charged that nothing was known about the contemplated operation in Washington "until rumors were received of its results." Halleck's reply was dated January 12—the day he removed the shackles from Grant's hands, the day probably when he had to give attention to Banks in New Orleans, and to Curtis in Missouri, and certainly to Burnside in front of Fredericksburg—and also the day he told Rosecrans to communicate directly with Wright about reinforcements. Occasionally Halleck's dislike of politicians was revealed in letters to his subordinates; but his reply to Maynard was a model of propriety and good temper. There was, however, no truckling in his statement: "It is not proper for me to say what plans have been formed in regard to East Tennessee, and why those heretofore formed were not carried out." Nor did he fail to uphold the dignity of his high office when he told the unhappy congressman that in his charges about the Carter expedition he was "greatly in error." [42]

There could well have been a touch of thankfulness in the ending of a dispatch that Bragg sent to Cooper on January 22: "The enemy has made no show of an advance from Murfreesborough." On the 11th he had written to Johnston that because of his casualties of 12,000 in the recent battle, he had only 20,000 effective infantry, and 1,500 artillery. Even before the letter had arrived, Johnston, on the basis of other reports, had wired to Richmond that Bragg thought 20,000 more men were needed to enable him to hold Middle Tennessee; but he had none to give. Bragg's direct appeal to Beauregard at Charleston had brought a disappointing response: "Sorry can't help you." The forces in his department were not, Beauregard said, half of the effectives on the first day at Shiloh, and the coast was heavily threatened. As if to discourage future entreaties, the Charleston general ended by himself requesting a little help: "Can you send me some rifled or Napoleon captured guns?" [43]

Although Rosecrans had reported on the 13th that there was no doubt that Longstreet was expected from Virginia, no help for Bragg would come from that theater for months. Rosecrans's apprehension was no doubt increased by a telegram from Wright on the 16th in which the Cincinnati general said, "Information, said to be from a reliable person, from Abingdon, Va., on the 8th, that fifty-five rebel regiments had passed there to join Bragg, and that more were to follow." The high-standing West Pointers should have known that this was utterly impossible, and should have recognized it as an effort to deceive. They knew that Carter had destroyed railroad bridges in East Tennessee and that Richmond could not have heard of Bragg's retreat until January 4 at the earliest. Acquainted as they were with the difficulties of railroad movement, and with the vast equipment needed, they should have realized that transporting fifty-five regiments from Virginia in four days was beyond all possibility, even if the regiments had been in Richmond, and not in Lee's lines at Fredericksburg; and even though they had not read a dispatch that a thoughtful citizen of Philadelphia had sent Stanton on the 5th:

> You need have no undue apprehension about the Richmond army reenforcing Bragg's Tennessee army. I have full lists of the machinery and rolling stock on the Virginia and East Tennessee road at the outbreak of the war, and they could not, even if the bridges were not destroyed as reported, send 20,000 men in three weeks from Richmond to Murfreesborough. At Lynchburg the gauge is changed, and no rolling stock or machinery can pass from one road to the other. All passengers and freight transfer at Lynchburg. If the bridges are burned, as reported, they cannot send any ammunition in ten days, and few regiments.

This message could well have been forwarded to Wright and Rosecrans, to quiet any fears, but commendably, when reporting to Halleck on the 17th that Wright would send him two divisions, Rosecrans, without outside help in adding two and two, showed a trace of doubt when he said, "*If* [emphasis supplied] Longstreet has brought fifty-five regiments west, this Middle Tennessee will be a great battleground." [44]

The Confederate general's resolve to harass the enemy had already made Middle Tennessee a minor battleground, and the occasion of Bragg's dispatch of the 22nd was a successful attack by a hundred of

Morgan's men upon a forage train not far from Murfreesboro, which had brought as net proceeds 150 prisoners and 30 wagons. Reconnaissances and skirmishes marked the succeeding days of January, but it was not until February 5 that Rosecrans could put on the wire some cheerful news; the Federal general radiated joy:

> Rebels—Wheeler, Forrest, Wharton, and Woodward—attacked Fort Donelson yesterday at 2 P.M. with 4,000 men and eight pieces of artillery. We have 800 men in the fort, under Col. A. C. Harding. They charged the fortifications several times, but were repulsed by our artillery and infantry with great loss.

Forces from Fort Henry, under Colonel Lowe, Rosecrans added, were pursuing the retreating enemy, while others had been sent to intercept them.[45]

It does not add commendably to the record of Academy graduate Wheeler that he put his name above those of Forrest and Wharton on the demand for unconditional surrender that was sent to Harding. Such a demand by itself would have been highly proper, and it was quite right—though ironic in view of the outcome—to speak of having the fort invested with a force sufficient to take it; but it was not in accord with the laws of war or the honor of a professional soldier to end with the threat: "If you surrender, you will be treated as prisoners of war; if not, you must abide the consequences." In view of this, what had transpired on the *Hastings,* with Wheeler not far away, becomes more understandable. There was no bragging, but only dignity in the answer that Harding addressed to Wheeler: "I decline to surrender the forces under my command or the post without an effort to defend them." (The reply is suggestive of that of the British commander of Boulogne to a German summons to give up, which so impressed the great panzer leader Guderian that he put it on record in his book: "The answer is No." [46]

The intercepting forces from Fort Henry of which Rosecrans spoke, but which may have raised slight hopes in Washington, failed. Wheeler, getting wind of what was up, changed direction and crossed Duck River at Centerville. Roads and weather were excessively bad, and Brigadier General Jefferson C. Davis, in command of the Federal column, had already marched seventy-five miles when he reported on the 8th from Franklin. Undaunted, he said that unless an order to the contrary arrived he would go on the next day to Columbia. Hazard lurked in such a move, and perhaps as Davis was writing, General Leonidas Polk was addressing a letter to Earl Van Dorn—who had moved from Mississippi into Tennessee—filled with a good churchman's hope of intercepting the interceptors. The message from Davis would not have been a good one for Rosecrans to send to Washington to support his plea for more horsemen—unless he omitted the concluding sentence: "My troops are all in good health, but our cavalry is too slow." [47]

More expeditions, more skirmishes followed. On February 11 Rosecrans sent a message which topped all his previous requests. This time he went directly to the President, and for nothing short of authority for generals or "commanders along the river districts," to give orders to naval officers—"absolutely necessary" for cooperation, he asserted. It was hardly a message to give a carefree feeling to Lincoln on his fifty-fourth birthday, when he called in the two Secretaries involved and the General in Chief. These men, the President said in replying to Rosecrans, promised "to do their very best in the case." And he was gentle when he left the Murfreesboro general off with the statement, "I cannot take it into my own hands without producing inextricable confusion." (He might have pointed out that Grant had been working harmoniously and successfully with the Navy, and still was, without any such extraordinary power, and without ever having suggested that it be given to him.)

The same February 12 saw Rosecrans reporting to Halleck that roads were impassable for wagons or artillery, except where macadamized; that the railroad was open to Nashville, and that he had at Murfreesboro supplies for fifteen days. Forgetful of the implied praise that lay in his recommendation that McCook be made a corps commander, he made a vicious attack upon that general: had it not been for McCook's errors there would have been no enemy after the first day's fight in the Stones River battle. (It may be recalled that earlier in this work it was suggested that it looked as though McCook's corps could have been reorganized, and with other troops, some fresh, could have made a counterstroke. But orders would have had to come from Rosecrans himself. It will also be recalled that McCook vehemently challenged the truthfulness of statements in the report that Rosecrans dated February 12.) At whom Rosecrans was aiming with the last part of his concluding sentence is not clear: "I believe the most fatal errors of this war have begun in an impatient desire of success, that would not take time to get ready; the next fatal mistake being to be afraid to move when all the means were provided." But it is safe to say that he did not suppose that his superiors might with justice think the second barb would become eminently applicable to himself.[48]

In addition to reconnaissances and skirmishes in Tennessee during the last half of February, there was an enemy operation into central Kentucky, which lasted two weeks and which brings to mind Wright's statement of the risk there would be to Kentucky after the depletion of his force, if Rosecrans did not move promptly. Well to the south, in northern Alabama, there was also activity, but this time it was Federal General Dodge who did the striking behind enemy lines. Under cover of gunboats that had ascended the Tennessee as far as Florence, Dodge's cavalry had taken Tuscumbia,* some two hundred prisoners, and a train belonging to Van Dorn, Rosecrans's old classmate, whom he had defeated in the sanguinary battle at Corinth. When Dodge last telegraphed to Rosecrans on the 27th, his cavalry was still pursuing the enemy.[49]

We interrupt the sketch of operations to tell about two officers who had recently joined the staff of General Rosecrans. One was Horace Porter, who had graduated from West Point in 1860 as Number Three man in the class—three places above James H. Wilson, who was seen playing an important staff part in Grant's Vicksburg operations. Porter was to serve the last year of the war on Grant's staff, and his postwar civilian career was one of great achievement and distinction. He came to Rosecrans as ordnance officer after initial service in the East that had given him brief but unusual personal contact with Lincoln in the crucial later days of April, 1861, when the Capital was cut off from rail communication with the North. Then followed duty on the Atlantic coast, where he had greatly impressed Wright by his energy and exceptional skill as an artilleryman, notably in the capture of Fort Pulaski. After a rather short period as ordnance officer under McClellan in the Army of the Potomac, he received an invitation from Wright to serve on his staff. Porter's request for transfer having been granted, he spent some busy and pleasant months in Cincinnati. As Porter never was a lover of ease, we may believe that he was content when he was assigned to the Army of the Cumberland,[50] for prompt and hard campaigning would have been a natural expectation.

* For Florence and Tuscumbia see map, p. 28, Vol. IV.

The gifted young officer was greatly impressed by Rosecrans. The men in the army were all in good spirits, he said in a letter to his mother on February 11; they had been largely reinforced, and if another general battle were fought there could be no doubt as to its outcome. Porter's enthusiasm for his new commander bubbled over in the sentence, "All hands would follow Rosecrans to the end of the world and further, if necessary." He was, he said, on good terms with his chief, and would often sit an hour or two in his room in the evening, talking about ordnance and other matters. The "old general" was always in fine spirits, and quite as his countenance suggested, was "very talkative." Rosecrans had said, "Porter, if you can get five thousand arms we'll put the Rebs up a spout." Porter, descendant of sailors prominent in the early days of the Republic, and son of a Pennsylvania governor, pronounced Murfreesboro "a beautiful little village," and said they were having "the most delightful spring weather"—a fact that Rosecrans did not mention when the next day he told Halleck that wagons and artillery could not move except on macadamized roads.

Working as industriously as he always did, life was again pleasant for Horace Porter, and his collection of weapons and ordnance stores had turned the courthouse into a veritable arsenal. John Morgan had been married in the courtroom; and it will be recalled that his nuptials were attended not only by two four-star generals, but by the Confederacy's President. Bragg's departure had been so hasty, Porter told his mother, that the courtroom had been found still "handsomely decorated." Not many citizens remained, he said, and those who did, did "not seem to rejoice much in the presence of the Yankees." Indeed, far from rejoicing, they must have felt outraged that the courtroom hallowed by the Morgan marriage had become the repository for Federal weapons and the host of lesser items and trinkets that a diligent ordnance officer amasses.

Not yet, Porter told his mother in his mid-February letter, was the entire army supplied with clothing, but in a few weeks it would be; he supposed there would then be a forward movement.[51]

On the month's last day Goddard gave way as chief of staff to Brigadier General James A. Garfield, in an order in which Rosecrans praised "the signal ability and untiring zeal" of the outgoing incumbent, now a lieutenant colonel. Garfield has been seen successfully prosecuting a campaign in East Kentucky, where he had to contend with a mighty flood on the Big Sandy. Then the future radical Republican congressman and President was seen arriving at Shiloh on the second day, in time to receive from Grant the order to march to where "the firing seemed to be hottest." [52]

John Beatty, now a brigadier, an incomparable commentator on military matters and a discerning judge of officers, was a little distressed that his fellow Ohioan had too many buttons on his coat. The splendor of the double row seemed to detract from the splendor of his remarks. After some months had passed, Beatty recorded, "Garfield gave us a grip that suggested 'vote right, vote early'." [53]

CHAPTER VII

EPISODIC WEEKS AND A FAMOUS RAID

I have no doubt but that Colonel Streight would have succeeded had he been properly equipped. *Dodge to Hurlbut*

THE FIRST operational directive from Garfield's pen led to unhappy consequences. Addressed to Brigadier General C. C. Gilbert, who was at Franklin with one of the divisions that Gordon Granger had brought from Kentucky, and dated March 3, the dispatch said that the commanding general directed Gilbert to send the next day a reinforced brigade out the Columbia Pike as far as Spring Hill. Thence one party was to proceed toward Columbia, while another went to Raleigh Springs on the pike to Lewisburg, there to meet upon the 5th a cavalry force from Murfreesboro. "We desire to know what is in our front," Garfield said quite reasonably. Something else was also wanted, and the new chief of staff directed, "Take a forage train along." Perhaps on direction of Rosecrans, perhaps on his own initiative—his experience as an independent commander was sufficient to prompt it—Garfield concluded, "Have you any news?" [1] (Gilbert was seen as a "corps" commander at Perryville, wearing, because of an unjustified order by Wright, the two stars of a major general.)

The next morning, 2,837 men and officers of all arms (five infantry regiments, 600 cavalrymen from three regiments, and a battery) marched from Franklin in weather that was "cool and favorable," with rations for four days. Commanding the force was Colonel John Coburn of the Thirty-third Indiana Infantry. Coburn's brigade actually belonged to the division commanded by Brigadier Absalom

Baird; but on February 21 it had been detached and sent from Nashville to Brentwood with orders to march to the assistance of Gilbert at Franklin, if summoned by that officer. Perhaps because he knew of enemy activity not far to the south, Gilbert called Coburn forward on March 2 and then handed him the task of executing the assignment that army headquarters telegraphed the next day, augmenting Coburn's combat troops by eighty wagons to "bring in the bacon." [2]

Coburn had advanced no more than four miles when he discovered a hostile force, which he estimated at 1,000 mounted men and two guns, deployed across the road. Long swells and ridges added interest to the terrain, but were annoying when their height or precipitousness prevented a good view except down the road. Coburn's action, however, was prompt and aggressive. A section of guns was soon engaging those of the enemy, while three regiments of infantry and some cavalry started forward, with one regiment of foot troops in reserve and one standing guard over the wagons. Obligingly the enemy fell back, disappearing for some time, only to reappear upon high hills to the left. As word came that another 1,200 to 1,500 Confederates were on the Lewisburg road only a mile to his left, Coburn called his advance troops back to the position from which he had first seen the enemy and sent Gilbert a message saying that the hostile force on the Lewisburg Pike was nearer than he was to Franklin. "What shall we do?" he queried. He thought he could advance but, should he do so, he said, there would at once be a force in his rear. A message sent at 7:30 P.M. gave more information. Now he was not so burdened by wagons, thirty-nine having been sent back filled with forage. But his artillery firing—which a woman had reported as killing four and wounding fifteen of the enemy—had reduced his ammunition to a hundred rounds; he sent back a call for more.[3]

Henry, in his justly highly esteemed book on Forrest, gives considerable attention to this operation and, pronouncing Coburn "a brave and determined commander," says he moved south the next morning without waiting for further instructions. It is possible, however, that Coburn had received a message Gilbert said he had sent, reminding Coburn that "he had quite a large margin and a wide discretion." In dispatching a captain of the Second Michigan Cavalry to investigate the situation, Gilbert took good action. But he may have given too much weight to that part of the captain's report—dated the 4th—which stated that he did not estimate the enemy at more than a thousand cavalry and three guns, and not enough to the concluding sentence that Coburn was "in a good deal of doubt as to the intentions of the enemy, and not over-confident." [4] In his evening dispatch Coburn had also said the Confederates seemed to be in camp "a few miles off" to his front, and that Negroes had reported infantry, cavalry, and artillery.

At daylight next morning two Negro boys reported that they had come from Van Dorn's "army"; it was north of Spring Hill and was moving to take Franklin. Van Dorn had on February 22 reported to Johnston his arrival at Columbia from Mississippi, and his readiness for operations. Unless otherwise ordered, he would "dislodge" the Federals from Franklin. Having told their story, the Negro boys were sent back to Gilbert; but Coburn later wrote that he heard nothing from the messenger who accompanied them. After patrols and scouts sent in all directions had reported that they had found nothing, Coburn at eight o'clock moved forward slowly, cavalry in front, followed by a line of skirmishers extending a half-mile on each side of the road, a gun with the reserve of the advance guard three-fourths of a mile ahead of the main body. Cautiously, but successfully, Coburn passed through a tricky gap in a ridge north of Thompson's Station after dislodging enemy skirmishers. Beyond the station and an open field, he saw the ground ascending to a wood, broken by irregular knolls. "Here the enemy lay," Coburn wrote—6,000 strong, according to Henry, all dismounted cavalry of Van Dorn's command, with Forrest on the right, and beyond him a battery.

Convinced that he was in the presence of an overwhelming force, Coburn decided to retire. In his report he charged that he was deserted not only by the cavalry and the battery—whose work during the advance he praised highly—but by the Ohio infantry regiment that was attached to but did not belong to him, and which was with the wagons. Had it not been for those defections, he could, he claimed, and with reason, have successfully extricated himself. On his part, the cavalry commander wrote, "Had Colonel Coburn retreated by the Franklin road, not a man would have been lost. My column never moved a step till long after he was out of sight on the hills to my right." But Van Dorn seemed to see things as Coburn did, for in his report he said, "The Federal cavalry, with one regiment of infantry, after offering some resistance to General Forrest, taking their battery and baggage train with them, precipitately left." That the fighting of the four deserted infantry regiments was most determined is fully attested to by Van Dorn and by Confederate casualties. The Southern commander spoke colorfully of charges up a "blood-stained eminence," which was "long and obstinately contested." Only when the hill had been taken, and a battery put in action upon it, and Forrest had gained the Federal rear and had charged them with two regiments, did Coburn's men, after firing a few volleys, lay down their arms in surrender.

Prisoners tallied about 1,050, with some 160 captured elsewhere. Among those taken was Coburn. He commended highly the colonels of his own four regiments for conspicuous daring and gallantry: "they did all that officers in their position could do." Among the five field officers who he said "were at their posts bravely doing their duty" was William R. Shafter, who in 1898 commanded American forces in Cuba.

When he wrote his report on August 1, after his exchange in May, Coburn described not only the battle but the hard journey to Richmond and Libby Prison. He paid high tribute to Union women in Shelbyville, who in spite of verbal abuse had ministered to the prisoners. The two days' march thence to Tullahoma was rendered terrible by a torrential rain that made streams waist-deep. Looking back in midsummer, Coburn recalled it in a sentence that lingers in the memory: "The water was chilling, and the night air as cold as March is in its most inclement moods." [5]

News of the disaster was in Murfreesboro on the 5th, through Gilbert's surely embarrassed pen. In a midnight message the next day to Halleck, Rosecrans, after quoting one of Gilbert's telegrams, sought consolation in the thought that according to the enemy the Federals had fought desperately and had given up only when surrounded. Then he said: "Information received to-day satisfies me they intend to fight us in Middle Tennessee, and that they will bring to bear upon us about 20,000 cavalry and mounted infantry. They are to-day superior to us in numbers." Only generals who *know* that they never weaken in resolve because of reverses should risk messages before they have had some sleep. Rosecrans was both "whistling in the dark" and announcing that it would be some time before he would venture southward when he said, "I am not, as you know, an alarmist, but I do not think it will do to risk as we did before." [6]

On the same day, sturdy Joe Johnston, now in Chattanooga, justifiably pleased, but not sufficiently enlightened as to discount the first reports of damage done to his opponent, wired Richmond: "Major-

General Van Dorn was attacked by the enemy at Thompson's Station yesterday, between Columbia and Franklin. He repulsed them handsomely, taking 2,000 prisoners." [7]

Baffling personality that he was, one must doubt whether Rosecrans really believed that the Confederate strength was superior to his own. The records, of course, contain nothing resembling a report of the enemy order in battle, with figures for various units made by a coolly analytical Federal intelligence officer upon his basis of reports that must have still been coming to headquarters in Murfreesboro. All we have are the actual figures from returns. That of Rosecrans for the last of February shows a present-for-duty strength of 80,124, out of an aggregate present of 98,073; while the comparable figures for Bragg are 49,068 and 59,053. Even after deduction for the garrisons that Rosecrans had to maintain, his field army was strong. In the newly designated Fourteenth Corps of Thomas, the Twentieth of McCook, the Twenty-first of Wood, and the three divisions headed by Granger, there were 65,752 present for duty and an aggregate present of 79,748. In horsemen Bragg was still the better off, any net gain that Rosecrans had made being more than offset by the coming of Van Dorn from Mississippi. The end of February saw the aggregate present in the commands of Wheeler and Van Dorn (to whom Forrest had been transferred) standing at no fewer than 15,625. Bragg's "effective" infantry was also well above the 20,000 he had gloomily reported to Johnston in mid-January. Now the figure for the corps of Polk and Hardee and the separate brigade of John K. Jackson was 31,924—much below Rosecrans's infantry strength.[8]

The defeat at Thompson's Station (or Spring Hill) came at an inauspicious time for Gilbert. The presidential appointment which had put stars upon his shoulders expired on March 4, and he was never confirmed by the Senate. Before too long he was once more captain of infantry—an honorable position, since next to first sergeants it is captains who make an army.

We shall pass on to the end of April, after describing the operation in which Granger soon drove Van Dorn south of Duck River; an action at Vaught's Hill near Milton (apparently the tiniest of more than a score of towns in the country with that distinguished name) in which Morgan was roughly handled; actions at Brentwood and along the Little Harpeth that caused Bragg to telegraph Cooper very happily and to praise Forrest in orders; an attack on April 10 in strong force on Franklin by Van Dorn that aroused in neither Bragg nor Johnston the desire to wire the result to Cooper; and successful, though not particularly damaging raids made the same day by Van Dorn's cavalry rival, Joseph Wheeler.

In recounting the prompt driving of Earl Van Dorn from the scene of his recent triumph, one can begin no better than by quoting what the editors of the *Official Records* compiled from the "Records of Events" in morning reports for Stanley's First Brigade, at whose head Colonel Robert H. G. Minty was riding:

> March 4, moved toward Rover, 863 strong, with about 300 men of the Seventh Pennsylvania and Fourth Michigan. Attacked and drove the enemy, 400 strong. Followed them up close to Unionville, 3 miles south, where we found an encampment of 600 more. The Seventh Pennsylvania charged them with the saber, and followed them to within 5 miles of Shelbyville, where they ran into the infantry pickets and captured 9. We captured the entire camp, camp equipage, and transportation of [A. A.] Russell's brigade (First and Fourth Alabama), together with 52 prisoners. Loss, 1 man slightly wounded.[9]

Taking his loot with him, Minty fell back to Eagleville, where Sheridan (still commanding an infantry division in McCook's corps) joined him the next morning. The ears of the Federal colonel took in more than the shouts and cheers and the sound of galloping horses and clashing sabers in his own exciting drive. "All day," he wrote, "heavy firing was heard south of Franklin"—Coburn's battle. Just how Federal cavalry command was being exercised is not clear; but on the 8th Sheridan sent Minty to Franklin, where Granger ordered him southward.[10] We quote again from the *Records* for Minty's activities:

> March 9, advanced from Franklin via Carter Creek pike [west of the main pike to Columbia]. Lieutenants Roys' and Rendlebrock's company, Fourth U.S. Cavalry, in the advance, drove the Third [Fourth] Mississippi Cavalry to Thompson's Station, where they were re-enforced by Starnes' regiment, Third [Fourth] Tennessee, all under General Armstrong. Attacked them with two companies Fourth U.S. Cavalry and 60 men Seventh Pennsylvania Cavalry. Drove them with a loss of 5 killed and 13 taken prisoners. Our loss, 3 killed and 1 wounded.

While Minty was advancing by the Carter Creek road, the Fourth Cavalry Brigade, under Brigadier C. Clay Smith, was following the direct road to Columbia with three regiments, while two others moved southward on the pike to Lewisburg. After danger of encirclement had compelled Smith to fall back to Thompson's Station, he learned of Minty's nearness and, upon once more advancing, found that Van Dorn had retired from Spring Hill. Then Minty and also Granger joined him. The 10th, a day of "terrible storm" in Granger's words, saw Minty and Smith moving ahead to Rutherford Creek, high, rapid, swelling, with all bridges destroyed. Across the angry waters, fine American cavalrymen shot at each other in full seriousness, Minty losing two killed and three wounded when opened upon from an ambush. Into the night the storm lasted; but in the morning Granger ordered his horsemen to get across Rutherford Creek and strike the enemy's right.

The record of events for Minty reads:

> March 11, crossed Rutherford Creek at Moore's Ford in the face of Forrest's forces, under Forrest in person, driving him from the field. Followed Van Dorn to Columbia. Found that he had crossed Duck River and destroyed the bridge.

Granger was apprehensive, a dispatch to Rosecrans shows, that Van Dorn's forces had crossed Duck River to safety during the night; should that be true, he would return to Franklin the next day. Just what force Granger had personally brought with him is not clear, but he ended his message, "Van Dorn greatly overestimates the strength of my force." [11]

From Tullahoma, Bragg was watching. A telegram to Wheeler directed that all the cavalry that could be spared should be sent to Van Dorn's support. Eager perhaps to get more good blue overcoats—as he had from Coburn's men—Bragg concluded: "Enemy is pressing him heavily, but are far from support. We ought to cut him off." [12]

Understandably, Rosecrans was much pleased, and as midnight neared on the 16th he telegraphed to Halleck:

> I have the pleasure to report the gallant conduct of our cavalry, under the brave Colonel Minty. They drove the rebel cavalry wherever they met them, captured one of their camps, 17 wagons, 42 mules, and 64 prisoners. They used the saber where the carbine would delay.[13]

The booty, though considerable for a small action, hardly paid for the thousand Federals captured not long before. Had Rosecrans written with morning freshness he might have made much out of Van Dorn's great eagerness to get across the Duck. The rough handling inflicted by Coburn's regiments, to say nothing of that dealt him by the small command of Colonel William H. Morgan at Davis's Mill, just after Van Dorn's success at Holly Springs, may well have made Van Dorn chary of infantry rifles. But Granger's infantry and artillery not having been able to pass swollen Rutherford Creek, it was from a cavalry force probably considerably inferior to his own in numbers that Van Dorn, in a manner, "escaped." [14]

Forrest, too, had memories going back beyond the recent rebuff at Fort Donelson. There was the recollection of Red Mound, the closing scene in his raid beyond the Tennessee, where Jeremiah Sullivan had taken from him quite a number of prisoners, horses, wagons, and small arms, to say nothing of Forrest's adjutant and an aide with the rank of colonel. Forrest's military talents have never been questioned; they were many and substantial. Yet he seldom if ever had to meet one of the hardest tests of a commander—operating in enemy territory. Not a day of his entire war career did he spend away from a countryside filled with friends eager to give him information about the Yankees—at times worth more than a goodly reinforcement of men. That the reports of civilians were often inaccurate—like the Negro reports that Van Dorn had infantry—and had to be checked against one another, is beside the point. One recalls Kirby Smith's desire to get away from Barbourville, Kentucky, where he encountered glum looks, and into the Blue Grass region of eager Secessionists.[15] Ahead of John Morgan, native of Lexington, whose operations had prospered partly because of easily secured information, was a novel experience, when, inadvisedly, he ventured into enemy terrritory across the Ohio, even though the region into which he went blossomed with Copperheads.

There is no gainsaying that throughout Granger's retaliatory operation the Federal cavalry was handled boldly and skillfully. Very pleasing to any soldier should be the thought of the Third Ohio Cavalry, with a captain in command, leaving the main body of Federal horse a mile and a half north of Duck River, with all infantry and artillery still farther to the north because of raging Rutherford Creek, and riding forward quietly and cautiously upon a nighttime reconnaissance. For some time the force waited at the river "to discover, if possible, any movement the enemy might be making, and finding all within his camp quiet"; then they returned to the main body of Federal cavalry and led its countermarch northward until midnight, when they went into camp.[16]

What has been just quoted is not from an undocumented regimental history written years after the event, nor from a laudatory work such as Duke's memoirs of Morgan or the early books on Forrest by Jordan and Pryor, written long before the publication of the *Official Records,* and with, one must believe, scant investigation of actual Federal situations. The quotation is from the day-by-day official record of Captain William M. Flanagan, of the Third Ohio Cavalry, dated March 15, 1863, the day after the last of the events he described. What a scene for an imaginative military artist if he had listened in the darkness at the side of the commanding officer, wondering at the balancing and the weighing that was going on in the mind of the soldier who had to make the decision, and then hearing quiet orders given to a waiting staff officer!

If Van Dorn lured Coburn through a defile and against a waiting battle line, so Colonel Albert S. Hall, of the 105th Ohio Infantry, enticed a goodly part of the two-brigade division that Morgan now commanded to attack a Federal brigade in a good position upon a hill. But there was a difference: Van Dorn exceeded Coburn's command by more than two to one, while Hall's men were probably fewer than those who assaulted them.

At the head of his four-regiment brigade, a section of guns, and a company of cavalry—totaling a little over 1,300 officers and men—Hall moved northeastward from Murfreesboro on March 18, his mission being to "reconnoiter the enemy and strike him, if the opportunity offers." Wagons were not to impede the column, for pack mules carried the two days' rations that supplemented a like amount carried on the persons of the soldiers.

After failing to capture a small Confederate camp on the night of the 18th because of a poor guide, Hall was on the road again early the next morning; he was soon skirmishing with 150 to 200 enemy horsemen, who fell back, Hall following very cautiously, with skirmishers carefully inspecting ravines. He had not gone far in this alerted manner when he saw a regiment of unfriendly cavalry in line of battle across a valley. For two hours he halted at a place ideal for rest and calm contemplation of the future—Prosperity Church.

"Becoming entirely satisfied that a large rebel force, under Morgan's command, was massed in the vicinity," and that not later than the next day he would be attacked, Hall decided to have any unpleasantness occur at a place of his own choosing. Leaving the enemy unmolested, he fell back and camped at Auburn, Confederate pickets confronting his own on every road, while a large hostile force bivouacked during the night at Hall's old position at Prosperity Church. As Hall wished to draw the enemy as near to Murfreesboro as possible, he again retreated in the morning to what he knew was a "fine position near Milton."

After making demonstrations as though he intended to halt at Milton—where indeed his men filled their canteens—Hall retired to the hill he had in mind, which he reached none too soon, for what he called heavy columns of the enemy soon were trying to get around him on the right and on the left. A gun opened on each column, and that on the right being compelled, probably by terrain, to come quite close, an infantry regiment poured in a volley that "extinguished its valor and boldness," so that a thin line from Hall's company of cavalry "was all that was necessary to control them thereafter."

Quite as he had directed, Hall's infantry regiments took position "without confusion or delay," and very timely upon the left. There the enemy dismounted "and advanced with all the precision, boldness, and rapidity of infantry drill"—high praise from a Federal colonel of infantry for Confederate cavalry. The first attack was broken quickly; but another of doubled force and greater determination advanced upon Hall's main line. When confusion developed in an Indiana regiment, line, field, and staff officers all played their parts well; and after sending to the Hoosiers' aid five companies of an Illinois regiment and one of his two guns, Hall checked the disorder, and subsequently wrote, "Every man returned to his post and fought to the last." An attack upon his rear was handled by a company of an Ohio regiment and some of Hall's dismounted cavalrymen, with aid from an unexpected quarter: "The enemy's artillery assisted in driving the enemy from my rear."

Every unprotected spot on the five acres where his command was surrounded was, Hall wrote, showered with shot, shell, grape, and canister. His own two pieces were, of course, busy, and though not a professional gunner, Hall had probably seen artillery in action sufficiently to give a measure of validity to his words: "Artillery was never better worked." The contest continued with renewed efforts to break Hall's "devoted circle" from 11:30 in the morning until 2:15 in the afternoon, when the Confederates gave up their efforts with small arms but continued artillery fire until 4:30, when their guns were also withdrawn. Though they took away the slightly wounded, they left many dead and mortally wounded, and Hall was told by an enemy surgeon that Morgan had been slightly wounded in the arm.

In Hall's judgment more damage should have been done to the enemy. At an early hour he had sent three messengers to Murfreesboro with information about his situation, and he believed that Cavalryman Minty had taken a very long time in covering the thirteen miles of one of the best roads in the state when he arrived at 7:00 P.M. Had Minty come earlier, he could, Hall wrote in his report, have taken many prisoners. Half an hour after Minty, a reinforcing infantry brigade arrived; but by then night had come. As if to atone for the lack of prisoners, Minty turned in a roster of the attacking force, and put the total at 2,250, with two brass pieces, one rifled, and one howitzer, and two other small howitzers.[17]

On the day of battle—March 20—a captain commanding the Confederate Ninth Tennessee Cavalry reported from Auburn: "We have had a rather warm time to-day. Our loss is great; do not know how much yet; perhaps 125 killed and wounded." Morgan himself reported the next day to Wheeler: "We attacked the enemy at Milton on yesterday morning; drove them 2 miles. They were largely reenforced, and maintained their position. The fight lasted six hours. Our loss heavy in officers." Though it may have been pleasing to Wheeler to think that the Federals had been strengthened before the battle had ended, as Morgan indicated, that was not the case. How annoyingly close was the scrutiny of Federal movements being maintained by Morgan's men, and how persistent were hopes that Rosecrans might yield the region he had won by heavy battle, seem indicated by the closing sentence of Morgan's message: "Colonel Martin, who has just returned from the Murfreesborough and Nashville pike, reports that the Federals are not falling back."[18]

Spring had lightly touched the region of delightful names—La Vergne, Triune, College Grove, Allisona, Eagleville, Rockvale, Overall, Readyville, Auburn, Gassaway, Liberty, Vaught's Hill, Prosperity Church—when on March 26 Union pickets south of Franklin were driven in. Granger, now personally in command at the place, directed G. Clay Smith (G. for Green) to reinforce the outposts sufficiently to press out and learn what was going on in front. Soon, however, word came that a brigade of Confederate cavalry under Colonel James W. Starnes had crossed the Harpeth some eight miles or so to the left and was moving toward Brentwood. Toward that place Smith hastened with the balance of his command—between 560 and 700 men—only to find that the railroad bridge just south of town had been demolished, the infantry garrison captured, and their camp destroyed, and that the enemy was moving westward with the handsome proceeds—wagons, arms, prisoners. After overtaking the retreating column and pushing a running fight, in which a considerable number of wagons were retaken, some laden with captured arms, Smith discovered that Starnes had brought his force to a halt six miles from Brentwood. After a general engagement, Smith according to his report drove the enemy from the woods, ravines, and brush, but only to find upon his right what he thought were cavalry and mounted infantry under Wharton, with Forrest and a sizable command upon his left. While Wharton was certainly not anywhere in the vicinity, there is no question about Forrest—now commanding the First Cavalry Division of Bragg's First Cavalry Corps. He was present and indulged in strong language to get his men back into the fight.

After another action of an hour and a half, Smith fell back, the enemy following with much loud shouting. Thus it was for two miles; then, still according to Smith, after he had checked enemy flank movements and repelled charges at all points, the Union column was allowed to continue unmolested. Three of the recaptured wagons, loaded with ammunition and rifles, had to be burned because their teams, in a display of pure mulishness, one may believe, had refused to pull. The other recaptured wagons were brought safely off, and the two "replevined" ambulances were matched by two the Confederates had brought upon the expedition.

In his report Forrest wrote that "not knowing what forces might be marching" on him, he deemed it "expedient to move off with the prisoners as rapidly as possible"—in number eight hundred officers and men. In doing this he disappointed the commander of the Sixth Tennessee Cavalry who, by Forrest's personal order, had ridden toward Nashville from Brentwood and, after doing some minor capturing, had circled westward across different turnpikes with "a plain view of the city and the capitol" until at 3:00 P.M. he struck the Cumberland. Patiently he waited six hours for Forrest, who had told him that his entire force "would certainly come to the point." Failure to send a message to the officer waiting to keep a rendezvous was not good procedure, and the commander of the Sixth Tennessee concluded his report with a note of diluted cheer: there had been no loss to his regiment "except the bad condition of horses." [19]

In an order on March's last day congratulating Van Dorn for his harvest of prisoners at Thompson's Station and Forrest for the accomplishment of his division on the 25th, Bragg said, "The skillful manner in which these generals achieved their success exhibits clearly the judgment, discipline, and good conduct of the brave troops of their commands. . . ." [20]

But Rosecrans could find nothing cheering in reports about Brentwood, and he said candidly to Lorenzo Thomas, "The block-house was one which could have been defended against any cavalry or infantry attack which they were able to bring against it." He drove home his point by relating how Colonel Innes and 290 men [First Michigan Engineers] had "defended themselves in a small corral of rails, brush, and wagons at La Vergne against a more formidable attack." The cavalry action on the 25th, however, did much to offset humiliation over the loss of the Brentwood garrison, and the Federal commander saw in the gallantry of his mounted arm promise for the future: "With proper officers and arms, it will soon be able to cope with its rebel foes effectually." [21]

Smith, who certainly had been greatly outnumbered, attributed his success not only to the good behavior of his men but to their fire power: the "five-shooters" of the Second Michigan Cavalry (doubtless the revolving rifles which Rosecrans had begun calling for soon after reaching Nashville), and the quick-loading Burnside carbines.

From Triune as well as from Murfreesboro reports reached Granger at Franklin that Van Dorn, back in his old Spring Hill camp after the fright that had sent him precipitately across the rushing Duck, was intending to attack him—retaliation for retaliation, one might say. To defend his position the Federal general had the divisions of Baird and Gilbert, largely raw men who had never heard the sound of hostile guns, and Smith's cavalrymen, who had heard them often. Protecting the town, which lay on the south bank of the Harpeth River, there were no works whatever, and the fort which was being built upon a 40-foot eminence across the stream was only partially completed, with an armament of two 24-pounders.

In spite of the fact that the town was wide open to approach from the south and that some reports had said that Van Dorn would bring 18,000 men to effect his conquest, Granger expected him to use an indirect approach, crossing the 30- to 40-foot-wide Harpeth, which at the time was running with a normal two to three feet of water, and then striking one of his flanks to gain his rear. When Stanley arrived on the morning of April 10—"a dark, smoky, and windy day"—bringing the Federal forces up to an effective total of close to 8,000, Granger ordered him to guard a ford four miles to the east; Baird, Granger directed to watch crossing points to the west; Smith he held as a reserve to help Stanley, if need be; Gilbert's division he kept as a general reserve.

But Van Dorn eschewed indirectness, and just before noon he arrived in two columns, one on the main Columbia road, the other by the Lewisburg pike, which for some distance from the town skirted the river. The sole Federal regiment south of the river—the Fortieth Ohio—after giving shelter to retiring pickets, proceeded to resist hostile entry into Franklin with firmness. A field battery of rifled guns that Granger threw into the fort aided in driving the Confederates back to a wood, where they put two guns in action and retaliated by throwing shells at the fort and at Granger's headquarters. At about this time there came over the wire from Brentwood the report that pickets there were being driven in. Sensitive about that position, Granger soon had Smith moving northward; but he found out subsequently that a panicky Federal outpost had fallen back before nothing more than three or four Negroes "walking along the road."

Though his force was now reduced, Granger decided to take the offensive by having Stanley ford the river, at the same time that Baird, summoned from below, crossed on a pontoon bridge at the town. But Stanley, having heard firing, had taken it upon himself to cross most of his command and attack the enemy in flank. At first he was successful, and an enemy battery and several hundred prisoners were soon in his hands. Then Van Dorn, not being held by anything near the town, and thus with an unendangered rear, struck heavily at the exposed Stanley, compelling the release of most of the prisoners, and recapturing the battery, but only after four of its guns had been spiked and had had their wheels broken. Part of the Federal horse was forced back over the river; but part advanced again, the commander of the Seventh Pennsylvania reporting that he met a heavy detachment of infantry and artillery under Baird. By then night had come, and Van Dorn was on the way back to Spring Hill. Only small casualties were suffered by either side in this "engagement at Franklin." But not always was it thus in contests for the town that was an important covering position for Nashville from the time Buell arrived there in February of 1862.

On the 13th Granger wrote to Rosecrans: "Baird and Gilbert, who met Cosby and Armstrong [under a flag of truce, to exchange wounded], report the rebels much dejected. Much reason to be; the bottom is about knocked out of the Southern Confederacy." Two days later he reported that Van Dorn had had 9,000 men, a total that looks high, but which is hard to check against reliable figures, for there is not a single report in the *Records* by a Confederate officer. The Union general ended his detailed account, which included an excellent map of the vicinity of Franklin, with the statement: "Since Van Dorn's repulse, he facetiously calls his attack an armed reconnaissance in force." [22]

Van Dorn's claim that he was only reconnoitering is quite unacceptable. He must have been well acquainted with the Federal situation at Franklin and in his command there must have been officers familiar with every road and lane in the vicinity. More than that, Rosecrans, according to a dispatch that Granger sent him on the 7th, had been keeping the Confederates posted. "I repeat again," Granger said, "that all your messages are taken off between here and Murfreesborough and communicated to the enemy by couriers." The Franklin general had bluntly asked the army commander, "Why not use the cipher?" [23]

In late February Van Dorn had told Johnston he meant to dislodge the Federals from Franklin, and it is probable that he thought that by seizing the town in force he would frighten Granger into giving up his position across the river, as he himself had recently been induced to abandon Spring Hill. Stanley's unexpected appearance upon his flank was certainly disconcerting; and Granger had reason for thinking that, if the cavalryman had not made the move until Baird had come from below and crossed the Harpeth, considerable loss would have been inflicted upon the enemy. At least Van Dorn would not have been able to turn upon Stanley with impunity. As for Granger, it is difficult to see why, when he realized that Van Dorn was doing the unexpected in moving directly on Franklin, he did not save time by having Gilbert's division cross, while Baird marched from the fords below to become a reserve. Certainly he was not excused by his statement that "it was a most propitious day for an attack," the wind raising so much dust that, even with field glasses, it was hard to distinguish at a distance of over a mile "a fence from a line of horsemen."

On the day of Van Dorn's effort against Franklin, Wheeler, rather quiet since his Fort Donelson repulse, struck a double blow at railroads. For the attacks and for covering and screening them, he used 1,900 men from Wharton's division and 600 under Duke from Morgan's, some of the protective force being in the vicinity of Andrew Jackson's well-loved "Hermitage" northeast of Nashville.

Taking advantage of a bend in the Cumberland that brought it close to the Louisville and Nashville Railroad across the stream, Wheeler shrewdly planted his guns to cover the tracks that were so important to the Federals throughout the war. While waiting at such a time may seem long, only two hours had to pass before "a very large locomotive came in view, drawing eighteen cars loaded with horses and other stock." The shooting of Wheeler's gunners at the moving target 700 yards away had, even according to Federal Brigadier E. A. Paine, a pinpoint quality. In all, thirty-five shots were fired, most of them striking the train, and some of them the engine. Wheeler, on his part, put it thus: "We also shot the horses in the cars, and retired." Federal soldiers had run back and had stopped three passenger trains; and evidently the hostile shells had caused no serious derailments or the piling up of much wreckage, for Paine closed his report, "After the rebels left, the three trains ran into Nashville about midnight."

While the affair at the bend was in process, a smaller body of Confederates ambushed a train guarded by forty-six Federal officers and men at a point five and a half miles on the Nashville side of La Vergne. Responsibility for protecting the line had rested on Colonel George P. Este, and he described how he had been scouring the country and had thought that he had "most satisfactory evidence from scouts, citizens, and contrabands that no rebels were in the vicinity in any considerable force." Timing was good, if indeed it was true, as Este said, that the ambushing party had arrived upon the scene only ten minutes before the train. While Wharton stated that the rails had been spread, Este reported that the evidence showed that the engine had been derailed by a "too sudden reversal . . . for the purpose of running back." Be that as it may, the booty was considerable: twenty officers, including—according to Wheeler—three from Rosecrans's staff; $30,000 in greenbacks—an item by no means despised within the Confederacy; and a large mail from which valuable information may have been secured. While both Wheeler's and Wharton's reports are open to some discounting, one can hardly challenge a sentence in Este's report to Thomas: "I need not assure you of my vexation at this successful raid." [24]

It was a strange coincidence that on the day of Wheeler's double strike at railroads, an expedition was embarking at Nashville for the purpose of cutting a rail line behind Bragg. One can imagine that the thought gave solace to Rosecrans on the evening when he learned that he had lost three staff officers, $30,000 in cash, and many letters.

Actually, the general who early in the war had dislodged the enemy at Rich Mountain by a bold flank attack had toyed with the idea of getting in his enemy's rear at least as early as January 17. When querying Wright that day as to the route by which he would send his two-division reinforcement, Rosecrans wrote, "If it were practicable, I should like to send them by the Tennessee, to operate on the rear of the rebel position behind Duck River." [25] Taking into account all that this implies, the idea may have struck Wright as fantastic, and as certain to end in the destruction of the commands that he was giving up to aid Rosecrans.

Whether Rosecrans himself continued to entertain these thoughts, he was probably from the first a sympathetic listener to a plan for a bold expedition laid before him by Colonel Abel D. Streight, of the Fifty-first Indiana Infantry. The target of the operation, which was the cutting of the railroad from Atlanta to Chattanooga, must have led to comments about the famous railroad raid just a year previously by James Andrews and his handful of brave Ohio soldiers—every one of whom, it will be recalled, was captured, and some of whom, including Andrews, were hanged. But Streight's operation was to be of an entirely different nature, though it was equally daring and not such as many officers would wish to undertake.[26]

Streight's energy and drive have been noticed in Buell's advance toward Chattanooga from Corinth, when dwindling supplies made it imperative to get a locomotive across the Tennessee at Decatur to draw on the abundance that was at Eastport. Slowly the building of a boat had dragged on until Streight took hold; then a craft was soon completed and the engine *Sam Cruse* was puffing westward.

Courtesy Library of Congress

COLONEL ABEL D. STREIGHT

Though not mentioned in this work, Streight was at the head of his regiment at Stones River. A sentence in the report of his brigade commander, Colonel Charles G. Harker, bears testimony to Streight's alertness: "My thanks are also due to Col. A. D. Streight, commanding Fifty-first Indiana Volunteers, for valuable information of the movements of the enemy during this engagement." [27]

Efficient handling of Harker's brigade during Wagner's peculiar January operation—peculiar because of the change in mission that Rosecrans suddenly gave it—had brought commendation to Streight, and he must have been recognized by all as one of the outstanding colonels in the Army of the Cumberland. For his far-off Georgia venture, a provisional brigade was put together: his own regiment; the Seventy-third Indiana, whose killed and wounded on December 31 had exceeded 20 per cent, and whose colonel, Gilbert Hathaway, Streight was to write later, was almost worshiped by his men; John Beatty's old Third Ohio (17 killed and 66 wounded at Stones River) now under Colonel Orris A. Lawson; and the Eightieth Illinois (under Lieutenant Colonel Andrew F. Rodgers), which had not been engaged at Stones River but had been with Colonel Hall on Vaught's Hill, where at exactly the right moment it had sent the five companies that had bolstered the One Hundred and First Indiana. To these fine regiments of infantry there was added a highly distinctive detachment: two companies of northern Alabama Unionists, belonging to the First Middle Tennessee Cavalry and riding under Captain D. D. Smith.[28]

Beatty's sorrow at the departure on April 7 of his beloved old regiment for Nashville was duly recorded in his diary; he never expected to see it again; it would get into another current and find itself in another brigade of another division of another corps. Even two red apples purchased for a quarter the next afternoon in Murfreesboro and a glass of wine with an authentic Kentucky colonel—which should have cured anyone of any discontent—did not cheer Beatty. A touch of complaint about inaction seems to lurk in his remark about the quiet time since the great battle, "each succeeding day seeming the dullest." Then on the 10th, while Wheeler was doing his railroad raiding, and Granger was repulsing Van Dorn, and Beatty's Third was embarking for its great adventure, Beatty recorded one of the saddest events in military life: "A soldier of the Fortieth Indiana, who, during the battle of Stone River, abandoned his company and regiment and remained away until the fight ended, was shot this afternoon." [29]

Streight later lamented that he was absent on the evening when the mules the expedition was to ride were taken aboard the steamers at Nashville—on the theory perhaps that an infantryman could travel as rapidly on a mule as on a horse, and no more uncomfortably. Not until he had disembarked his command at Palmyra—a few miles below Clarksville—to march across and re-embark upon the Tennessee, did Streight discover that the mules were poor, wild, unbroken colts, many only two years old, and some afflicted with horse distemper. The letter of instructions that Garfield had given Streight bade him not only to live upon the country, but to keep himself "well mounted"; and the expedition quartermaster had money to "make cash payments in full to men of undoubted loyalty," from whom property was taken, but giving the usual conditional receipts to those whose allegiance to the Union was suspect, and "to rebels nothing." So parties were dispatched to hunt for animals, and 150 very good ones were brought in, "but mostly barefooted." Although 100 mules broke down upon the march to Fort Henry, Streight reached there with 1,250 animals for his 1,700 officers and men.[30]

April 19 saw the expedition arriving at Eastport * under the guardianship of two gunboats, unnecessarily accompanied by the Marine Brigade. When Brigadier General Alfred Ellet took over command and refused to run at night because of low water, there was nothing that Streight could do but prod a little, and fret. Upon returning to Eastport about midnight, after a conference with General Dodge, Streight got the unpleasant news that there had been a stampede; and a morning check showed that about 400 animals were gone, naturally the most enterprising ones. Nearly two days were spent in the fatiguing work of rounding up about half the missing animals, the others ending up in the possession of the enemy, according to Streight, who may have suspected that the stampede had been caused by guerrillas or regular Confederate horsemen who prowled the region. Some of the Nashville mules took advantage of the delay and died; others with distemper were left behind when Streight departed on the afternoon of the 21st to join, the next morning, Dodge's column of 8,000 (Streight's figure) twelve miles up Bear Creek.

In accord with Garfield's instructions to make it appear as if his force were only a reinforcement to Dodge, Streight followed in the rear of the latter, scouring the country for animals as far as the river

* Eastport, Tuscumbia, and Bear Creek will be found on the maps on pp. 28 and 77 of Vol. IV.

to the north and the mountains to the south. At Tuscumbia, which was reached late on the afternoon of the 24th, Dodge gave Streight 200 mules—200 according to Streight, but many more according to Dodge—and six wagons for ammunition and rations, while Streight's surgeons cut his force to 1,500 by eliminating men unfit for the arduous march ahead. It being by this time certain that Forrest had crossed the Tennessee, Dodge agreed to give diversion and protection by marching on to Courtland (a good half of the way between Tuscumbia and Decatur), while Streight, after writing a dispatch to Garfield, at 11:00 P.M. of the 26th, headed southward to Russellville, there to turn eastward to Moulton (twenty miles southwest of Decatur). Rain was falling heavily and 300 of Streight's men were afoot, half of them because mules they might have ridden could carry nothing more than a saddle. Terrible roads made speed impossible; then a turn in the weather on the evening of April 28 gave "strong hopes of better times." [31]

The next day found every man mounted, and the expedition made thirty-five miles in the direction of Blountsville (fifty-five miles southeast of Decatur), halting for the night in a mountain region of devoted Unionists. Here it was that a goodly number of Smith's men had been recruited, "and many were the happy greetings between them and their friends and relations." Blountsville was reached at 10:00 A.M. of May 1, but only after very hard marching and fights with pursuers led by Forrest.

No glimmer of an idea that Streight's stroke was to be carried out was responsible for Forrest being close upon his heels. He had been sent south from Spring Hill to join Colonel P. D. Roddey, who commanded in northern Alabama. Together they were to oppose an advance by Dodge, while regular and irregular horsemen harried Dodge's rear. But the reports of scouts and his own appraisal of the fighting that Dodge had done on April 28 convinced Forrest that Dodge's move was merely a blind and that the real threat was Streight. Sending word to the cavalry behind Dodge to continue their annoying tactics, and after a night spent shoeing his horses, Forrest turned his personal attention to the column whose purpose, a mystery when it headed due southward from Tuscumbia, began slowly to acquire meaning after it turned eastward into desolate mountain country.

The first clash occurred soon after Streight had passed through one of the mountain gaps. Having learned that hostile columns had gone through openings to his right and to his left with the purpose of joining at a crossroad to head him off, he pushed rapidly past the danger point, and, upon finding a good defensive position, made ready for battle. The mules were sent to a ravine for safety, and behind a concealing ridge Streight deployed his infantry. When Captain Smith's cavalry, luring the pursuers on, passed through an opening left for him, battle-tried rifles opened a devastating fire, which was thickened by the blasts of two concealed 12-pounder howitzers, commanded by infantryman James Vananda, major of the Third Ohio. Driven back and leaving Forrest's brother, Captain William Forrest, badly wounded on the field, the Confederates got off their horses and, reinforced by some newly arrived units and two guns, attacked again. Even if the attackers had equaled Streight in numbers, they could not have handled such foot soldiers as they were attacking. Just as Streight had kept a keenly discerning eye on enemy movements at Stones River, so here in a desolate region of northern Alabama he watched the effect of the fire of his steady riflemen; and as soon as he saw signs of wavering by the attackers, he threw his men into a counterattack that drove the enemy backward in confusion so precipitate that their guns and caissons were left behind. In a few minutes Major Vananda, who had well played an artilleryman's part with two pieces, had a total of four to aid the infantry in the next clash.

According to his biographer, Henry, Forrest was thrown into a towering and thundering rage, which hardly reflects well on him as a battle commander, though other generals have had a blustering and cursing style. While Michigan infantry had handled him roughly at Murfreesboro on his forty-first birthday before he got their surrender by a note that promised to put them to the sword if they did not yield, and although he had recently been humiliated at Fort Donelson, Forrest had never experienced anything like this fight in the inhospitable region where his trained cavalry had caught up with Streight's incongruously mounted men. It was a time for a commander to assess coolly what was and what was not possible. But Forrest, dominated apparently by overweening eagerness to get back the two lost guns, formed his men for another assault, "raging up and down the line," in Henry's words. Streight, who had reason to believe that another column was on his northern flank, withdrew, saving Forrest, one must believe, another repulse.

Skirmishing soon began with the column on the left, and an hour before sunset Streight once more prepared for battle in a good position on Hog Mountain. The force which Forrest had led in the five-hour morning contest—apparently largely Roddey's—was sent to the rear, ostensibly to keep Dodge from striking Forrest's rear, but more likely, and this without reflecting upon them in the least, because Forrest believed that for the moment they had lost real combat value. After Streight had beaten back until 10:00 P.M. bold assaults by two regiments that had failed to get in his front, which had been joined by Forrest and his escort, his wounded brother's company of scouts, and a battery, Streight again took up the march. On the deserted battlefield, lighted by a kindly moon, Forrest found his two guns, but hardly in a condition to cause rejoicing. When captured ammunition had been exhausted, they had been spiked and their carriages broken by men who could injure guns with less compunction than regular artillerists. When word came from his rear guard that the enemy was still following, Streight prepared another ambush, using for it a different pattern from the first. Though it damaged the enemy, a third ambush was needed to cause his pursuers to disengage.

Many men were afoot because their mules had given out when Streight reached Blountsville in midmorning; but enough corn was found to feed the tired and hungry animals. Upon learning that wagons could not negotiate the roads ahead, rations and ammunition were distributed among the men and packed on mules. Then, after burning his wagons beyond redemption, Streight started his column toward Gadsden, thirty-five miles to the east. Even a halt for rest of only two hours had enabled Forrest to catch up, though apparently he followed this day with the experience of the day before in mind. His advance guard contented itself with skirmishing with Streight's rear guard until the Federal column reached Black Creek, just west of Gadsden, at 9:00 A.M. of May 2; there a sharp attack had to be beaten off.

Informed by scouts that a column was moving on his left, Streight now began to bend every effort to reach Rome, where he thought that by destroying bridges over the Oostanaula he could gain a respite. But without a little rest another night march was impossible, so, after turning northeasterly at Gadsden—where he tarried only long enough to destroy a quantity of arms and commissary stores—Streight halted at four o'clock a little beyond Turkeytown, a name that probably elicited wise comments from weary Buckeyes, Hoosiers, and men from the Prairie State. While a detail fed the animals,

Streight formed the balance of his command to receive the attack which he expected and which soon came. In repelling it, Colonel Hathaway was mortally wounded, to die in a few minutes. One can

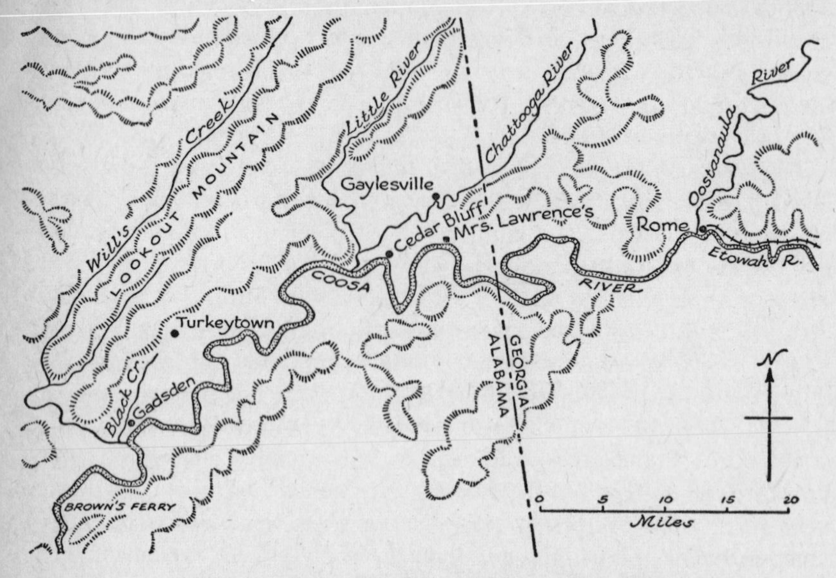

THE REGION OF STREIGHT'S CAPTURE

From Tuscumbia on the Tennessee, 115 miles to the west, Streight turned south and then east. He had rear-guard actions with pursuing Confederate cavalry under Forrest at several places. At Gadsden he turned north through Turkeytown, and was surrounded and captured east of Cedar Bluff, at Mrs. Lawrence's farm.

imagine the gloom that gripped the men who had marched and fought under such a leader. In this fight the painful discovery was also made that a large part of the ammunition had been spoiled in fording deep streams, while much of what had been carried by the men had been ruined by the wearing through of the paper cartridge cases and the sifting away of the powder.

After the failure of his own ambush which he laid after taking to the road again, Streight skillfully avoided one set for him, of which he was informed by faithful scouts. Then, as his weary men toiled through the night up a valley road just to the east of the southern reach of famed Lookout Mountain, their commander began really to hope that he would reach Rome ahead of the enemy. His principal guide, who thus far had proved reliable, had reported that no difficult streams lay ahead and that the road was good. The Chattooga River, however, was found to be unfordable and the ferryboat had been removed. Strangely enough, a detachment of two hundred men mounted on the best surviving animals, which Streight had sent ahead to seize bridges at Rome, had finished crossing only an hour before, but the detachment commander had failed to leave a guard over the precious ferryboat. By such a minor oversight can an operation be thwarted.

Night though it was, and hostile though the countryside now was, Streight learned of a bridge seven or so miles up the Chattooga, not far from Gaylesville, and thither, with the help of new guides, he led his column, which, though scattered by a confusing labyrinth of roads, arrived in time to cross safely. After burning the bridge, Streight turned southward, then toward the east, passing the village of Cedar Bluff just as light was breaking on May 3. Only twenty miles lay between him and Rome. But neither men nor animals, which had both been giving out after the crossing of the Chattooga, could cover the distance without rest. So at nine o'clock Streight halted. Even as they fed their mules, men fell asleep, and consciousness quickly left every man except the pickets that any commander hates to detail at such a time. Soon the pickets were driven in, and Streight ordered his command into line. While every effort was made to rally the worn-out soldiers, a large part of Streight's "best troops actually went to sleep while lying in line of battle under a severe skirmish fire." Aware that his men were exhausted and outnumbered, their mounts "in a desperate condition" and their ammunition worthless, Streight had no course but to listen to Forrest's demand for surrender.[32]

Upon receiving the demand, Streight assembled his regimental commanders. All of them expressed the belief that unless it was possible to reach Rome and destroy the bridges behind them as they crossed (bridges over the Oostanaula without doubt), surrender was advisable. But already word had come from Captain Russell, commander of the two hundred, that he had been unable to seize these invaluable structures. Whether he had been deceived as to the strength of Confederate forces in Rome is immaterial, though it is an interesting point. Yielding to the views of his subordinates rather than to his own inclination, Streight at once entered into negotiations with Forrest, and about noon the command "surrendered as prisoners of war."[33]

In his report Streight did not, as Coburn had done, recount the story of the trip to Richmond and Libby Prison. The men were exchanged; but, unlike Coburn, Streight and his officers were held. On June 3 the Federal agent of exchange made a formal demand for their release, tendering their equivalents in Confederate officers in Federal hands. Two days later the Confederate agent replied:

> Allegations have been officially received from the highest authority in Alabama charging these officers with grave offenses as well against the laws of that State as the usages of civilized warfare. They are detained until the proper inquiry can be made and the fact ascertained when a determination will be made by the Confederate Government whether they come within the obligations of the cartel as prisoners of war or are to be dealt with as criminals against the laws of war and the State.

This explanation the agent pronounced more detailed than the one that had been given him when he had inquired about a Confederate colonel and other officers since exchanged. Though it seems to have been decided that Streight and his officers were not criminals, they continued to be held, and the correspondence in the case was voluminous. So far as the colonel and four of his subordinates were concerned, all dispute was terminated when they appeared in Washington on March 1, 1864. They had escaped.[34] (On August 30 Streight had written the Confederate Secretary of War that accommodations in Libby were inadequate and its cuisine poor.)[35]

Having been the proposer of the operation, Streight could hardly be expected to say that success had not been possible, a fact one should keep in mind when reading the comment in his report:

> In reviewing the history of this ill-fated expedition, I am convinced that had we been furnished at Nashville with 800 good horses, instead of poor, young mules, we would have been successful, in spite of all other drawbacks; or if General Dodge had succeeded in detaining Forrest one day longer, we would have been successful, even with our poor outfit.

Dodge's movement eastward having been the cause of Bragg's sending Forrest to northern Alabama, one can question whether this operation was in all ways well advised. As there were Confederates in the region, some clearing of the way was essential, or Streight would not have been able even to start; but whether Dodge's move was in too strong a force is an interesting though difficult question. Dodge sent a full and excellent report to Hurlbut at Memphis, supporting it by two good ones from subordinates, one of special merit from the commander of his cavalry brigade. At Tuscumbia, Dodge claimed he gave Streight 600 horses and mules, and inasmuch as Dodge wrote on May 5—over fifteen months before Streight did—his figure may be the better. He also turned over to Streight all the hard bread he had, 10,000 rations. He put at 5,500 the strength of the enemy that he forced back on Decatur, after having passed Town Creek, which in a morning had been raised ten feet by the torrents that had impeded Streight. For an operation such as Streight's to succeed there must be perfect timing of collaborating columns, difficult in this case because of the long river movement involved. Punctual himself, Dodge had actually fallen back to Bear Creek to await Streight, who was late, though not through any fault of his own. How well the fine soldier and future great railroad builder could appraise a situation is shown by a paragraph Dodge wrote before he had actually heard of Streight's failure:

> I have no doubt but that Colonel Streight would have succeeded had he been properly equipped, and joined me at the time agreed upon. The great delay in enemy's country to fit him out gave them time to throw a large force in our front. Although Colonel Streight had two days' start, they can harass him, and perhaps check his movements long enough for them to secure all their important bridges. If he could have started from Bear Creek the day I arrived there, then my movements would have been so quick and strong that the enemy could not have got their forces together.[36]

Knowing Hurlbut, it will be no surprise to the reader to learn that the Union commander in Memphis telegraphed all the information he had to Rosecrans on Friday, May 1: Streight had left Tuscumbia on Sunday night; Dodge had gone forward the next day and had driven the enemy from Town Creek; "Streight got two days' march on them and went toward the mountains." Van Dorn had appeared in force and with fifteen guns at Florence on the 28th; Dodge had fallen back to Tuscumbia; then to Little Bear Creek; the night before to Big Bear Creek; that night he would return to Burnsville; Van Dorn was presently not far from Eastport. All this was encouraging enough. But the last sentence of Hurlbut's dispatch might have made Rosecrans uneasy: "Roddey fell back to Decatur, and is not following Dodge." Replying at 2:00 A.M., Rosecrans said that Van Dorn was probably not at Eastport; only "Forrest, with 3,000 or 4,000 men" was there.[37] Even with this misconception, Roddey remained a potential threat to Streight.

Waiting for news about a hazardous operation is a trying thing for the responsible commander. But Rosecrans had diversions. A message from Granger on April 30 reporting the departure of Forrest for Florence had ended pleasingly: "All quiet in front. Rebels mighty vigilant and mad since our last rampage." On May 2 Brigadier General James B. Steedman, the energetic and outspoken brigade commander who was seen in Buell's advance eastward from Corinth and in the Battle of Perryville, but who had not been present in the great contest near Murfreesboro, reported on the second of two highly successful foraging expeditions he had made across Stones River. Not only had he been in a region of seemingly plentiful corn but he had "patrolled a section which has been a place of resort and concealment for the rebels who have made the raids upon the railroad and pike between this post [La Vergne] and Nashville." Inactivity being something Steedman did not relish, he concluded, "On Monday, I will go over the river again with a large train." On Sunday, Schofield, then commanding the division in Thomas's Fourteenth Corps to which Steedman's brigade belonged, reported from Triune about a scout to Eagleville; while from Carthage on the Cumberland, George Crook was writing that his brigade was suffering greatly not only from lack of antiscorbutics—a boat loaded with them had sunk —but from lack of blouses and pants, of which elementary garments "many of the men" had "none." More than that, the Rebels were again appearing in the Alexandria country and were scattering in all directions; without cavalry he could do nothing. From Rosecrans's own headquarters there issued a long and important order about the duties and procedures of inspectors of different units, while to the Adjutant General of the Army the general himself grumbled a little about an order to turn over to Andrew Johnson the First Tennessee Infantry; he was carrying out the direction, but he thought the arrangement "far more likely to beget discord and trouble than anything else." [38]

Overshadowing these matters in many ways were conferences between Rosecrans and Major General George L. Hartsuff, an envoy from Burnside, new commander of the Department of the Ohio.

Replacement of Wright had been necessary when the Senate on

March 12 failed by a vote of 20 to 15 to confirm Lincoln's appointment of the Cincinnati commander as a major general of volunteers. Perhaps Senator Sherman who thought criticism of his brother's administration in Memphis had been unjust, and who had spoken in a letter to his brother of a thousand evidences of Lincoln's unfitness for his office, had not liked Wright's military philosophy as expressed to Thomas Ewing, General Sherman's father-in-law, "The citizens living upon the border must aid in their own protection." Inasmuch as Wright has been praised in these pages, it will be noted that he was subsequently given the rank denied him in March, 1863.

March 25 saw Burnside assume command of the department, and five days later he was telegraphing to Stanton that there were Cincinnati persons who wanted to go South, and that he thought they should be sent because they were doing harm. As yet, however, there was no real excuse for arresting them; nor did Burnside desire to pass them through his own lines. So he requested authority to ship them to City Point (an exchange point, it will be recalled) by way of Baltimore and Fort Monroe. He must have been more than eager to get them on their way, and when his question, "Can I have an answer from this to-night?" brought no response, he wired again the next day the announcement that the next morning he would start "some females in charge of an officer to care of General Dix." Should the ladies remain longer in the Queen City, they would certainly cause mischief; but no good would come from locking them up—they rather courted martyrdom. If it seemed that the Secretary had been dilatory, the fault had been with the telegraph, for on the 31st he wired: "Your proposed disposition of secesh women is also approved. They should be cleared out and sent home. The telegram you mention as being sent yesterday did not reach here" (which raises the disquieting thought that the "females" had male friends in the telegraph office).[39]

As March was ending, the First and Second divisions of Burnside's old Ninth Corps arrived by rail in Cincinnati after some excellent logistics. (The Third Division remained with Dix at Fort Monroe.) Soon they were at various Kentucky stations, a brigade and a battery at Mount Sterling being quite ample to prevent any more raids upon that place: the veterans of many battles were not men upon whom one could easily play tricks. Even before the order had been issued sending Burnside to Ohio, Jefferson Davis had seemingly learned that the concentration of the Ninth Corps at Fort Monroe presaged its dispatch to Kentucky. The news did not make him happy; it spoiled, he wrote to Johnston on March 6, the hope he had been entertaining that a move into Kentucky—probably by Humphrey Marshall from Virginia—would force Rosecrans to send back troops to protect the Bluegrass State.[40]

Like Wright before him, Burnside wanted to cooperate effectively with Rosecrans. To Boyle, whom he had retained at Louisville only by protesting against Stanton's explicit order that he be removed, Burnside telegraphed on April 25, "We must occupy the enemy, and keep them from flanking Rosecrans." Then in early May he dispatched Hartsuff, whom he had requested to have assigned to him, and who on April 27 was made commander of the Twenty-third Corps—the troops in Kentucky that Burnside had found upon his arrival—to Murfreesboro for a conference. The New York-born general, whose service had all been in the East and who carried a severe Antietam wound in addition to one received fighting Indians in Florida, must have ridden southward with keen anticipation of meeting friends. Alexander McCook and David Stanley had been in his class of 1852 at the Academy, as well as George Crook, who has the distinction of being described in the West Point register of graduates as the "ablest of all men in dealing with the Indians." (Milo Hascall was likewise a classmate, but he had been sent by Rosecrans to round up deserters in Illinois, Indiana, and Ohio, and before long was to be transferred to Burnside.) More important than this, Hartsuff, while still a captain, had been adjutant to Rosecrans when on September 10, 1861, the latter had defeated the entrenched force commanded by John B. Floyd at Carnifix Ferry on the Gauley River—an action that brought peculiar satisfaction to people in the North because of their great dislike for Floyd. In his report, Rosecrans had given generous praise to Hartsuff, who, during the general's absence reconnoitering, seems to have had to make decisions for the deployment of the attacking column as it emerged from a wood.[41]

The conference was certainly conducted in a favorable atmosphere for Rosecrans, and Burnside may have been surprised at the telegram he received from Hartsuff not long after noon on May 4: "Conference just ended. It was decided that it would be most advantageous to this army now for the Ninth Corps to come to Carthage immediately, via Glasgow, and relieve the force at Carthage. Reasons and particulars when I arrive." As Hartsuff was not leaving Murfreesboro until the afternoon of the 5th, he asked Burnside to telegraph immediately if further information was to be obtained or given before he left.

He was not, it should be noted, asking for approval of the conference decision, and Rosecrans on his part took it for granted that it was final, for he at once queried Burnside by telegraph as to when his corps could take over at Carthage. His eagerness for the arrival of the Ninth was probably only increased when a dispatch the next day from Crook stated that the enemy had appeared across the river, and seemed to be present in squads all the way to Gallatin.[42]

The 7th brought dispatches from Burnside not entirely agreeing to the Rosecrans-Hartsuff decision. Burnside wanted to move to aid Rosecrans, but he ended his second dispatch, "I will add that there is a very heavy pressure in favor of a movement on Knoxville." Evening brought Rosecrans a note from McCook: Sheridan had reported recent Shelbyville news; two words were cheering—"No arrivals." McCook wrote that Stonewall Jackson had been wounded, but that Chancellorsville was yet undecided. The ending of the dispatch should have sent Rosecrans to bed with unquiet thoughts: "Rumor says Forrest has made a large capture of our men in Alabama." [43]

On its part, Confederate headquarters at Tullahoma had unexpected and upsetting information to put on the wire on the 7th to Cooper. The "painful intelligence" had just come, Johnston said, of the death at Spring Hill "of the distinguished Major-General Van Dorn." While there is no doubt that Van Dorn was the victim of an angry bullet, there has been dispute as to whether the cause was an argument over politics, or a husband's belief that the Mississippi cavalryman had interests in Spring Hill other than military affairs.[44]

As Murfreesboro struggles on May 8 against belief in mounting rumors from the south about Streight, and as Johnston and Bragg give thought to the replacement of an important cavalry general, perhaps now is the moment to view other theaters and to read the dispatches and estimate the views of other commanders.

Sherman, bringing up Grant's rear in his move southward from Vicksburg and across the Mississippi, is over the great river and with two divisions is at Hankinson's Ferry, where he doubtless read the order that Grant had issued the day before to his troops. Grant's quartermaster back at Milliken's Bend is sending him a dispatch laden with ration figures that will be anything but dull reading to the general already well launched in the operation which even Sherman had thought too hazardous. Richmond not only knows the seriousness of Jackson's condition to balance the rejoicing over Lee's brilliant defeat of Hooker; it knows of Grant's move and is much worried because he has at last secured a firm footing east of the Mississippi and has won the first battle. While the Federal High Command is well aware of the disappointing outcome of Hooker's move that had begun with brilliance and high promise, it has no recent cheering Vicksburg news —except perhaps as some has come from Richmond papers. In due time, however, Washington will be reading the confident dispatch that Charles Dana wrote on May 8 which ended with a good augury: "The weather is cool and splendid." [45]

The Burnside threat to East Tennessee was ably discussed on May 8 in a letter by Joe Johnston to Major General Dabney H. Maury, who was then commanding the Confederate Department of East Tennessee but would in a few days change places with Simon Buckner at Mobile. Johnston's letter of May 8 is of special interest because no Federal commander described better the difficulties that confronted a Union army bent on carrying the war of conquest to a point far from its base.[46]

An army invading East Tennessee would—if Johnston was correctly informed—have to bring with it supplies of every kind, for the country was completely exhausted. Thus the best mode of opposing Burnside would be to strike his trains with as large a force of cavalry as possible, while other troops impeded his progress by frontal action, especially in the Cumberland Mountains. Even should Burnside reach his destination, an attack on his trains ought to compel his withdrawal, for in spite of Northern superiority in manpower Burnside could not, in Johnston's view, "be strong enough to guard so long a route of communication, and at the same time hold that country." Nonetheless the eminent general wished confirmation of his views, and he ended his letter, "Do let me hear from you on these subjects." [47]

As an excellent cooperator with Maury's cavalry in the task of harrying Burnside's communications, Johnston suggested John Morgan. But on that same day Hardee was writing Johnston about Morgan, and one cannot believe that he did so without mature and disquieting thoughts:

I learn that Morgan's command is in bad condition and growing worse. I judge from all I hear that he is greatly dissatisfied with being under Wheeler. His conduct, if this be true, cannot be justified, and he has suffered, and will continue to suffer, in public estimation. I dislike to see his usefulness impaired and his reputation sullied by mistaken notions of pride and duty. Would it not be well for you to send for Morgan and have some talk with him. [?] He likes you and will receive kindly any suggestions you may make to him. I have had no intercourse, direct or indirect, with Morgan, and write only from a sense of duty to the public.[48]

Johnston would have felt even better about a Federal advance into East Tennessee if he could have seen a dispatch that Rosecrans sent to Burnside on the 8th. Burnside's proposal of the day before, that he send the Ninth Corps to Jamestown, Tennessee, did not please Rosecrans. It would be too remote to cover his flank even from infantry attack, "aid in battle, or succor in disaster." If Burnside could reach Jamestown soon enough and supply himself, it might be all right (a raid deep toward Chattanooga was suggested); otherwise the Ninth should come to Carthage. The general who was always calling for horses, and who a month previously had equipped Streight with unfit mules, now apparently had plenty of the animals favored by the army to haul wagons and carry burdens, and he offered Burnside his pack train of 2,000 mules. On the same day when Rosecrans clearly indicated to Burnside a gnawing doubt as to the outcome of a battle with Bragg, he telegraphed to Stanton, ". . . What we want is to deal with their armies. . . . We shall soon be ready here to try that." [49]

The Secretary himself on this eventful May 8 sent a dispatch to Burnside that the latter must have appreciated highly. On the previous day Burnside had telegraphed to Halleck that on the 5th he had "caused the arrest of the Hon. C. L. Vallandigham," who was now in Cincinnati undergoing trial by a military commission for uttering sedition. Some trouble had been caused in Dayton where the arrest had taken place, but all was now quiet, and Burnside hoped to maintain perfect order in other areas of his department, though among the arrested man's friends there was, Burnside said, necessarily much excitement. (The Vallandigham case has been discussed in an earlier volume.) Smooth working between the General in Chief and the Secretary of War was indicated when the higher official replied: "In your determination to support the authority of the Government and suppress treason in your department, you may count on the support of the President." [50]

The next evening—May 9—the commander of one of Wheeler's brigades which was near Liberty reported, according to a scout, that the Cumberland was now fordable; but there were no enemy movements to report, other than those of Burnside in Kentucky. With a quiet nearby front, the brigade commander's mind was dwelling upon the great Confederate victory at Chancellorsville, and he craved more news. From what source it had reached him he did not say, but he also had the rumor that Price had won a great victory in Missouri. Skepticism seems to have been behind the question, "Is the report reliable?" (Doubtless what had reached Liberty was merely a report exaggerated by time and space of Marmaduke's recent raid and his unsuccessful attack on Cape Girardeau. Actually, Price seems to have been quietly at Little Rock; and on May 9 Kirby Smith, then at Shreveport, wrote to Holmes at Little Rock that he could expect no support and that if the Federals advanced in overwhelming numbers he might have to give up the valley of the Arkansas and concentrate at Shreveport in order to oppose Banks, who, it may be recalled, had advanced up the Red River as far as Alexandria before turning back to Port Hudson.) [51]

More happily, Gideon J. Pillow, now on conscript duty, was writing from Huntsville to Isham G. Harris, roving Confederate governor of Kentucky. Said the general who upon receiving from Floyd command at Fort Donelson had at once relinquished it to Buckner, and who had then escaped across the Cumberland upon a raft in order to avoid surrender to Grant: "I am happy in the belief that I see the dawn of our independence breaking in the future. We have got to kill off and wear out the army now confronting us, which the work of this summer will accomplish, and peace will soon follow." Pillow did not approve of Johnston's and Bragg's defensive policy: it would protract the war and greatly increase the public debt. Blood he knew would be the inevitable price for the offensive which he advocated; but the policy of merely wearing down the Federals would in the end cost as many lives and would cause "suffering and losses infinitely greater than any battle would occasion." [52]

In Richmond, Secretary Seddon was issuing an order relieving Humphrey Marshall from command in western Virginia, and assigning his position to William Preston.[53] But more important was the telegram Seddon put on the wire to Johnston directing him to proceed at once to Mississippi and take personal command of the situation that had become alarming since Grant had landed on the east bank of the great river.[54]

Already, in response to the clamor raised by Grierson's ride through the length of Mississippi, Johnston on May 5 had ordered Roddey into that state with the rather indefinite remainder of his own and Forrest's commands. As previously noted, the order sending Johnston to Mississippi bade him take with him, or to have follow him without delay, 3,000 good troops from Bragg's army, the same to be replaced by a like number of recently exchanged men who had been captured at Arkansas Post and who were on their way to Pemberton. Johnston's reply to Seddon of 6:40 P.M. will be given exactly as he wrote it as an important part of the picture of May 9: "Your dispatch of this morning received. I shall go immediately, although unfit for field service." [55] (No chance would there be for the conference with Morgan that Hardee had urged, which Hardee doubtless regretted a few months later on the occasion of Morgan's great insubordination.)

By the time the ailing Johnston had begun to pack, uncertainty in Murfreesboro over Streight's fate had been dispelled by the passage through the lines of a copy of the *Chattanooga Rebel* for May 7, which some Southerner was doubtless more than eager to send northward. There was no delay on Rosecrans's part in sending the paper to Adjutant General Thomas, with a letter whose opening sentence suggested Halleck's tacit approval of Streight's venture: "I informed the General-in-Chief that I proposed to send out an expedition to cut the Georgia Railroad south of Dalton. . . ." Surely Streight, who before long would be en route to Libby, would have liked to add a qualifying clause to the sentence: "They were provided with pack animals, and mounted with the best we could furnish." [56]

"To cut the railroad south of Dalton!" Certainly the Confederates would have found even a temporary breaking of the rail line from Chattanooga to Atlanta discommoding. But they very likely had considerable stores amassed in Chattanooga; and they would still have had the route used heavily from the first days of the war, connecting Bragg's actual base with Richmond by way of Knoxville and Lynchburg, as the venerable Adjutant General of the Army and others in Washington must have observed.[57]

CHAPTER VIII

ROSECRANS OUTMANEUVERS BRAGG

Frequently I have great trouble in making out your exact meaning, owing to the haste or imperfect manner in which dispatches are written or copied. *Granger to Rosecrans*

JUST WHAT did Rosecrans mean when he ended his telegram to Stanton on May 8 with the encouraging pronouncement that he would soon be ready to try dealing with the enemy in his front? The War Secretary had not been goading him; he had in fact not even made a quiet, apologetic inquiry. He had merely sent Rosecrans the same telegram that had gone to other department commanders and to the Northern governors to keep them in good cheer in spite of the bad news in the papers about Hooker and Chancellorsville. While the telegram candidly stated that the principal operation had failed, it reported that Hooker was safely back over the Rappahannock with an army not a third of which had actually been engaged. Thus the readers of his messages could see that in spite of a most humiliating defeat there had been no great disaster. Stanton, however, did not let the matter rest there; he wanted it to be believed that something had actually been accomplished besides the rescue of an army that had launched an offensive stroke intended to wreck an inferior enemy, or at least force it to make a significant retreat from the strong position in which he had for a number of months been barring the road to Richmond. So Stanton pronounced Stoneman's cavalry operation toward the Confederate capital "a brilliant success." In concluding, the Secretary went even further: he planted a sanguine hope for the future. "The Army of the Potomac will speedily resume offensive operations." [1]

There is little evidence that Rosecrans ever felt that his actions were open to just criticism and that the High Command had been lenient and indulgent toward him. But he may have felt that Stanton's concluding sentence posed the question: "What about the Army of the Cumberland?" It would be to his credit if he had a twinge of conscience.

If thoughts that flitted through Rosecrans's mind are important, so too are those that passed through Bragg's. What judgment of his adversary had he formed during Rosecrans's long stay at Murfreesboro? He had not read Rosecrans's boastful statements about pushing the Confederates to the wall when once he started from Nashville; he had not seen that delightful expression to Halleck's chief of staff when arguing the virtues of iron pontoons over wooden ones that required caulking—that after he moved he "did not want to stop and tinker." Though Bragg had never read such pronouncements, it was natural that he retreated from the battlefield near Murfreesboro not only with a mind burdened by the thought of his heavy losses but with the belief that the Federals were capable of prompt and energetic pursuit. Certainly a change had already taken place in his thinking when, finding that he was not being followed, he reversed his march and returned to Shelbyville and other advantageous positions. Knowing as we do that Bragg could swing from optimism to pessimism or back again with equal facility, it is not surprising to find him indulging in thoughts of more than harassing Rosecrans and his communications. Johnston, aware certainly of Bragg's temperament, was probably prepared for the ending of a message sent him at his Chattanooga headquarters on February 25, "I have strong hopes of breaking the enemy lines soon." [2]

Yet, in spite of his increase in strength, such ambitious thoughts could hardly have been a day-by-day matter with Bragg; and Johnston, on his part, could hardly have expected any offensive stroke of magnitude when, in early March, apprehensive because of Grant's persistent efforts at Vicksburg, he started out for Mississippi, where he felt his presence had become necessary. Mobile, however, was the limit of his journey, for a telegram received there on March 12 turned him back with instructions to take personal command in Middle Tennessee, so that Bragg might come to Richmond for a conference. What thoughts were stirring in the minds of the Confederate High Command is another mystery; but on reaching Tullahoma, Johnston found that Bragg was at the bedside of his wife, critically ill in Winchester. A telegram on March 19 informed Seddon of the fact, and added: "The country is becoming practicable. Should the enemy advance, General Bragg will be indispensable here." However disappointed the Secretary must have been at the impossibility of a conference with Bragg, there was reason for satisfaction; the tone of Johnston's dispatch suggested that there had been a turn in the feeling toward Bragg by his subordinates. It was, it may be recalled, the dissatisfaction among higher officers of the Army of Tennessee which had caused Richmond to order Johnston from Mississippi to Tullahoma on January 22. Weeks were to pass before the Davis-Johnston quarrel—in which the President showed an uncompromising self-righteous strain, and the general revealed himself as petulant—was to burst forth. Though there had been misunderstandings from the early days of the war, with some disapproval of Johnston by Davis, the January order that had sent him to Tullahoma was clear recognition of his merit as a higher commander. And as Davis himself had been a supporter of Bragg when others were heaping abuse upon him, Johnston's March telegram should have pleased him, even if it did not actually give the warming feeling of having been right when others had criticized Bragg.[3]

Though drying ground obviously made Johnston expect the advance of blue-dressed columns, Beatty, five days after Johnston's dispatch, was writing in his diary a strange entry: "There are no indications of an advance. The army, however, is well equipped, in good spirits, and prepared to move at an hour's notice. Its confidence in Rosecrans is boundless, and whatever it may be required to do, it will, I doubt not, do with a will." Beatty's own brigade had been building a strong earth fort at Murfreesboro—certainly not an invaluable item, but one requiring far more "tinkering" than the keeping of wooden pontoons in order. When visiting Beatty on April 10 Rosecrans expressed pleasure with the fort and had even queried Beatty as to whether he did not think it looked like "remaining." To Beatty's reply that a small force could hold the work and that he wished the enemy would attack, instead of compelling the army to go farther south, Rosecrans had replied that he wished the same. Only a few days previously the sharp-eyed, and at times restless and bored Beatty had indicated that Murfreesboro had become quite a base of supplies. In a single stack there were 40,000 boxes of hard bread, while flour, pork, vinegar, and molasses were in such quantities as he had never seen before.[4]

Supplies well forward would be a necessity when the Army of the Cumberland started to advance, but the day after Rosecrans had asked the rather strange question of Beatty, Bragg's assistant inspector general ended a letter to "Dearest Friend":

> We are not expecting a fight soon. General Rosecrans is badly frightened. Such cavalry as we have here never has been known before. Our little Texan, General Van Dorn [actually a Mississippian by birth], is playing the wild work with the Yankees with his cavalry. Forrest, Morgan, and Wheeler are equally as good.

This letter, with its reflection on Rosecrans, its praise of the South's cavalry leaders, its description of an impressive review of Bragg's army on the morning that had just ended, and its account of the serenade being given to Generals Hardee and Breckinridge by a band that played so beautifully that the writer had to lay down his pen occasionally in order to listen, was, however, destined not to reach the lady for whom it was composed. It was in one of the mail bags that the Federals seized at Simmesport—and on June 3 Banks sent it to Army Headquarters. War being the indelicate business that it is, Halleck no doubt read it with interest and no feeling of guilt, though the editors of the *Official Records,* if the letter came to them in the original envelope, dealt unkindly with history by not revealing the identity of "Dearest Friend." [5]

Since we have turned back in time from May 9 when the last chapter ended in order to round out the picture, something more may now be added as to what was transpiring within the enemy lines during the month of April.

Doubtless it was to spread encouragement and good cheer in Texas that "Dearest Friend" was told that 60,000 infantry had "marched in the grandest order before that old chieftain"—General J. E. Johnston. But Washington was saved the trouble of deciding how much of an exaggeration this was, for a letter forwarded coincidentally by Banks that had been written by Captain C. F. Sanders, and which also was in the Simmesport acquisition, put Bragg's infantry at from 35,000 to 40,000, the first figure being very close to his present-for-duty strength in foot soldiers on April 10. In spite of the impressive review that morning the "old chieftain" was in a depressed state of mind on the 11th and for some days thereafter. To Simon Buckner—who, it will be recalled, was still at Mobile—he telegraphed that intelligence from Louisville, Nashville, and Memphis indicated that Grant's army might join that of Rosecrans. The beginning of such a movement could, Johnston said, be discovered by Pemberton; in case it took place, he had been instructed to return Stevenson's division to Bragg. Buckner himself was alerted to entrain infantry as expeditiously as possible, for he could get troops to Tennessee more speedily than Pemberton. While Johnston's alarm was based solely on Federal talk—probably growing out of the fact that Grant's Vicksburg operations had, up to the moment, netted little—Pemberton at Vicksburg had been completely deceived. It was, in fact, on this same April 11 that he reported to Johnston that a large part of Grant's army would reinforce Rosecrans. This erroneous belief, it will be remembered, actually caused him to start troops to the aid of Bragg, which were, however, stopped en route and returned to Mississippi.[6]

At this time Johnston had by no means reached the view about the difficulty of a Federal invasion of East Tennessee that he revealed in his previously quoted dispatch to Maury on May 8. He was so alarmed, in fact, that he telegraphed to Cooper that indications in Kentucky pointed to an early invasion of East Tennessee. It could, he thought, be forestalled by a thrust into Kentucky by troops from East Tennessee in cooperation with some furnished by Humphrey Marshall (still an independent commander at that time in the Abingdon region). Johnston's fear was not limited by what was transpiring in Kentucky. Accepting Pemberton's erroneous appraisal, he made the categorical statement, "Intelligence from Mississippi is that Grant is re-enforcing Rosecrans strongly, probably with his main body." [7]

It is likely that one cannot exaggerate the relief that it was to Richmond to think that the Federals, who had given up efforts to take Vicksburg in the summer of 1862, had again decided that the great bastion was too strong for them. But disillusionment, of course, came rather promptly; and even while the cheering thought prevailed it must have been mixed with the fear that an attack against Chattanooga and Atlanta with great weight could be devastating. Here there enters the question whether even Joe Johnston, a former quartermaster general of the United States Army, realized the multiplication of logistical difficulties that would confront the Federals if they increased greatly their force in Middle Tennessee.

Those 40,000 boxes of hardtack, as well as the mountainous accumulation of flour, pork, vinegar, and molasses that had awed

Beatty, makes one wonder as to the supplies possessed by the Confederate army. But before looking at that question, one should not dismiss the Murfreesboro stocks with a wave of the hand and the remark that the North was rich. More was involved than protecting 220 miles of railroad and guarding transports on a river. The men of the Army of the Cumberland came from the states which were full of opposition to the war. As supplies came forward, there went back home a flood of soldier mail combating the antiwar spirit and denouncing men like Vallandigham. These letters, Beatty wrote on April 10, had done much good, but he gave a peculiar explanation to his own failure to participate in the campaign: "A Republican has not much need to write. His patriotism is taken for granted." [8] Perhaps he merely meant that the voices of ardent "War Democrats" could do the most good. But be that as it may, as one thinks of soldiers unloading and stacking provisions one should not forget that they were also sending letters to editors and to their families that would prevent a betrayal of the army by the home front.

The South never had the highly efficient quartermaster and commissary departments that sustained the Northern Army, but just as Jefferson Davis kept a tight hand on military operations, so he tried to keep posted about the supply situation. (Whether he attempted to institute proper reforms is a question beyond the compass of this history.) To this end his military aide, Colonel William Preston Johnston, was dispatched on March 12 upon an inspection trip to Atlanta, Montgomery, and Tullahoma. The emissary's duties at the latter point were set forth in a single sentence: he was to make himself "acquainted generally with the condition of the army." In just a little over a month Johnston was back writing a report at Richmond, supplementing it with documents from various responsible officers. While he pronounced Bragg's army well clad and armed, of good discipline, high courage, and possessed of capacity for endurance, and living with little sickness in camps well laid out and clean, his words about subsistence were disillusioning and pessimistic.

Only a little beef supplemented the monotonous ration of corn bread and half a pound of bacon. Yet the President's aide reported that he had heard little grumbling. Perhaps it was natural that hope or optimism should burn brighter in the breast of bishop-general Polk than in those of other high officers. By pushing trains up toward Fort Henry, Polk thought that much more in the way of supplies could be obtained than from the three counties then being relied upon; if that were done the present line could be held for three more months. That the haul would be long and that there would be danger of interception must have been considered; but Polk may have been inclined to minimize a point made by Colonel Johnston: "One obstacle is the inability to use Confederate money to advantage." State money would be more advantageous, Colonel Johnston said, while a gallon of molasses would bring forth eight pounds of bacon where "neither force nor persuasion" could obtain it. It might, Johnston wrote, even coax it from behind the Union lines. The prospect with regard to beef was, however, gloomy. Both General Johnston and General Bragg thought that beef would in large part have to be obtained in far-off Kentucky under the protection of raids.

"Our battle against want and starvation is greater than against our enemies"—such was the description of the situation in a report that the Atlanta commissary of subsistence sent on April 4 to Colonel Johnston. The people of Middle Tennessee were, he thought, devoted to the South, and Richmond would doubtless think his own heart was in the right place when he said that a further retreat of Bragg's army would leave them "to the mercies of the foul invader." Among other things, the Confederate money that was being given them for supplies would be worthless. The commissary major should have been embarrassed in reporting that "considerable quantities of supplies" had been stolen during a two- or three-week period when some dozen of his eighteen warehouses were left unguarded by the provost marshal, and he himself had not hired watchmen. Perhaps the most interesting of his revelations was that he had been approached by persons eager to set up a procedure to get supplies out of the North by an offer of cotton.[9]

April was ending as Joe Johnston in a dispatch to Seddon ruled out the possibility of getting supplies out of Kentucky in exchange for bacon. The haul from any railroad held by the Confederates was too great; it was also only at great risk that small quantities of meat were being procured from behind the Federal lines. There was still an abundance of corn in the region to the southwest, but the haul was long, and Dodge's advance, of which he learned that day (April 28) from Forrest, he interpreted not as a blind to cover anything like Streight's raid but as a thrust into a region of potential supplies. About the only cheerful note in the Johnston dispatch was that sugar could still bring out bacon.

More was at stake than subsistence. If Bragg were forced from

Middle Tennessee, it would be very difficult to defend East Tennessee "against an enterprising enemy." [10] But ill though he was, Johnston, as has been seen, was soon to be more cheerful: the Federal effort against his communications had ended most happily for the Confederates; and Rosecrans was showing no signs of stirring from his Murfreesboro lines.

On May 9, the very day that Rosecrans received the copy of the *Chattanooga Daily Rebel* with the account of Streight's capture, he read in a letter from Montgomery Meigs the shattering sentence, "The rebels will never be conquered by sitting in their front."

For the quartermaster general to criticize the operations of a field army commander is certainly irregular. But the long letter that Meigs wrote to Rosecrans on May 1 grew in general out of Rosecrans's continual demand for more horses, which Meigs knew were difficult to procure of required standard, and which greatly added to the cost of the cavalry arm, a consideration he could not dismiss, though Rosecrans might. Using figures that the general had himself furnished Halleck—which shows close collaboration between different Washington offices—Meigs wrote that since December 1, no fewer than 18,450 horses and 14,607 mules had been sent to Rosecrans. This, Meigs thought, was a large supply, and if his figures were correct, Rosecrans had on March 23 a total of 43,023 animals—19,164 horses—or about an animal for every two men. The supply of new animals was, however, perhaps not the main point. Rosecrans had evacuated over 9,000 horses as unserviceable, and had just reported that a quarter or even a third of those he had were worn out. Not unnaturally Meigs concluded that the horses were overworked, underfed, neglected, or abused, and he pointed out that not in the entire war had cavalry decided a battle other than a skirmish. The 126 cavalry regiments then in Federal service had killed, he said in concluding, ten of their own horses for every enemy animal they had eliminated. When he asserted that infantry could often be employed where cavalary was being used, Meigs was merely anticipating what Sheridan did—after convincing Meade of the soundness of his idea—when he took command a year later of the cavalry of the Army of the Potomac. In two weeks' time he nursed back into condition a mounted corps which had been run down through constant outpost and other duties by an army commander who did not properly understand its function.[11]

Much to his credit, Rosecrans replied very temperately, without any suggestion that Meigs had intruded into a realm outside his proper office. (There was no trace of the indignation that was in his telegram to Halleck sent two months previously, in reply to the dispatch that a vacant position as major general in the regular army awaited the field commander who first won a decisive and important victory.) Correct though he might have been when he said in concluding that he knew he was "not mistaken in saying that this great army would gain more from 10,000 effective cavalry than from 20,000 infantry," he ignored a large part of the question. The government, from a pure dollars-and-cents standpoint, might prefer to furnish the infantry, which Rosecrans clearly admitted could do the work.[12]

Soon there came a series of nudges from Hurlbut. Quite naturally, the commander of the Sixteenth Corps, to which Dodge's force belonged, thought that the wholehearted aid that had been given to Streight would be reciprocated. Out of close touch with Grant below and behind Vicksburg, he telegraphed to Rosecrans on May 12 that his chief had sent word that the Confederates were expecting aid from Tullahoma. After stating that he was sending sixteen regiments down the river, he said, "If Johnston is permitted to throw a force on Grant, the consequences may be disastrous." Five days later the Memphis general wired to Rosecrans news of Grant's victory at Raymond, and the entry of his cavalry into Jackson. Johnston himself, according to Hurlbut, had reached Jackson on the 13th—which was correct, as was the statement that the reinforcements which had already arrived were from Charleston. Heavier forces were expected from Tennessee and Virginia; should they come, they would be too strong for Grant, inasmuch as the Vicksburg garrison numbered not fewer than 35,000, a figure which Hurlbut said could be relied upon since it had just been brought by his best scout—and it was indeed near the truth. Realizing that the Confederates had the advantage of interior lines, Hurlbut told Rosecrans that it was the enemy intention to crush Grant and then turn back on him. As if to spur Rosecrans with the knowledge that other commanders were accomplishing things, Hurlbut ended his dispatch, "Banks has taken Alexandria." As the next midnight was approaching, Hurlbut wired a third time: Grant had certainly taken Jackson; but Mobile papers of the 14th were saying that heavy reinforcements from South Carolina, Georgia, and Tennessee were on the way to Johnston.[13]

Gently, very gently indeed, Lincoln entered the controversy with

Courtesy Library of Congress

MAJOR GENERAL STEPHEN A. HURLBUT

a telegram to Rosecrans on the 27th: "Have you anything from Grant? Where is Forrest's headquarters?" Rosecrans replied the same night that according to the latest news Forrest had that day moved his headquarters from Spring Hill to a crossroads eighteen miles southwest of Murfreesboro. The most recent news about Grant was in a Rebel dispatch the night before: Johnston had crossed the Big Black with 20,000 men. As if to allay any disturbing effect of this news, Rosecrans said that the enemy was not jubilant at two o'clock that afternoon—according to a report of Rosecrans's provost marshal who had talked with Bragg's chief surgeon. The answer merely brought another message from Washington the next day, restrained yet showing apprehension by the President: "I would not push you to any rashness, but I am very anxious that you do your utmost, short of rashness, to keep Bragg from getting off to help Johnston against Grant." The reply was prompt and short: "Dispatch received. I will attend to it." [14]

One would like to know just what thoughts this telegram stirred. But it has already been told how vigorously Halleck entered the picture when Grant's dispatch of May 28, saying he must have some reinforcements from outside his department, reached Washington on June 2. The telegram he sent to Rosecrans was in the temperate tone proper for a General in Chief, but its ending put the cards on the table: "If you can do nothing yourself, a portion of your troops must be sent to Grant's relief." The master of deceptive and ambiguous sentences had no special trouble handling this new urging, and a sentence of his reply has already been quoted: "The time appears now nearly ripe, and we have begun a movement, which, with God's blessing, will give us some good results." While Burnside's Ninth Corps was halted in its advance toward East Tennessee and hurried to Vicksburg under Major General Parke, and while Herron in Missouri pushed his veteran division in forced marches to embark for the same place, Rosecrans's army was left untouched.[15]

Uneasiness as well as doubt about the general must have mounted in Washington as days passed with no word of anything significant transpiring in Middle Tennessee. On June 11—ten weeks after Beatty had recorded that the Army of the Cumberland was well equipped and prepared to move on an hour's notice, Halleck wired to Rosecrans forthrightly: "I deem it my duty to repeat to you the great dissatisfaction felt here at your inactivity. There seems to be no doubt that a part of Bragg's force has gone to Johnston." The General in Chief was surely not depending solely on information that Grant had sent or upon his mild plea of May 6 which had been telegraphed from Memphis on the 12th, "Should not General Rosecrans at least make a demonstration of advancing?" Looking across the lines for the actual situation, we find Hardee wiring to Davis on May 27, "Breckinridge, with greater part of his division, has left for Mississippi." (To take its place another division would, Hardee said, be immediately organized, but he did not specify whether other divisions would be levied upon and therefore depleted, or whether new conscripts would be employed.) [16]

A long telegram from Rosecrans to Halleck was on the wire before the day had ended. He reminded Halleck of his statement that an adequate cavalry force was a condition of success—which brings up the important question of the actual mission assigned Rosecrans, a matter to be considered later. He had not lost a moment in mounting dismounted cavalry; in addition, the Fifth Iowa Cavalry, ordered up from Fort Donelson, had arrived that day, and the First Wisconsin would be on hand on the 13th. Preliminary infantry moves were about complete, and he was preparing to strike a blow that would "tell."

To enlighten the General in Chief on how differently matters were viewed in his army than in Washington, Rosecrans reported on the vote upon three questions he had submitted to corps and division commanders. To the question: "Do you, from your best information, think the enemy materially weakened in our front?" he had received eleven negative and six affirmative answers, in which the enemy weakening was put at 10,000 men. To the question whether the army could advance "with reasonable prospect of fighting a great and successful battle," four subordinates had answered yes, with doubts; thirteen had replied negatively. The simpler, but crucial question, whether they thought an advance "advisable" at the present time, had not brought a single affirmative vote; all seventeen queried officers had said no.

It was bad enough that Rosecrans had abdicated as a commanding general and resorted to balloting by officers, many of whom doubtless did not want to give up the comfortable conditions under which they were living. But almost unbelievable was the statement: "Not one thinks an advance advisable until Vicksburg's fate is determined." Rosecrans's subordinates were arrogating to themselves the role and responsibility of the High Command; and in addition they were coolly shrugging off the possibility that success at Vicksburg might depend in part upon a strong move by the Army of the Cumberland. Lincoln clearly thought so, and it may be recalled that he believed that the Army of the Potomac had lost battles because commanders had failed to get all their men into the fight—either from timidity or from ineptitude. As a matter of fact, Parke was expected at Vicksburg on the day Rosecrans telegraphed; Herron had already arrived from Missouri. The departure of the Ninth Corps must have been well known at Murfreesboro, and with ample time to read the newspapers the voting generals should also have been aware of Herron's move. Thus the fate of Vicksburg was already decided unless Johnston succeeded in building up a large and effective force that could raise the siege; and if he did that, part of the force would have to come from Bragg. (That Gardner, shut up in Port Hudson by Banks, could not contribute to a relieving force was certainly known.) Even if this had not been the case, it was not the business of Rosecrans's officers to say, "Don't strike here until the Vicksburg matter is settled."

After reminding Halleck that it was a great military maxim not to fight two battles on the same day—thus clearly lining himself up with his subordinates—Rosecrans concluded by asserting that he must have such ground that when he said, "Forward," his word would inspire conviction and confidence where both were currently wanting.[17] Recalling what both Horace Porter and Beatty had written about the army's willingness to follow him, here is revealed in Rosecrans another strange weakness.

The obvious answer to Rosecrans's citation of a military maxim did not escape Halleck, and in his reply the next day he stated that while the quoted maxim about two battles in one day might apply to a single army, it did not to two armies such as his and Grant's. The General in Chief hurled back at Rosecrans another maxim: "Councils of war never fight." Assuming that Rosecrans had reported correctly, and that none of his subordinates—including George Thomas—thought an advance should be made pending the outcome at Vicksburg, Rosecrans, however, had the High Command at a disadvantage, if they considered the question of a replacement. The authorities at Washington would not, Halleck said, make Rosecrans fight against his will. Though he had, quite as Rosecrans had wished, often advised caution and patience on the part of the government, after six months of inactivity on Rosecrans's part it was not strange that the government's patience was "pretty well exhausted." Halleck was reduced to making a minor suggestion: if Rosecrans did not deem it prudent to risk a general battle with Bragg, why could he not do something to harass his opponent, or make demonstrations that would prevent his sending more reinforcements to Johnston? [18]

Even while Halleck was telegraphing to Rosecrans, Garfield may have been at work on an estimate of the situation for his chief, and the long document that came from his pen must be rated highly. Whether it had been requested is a natural question. The Rosecrans telegram to Halleck of the 11th practically rules out an affirmative answer. It seems unlikely that the telegram—which must have been read by Garfield—pleased him any more than it did the General in Chief. One recalls that Garfield had not always been a staff officer, but had had a respectable experience as a responsible commander who had had to make some hard decisions.

Actually, five, rather than three, questions had been submitted to Rosecrans's subordinates, and Garfield stated that the answers were not categorical. One officer, for instance, who thought that Bragg's command had been reduced by 10,000 men, did not consider that it had been "materially weakened." On the question whether an *immediate* advance should be made by the army, there had—according to Garfield's tabular compilation—been two abstainers, though all voters had cast negative ballots. On the related but different question whether an *early* advance was advisable, only two officers had committed themselves—both unfavorably. (In his report to Halleck, when he replaced the two questions by a single question not identical with either, Rosecrans had tampered with the truth.) In giving the reasons that had been urged against an advance "at the present time," Garfield included not one mentioned by Rosecrans: a failure in Middle Tennessee would have disastrous effects on lines of communication and on the politics in the loyal states. Entirely neglected was the fact that the long sojourn of the Army of the Cumberland at Murfreesboro had already had an effect both North and South. Stout-hearted Unionists must have often been more emphatic even than Bragg's assistant inspector general when he said to his Texas friend: "General Rosecrans is badly frightened."

The analysis by Garfield of Bragg's strength revealed full knowledge of his weakening through sending aid to Johnston in Mississippi. (In view of Sheridan's past performance, as well as his future career, it is not surprising to find in Garfield's report that Sheridan had been taking great pains to collect evidence as to the enemy force, which, in total, he put lower than Garfield did.) After setting forth the figures for the Federal army, with the elimination of all officers as well as men on special duty, and likewise the garrisons for eight places —including 2,500 efficient men and 2,394 convalescents to be left at Murfreesboro—Rosecrans would have 65,137 bayonets and sabers to throw against Bragg's 41,680 men. As lines of communication would lengthen, and since Bragg held prepared positions, the disparity cannot be looked upon as excessive, even though it was substantial. It is also to be recalled that in spite of difficult features of terrain, there was nonetheless opportunity for maneuver.

Real courage on the part of the chief of staff was required for him to write bluntly: "The Government and the War Department believe that this army ought to move upon the enemy; *the army desires it, and the country is anxiously hoping for it.*" (Emphasis supplied.) It was not strange that, having said it, Garfield appeased his chief by writing that he had been wise to wait until his army was massed and his cavalry mounted. Concentration of the mobile army, Garfield continued, could be accomplished within twenty-four hours. While he admitted that the Federal cavalry was not equal in numbers to that of the enemy, he pronounced it "greatly superior in efficiency and morale." (It would seem that Garfield could also have stated that Rosecrans's cavalry had greater fire power than Bragg, and fire power, rather than numbers, could be the real determining factor.) It is difficult not to believe that Garfield looked with disillusioning disfavor upon Rosecrans's council of war when he concluded that an immediate advance with all available forces was advisable.[19]

When did Captain Sanders's intercepted letter from Tullahoma reach Washington? No positive answer to this interesting question seems possible, but inasmuch as Banks had forwarded it more than a week after he had invested Port Hudson one would expect that it had been read by Halleck by the middle of June. That letter, written two months previously, had pictured a Confederate army in good health and spirits, and confident of success in any engagement—and one was expected soon if the weather continued favorable. But when the letter was read, Halleck knew that the 35,000 to 40,000 infantry of which Sanders spoke had been further weakened by detachments; and he was probably aware of the fact that cavalry had been sent from Tennessee to Mississippi. (Garfield said that it had been clearly ascertained that two brigades had gone from Van Dorn's old corps.)

In Washington patience with Rosecrans continued to wear thin, and none of the moderation of tone that characterized Halleck's dispatch of June 12 was in that of the 16th, which was perhaps the curtest he ever sent to an army commander: "Is it your intention to make an immediate movement forward? A definite answer, yes or no, is required." Four and a half hours later—at 6:30 P.M.—Rosecrans answered: "In reply to your inquiry, if immediate means to-night or to-morrow, no. If it means as soon as all things are ready, say five days, yes." [20]

Probably Army Headquarters wrote down on its mental calendar June 21 as the day that would finally see a movement against Bragg. Actually, the 21st merely brought another telegram from Rosecrans, with further discussion of military maxims, ending: "We ought to fight here if we have a strong prospect of winning a decisive battle over the opposing force, and upon this ground I shall act. I shall be careful not to risk our last reserve without strong grounds to expect success." [21]

Who had told him that the Army of the Cumberland was the last reserve? On June 9 Pleasonton's cavalry of the Army of the Potomac had inflicted a humiliating defeat on Stuart's celebrated horsemen at Beverly Ford and Brandy Station. Though the capture of Winchester by Ewell's corps of Lee's Army of Northern Virginia soon followed, and excitement rose in the North because of the Confederate thrust toward the Potomac under cover of the Blue Ridge Mountains, June 21 saw the strong Army of the Potomac in positions to cover Washington and ready to move farther northward if need be. In addition to the tightening hold that Banks had on Port Hudson, Grant at Vicksburg was not talking as if there might be failure. When on the 22nd it looked as if Joe Johnston might be moving to the relief of Pemberton, no questions were submitted by Grant for the decision of a council of war. Sherman was merely informed of the situation and told that he would command the entire force that would meet such a threat, while a note to Parke had the delightful ending, "we want to whip Johnston at least 15 miles off, if possible." [22]

But at last, at long last, the desired news came to Washington from Rosecrans, and Halleck may have read it before he had lighted his first cigar on June 24: "The army begins to move at 3 o'clock this morning." As the telegram was marked 2:10 A.M., there was not much time for miscarriage of plans, and leading elements should have been finishing their breakfasts when Rosecrans laid down a pen worthy of preservation as a historic item.[23]

No general written order for the operation was issued. Though time had certainly not been wanting, if one takes a long view, some details may not have been fully worked out until the last minute. Secrecy also may have been an element; but here one must note that alerting orders prescribing that troops have twelve days' rations of bread, coffee, sugar, and salt, together with six days' pork or bacon, with fresh beef for an equal period, alerted every man that a movement was imminent, even though corps commanders were not taken into the army commander's confidence until time for starting was only a matter of hours away. Having described a preliminary movement on June 23 by Gordon Granger, commanding now a three-division "reserve corps" organized on June 8, Rosecrans said in his report that corps commanders met at his headquarters on the evening of the 23rd, "when the plan of the movement was explained to them, and each received written plans for his part"—which he then outlined.

It will be recalled that in his report on the Battle of Stones River, Rosecrans claimed that he had called his corps commanders together on the evening of December 30, 1862, and had gone over with them his plan of attack for the next day—forestalled by Bragg's heavy assault against the Federal right early the next morning. Likewise it will be recalled that McCook, though asked to confirm Rosecrans's statement, vigorously denied it: he had gone to headquarters solely from a sense of duty, along with Stanley, and had found no general officer there except Rosecrans. More than that, McCook challenged the accuracy of the conversation the army commander had written into his report. With regard to the meeting on June 23rd, history seems to repeat itself. McCook spoke in his report only of having received "verbal orders and instructions"—with no allusion whatever to written directions. Crittenden, back in command of the Twenty-first Corps—Wood having reverted to commander of the corps's first division—launched his report with the statement that he moved in obedience to orders received at 2:15 A.M. on the 24th. From the report by George Thomas one can infer nothing one way or the other as to any meeting and orders on the evening of the 23rd; but the move made by Thomas's third division under Brigadier John M. Brannan on the 23rd from Triune to Salem was, Brannan explicitly stated, in accordance with orders from Granger, and his march the next day as part of McCook's column must have been directed either by the latter or by army headquarters. Stanley—one of whose cavalry divisions was under Brigadier General Robert B. Mitchell, last seen as Nashville commander, while the second division was under the controversial Brigadier General John B. Turchin—says nothing whatever in his report about a meeting of corps commanders on the evening of the 23rd. Finally, Granger speaks of instructions for the preliminary moves on the 23rd reaching him at Triune at 2:00 A.M. of that day, and says that orders for the 24th reached him during the preceding night at Rover.[24]

No subordinate except McCook set down the objective with which the army marched. And, either because it had been poorly explained at such meeting as may have occurred, or because he had listened inattentively, McCook described the purpose very differently than did Rosecrans in his report. The commander of the Twentieth Corps stated that he was ordered to put his command "in motion to co-operate and take part with the other corps of the Army of the Cumberland in an attack on the rebel army under General Bragg, posted in force at Shelbyville and Wartrace." According to Rosecrans, this was precisely what he meant not to do. He had set out, he wrote in his report of July 24, with the determination of rendering the Confederate entrenchments useless; by turning their right he would force "a battle on our own ground or drive them on a disadvantageous line of retreat." His movements from the beginning indicate that such indeed was his intention.

Turning the Confederate right was rendered difficult by the terrain, though there was relatively easy access to the left. The right, however, was more weakly held than the left. According to Rosecrans, Hardee's corps, at and in front of Wartrace, was generally estimated "by intelligent rebels and Union men" at about 12,000 infantry and artillery, while Polk's corps at Shelbyville was put at 18,000. On his right at McMinnville, Bragg had cavalry, just as he had on his left at Columbia and Spring Hill (Van Dorn's old corps, now under Forrest). Remembering the exorbitant figures that Rosecrans had sent to Washington about the hostile mounted strength, one is a little surprised to find that Bragg had "probably 8,000 effective cavalry." Though it looks as if the strengths he set down were what Rosecrans expected to meet, one cannot be certain. They may have been figures given him after he had, by skillful maneuvering which has won high praise, forced the Army of Tennessee to abandon its position and retire across the Tennessee River and to its base at Chattanooga.

Four gaps led through the considerable ridge that covered Bragg's army in its position north of Duck River—"a deep, narrow stream, with but few fords or bridges," which could, of course, be an embarrassment to an army placed where Bragg's was. Counting from the east they were: Hoover's Gap, on the pike from Murfreesboro to Manchester; Liberty Gap, on the road to Wartrace; Bellbuckle, farther south and threaded by the railroad as well as by a wagon road; and Guy's Gap, on the Murfreesboro-Shelbyville pike. Westward from

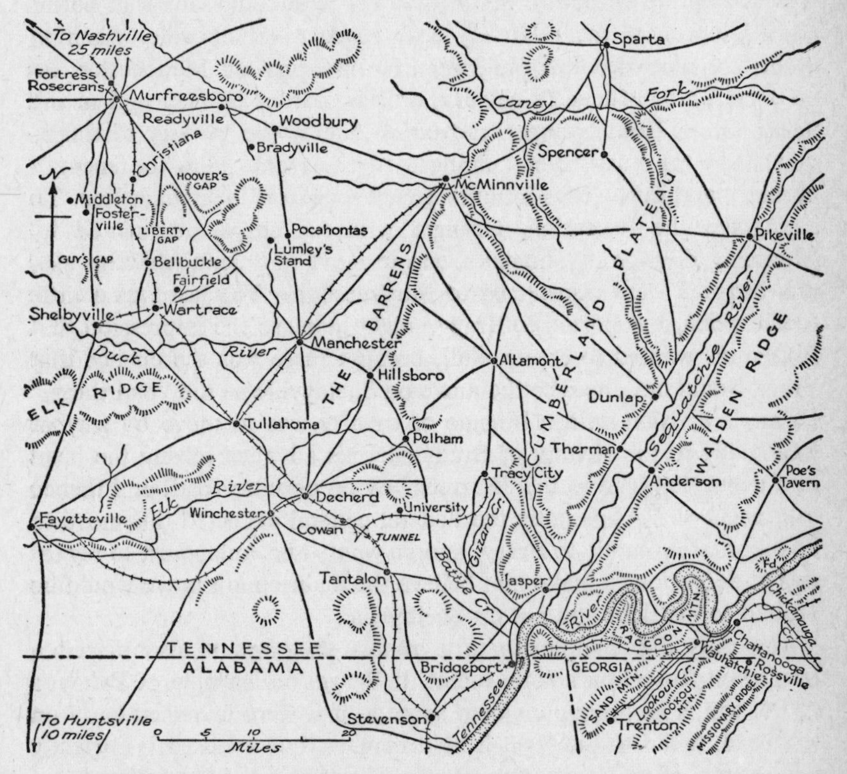

THE REGION OF ROSECRANS'S ADVANCE ON TULLAHOMA

the latter were roads that led to Shelbyville, which avoided passes and had few defiles. Rosecrans knew that the hills flanking the gaps were held by enemy covering forces, and not so far from the main bodies but that they could be rather quickly reinforced. Actually, some cavalry was holding Hoover's Gap, while a brigade of Cleburne's division of Hardee's corps held Liberty and Bellbuckle, with troops from Polk's corps outposting Guy's Gap. Rosecrans may have been indifferent to these terrain features when he spoke of pushing the enemy to the wall if he defeated him at Murfreesboro, but they loomed large in his thoughts once he had established himself there, for on January 11 he had said in a dispatch to Stanton, "The country is full of natural passes and fortifications, and demands superior forces to advance with any success." [25]

Deception as to his point of attack was what Rosecrans relied upon for success. He wished to plant in Bragg's mind the idea that he intended to follow the relatively easy roads to Shelbyville, when in reality he purposed throwing most of his army on Manchester. So on June 23rd, Mitchell's cavalry, detached from Stanley and acting under orders from Granger, moved on Shelbyville by way of Eagleville, with the mission of making a "furious attack on the enemy's cavalry" and driving his infantry guards back on their main line. To strengthen the deception, Granger with his corps, augmented by Brannan's division of Thomas's, was to move to Salem, while his sick and baggage were transferred to Murfreesboro. The last was a little touch which, if reported to Bragg, might increase the impression that Rosecrans wanted to create. Still, because there was the chance that Bragg would not appraise the move on Shelbyville as the "real thing," Palmer's division with a brigade of cavalry was to move by way of Readyville to the vicinity of Bradyville, his advance seizing the head of a defile that lead to the "Barrens" by an obscure road, and thence to Manchester. Apparently the Federal general expected this move to be reported promptly to Bragg, and he wanted his antagonist to regard this as deception to make him believe the main Union move would be around to his right and not on Shelbyville.

Not only did complexity lurk in this program, it also placed a hazard on Rosecrans's main intent. If Bragg, on learning of Palmer's move, which he probably would soon do if it were launched early on the 23rd, failed to interpret it as deception, but assessed it correctly as the start of the main Federal effort, in spite of the fact that it led through difficult country, he might be prepared for the intended thrust at Manchester. One need not ponder this too much, however, for on June 23 little, if anything, seems to have happened as intended.

Mitchell fell far short of driving the enemy cavalry and infantry guards back on "their main line." After a severe skirmish in and beyond Rover all he could do was compel retirement on a "strong force" at Unionville, whose pickets he felt. When he got the report that three brigades were entrenched one mile beyond the town, Mitchell rather naturally desisted—especially since he was sick himself. Surprising as it may seem, it was not until 3:00 P.M. of the 23rd that Palmer received preliminary orders from corps headquarters (that of Crittenden), and as he was camped at a considerable distance from Murfreesboro, whence the prescribed supplies for twelve days had to be drawn, the rest of the afternoon and the night were consumed merely in making preparations. It was 4:00 A.M. on the 24th when there came to Palmer a corps order marked 2:15 A.M. directing the move that Rosecrans indicated was to be made on the 23rd. Corps specified that Palmer was to march at 7:00 A.M., which was four hours after the starting time that Rosecrans had telegraphed to Washington. Thus in spite of what the Federal commander later wrote, Palmer gave Bragg no puzzle to unravel.[26]

As Rosecrans opened his campaign in full force, the sky opened in equal earnestness. "During the 24th and 25th it rained incessantly," Brannan wrote on the 28th. "June 26, rained nearly all day," was a comment by Stanley. Lovell Rousseau, still commanding one of Thomas's divisions, wrote on July 6, "It began to rain just as my division was being formed to march out of Murfreesboro on the 24th ultimo, and it has rained heavily every day since but one." Unimpressed or forgetful of any temporary letup, Crittenden recorded on July 13 that after commencing on the morning of June 24 it "rained incessantly for fifteen days." Though the main movements took place on pikes, with a minimum employment of dirt roads that quickly became all but impassable, there is no discounting the difficulty under which the campaign was carried on. Cooked rations were certainly soon exhausted, and no one not familiar with the problem can imagine the difficulties in distribution of rations in the form in which they then existed, or of their preparation for eating with the facilities possessed by the soldiers of the 1860's. Thus, to the hardships of mud and soaked camping ground, there must have often been added the debilitating effect of inadequate and poor food.[27]

One unit that got in a few road-hours before the torrents struck was Wilder's brigade of mounted infantry, of Reynolds's division of Thomas's corps, which left its camp six miles north of Murfreesboro sharp on the stroke of 3:00 A.M. of June 24, to be the leading element of the corps on the pike to Manchester. Wilder was seen in the last volume at Munfordville, where, before capitulating to the greatly superior force that Bragg had thrown around him, he insisted on proof of Bragg's numbers and in the dead of night was given a personal tour of the enveloping lines by no less a person than Simon Bolivar Buckner. Still a colonel, Wilder now commanded two Illinois and two Indiana regiments. During the winter and spring they were mounted, and on March 23 John Beatty told his diary: "Colonel Wilder expects to accomplish a great work with his mounted infantry. He is endeavoring to arm them with the Henry rifle, a gun which, with a slight twist of the wrist, will throw sixteen bullets in almost that many seconds. I have no doubt he will render his command efficient and useful, for he has wonderful energy and nerve, and is, besides, sensible and practical." [28]

As a matter of fact, the weapon with which Wilder's men rode southward in the still, dark hours of that June morning was not the low-powered Henry rifle, 1,200 of which had been purchased for use in the East as early as 1861 at $36 each (in contrast to the average cost of $10.69 at which the Springfield armory produced in 1864 no fewer than 276,200 of the muzzle-loading, but long-range and hard-hitting regular infantry rifles). The Hoosiers and the Prairie Staters had the seven-shot Spencer carbine, which, with the Spencer rifle, became the best known of the repeaters used in the war. Though the Spencer's power charge and bullet were heavier than those of the Henry, it was, as one authority puts it, in range and muzzle velocity "decidedly inferior to the rifle musket." The fewer number of rounds that its magazine carried, when compared with the Henry, was compensated for by the fact that the soldier could start a day's work with ten loaded magazines. Decreased range and hitting power were of little moment when firing lines were close together, but recent enthusiasts for the Spencer have not revealed a comprehensive grasp of the problems facing the ordnance department at the beginning of the war when they accuse General Ripley of stubborn opposition to progress and improvement. It was, it will be recalled, neither the Henry nor the Spencer that Rosecrans called for in November, 1862, and again in January, 1863, but the five-shot revolver-like Colt—a few of which had been supplied to the army as early as 1857 at $50 each, probably for experimental purposes. According to Stanton, Rosecrans had received all the Colts that could be purchased. Bankers in Wilder's home town of Greensburg, Indiana, had advanced funds upon the security of his note for the purchase of the Spencers, the men in his command agreeing to deductions from their pay to reimburse their commander, they, on their part, being ultimately repaid by the government. Dipping into his own pocket for the benefit of his men was nothing new to Wilder. Previous to this, according to his biographer, he had spent over $7,000 upon needy soldiers.[29]

When he had advanced seven miles beyond Murfreesboro, scouts sent ahead informed Wilder of the proximity of enemy pickets. Though he had at least six pieces of artillery in addition to shoulder arms unique in fire power, Wilder waited for the infantry to close up—quite as if he could take comfort in the presence of foot soldiers with hard-hitting weapons. Hostile fire greeted his resumed advance. The disputing pickets were driven back on their reserves in a grove upon a hill, and after energetic action had put this forward Confederate position in Wilder's control, he ordered his advance to push on speedily and prevent, if possible, the enemy from occupying fortifications which he learned had been constructed at the narrowest part of Hoover's Gap. The works were taken, and along with them a set of silk-embroidered colors that had been presented to the defending regiment—First Kentucky Confederate Infantry. Wilder also learned that a brigade of infantry was encamped two miles to the right, and by the time he had pushed on two miles to the end of the three-mile-long narrow gap, the long roll was heard from that direction. Wilder then prepared to hold the gap against the attack he was sure would come.

In their determined efforts to regain the all-important position that Wilder had seized, the Confederates struck not only with infantry; they used two batteries also. One of their guns, however, was soon dismounted, and the others were compelled to change position several times by the fire of the four 10-pounder rifled Rodmans of Captain Eli Lilly's Eighteenth Indiana Battery (two mountain howitzers with the Seventy-second Indiana in support were on a "hillock" also on the right of the gap). When on one occasion the attackers got very close, Lilly gave them a few rounds of double-shotted canister, while the Seventy-second Indiana "opened an enfilading fire upon them, which caused them to first fall to the ground to escape the tornado of death." Finding no cessation of the "leaden hail," the Confederates "crawled back as best they could" to the cover of the hills, and gave up their efforts against Wilder about the time that Reynolds arrived with two infantry brigades, one of which was so placed as to support and prolong Wilder's right.[30]

One might, or might not, infer from Wilder's words that his men were unusually well armed; but it seems strange that he does not even mention the Spencer in his report, especially since this was the first time the weapon was used in the West. One recalls that C. Clay Smith, in his report about his fight with Forrest west of Brentwood on March 25, spoke of the "five-shooters of the Second Michigan," and the rapidity with which the Burnside carbine could be loaded, as contributors to success. While Wilder gave great praise to his officers and men, he said not a word to indicate that eagerness for battle and élan were in any way attributable to confidence in the superiority of weapons. One might explain this by saying that, having armed his regiments in an irregular manner, Wilder did not want to leave an official record. But the old weapons of his regiments must have been turned in to Rosecrans's ordnance officer, Horace Porter, through whom ammunition, however it was financed, would also have to pass, and Porter was hardly a man to be bribed into silence.

Nor did Reynolds nor Thomas nor Rosecrans mention the Spencers in their reports, though one would think that they would have thought Washington would be pleased to learn of the field performance of the new weapon. It may be recalled that Rosecrans, when asking for more Colt revolving rifles, said that each one would add a new man to his command.

By the time that night had fallen on that long, dripping June 24 Liberty Gap was also in Union hands, the prize largely of the brigade of August Willich, himself not long back from the captivity which had followed his humiliating capture in the early hours of the Battle of Stones River. Unlike the advance upon Hoover's Gap, that upon Liberty had not been straight down the pike that led to it. Instead, Sheridan's division, keeping up the appearance of a move on Shelbyville, led McCook's corps down the main road to that town for a distance of nine miles, when it halted. Robert Johnson's division, following Sheridan, turned eastward after a march of six miles, to make the attack upon the gap, with Post's and Carlin's brigades of Jefferson C. Davis's division following close behind, so as to be ready to lend a hand. Soon the five companies of the Thirty-ninth Indiana Mounted Infantry covering Johnson encountered the enemy, and three captured Confederates who had been harvesting in the vicinity obligingly gave information about the forces holding the gap. Army headquarters were not long in knowing what was transpiring, for at 6:35

P.M. there came a message that McCook—riding with Johnson—had written at 5:15, which began, "We are in the act of driving the enemy from the Liberty Gap. It is a strong place. We will have it in half an hour. The Fifth and Fifteenth Arkansas are in the gap. Liddell is back at Bellbuckle." [31]

After Willich—whose prison experience had dulled neither his zest nor his tactical skill—had swept up a steep hill under heavy fire and captured one encampment with tables set for supper, Johnson reinforced him with two other regiments, and before night all the camps with the equipment accumulated for gracious living during six months of undisturbed occupancy were in Johnson's possession. But the enemy, reluctant to yield the position, were not entirely driven away until Johnson had committed Baldwin's brigade. After describing the deployment that that officer made of his four regiments, Johnson said in his report, "It was a pleasing sight to witness the promptness with which these regiments advanced."

The McCook dispatch to Garfield had said, "Sheridan has just come." The covering of that general's advance down the Shelbyville Pike had been in charge of the remaining five companies of the Thirty-ninth Mounted Indiana Infantry. Hostile pickets early encountered had been driven back "with scarcely any effort"; but when Sheridan halted at Christiana, partly to cover the march from the west of Brannan's division en route to Thomas on the Manchester Pike, he was assailed by Confederate sharpshooters and a section of guns. To the minor annoyance he made no reply, as he wished to conceal the strength of his force. After Brannan's column had arrived, Sheridan swung to the left, to encamp, as he put it, "at the little town of Millersburg, in the vicinity of Liberty Gap." [32]

The objective of Crittenden's corps, like that of Thomas, was Manchester from the start, but it moved by way of Bradyville. Considering the ruggedness of the road and the heavy rain, Crittenden seems to have made as much progress as possible with the divisions of Palmer and Wood, that of Van Cleve having been left at Murfreesboro as garrison for Fortress Rosecrans. When the day began, Manchester was also the objective of Turchin's division of Stanley's cavalry corps, though the move was to be roundabout through McMinnville. Upon learning in midmorning of Mitchell's troubles the day before, Stanley withdrew Minty's brigade from Turchin, and with it and a battery hastened to Mitchell's support. Before the forces had been united, Mitchell, however, had engaged and routed the enemy at Middleton. "The rain poured in torrents the entire night," was Stanley's comment. With McCook swinging over to the left, Rosecrans's effort to make Bragg think he was moving on Shelbyville had really devolved upon Granger, who that day reached Christiana.[33]

The 24th saw two interesting dispatches from Murfreesboro. One was from Garfield to John C. Van Duzer, the telegraph operator whom Grant had expelled from his department the preceding fall, and who was now in charge of the Nashville office. Said the chief of staff:

> The general commanding directs that no dispatches for the press be sent over the lines till further orders, and no military intelligence sent without authority from these headquarters. Communicate this order to all your subordinates.

While thus seeking to guard against leaks of information to conscienceless newspapers, Rosecrans sent to Halleck a report that should have delighted the Washington authorities. In an endorsement he said: "These facts were obtained by Dr. McGowan, a Union man of East Tennessee, whom Major-General Thomas sent for the special purpose of reporting the condition of railroads in Georgia, Alabama, and Mississippi. The doctor traveled over the whole route, and his report is very reliable." In the amazing document there was a wealth of information about the number of locomotives on different lines, their condition, and that of the tracks—all tending to show that the general diagnosis "pretty sick" would have been in order. After giving the location of the two pontoon bridges over the Tennessee above Bridgeport, the doctor wrote, "They could be destroyed very easily, as there are only some 15 or 20 guards at each place."

Looking across the lines we find that Manchester was in Bragg's mind, quite as well as Shelbyville. About the time that McCook's Liberty Gap message reached Federal headquarters, Mackall telegraphed to Polk:

> General Wharton has been ordered to take two regiments of cavalry from the front and move toward Manchester. Please put another regiment of infantry on the Murfreesboro pike, to support your outpost, now weakened by the withdrawal of the cavalry and by being more advanced to the front on the call of General Wharton.

While two regiments of horse could do nothing to stop Rosecrans's strong movement, they could help discover what he was up to.

Polk at Shelbyville was alert, and at 10:15 P.M. had orders sent to his division commanders to be "in readiness for any movement"; any men who had been sent out to cut wheat were to be called back. Deception too was part of the Confederate game, and from Shelbyville, Bragg's (or Polk's) provost marshal general telegraphed to the editor of the *Chattanooga Rebel:*

Publish an article to this effect: "We are happy to see that re-enforcements continue to arrive for Bragg's army. Our trains to-day are loaded with troops," &c. Don't mention the names of the commanders.

A dispatch the next morning explained: "They get all our papers. Yours being the nearest, and, of course, the latest, appears to be looked upon by them as the best information." [34]

What happened at the gaps and in the thrust toward Shelbyville is an especially important question. After having been relieved for some hours by a brigade of Rousseau's division, Wilder's regiments were again in line at 2:00 A.M. of the 25th, but as a reserve. There was no advance beyond Hoover's Gap, nor any notable enemy reaction. At Liberty Gap, however, there was some sharp action after the Confederates had attacked late in the afternoon, and had been driven back by counterattacks, in which Johnson noted that three "fine regiments lost heavily." In the evening McCook received an order from Rosecrans to make a demonstration in force to cause the enemy to believe that it was his intention to march through the gap to Bellbuckle. Carlin's brigade of Davis's division was given the mission, and McCook recorded: "The enemy was met in such force and so strongly posted that General Davis did not persist in this attack. His action was approved by me, as the spirit of the instructions had been carried out. After Carlin's attack ceased, everything was quiet save with the sharpshooters of either side." [35]

The advance on Shelbyville that was meant to deceive Bragg was stalled, it would seem, by Mitchell's failure, for a reason that is not apparent, to take either rations or forage, so that both his men and animals were soon hungry. In a 7:00 A.M. message on the 25th from near Christiana, Granger informed Rosecrans that he had sent subsistence to Mitchell, who was returning to join him, and was sending back to Murfreesboro for an additional supply for the cavalryman. The message closed, "His command will not be fit for service before to-morrow night, and I will retain it here awaiting your orders." After

Stanley had joined him with Minty's brigade, Granger some time before noon sent two of the latter's regiments "to observe the enemy at Fosterville." According to Granger, the Federal horse by a bold dash drove a strong hostile force beyond the town. But when the Confederates made a stand and opened with artillery, the two regiments, in obedience to Granger's instructions, returned to Christiana.[36]

That the Confederates were prepared for warning of an advance around their right is shown by a paragraph in the report of Colonel Eli Long, Fourth Ohio Cavalry, who was riding at the head of Turchin's division. On the night of the 24th he had camped near Bradyville in close proximity to Palmer's division. That Long was equal to the responsibility of covering the advance of Crittenden's corps seems indicated by this:

> On the 25th, I marched out at 6 A.M., going by easy motion toward Manchester. Passed Hollow Springs and halted at Lumley's Stand, junction of Bradyville, of Manchester and Shelbyville, and of McMinnville roads. Three suspicious appearing persons were here taken, one of whom proved a notorious character, and I then sent parties to reconnoiter as far as Noah's Fork, 3 miles to the west, and Pocahontas, lying 6 miles eastward. Courier stations were found at each of these points, and 1 rebel courier captured at each, together with 3 other prisoners near the latter point. Left the Second Kentucky Cavalry on picket, and retired 2½ miles to camp. Wet weather all day, and my train not up in consequence of difficult traveling.

That there was a heavy Federal advance upon the right seems to have been known at Tullahoma, thanks perhaps to the functioning of the courier stations that Long discovered. At an unspecified hour, Mackall directed Wheeler's adjutant:

> Report facts of the advance of the enemy to General Morgan. Order him to assemble his force, and fall on their rear if they pass him. Notify all commanders of the corps, and have them move en masse in the same direction. Report every half hour, and state hour in your telegram.[37]

But probably by this day Morgan was entertaining the idea of an operation of his own.

Brannan's division having finally joined Thomas after a hard struggle through rain and mud was thrown into an attack in the direction of Fairfield on the morning of the 26th, along with Rousseau's troops. The attack was successful, though Thomas said the Confederates had evidently intended obstinate resistance, and when forced to retire did so under cover of two batteries, with cavalry operating on a flank. Reynolds's order was to push on through Matt's Hollow—a long and narrow gorge beyond Hoover's Gap—and, if possible, reach Manchester. Wilder, once more in the lead after driving back some infantry that might have hampered Reynolds, skirted the gorge, and on reaching the pike after it had ascended to the plateau on which Manchester stood, found that Reynolds was passing through Matt's Hollow without any resistance. While the goal was not gained, Wilder camped only six miles from the coveted town. During the day and night McCook's corps gave up Liberty Gap and moved over to the Manchester Pike. The postscript to a message that McCook had sent Garfield an hour before noon must have made Rosecrans believe that his deception was working: "I think the enemy are fighting for Wartrace, thinking we will come that way." There still was nothing, however, to make Bragg believe that Rosecrans intended a strong move on Shelbyville. It was, in fact, not until early on the 27th that Granger received an order "to feel the enemy at Guy's Gap." [38]

In the report on his western trip which Colonel William Preston Johnston addressed to Davis on April 15, he pointed out that though Tullahoma was regarded as the central point of the Confederate defensive line, the greater part of the army was to the left of it. Then the colonel made a significant remark, overlooked certainly in many accounts of the campaign: "It is not the intention or expectation of Generals Johnston and Bragg to await attack there, unless made in front, and this they do not expect. They believe that Rosecrans will attempt to pass our flank, most probably our right flank; in which case we would go out and attack him." [39]

Late afternoon and evening of the 26th saw a change in Bragg's immediate purposes. At 4:00 P.M. Mackall, himself at Shelbyville, informed Polk that the movement proposed for the next day had been abandoned. Nevertheless, Polk's corps must be ready, with cooked rations, for a prompt movement. Four and a half hours later Hardee wrote to Stewart (one of his division commanders) that the move scheduled for the next day against Liberty Gap had been canceled. Should the enemy show any inclination to press, Stewart was to withdraw to Wartrace for a march on Tullahoma. Cleburne, Hardee said, had been directed to withdraw his two brigades from near the gap and march on Bellbuckle early in the morning. A dispatch on the same day from Buckner at Knoxville shows conclusively that Bragg meant to give battle. Actually, he had early called on Buckner for aid, but as so often, the Confederates had trouble with their ciphers, and a telegram from Buckner on the 25th began, "I have at last made out your dispatch." He could send two batteries and nearly 3,000 infantry, and he would personally accompany them. Not only was Buckner not deterred by a brilliant raid just made against the railroad through Knoxville by 1,500 cavalry and mounted infantry under the command of Colonel William P. Sanders of the Fifth Kentucky Union Cavalry, he was not deflected from his purpose when he learned on the 26th of a large body of Federal cavalry near Jamestown, a little beyond Wartburg.* He would join Bragg, he said in a dispatch to Mackall, unless the Federals moved first, and he was waiting only for requested transportation. A highly understanding and cooperative soldier was revealed by the closing sentence: "Yours is the decisive point, and you may expect me." [40]

Wilder was in Manchester so early on the 27th that he took the enemy pickets by surprise, capturing no fewer than forty men, including a captain and three lieutenants. Then, after the arrival of Reynolds's division, he sent four companies of the Seventeenth Indiana with a detachment of pioneers to destroy the trestle work on the railroad to McMinnville, four miles from Tullahoma; the expedition returned that night with a report of success. During the day army headquarters arrived, and during the night the balance of Thomas's corps. The Manchester Pike had been so full of trains that some of McCook's corps was ordered around by way of Fairfield, and at 10:00 P.M. Garfield instructed Crittenden to lighten his wagons by throwing out everything but rations, forage, and ammunition. Said the chief of staff: "A serious mistake has been made by all our commands in bringing too much baggage." Rosecrans's intentions were now, Garfield said, known to the enemy, and he was "gathering his forces for a retreat on Tullahoma." Probably it was the shorter distance that lay between Tullahoma and Manchester than between Tullahoma and Shelbyville that caused Garfield to say, "If the army were here, it could be there before him." (Garfield reported that one division of McCook's corps in addition to the corps of Thomas had arrived.)

* See map, p. 134, Vol. III.

At the moment it would look as if the intention had been, not to cut Bragg's communications, but to give him battle in his prepared position, for Garfield said, "The success of our whole movement depends upon throwing our forces upon that place at the earliest possible moment." [41]

Had the entire army been present at Manchester it would not have been possible to strike at Tullahoma without a distribution of rations and some reorganization, as Rosecrans's report makes plain. The difficulty that subordinate units were having seems not to have been fully realized at army headquarters, for a dispatch to Turchin on the 27th bade him forward with his command—a single brigade—"at once and rapidly," and it ended with the statement that it was hoped that Crittenden would reach Manchester "this evening." Actually, it was not until the 29th that Crittenden was on hand with his two divisions, "badly worn," nor until that night that all of McCook's corps was present, "troops and animals much jaded." On this day a dispatch went to Halleck from Murfreesboro that must have helped raise drooping spirits in Washington in the tense hours of Lee's advance into Pennsylvania. Bragg, Rosecrans said, had put his whole army into retreat upon Tullahoma the morning before the writing of the message—the 28th. Evidently in good touch with the right column of his army, Rosecrans wrote: "General Gordon Granger and General Stanley advanced from Christiana yesterday morning, and entered Shelbyville at 6 P.M., capturing three pieces of artillery and 300 prisoners. The bridge across Duck River was saved. At 9 P.M. last evening Granger started in pursuit of Bragg's train, not then more than 9 miles from Shelbyville. He has not been heard from." Polk saved his train, and in view of the fact that Polk was alerted for prompt movement on the afternoon of the 26th, Rosecrans was probably stretching things when he closed his message to the General in Chief, "Nothing but heavy and continued rain has prevented this army from reaching Tullahoma in advance of Bragg."

Guy's Gap had been found deserted, but the enemy was encountered in fortifications four miles north of Shelbyville, where they opened artillery fire on the advance of Minty's brigade, which had ridden through the gap, while Mitchell's division, in anticipation of resistance, had ridden off on a road that would turn the position. The Confederates were dislodged principally by the Fourth Michigan, which "attacked them with revolving rifles." When a second stand was attempted on the line of the public square and railroad depot, part of Minty's command charged boldly up the pike, while a brigade of Mitchell's division cut off the enemy retreat by the upper bridge over Duck River. Stanley stated that 591 of the enemy were captured, including six field officers; and he estimated as high as 200 the number of killed, wounded, and drowned. Rosecrans wrote, "It was worthy of note that the waving of flags and cheers from the inhabitants of this unconquerable stronghold of loyalty doubtless gave added vigor and energy to the advance of our troops." [42]

Rosecrans's statement in his report that the result of the cavalry battle revealed the general expectation that Bragg would fight at Tullahoma was at variance with a dispatch from Granger. Because his orders required him to return to Murfreesboro if no battle was fought north of Duck River, Granger was back at Christiana in the early hours of the 29th, after having ordered Stanley to report directly to Rosecrans by way of Fairfield. "From the best information I can obtain," he said in a letter to the army commander, "Bragg's army, in mass—horse, foot, and dragoons—are falling back as rapidly as possible upon Bridgeport." Respectfully Granger took his superior to task for his tendency to issue ambiguous orders and his still more pronounced habit of encroaching on the province of subordinates by prescribing details:

> Please make your instructions to me, in reference to all that you wish done in the rear, as clear and definite as possible. Frequently I have great trouble in making out your exact meaning, owing to the haste or imperfect manner in which dispatches are written or copied. If you will keep me advised of your wants and wishes, and leave the execution to my direction, we will do the best we know how. I shall be in Murfreesborough to-night, to put things in shape, and get everything fairly and properly started.

In the second sentence there was a warning, if Rosecrans had cared to interpret it as such, and in view of what lay ahead it would have been well if he had let it burn into his consciousness.

Garfield was also up late, and at 12:30 A.M. of the 29th—an hour and a quarter before Granger wrote—he closed a dispatch to Granger, "It is doubtful whether Bragg will make a stand at Tullahoma or fall back on Chattanooga. What do you think?" The message also apparently reveals a lack of agreement as to the orders under which Granger was operating. So far was Garfield from suspecting that Granger may have fallen back because he believed his mission had been accomplished that he stated that the commanding general thought it would be best if Granger ordered up from Nashville his second division, commanded by Brigadier General James D. Morgan. (Granger had made his advance with only Baird's division, his third division, commanded by Robert Granger, being also at Nashville.) Then Garfield queried, "Can you hold Wartrace?"

The restrained complaint over excess baggage that Garfield had expressed to Crittenden on the 27th was replaced by sharp criticism in letters that he sent to Thomas, McCook, and Crittenden, bearing the date 2:15 P.M., June 28:

> The general commanding has noticed with great regret the criminal neglect to obey department orders in reference to the reduction of baggage. If this army fails in the great object of the present movement, it will be mainly due to the fact that our wagons have been loaded with unauthorized baggage. Officers and soldiers who are ready to die in the field do not hesitate to disgrace themselves and imperil the army by luxuries unworthy of a soldier.

The actual prescription of loads was a detail not only justified but necessary for army headquarters, for in such things uniformity is essential, and this will not be attained if the army commander merely gives a general direction. Now Rosecrans did away with company wagons, and allowed only seven to a regiment. Excess wagons were to be turned over to division quartermasters for organization into division trains, while surplus baggage was to go back to Murfreesboro. Knapsacks were to go to the rear, soldiers carrying nothing except shelter tents (a half-tent each, perhaps), a blanket, one pair of socks, and one pair of drawers. Unauthorized articles were simply to be thrown away, and the letters ended: "Any quartermaster whose train shall be found carrying chairs and such other needless weight, usually the fruit of thieving, will at once be arrested, and the officer claiming it be severely punished."

Of course, the heavy and continuous rain which no one could have foreseen had greatly aggravated the handicap of excess baggage and wagons. But it is still interesting to note the contrast between the second sentence of the letter to his corps commanders, and the closing one of the dispatch sent by Rosecrans the same day to Halleck.[43]

When telegraphing to Halleck on the 28th Rosecrans had said, "A cavalry force was sent from here last night, to cut the railroad toward the Tennessee." That the assignment was handed to Wilder and the command newly christened "The Lightning Brigade" is hardly surprising. Actually, it was not until the morning of the 28th that Wilder mounted his men and rode away, moving by way of Hillsboro, where John Beatty's brigade was sent to cover his operation. One of Wilder's regiments having been foiled in its effort to reach the railroad bridge over the Elk River by what appeared to be an infantry division, he moved with his command in the direction of Pelham. After swimming some streams where ammunition for his howitzers was carried over on the shoulders of his men, by a quick dash he saved the road bridge that an enemy detachment was supposed to destroy. There was also a handsome bonus: seventy-eight mules that were at once sent back to Hillsboro under the guardianship of a company. The south fork of the Elk was encountered at a point where the stream, though rapid, could be swum by crossing diagonally. An old mill good-naturedly furnished timber for a raft on which the howitzers were towed over. Then, after the loss of three hours in which thoughts of what the enemy might be doing must have often crossed his mind, Wilder started toward Decherd, where Beatty during Buell's operations the previous August had recorded that he was discouraged and worn out with idleness, and that in addition to water being bad, whisky short, and dust abundant, "the air was loaded with the scent and melody of a thousand mules." There was now no scarcity of water and another stream had to be crossed, half by swimming, half by fording, before the Federal column struck the railroad at a point defended by about eighty men who had the benefit not only of a stockade, but of a railroad cut. After they had been dislodged, the Confederates took position in a ravine that gave them good cover, from which they could bring sharp fire at a distance of sixty yards on those who sought to attack them over the intervening bare ground. Doubtless the Spencer rifles had largely helped in driving the enemy away from the stockade and railroad cut, but Wilder again said not a word about them. He did, however, report how he solved his problem after his brigade had taken shelter in the ravine: "I ordered up our howitzers, and a couple of rounds of canister silenced them and drove them out."

No time was lost now in destroying railroad track and water tanks, blowing up the trestle on the branch line to Winchester, and burning a railroad depot filled with commissary stores. Even such items as telegraph instruments did not escape. There was some skirmishing with the advance guard of a hostile force approaching from the north; and four or five prisoners, when questioned separately, stated that six infantry regiments were making ready to attack. Even with his Spencers, Wilder did not believe he could stand against the enemy with success because of darkness and complete ignorance of the ground, so he struck off in the direction of Pelham, to bivouac about 2:00 A.M. off the road without any revealing fires, after he had gone about six miles.

One day of good work did not satisfy Wilder, and in the morning he once more started up the Cumberland Plateau, with the intention of breaking the railroad again below Cowan. He reached the Southern University and did some demolition to the branch line at Tracy City. Then a detachment of 450 men under Colonel John J. Funkhouser of the Ninety-eighth Illinois was sent to break the main line at Tantalon, while Wilder with the balance of the command moved toward Anderson, just over the line in Georgia, for a like purpose. Soon from Funkhouser there came the report that three trains loaded with troops were at Tantalon, while Wilder's scouts reported that there were two more at Anderson. As both places were approachable only by bridle paths, Wilder decided that he could accomplish nothing further. More than that: the picket force that he had left near the university had been driven in by cavalry preceding a train of infantry.

It was clearly time to extricate his command, which Wilder did by taking the road to Chattanooga. Having gone some distance he turned off into the woods, the task of deceiving his pursuers being left to his rear guard, which did not rejoin him until the next morning. At the last a tremendous rain was helpful; it obliterated Wilder's trail. As soon as the enemy column had passed, he struck through the mountains in the direction of Pelham, over a very rocky and steep road; and though he had no guides he came out where he wanted, to bivouac at 10:00 P.M. at the foot of the final mountain. Daylight found Wilder on the road again, headed for Manchester—and just in time to get ahead of Forrest, who had been sent out with nine regiments of cavalry and two guns to intercept him at Pelham.

Noon of the 30th had come when Wilder reached Manchester with a command which, he indicated in his report, had been in the saddle or fighting for about twenty hours out of each twenty-four since the 24th, "All the time drenched with rain, our men half starved and our horses almost entirely without forage." Yet not a single man had been lost in the expedition to the rear of Tullahoma. Naturally Rosecrans was delighted, and in a dispatch to Burnside reporting the success of his operations to date, he stated that at Tantalon, Wilder had "found Buckner's troops on cars coming this way." Then he closed his dispatch, "Would it not be a good time for you to clean out East Tennessee?" The possibility of aid from the Navy also came into Rosecrans's mind, and a dispatch to Pennock at Cairo reporting that the enemy had been driven back upon Tullahoma concluded: "Can't you come up the Tennessee, and head off any attempt they may make to cross at Florence or Decatur? Do so, if possible."

Granger, back at Murfreesboro, was on his part sending Rosecrans some information which he could well heed. Van Cleve had been ordered forward, and Granger said he could not be relieved for two or three days; he suggested that his troops be left, for he did not consider that there was any probability that the enemy would make a stand at Tullahoma. Then he made bold to tell Rosecrans that he already had more men and animals than he could possibly take care of or feed until the railroad was finished. "The dirt roads are impassable; the Manchester pike is worn out, and even worse. Broken-down animals and unloaded ammunition, provisions, forage, &c., are strewn along the whole length of the road." More than that there was to report, and Granger ended his letter, "There is a stampede in town about Morgan being in the vicinity to-night." [44]

On this same June 30, Rosecrans directed that Morton ascertain if it were possible to make a flank attack that would dislodge Bragg from Tullahoma. Detachments from Morton's Pioneer Brigade had been covering the various columns in their advance southward and, as at Stones River, where Morton's service had won such great praise from Rosecrans, had given much assistance. After Morton had reported favorably, preparations were made for an attack, but this was unnecessary, for the enemy withdrew his infantry during the night, the cavalry following at daylight. It was Thomas who learned of Bragg's retirement in a report made to him early on the 1st by a citizen. By noon he had some troops in Tullahoma, and Brannan's and Reynolds's divisions were in possession by night. Negley, in assuming a position assigned him by Thomas, came upon the retreating enemy and encouraged the continuation of his march. In one place, however, the Confederates made a stubborn resistance, and wounded a number of Federals who were driving them southward.

His experiences during these days undoubtedly served Thomas well in the great test which would fall upon him at Chickamauga. In his report he praised warmly his soldiers who marched "day and night, through a most relentless rain, and over most impassable roads, bivouacking by the roadside, ever ready and willing to 'fall in' and pursue the enemy whenever ordered, with a cheerfulness and determination truly admirable, and no less commendable when confronting the enemy; fearless and undaunted, their columns never wavered, giving the highest proof of their veteran qualities, and showing what dependence can be placed upon them in time of peril." [45]

Thus ended the Middle Tennessee campaign, or, as it is also called, the Tullahoma campaign. For successfully maneuvering Bragg out of position great praise has been given to Rosecrans. Even Halleck, who was critical in his report of Rosecrans for his long stay at Murfreesboro, spoke well of the operation. Others have gone much further. Horn calls Rosecrans's campaign "a masterpiece of offensive strategy." The editor of Beatty's *Memoirs* not only describes it as "Rosecrans's finest achievement" but adds that it is "in some respects the outstanding operation of the war." How thoroughly the campaign has actually been studied by those who have so highly praised it is open to question. Skill and good thinking were undoubtedly revealed, but some of Rosecrans's usual faults were manifested. How much traffic the Manchester Pike could actually handle without great confusion was probably never investigated. In the communication in which Rosecrans told his corps commanders that if the operation failed to achieve what it should, it would be because of an inordinate amount of baggage, he showed clearly that he had not learned the lesson of Corinth where, it will be recalled, the pursuit had to be halted in order to straighten out the crowded trains. The exasperated orders which he sent his division commander on October 5, 1862, were similar to the notes he addressed to Crittenden, McCook, and Thomas on June 28, 1863.[46]

Nor was the campaign so bloodless as is sometimes made to appear, although casualties were far below what had been anticipated and provided for. They were by no means uniformly distributed; 39 of the 84 killed and 200 of the 473 wounded were suffered by Johnson's division in its operation against Liberty Gap.[47]

By way of epilogue one can well glance at Richmond and Washington, and then at Chattanooga, after Bragg had found himself secure with his army in that strong position, following what Horn calls "an ignominious retreat before Rosecrans's flanking strategy." [48] Bragg, after having informed Richmond on July 1 that he was retiring and was losing nothing of importance, telegraphed from Bridgeport on the

3rd that he had retreated because he had been unable to obtain a general engagement without sacrificing his communications.[49] He had not heard, he said, of any formidable pursuit.

Buckner, on his part, had not failed to inform Cooper of his movement to reinforce Bragg. "I leave with my disposable force to reenforce General Bragg," he telegraphed on June 27, adding reassuringly, "Louden and Knoxville are left strong garrisons." Soon a dispatch was on the way from Pegram to Cooper, to say that Buckner had left and that Pegram was temporarily in command of the Department of East Tennessee.[50] Jefferson Davis soon had a message on the way to Lee, informing him of the Middle Tennessee situation. As luck would have it, the courier was captured by Federal troops. Stanton—understandably at his desk at 8 A.M. on July 4—informed Burnside in Cincinnati. Said the Secretary in closing: "From the letter of Davis you will understand in how tight a place Bragg and Buckner are, and will know whether and how to strike Buckner and prevent him aiding Bragg." About three hours later Halleck was on the wire, informing Burnside that there could not be any considerable force now in Tennessee to prevent an advance. His message closed: "A rapid movement, living as far as possible on the country, may produce important results. It is not possible for Bragg to make any considerable detachment to oppose you." [51]

Richmond, aware of unprecedented disasters in Pennsylvania and at Vicksburg, could at least feel that in Tennessee actual calamity had been avoided when, on July 8, it read the following dispatch:

> Since my report from Bridgeport the whole army has crossed the Tennessee. The pursuit of the enemy was checked and driven back at University Place, on the Cumberland Mountains. Our movement was attended with trifling loss of men and materials.
>
> BRAXTON BRAGG [52]

While in Richmond there must have been sighs of relief, it would have taken a bold person indeed, at a moment when the raging Potomac was barring Lee's return to Virginia, pressed, as seemed inevitable, by the victorious Army of the Potomac, to see in Bragg's salvaged army a possibility of a counterstroke. Still, Rosecrans had unexpectedly tarried for months at Murfreesboro. If he should find the Cumberland Plateau in the vicinity of Manchester congenial in the summer, and if Lee should miraculously escape, and if Federal pressure generally should not be kept up, there might be an opportunity.

CHAPTER IX

CHICKAMAUGA

"And now be assured once more that I think of you in all kindness and confidence, and that I am not watching you with an evil eye." *Lincoln to Rosecrans*

According to Halleck's report, the actual destruction of Bragg's army by Rosecrans had not been expected. The Federal general was supposed merely to drive the Confederates from Middle Tennessee and far enough into Georgia so that the long-cherished hope of liberation of East Tennessee Unionists could be carried out.[1] An advance as far as Manchester as the first stage of such an operation was all that could well have been expected. Before renewing his forward motion, it would be necessary to bring the railroad up to a more advanced base than Murfreesboro. In accordance with orders received the day before, Colonel William P. Innes's First Michigan Engineers, seen frequently in the story of Buell's advance toward Chattanooga, left Murfreesboro on June 29 to carry out necessary railroad reconstruction. Directions to replace 2½ miles of iron which had been removed between Bellbuckle and Wartrace went to Colonel J. B. Anderson, whom the reader will also recall. Then the Michigan men took over the task of repairing and rebuilding the 350-foot bridge over the Duck River, which had been burned and chopped down, as well as a long trestle farther south, and soon had everything in order as far as Tullahoma. Necessary repairs were also made on the branch line to McMinnville, on which Manchester was located, and a mile and a half of new corduroy road was constructed for the use of wagon trains.[2]

But Washington was not in the humor for a long delay. On July 24 Halleck opened a telegram to Rosecrans with the blunt statement: "You must not wait for Johnston to join Bragg, but must move forward immediately against the latter." After telling the general to take only minimum supplies and to live on the country as much as he could, Halleck added: "Reduce your trains to the lowest point possible, and move rapidly. There is great disappointment felt here at the slowness of your advance. Unless you can move more rapidly, your whole campaign will prove a failure, and you will have both Bragg and Johnston against you." There was even greater frankness in a private and confidential letter on the same day: "The patience of the authorities here has been completely exhausted, and if I had not repeatedly promised to urge you forward, and begged for delay, you would have been removed from the command." After admitting that there were difficulties not perceptible except near at hand, Halleck concluded that he felt it his duty as a friend to inform Rosecrans of the exact feeling in Washington.

The following day Halleck assigned a precise mission to Rosecrans: "The great object you will have in view is to drive Bragg from East Tennessee before he can be re-inforced by Johnston." According to information in the Capital, abundant supplies would be found in the valley, if time were not given the enemy to remove them.

It is impossible to reconcile Rosecrans's previous denunciation of his corps commanders for having too much baggage with the statement in his dispatch to Halleck on the 25th, "We never think of moving with any but the minimum baggage." He thought the General in Chief was exaggerating the degree to which supplies could be found locally. He promised to move promptly and inquired as to the effect of movements by Grant upon his own operations. This brought from Halleck another confidential letter: "I perceive from the tone of your dispatch today that you are displeased at my urging you to move forward your army against Bragg. . . . Having now explained to you frankly that you can have no possible grounds for your tone of displeasure toward me, I shall not again refer to this matter." [3]

Within a week Rosecrans wrote at length to Halleck. He expressed gratitude for the latter's notes; he was relieved that the injustice he had experienced from the War Department did not extend to Halleck; he thought he should be removed if the Government had a commander in whom they felt more confidence than in himself. Then followed an impressive list of difficulties that he faced.

Well before his letter to Halleck was received, he had read Halleck's blunt dispatch of August 4: "Your forces must move forward without further delay. You will daily report the movement of each corps till you cross the Tennessee River." Rosecrans's acknowledgment the same day stated that the movement across the Tennessee was under preparation, and ended: ". . . I wish to know if your order is intended to take away my discretion as to time and manner of moving my troops?" Halleck's reply of the next day was short: "The orders for the advance of your army, and that its movements be reported daily, are peremptory."

A long telegram from Rosecrans to Halleck on the 6th, saying that it had not yet been ascertained where the Tennessee could best be crossed and amplifying other difficulties, brought from Halleck an answering dispatch on the 7th:

> I have communicated to you the wishes of the Government in plain and unequivocal terms. The object has been stated, and you have been directed to lose no time in reaching it. The means you are to employ, and the roads you are to follow, are left to your own discretion. If you wish to promptly carry out the wishes of the Government, you will not stop to discuss mere details. In such matters I do not interfere.

Rosecrans answered on the same day that his army would move with all the dispatch compatible with success. Forage was being brought forward, and while the rolling stock of the railroad barely sufficed for his needs where he was, he had bought fifty additional freight cars, some of which had arrived.[4]

Extremely kind, but inflexibly firm, was Lincoln's reply to a letter which Rosecrans had written directly to him. He had, he said, seen Rosecrans's correspondence with the General in Chief. Then he sought to mollify Rosecrans with the words: "And now be assured once more that I think of you in all kindness and confidence, and that I am not watching you with an evil eye."[5]

Mid-August had barely passed when the Army of the Cumberland began to move. Ahead was the crossing of mountains by steep and narrow roads, the passage of a great river, and finally the mastery of a still loftier mountain. Crittenden's corps, his left covered by Minty's cavalry, went by way of the Sequatchie Valley, down which he turned to cross the Tennessee in the area of Bridgeport, except for a substantial detachment under Hazen charged with the important duty of making Bragg believe that a major crossing would be attempted above

Chattanooga. Thomas was to move to the general vicinity of Bridgeport, and McCook was to move two divisions toward Bellefonte and Stevenson. Logistically the operation posed many problems. Henry Cist stated that ammunition for two battles and rations for

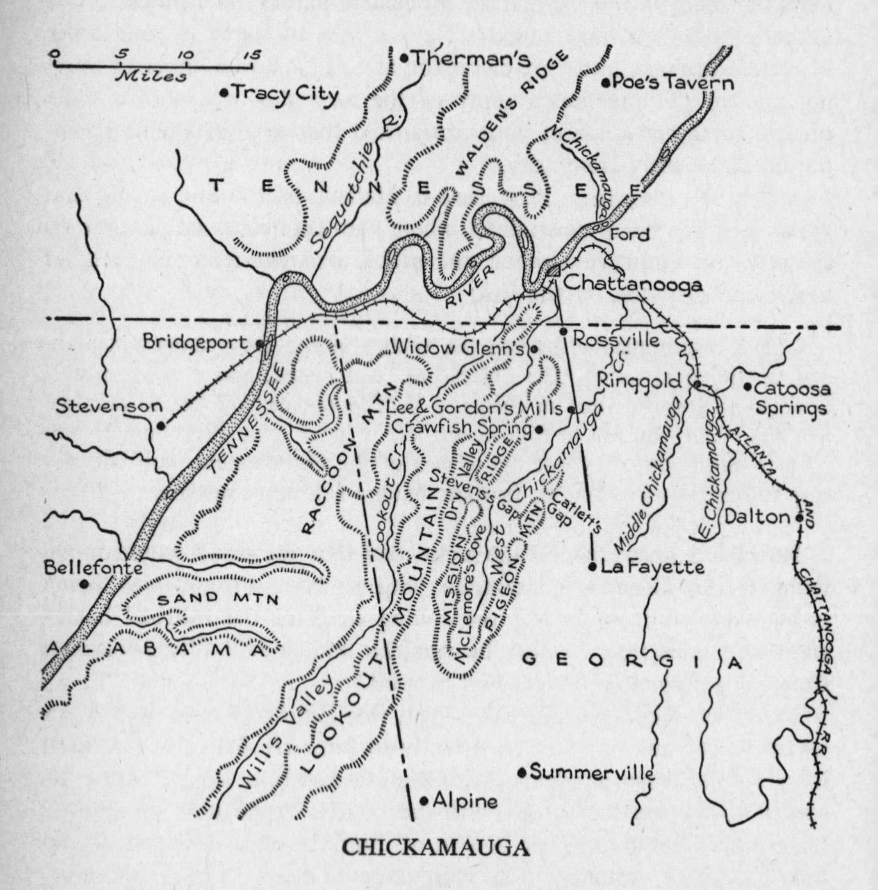

CHICKAMAUGA

twenty-five days were taken. Whether superfluous baggage was eliminated in accordance with Rosecrans's orders cannot be said.[6]

Hazen, who, it will be remembered, held the "round forest" in the hard fighting at Stones River in the late afternoon of December 30, 1862, and thereby saved the left of Rosecrans's line, performed his duty well. To him had been assigned Wilder's Lightning Brigade. After moving through Tracy City down into the valley, where he repaired roads for his artillery and trains, Wilder surprised and captured fourteen Confederates who were on the point of hanging five Federals at Therman. Then he ascended Walden's Ridge on the heels of Hazen's brigade, and after taking the lead in the march to the summit of the mountain, he struck for the Tennessee River, capturing en route some more of the enemy and releasing three more Federals. Upon reaching the river south of North Chickamauga Creek, he captured the animals and some of the men of a battery, and some pickets, and brought fire to bear upon Confederates who were crossing in boats. Soon hostile guns opened on Wilder, only to be silenced promptly by Captain Lilly's Eighteenth Indiana Battery. When a rifled 32-pounder joined in the action, it too fell mute after firing only four shots, one of which, however, killed four horses and mortally wounded a Federal corporal. In addition to beating down the enemy fire, Lilly's guns also sank the *Paint Rock,* disabled another steamer, and sank a number of the boats of a pontoon bridge which the Confederates were apparently about to lay. Then Wilder began activities by day and night calculated to make Bragg think a major crossing was to be attempted at some point above Chattanooga.[7]

Shells from Yankee guns had previously been heard in Chattanooga, for it will be recalled that on June 7, 1862, Negley, operating under orders from Hornsby Mitchel, had reached the Tennessee and for three hours engaged Confederate batteries across the river.

Soon after the Federal appearance opposite Chattanooga on August 21, Bragg ordered Anderson's brigade to withdraw from Bridgeport, facilitating thereby Rosecrans's operation. Crossings at four points were begun on August 29 and completed on September 4. Skirmishing was involved, but no heavy actions occurred. McCook's corps headed for a gap in Lookout Mountain, forty miles southwest of Chattanooga, and Thomas's corps for Stevens's Gap, twenty miles farther north, while the remainder of Crittenden's corps was to move closer to the river.

Well before the Fourteenth and Twentieth corps had started up the rough roads in the gaps over Lookout Mountain, they had crossed into the state of Georgia. They constituted the first Federal forces of any size to penetrate this critical region since the beginning of the war. While they were not within supporting distance of each other, both were protected by the mountain ahead. Not until they had descended the eastern slopes of Lookout could danger come from dispersion. Rosecrans's strategy is clear: McCook's column on the right, headed toward the Atlanta and Chattanooga Railroad well south of Bragg's position in Chattanooga, would pose a threat that might cause the Confederate commander to abandon the long-sought city.

Thomas had little more than reached the south bank when he picked up the report—according to Cist—that Joe Johnston was sending 15,000 men from Mississippi to reinforce Bragg. Washington's fears were justified.[8]

Few operations of the war are more inspiring to contemplate than those of the Army of the Cumberland during the days under consideration—columns of troops descending mountains to cross the Tennessee by pontoon bridges, fords, and boats, followed by batteries and wagon trains, all against a superb setting of river and mountain. Soldiers are often reminiscent. While some are boastful, through the minds of others there pass quiet thoughts. Many must have recalled what they were doing exactly a year ago: beginning their retreat, as the Army of the Ohio under Buell, from the very place from which they had just started their advance, a retreat which, because of Bragg's outflanking operation and invasion of Kentucky, had taken them all the way back to Louisville.

Simultaneously with Rosecrans's advance, the long-desired invasion of East Tennessee had begun under Burnside; his movements gave security to the Army of the Cumberland's long line of communications.

On August 5, the day Halleck gave Rosecrans a blunt order to advance, he sent an equally blunt order to Burnside. Burnside was told to "immediately move with a column of 12,000 men by the most practicable roads on East Tennessee, making Knoxville or its vicinity" his objective. When the two divisions of the Ninth Corps returned from Vicksburg they should follow as a reserve. Burnside was to telegraph his troop movements. Upon reaching East Tennessee, he was to try to connect with the troops of Rosecrans, who had received "peremptory" orders to advance. The dispatch had the unhappy ending: "The Secretary of War repeats his orders that you move your headquarters from Cincinnati to the field, and take command of the troops in person."

Stung by the implication that he had failed to obey an order previously given to him by Stanton, Burnside denied ever having received any direction to leave Cincinnati. He reminded the General in Chief that he had voluntarily done so and was in the field preparing to move on East Tennessee when, in early June, he had received from Halleck orders to send troops to aid Grant at Vicksburg. Concentration and forward movement of his forces were being made as rapidly as possible.[9]

The three infantry divisions and the cavalry of Hartsuff's infantry corps (the Twenty-third)—portions of which were recovering from their exertions during John Morgan's raid—numbering about 15,000 men in all, comprised Burnside's striking force, the department commander himself taking the field on August 20th. Rugged terrain lay ahead, and a lieutenant of infantry in the 111th Ohio wrote of the great difficulties involved in getting the artillery over the mountains. In due time Northern readers would see in *Harper's Weekly* an artist's portrayal and a correspondent's description of the hardships that had to be met.[10]

In addition to the veteran troops that formed the main columns, a new division, under Colonel John F. De Courcy, was to move directly against Cumberland Gap. Colonel De Courcy would be glad to get another look at it. He had been in the column from George Morgan's division which had seized the crucial position in July, 1862, and which two months later had had to retreat to the Ohio.[11]

From Williamsburg a cavalry force, under Colonel Robert K. Byrd, of the First Tennessee, was dispatched to move through Big Creek Gap and demonstrate against Knoxville; while from Montgomery a second body of cavalry, under Colonel John W. Foster, was sent to seize Knoxville, moving by way of Winter's Gap. The main body of invasion reached Kingston on September 1st and Knoxville on the 3rd, finding the city secure in the possession of Foster, who had arrived the day before.[12]

It was to the operation by Burnside, now squarely across his direct communications with Richmond, that Bragg devoted the beginning of his letter of September 4 to General Cooper. Burnside's move, coincidentally with Rosecrans's advance, had caused Buckner to draw back his forces, except for those at Cumberland Gap, to Loudon; Bragg had ordered him to continue his retreat some thirty miles to the Hiawassee. After indicating that the surrender of so much of East Tennessee had been made only reluctantly, and solely because of his inability to hold a long line with the forces at his command, Bragg turned his attention to the advance under Rosecrans. Though the Federal columns posed a direct threat to vital communications, Bragg closed on a hopeful note: he would spare no effort to bring the enemy to an engagement whenever there were favorable chances. Eight days later Jefferson Davis's endorsement on the Bragg letter—which had noted that not all the reinforcements from Mississippi had arrived—began: "The case demands great activity, with which it is hoped the enemy's purpose may be defeated by fighting his two columns separately." [13]

In accordance with orders received from Wilder at Poe's Tavern, Colonel S. D. Atkins, of the Ninety-second Illinois Mounted Infantry, which had been added to Wilder's brigade, returned to General Thomas, reporting to him on September 7th at 10:00 A.M. at the foot of Raccoon Mountain. (Raccoon Mountain forms the northern extremity of Sand Mountain, the range to the west of Lookout, Sand Mountain and Lookout Mountain forming Lookout Valley, also called Will's Valley, down which flows Lookout Creek on its way to the Tennessee.) The next day, on orders from General Reynolds to whom Thomas had assigned him, Atkins with two companies made a reconnaissance on Lookout Mountain, but nothing was ascertained about the enemy.

Rumors of evacuation of Chattanooga were nonetheless received, and at 1:00 A.M. on the 9th, Garfield wrote to Crittenden that the commanding general directed him to move "around the point of Lookout Mountain," prepared to occupy Chattanooga if he should find it evacuated. Crittenden was cautioned not to expose his artillery until he was certain that there was no ruse; a regiment of mounted infantry, he was told, had been ordered to move over the ridge and to report news of his advance to the commanding general. The mounted infantry, Atkins's Ninety-second Illinois, received their orders at 3:00 A.M. from Reynolds. Apparently a detachment of the regiment placed itself at the head of Crittenden's column, while Atkins led the remainder across Lookout. Undaunted by picket fire not far to the west of Lookout, the detachment with Crittenden pushed on and was in Chattanooga at 9:15 A.M.; and at 10:00 A.M. Atkins, who had seen clouds of dust above the road to La Fayette, raised the colors of his regiment "on the third story of the Crutchfield House, the first to float over the evacuated town." The remainder of Wilder's brigade crossed the river at a ford eight miles above the city and was joined by Atkins.[14]

Coincidentally with the evacuation of Chattanooga the Confederate force at Cumberland Gap capitulated to Burnside, who, after learning that the Confederates were too strong for De Courcy and the cavalry from Knoxville, proceeded to the position at the head of Colonel Gilbert's brigade. Arriving on the 9th, after a march of sixty miles in fifty-two hours, he summarily demanded enemy surrender. Stonewall Jackson would have been thrilled over such "fruits of victory" as fell to the Federal commander: 2,500 men, with all their matériel and armament intact. Burnside, it may be added, refused to parole the Confederate command, on the basis that he did not have such authority under the Dix-Hill cartel.

Before leaving the gap, Burnside received a dispatch written by Crittenden, at Rosecrans's direction, at 2:00 A.M. on September 10th. The enemy, Crittenden said, was in retreat upon Rome. He would start pursuit at daylight. It was Rosecrans's desire that Burnside send cavalry to occupy country recently protected by Minty, who would furnish particulars and then cross the river.

Believing from this that Rosecrans had the situation in his front well under control, Burnside gave his attention to the occupation of East Tennessee, planning even to seize the important saltworks near Abingdon, Virginia. He sent, however, sufficient forces to occupy Kingston and Loudon, while Byrd's horsemen continued south in fulfillment of Rosecrans's request for cavalry.[15]

At 9:00 A.M. of the 9th, Garfield wrote to McCook about the orders given Crittenden, described the movement being made by Thomas, and directed McCook to move as rapidly as possible on Alpine and Summerville, in order to intercept the retreating enemy. McCook was enjoined to strike the enemy in flank if possible, directing his march by information that he could himself pick up. According to Garfield the main body of the enemy could not be more than two days' march from Chattanooga, and it was Rosecrans's hope that McCook could inflict serious injury upon them.

The order did not reach McCook until 6:35 P.M., but he made haste to write that he would push on and carry it out. He would march at 3:00 A.M., and would pursue the enemy and attack him when he had "a reasonable hope of success." During his absence from headquarters a resident of Lookout Mountain had reported that he had been in the valley and had learned from a Mr. Robertson that the Confederates were moving by train and road for the purpose of concentrating at Rome to give battle. This and other dispatches show that

Rosecrans's corps commanders stimulated his belief that Bragg was in full retreat, the outcome no doubt of planned deception by the latter.[16]

By the night of the 11th, however, Rosecrans, whose headquarters were then in Chattanooga, had a premonition that Bragg was not in full retreat, but was probably concentrating for the purpose of striking some part of the Federal army, now dispersed in order to cross the mountain. Such is the unquestionable testimony of Charles Dana.

The Assistant Secretary of War arrived at Chattanooga during the evening of the 11th. Upon being presented with Stanton's letter of introduction, Rosecrans, according to Dana's well known *Recollections of the Civil War,* burst out in a torrent of abuse of the Washington authorities: both Stanton and Halleck had tried to prevent his success. The tirade was stopped by Dana's telling Rosecrans that he had not come to listen to such talk but to learn what the Government could do to aid him. Quieting down at once, Rosecrans then explained the situation fully. Part of his explanation involved a detailed description of the valley that lay ahead, with which the reader should also be familiar if he is to understand what is to follow.[17]

East of Lookout Mountain lay Missionary—or Mission—Ridge. Beginning at the northeast of Chattanooga, it continued southward to the general vicinity of Summerville and Alpine, the objectives that had been given to McCook. At Rossville, not far to the south of Chattanooga, the road to La Fayette and Rome passed through a gap. To the east of Missionary Ridge flowed Chickamauga Creek, formed by the union of East, Middle, and West Chickamauga creeks, and emptying into the Tennessee above Chattanooga. After passing through the Rossville Gap, the La Fayette road crossed Chickamauga Creek at Lee and Gordon's Mills, thence continued east of Pigeon Mountain, a short range to the east of Missionary Ridge, the region between the two ridges being called Chickamauga Valley. In this valley lay McLemore's Cove. Into this cove one could penetrate from La Fayette only by gaps, but it was to be one of the great battlefields of the war. From Summerville, where Rosecrans had been so hopeful that McCook might strike a heavy blow at Bragg's retreating army, it was about twenty-five miles to both La Fayette and Rome. Dalton, but not La Fayette, was located on the railroad from Atlanta.[18]

Like his dispatches from Vicksburg, Dana's dispatches to Stanton from the headquarters of the Army of the Cumberland were masterful reporting. They laid bare the most important things: Rosecrans's thoughts, his sanguine hopes, his sudden fears. Already Dana had put on the wire to Washington important news: Governor Andrew Johnson was very hopeful about the prospects in Tennessee; he was intending to call a general election, taking care that only Unionists would vote; Tennesseans generally, the governor had said, accepted the end of slavery and were concerned only about the future of the Negro; commissary supplies in Nashville were not so abundant as believed in Washington, only 16 cars a day were arriving from Louisville instead of the requisite 65 (later Dana repeated a charge made the summer before, that the Louisville and Nashville Railroad authorities preferred private to Government business); it would require a month to repair the bridge at Bridgeport, badly damaged by the retreating Confederates; the reserve ammunition train of 800 wagons would have to clear the road before Granger's corps could advance.[19]

The first dispatch from Chattanooga, at 11:00 A.M. September 12th, reported that McCook and Thomas were through the gaps on Lookout Mountain, while Crittenden was at Ringgold. Dana might have added that Wilder was with Crittenden. In fact, Wilder had on the 11th driven Confederate cavalry back as far as Dalton, where he was halted finally by Forrest's command, only returning, however, to Ringgold when called back on the morning of the 12th by Crittenden. The appearance of hostile cavalry on the road to La Fayette was not a thing to cause surprise; it could well be covering a retreating enemy. But an attack westward against Negley, who was leading Thomas's corps, was another matter. Then it was that the thought came to Rosecrans that Bragg might have abandoned his retreat and returned for the purpose of striking the Army of the Cumberland in detail. By the 12th, however, it looked as if the attack on Negley had subsided, and it was concluded that it had been made merely for the purpose of checking pursuit.

Dana indicated there would be communication between Crittenden and Thomas, and that the latter would push eastward toward Catlett's Gap in Pigeon Mountain; while McCook, resting his left flank on the southern end of Missionary Ridge, would reach toward Summerville. It seemed probable, however, Dana continued, that before all of these things could be done the enemy would have made good his escape to Rome. Everything seemed satisfactory on the 13th, and Rosecrans and Dana proceeded to Thomas's headquarters in front of Stevens's Gap, Dana explaining to Stanton that inasmuch as the telegraph ended at Chattanooga there would be a delay in the transmission of his future messages.

In a dispatch at 11:00 A.M. of the 14th, Dana reported: "Everything progresses favorably; concentration of the three corps already substantially effected." The enemy was abandoning "this basin," and Federal scouts had reported that he was evacuating La Fayette and moving toward Rome. The Federal advance toward La Fayette would be continued, and the place would probably be entered the next day. The army had supplies for ten days, and forage was abundant. Optimism continued to mount. Dana's second dispatch reported that a steamer taken at Chattanooga, along with barges, could be used to bring supplies from Stevenson, thus freeing the roads from many wagons. Still later in the day, Dana asserted that the army had gained a position from which it could effectually advance even as far as Atlanta, and "deliver there the finishing blow of the war." A tinge of apprehension, however, appeared. A sudden move by the enemy to the Federal right would endanger the long line of communication and compel retirement to the Tennessee. Dana suggested that it might be desirable to stop Steele's advance on Little Rock, so that all available men could be moved eastward through Memphis and Corinth in order to give security to the operation that was aimed at the "heart of rebellion."

By the 15th, if not late on the 14th, the truth was realized: Bragg was not in retreat but was preparing to strike a blow from La Fayette. Reports from corps and division commanders clearly indicated this. One from Wood, on the 14th, giving information communicated by "an intelligent contraband," spoke of a movement toward Lee and Gordon's Mills of a force of 10,000 men under General Hindman; bafflingly, they had later retired, and the contraband ended by saying he had heard talk of a retreat to Atlanta. At 8:00 A.M. the next morning Negley reported to Thomas that a "reliable lady" had seen "right smart" forces at various places, as well as a battery. A rebel lieutenant had told her that they had heavy forces at all the gaps at Pigeon Mountain. Some time during the day a signal sergeant flashed to Thomas the word that a rebel prisoner who had left the enemy at daybreak said there were 80,000 men on Pigeon Mountain. A dispatch from Negley at 8:00 P.M. describing terrain in his front ended:

> Later: Away up in the gap is a small dust. There is an immense dust in the east, north of Pigeon Ridge, as if a large party of cavalry were charging this way. It was very rapid in its approach; at the same time a dust raised in the gorge of Dug Gap, coming this way. A great many fires on the Chattanooga road near the end of Pigeon Ridge.

Also at 8:00 P.M. a signal officer sent directly to Rosecrans a message about the ability of Confederates to concentrate in McLemore's Cove and advance on the position where he was stationed.[20]

Discretionary power having been given to Thomas to order McCook to his support if he thought best, instructions had been sent the latter on the 13th. Confusion was to follow because of orders to McCook from both Thomas and Rosecrans, but in the end McCook, moving his ammunition and rations along Lookout Mountain, marched two divisions through Lookout Valley to Stevens's Gap, Sheridan's division moving east of the mountain. The full picture begins to emerge when Thomas writes in a dispatch to Reynolds on the 15th: "General McCook arrived today. Troops will be here tomorrow." Unfairly, Dana opened a dispatch from Crawfish Spring at 1:00 P.M. of the 16th: "McCook mistook the order of march prescribed for him to concentrate upon Thomas. . . . This mistake has caused two days' delay." [21]

The telegraph at Chattanooga was also bringing important information and warnings from Washington. On September 13 General Foster reported to Halleck from Fort Monroe that there were heavy train movements on the railroad from Richmond and Petersburg, following this the next day with a categorical statement that Longstreet's corps was reported to be going southward through North Carolina. On the 13th Halleck had telegraphed to Sherman or Grant (he did not know whether Grant had returned from New Orleans) about the danger to Rosecrans's right flank, directing that all available troops should be sent to Memphis and thence to Corinth and Tuscumbia. Now, on the 15th, the General in Chief telegraphed to Rosecrans that information received in Washington indicated that three divisions from Lee's army were on the way to reinforce Bragg. All possible forces in the departments of the Ohio and the Cumberland should be brought forward; Sherman and Hurlbut would bring reinforcements. To General Allen, quartermaster at St. Louis, there went the dispatch: "All available troops at Vicksburg have been ordered to Tuscumbia, via Memphis, to re-inforce Rosecrans. Give immediate attention to the matter of transportation." Nor did Halleck overlook the question of supplies. A similar dispatch, ending with the injunction "See to the supplies," went to the chief commissary officer.

After two dispatches to Burnside on the 13th and 14th directing him to move to Rosecrans's support, Halleck sent an even more urgent telegram, that in view of the probability that three divisions had gone from Lee's army to the assistance of Bragg, it was important that all the troops in Burnside's department should be "brought to the front with all possible dispatch, so as to help General Rosecrans."

Even to Pope, in Milwaukee, and to the adjutant general of the Department of the Ohio, at Cincinnati, there went telegrams about sending reinforcements.[22]

Though he has been frequently blamed for not moving to Rosecrans's assistance, Burnside was in fact quite without fault, in regard to both Halleck's telegrams and the message sent him on the 16th by Rosecrans himself asking for cavalry support and saying, "I want all the help we can get promptly." After receiving Crittenden's dispatch of September 10 that Bragg was in full retreat, it was natural that Burnside should throw himself wholeheartedly into the task of operating eastward from Knoxville. This would not only free an area of strong Union sentiment but would pose a threat to one of the Confederacy's sensitive points, the salt springs at Abingdon, Virginia. Garrisons had always been detailed to protect these works, but only against raids. Union troops up toward Virginia would be a greater menace. When Burnside on the 16th received Halleck's dispatch of the 13th, his troops were utterly incapable of taking aid to a battle that was about to develop in McLemore's Cove, miles upon miles away. Burnside pointed this out clearly in his report, and it is only those who ignore all logistical matters who could censure Burnside. When Dana came into possession of the dispatch that Crittenden had sent to Burnside, he at once saw the bearing that it had had on operations, and he sent a copy of it to Stanton with the statement that Halleck might wish to include it in his report. The Assistant Secretary commented to his chief: "The letter made Burnside believe Rosecrans perfectly successful, needing no assistance whatever." [23]

In his dispatch of the 16th which so harshly criticized McCook, Dana indicated that the concentration of the army would be complete upon the arrival of the balance of McCook's Twentieth Corps. The latter would hold the right, and Thomas would remain in the center, while Crittenden held the left. On the extreme left, guarding the road to Chattanooga at Rossville, there would be Steedman's division and Daniel McCook's brigade of Granger's Reserve Corps. There was no evidence as yet of the arrival of Longstreet's troops, but the enemy was clearly concentrated at La Fayette. It was not, however, Rosecrans's intention to wait for Bragg to strike. He himself planned an offensive blow. Leaving campfires burning so as to deceive the enemy, he would march around Pigeon Mountain and throw himself on the Confederates. Everything would be ready for a start by the next night—"should no new development prevent."

At 5:00 P.M. on the 17th reports that Longstreet had reached Atlanta were brought to Rosecrans's headquarters. Twenty-four hours later, Rosecrans was in a state of indecision. Enemy activities on his left earlier in the day had been diagnosed as a "reconnaissance in force." The Confederates had made no headway against Wood, who held Crittenden's left, but had forced Wilder and Minty to retire to the west of Chickamauga Creek. Said Dana: "Rosecrans has not yet determined whether to make a night march and fall on them at daylight or to await their onset."

All idea of taking the offensive would seem to have been given up when during the night of the 18th Thomas was shifted to the left of the Federal line so as to cover the critical road to Chattanooga. A little ambiguously, perhaps, Dana reported that Crittenden had been pushed up behind Thomas, while McCook had been brought to Crawfish Spring as reserve. In communicating this information Dana stated that battle had been started at 9:00 A.M., September 19, by an enemy attack against Rosecrans's right, indicating in a subsequent dispatch that he should have said the left. Optimism at the moment —10:30 A.M. on September 19th—seemed to prevail at Federal headquarters, and Dana commented: "Rosecrans has everything ready to grind up Bragg's flank." In successive dispatches, Dana described the heavy blow against the Federal left which had been repulsed, and an enemy diversionary stroke against the Federal right which had also been thrown back. Then there was an artillery attack against the center, the most furious of the day. Rosecrans's headquarters were shifted northward to the Widow Glenn's, leaving Negley and Sheridan on the right. The intention had been to have Negley hold the fords on the right and for Sheridan to report to the Widow Glenn's. Because of the distances, the roles of the two division commanders were interchanged, and it was Negley who came to give support in the vicinity of army headquarters.

There was continued hopefulness over the great battle which was being fought along a line two or three miles long in a forested region where the undergrowth was so dense that it was difficult to appraise the vicissitudes of the struggle, and in his dispatches to Washington Dana said, at 2:30 P.M., "Decisive victory seems assured to us"; at 3:20 P.M., "Thomas reports that he is driving rebels, and will force them into Chickamauga to-night"; at 4:30 P.M., "I do not yet dare to say our victory is complete, but it seems certain." But at 5:20 P.M. doubt began to appear: "Now appears to be undecided contest, but later reports will enable us to understand more clearly."

Two hours later there was a lifting of spirits. Negley had attacked, driving the enemy back for half a mile, the fighting continuing after dark by moonlight. The enemy had been frustrated, Dana said, in his effort to cut the Federals off from Chattanooga. Rosecrans would renew the combat in the morning unless the enemy retreated. In addition to minor unengaged units on the battlefield, there were 8,000 fresh men.[24]

At a council of war of corps and division commanders, which Dana described in his postwar recollections, higher officers were canvassed as to the situation, and their suggestions were requested. To all inquiries Thomas, in hard battle all day after a night without sleep, would reply, "I would strengthen the left," and then drop again into unconsciousness. The army commander invariably responded: "Where are we going to take it from?" Written orders, read to all present, were given to corps commanders. Thomas would hold the left, with McCook to close and cover the Widow Glenn's position, and Crittenden to have two divisions in reserve near the junction of Thomas and McCook. About midnight, after coffee had been passed around, and McCook had sung "The Hebrew Maiden," the council dispersed, with Dana sleeping on the floor beside Horace Porter.[25]

The knowledge that Bragg was being reinforced must have spurred efforts at Federal headquarters to identify enemy units. Dana, in fact, reported prisoners from thirty regiments. "Is Longstreet here?" must often have been anxiously asked. This hard-fighting general was bringing two (not three) divisions. When his movement westward was decided upon, the railroad through Knoxville was still open. But so much time was required to accumulate rolling stock that Burnside had possession of the line before the movement from Virginia was begun on September 9. Thus it was necessary to use the long route through the Carolinas and Georgia described in a previous volume. Three of Hood's brigades had arrived in time for the preliminary fighting on the 18th, but the balance of the infantry and all of the artillery was still en route. According to Livermore, the Confederates would have a grand total of 66,326 "effectives" in the great battle, against 58,222 Federals; but it is impossible to give with precision the times of arrival of different units. In one of his dispatches Dana referred to D. H. Hill. But this officer, frequently seen in the East, had brought no troops. Freshly raised to "three-star" rank by Jefferson Davis, he had been rushed westward to take command of Hardee's corps when that officer was sent to Mississippi. In addition to Buckner's corps and that of Longstreet, Breckenridge's division, which had been with Bragg at Stones River, had, after being sent to Mississippi, returned eastward; and T. C. Hindman (ardent secessionist but contentious general previously seen west of the Mississippi) was there with a division from the West to help save the gateway into Georgia and the heartland of the South.[26]

With his right covered by Forrest's cavalry, which was observing toward Rossville, Bragg had purposed to turn Rosecrans's left flank on the 19th, cutting him off from the road to Rossville. Then continuing the movement so as to uncover the gaps in Missionary Ridge through which the Federals might retreat, he hoped to roll the Federal army back into eerie McLemore's Cove and there destroy it at leisure.

While Dana's report to Washington was quite sufficient for his purpose, it did not include some interesting aspects of the opening of the battle on the 19th. Pugnacious Daniel McCook, of the famous Ohio family of generals and colonels, had reported that there was an isolated Confederate brigade that might be captured. This seeming to Thomas a desirable thing, Brannan was assigned the task. The nature of the terrain and the lateness in reception of orders made his movement somewhat slow, and, when he struck, he found not a brigade but a strong enemy division attacking. Though he fought stubbornly, Brannan was forced back; and Baird, who had been moved to assist Brannan, was likewise driven, at least some of his units breaking in confusion. Then the Confederate effort to gain the Federal left continued, and Dana's description of what took place can be accepted as adequate. But Baird had the satisfaction of bringing off two hundred Virginia prisoners.[27]

On the afternoon of the 19th, at the tiny village of Catoosa, Georgia (no longer existent), Longstreet stepped from a train and found to his amazement and almost unbelief that no officer from Bragg's staff was there to receive him. Nor did one appear while he waited from two to four o'clock for the next train, with his horse and his staff. From the north there came the sound of battle, but Bragg had left Lee's "old war-horse" to his own devices in bringing aid to the Army of Tennessee. Longstreet's conduct on this afternoon, this evening, and the next day are to be carefully observed, for it will be recalled that he has been made the scapegoat for Lee's defeat at Gettysburg, the charge being that his tardiness on the second day was responsible for failure. (It has been pointed out that in his second treatment of Gettysburg Freeman admitted the baselessness of the charge.) With the members of his staff accompanying him, Longstreet rode northward, twenty miles lying between him and Bragg's headquarters at La Fayette. Night had come, with moonlight, when an answer he made to a picket's challenge evoked a reply that suggested a Federal, not a friendly outguard, but an adroit side remark by Longstreet to his staff enabled the little group to retire to another road. Midnight was only an hour away when Longstreet reached Bragg's headquarters, to be informed by the latter that he was to command the left wing in the next day's battle. While the South Carolinians and the Georgians who had comprised Longstreet's reinforcements had had food given to them by well wishers along their route, Longstreet could justifiably have pleaded the necessity of rest before battle for men who had traveled so far in uncomfortable cars. Seemingly he did not.

With nothing more than a map, an indication of the plan of battle for the next day, and a listing of the main units on the Confederate left, which had been only moderately engaged that day, Longstreet rode into the moonlit woodland to discover what he could. By dawn he had succeeded in locating his command. On the extreme left was one division of Buckner's corps, the other division forming the right of the left wing where it joined the Confederate right under Polk, the two wings meeting at a rather sharp angle. He found Hindman's division and a new division under Bushrod Johnson, as well as the three brigades of Hood's division, which had been in action that day on the right but had then been moved to the left. In order to have a striking force with depth and power, Longstreet ordered the two brigades of McLaws' division, whose arrival from Ringgold was anticipated, to form behind those of Hood. All of Longstreet's artillery was miles to the east, but Buckner reported some twenty guns with his corps, and other batteries were present with the left wing. At first, all of Hood's division appears to have been formed behind Bushrod Johnson, to be later, however, put in line to the right of Johnson, without this general being fully aware of the change.[28]

Not until 4:00 P.M. did Dana send his first dispatch of the next day, the 20th. Headed "Chattanooga," it was one of the most melancholy and dismal reports of the war. Yet, though noticeably shaken by the swift transformation of an undecided but favorable contest into a tragic defeat, Dana's report contained elements of accuracy. Unaware he was at that time, however, of the ambiguous order which had been so catastrophic in its consequences. The day had not opened with a crash of musketry as was sometimes the case, and though there had been firing earlier, it was not until 9:00 A.M. that Dana said the first cannon had been fired. It would seem that at an early hour Rosecrans started on an inspection of his line, giving orders here and there, and perhaps returning from time to time to check on their execution. According to Dana's *Recollections,* McCook received a severe castigation for a movement which had actually been ordered in writing the night before, and it would appear from Dana that Rosecrans then took position upon the extreme right, well before noon. Having received repeated calls from Thomas for reinforcements, Rosecrans—according to McCook—at 10:10 A.M. directed him to be prepared to start reinforcements to Thomas at a moment's notice. Twenty minutes later, McCook was directed to send two of Sheridan's brigades at once and to follow with a third as soon as lines could be properly contracted. At about this time there was brought to Rosecrans a report that Brannan (seen on the 19th on the extreme left, but now in the center) was not in position in line, leaving Reynolds's right exposed. Actually, Brannan was in position, though withdrawn slightly into a wood. Without checking, Rosecrans caused a staff officer to deliver the following message to General Wood, who was on Brannan's right: "The general commanding directs that you close up on Reynolds as far as possible, and support him." Having to choose between two contradictory things, Wood chose to withdraw his brigade from line and march to the rear of Reynolds. As Sheridan's brigades, which had been ordered to Thomas, were at this moment in motion toward the left, little of the Federal army remained to the right of the gap created by Wood's withdrawal. Without much success Davis, according to McCook, sought to fill up the space into which Longstreet would soon hurl a column of attack with devastating fury.[29]

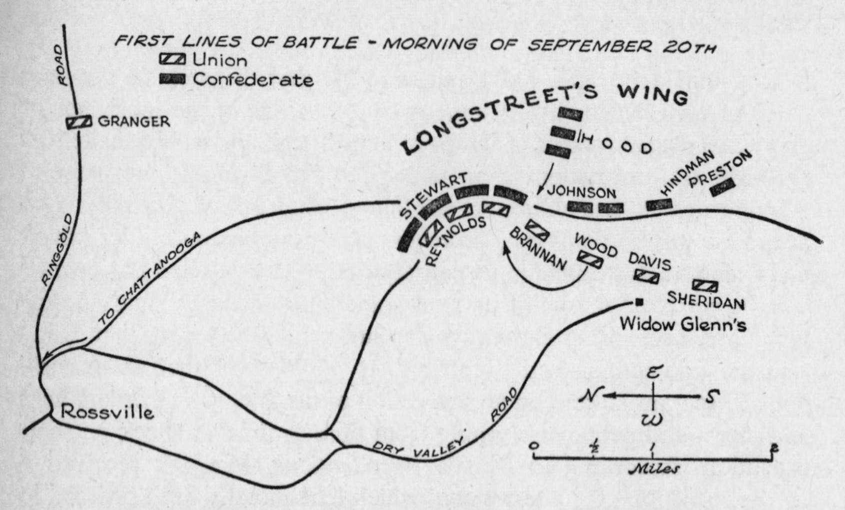

LONGSTREET'S ATTACK, MORNING, SEPTEMBER 20

At 10 A.M. the attack of Stewart's division caused Brannan to be drawn to the support of Reynolds. Johnson and Hindman were ordered by Longstreet to follow in close echelon on Hood's left.

But it is not to be thought for a moment that Longstreet achieved his success without terrific losses, bitter fighting, and moments of apparent failure. Toward eleven o'clock, when it was manifest that the attack of the Confederate right was not rolling up the Federal left, Longstreet sent a message to Bragg indicating that an attack by the left might be helpful. Bragg replied that the division to the right of where Longstreet had formed Hood's column had already received orders, and that orders would come to successive divisions on the left. Shocked by the thought that the army commander was planning consecutive assaults by divisions, Longstreet interposed and issued orders that would coordinate under his direction the efforts of the left. When Hood went in, his leading brigade was decimated by the fire of rifle and cannon from good positions behind rail defenses. Hood, who had lost an arm at Gettysburg, received here the wound that cost him a leg as well. Units to the left of Hood also staggered under the volleys poured against them, one normally composed brigade commander reporting to Longstreet that he had not a single man left. Federal cavalry upon the right also struck at the Confederate left and were held off only with difficulty. At no place in his *From Manassas to Appomattox* does Longstreet in fact indicate the knowledge of a gap caused by the withdrawal of Wood's division. He speaks merely of finally breaking the Federal line, and of Bushrod Johnson going through a breach. It was then clear to him, however, that he had achieved a notable result, for he became aware of the fact that the Federal right wing had completely given away and that men of the Twentieth and Twenty-first Corps were escaping in panic over Missionary Ridge, while wagons were extricating themselves as best they could. Grant's old classmate realized it was a time to assess the situation fully and get things well in hand before continuing. After giving orders for troops to be straightened out and fed, he sent for his own lunch, probably about one o'clock, and had it spread at a convenient place while he rode with Buckner, still on the extreme left, to view the changed conditions. After some close calls from sharpshooters' bullets, Longstreet was back and eating the Nassau bacon and Georgia sweet potatoes that were waiting for him. It was not to be a quiet, uneventful meal, for a fragment of shell struck down his chief of ordnance. Some present believed the officer was dying, but when the corps commander examined him he discovered an unconsumed piece of sweet potato which, when removed from the gasping man's mouth, brought such relief that he could be sent to a hospital, where he recovered.

Upon reporting to Bragg in consequence of an order that arrived even before his bacon and sweet potatoes had been completely disposed of, Longstreet explained the necessity of the change he had made in Bragg's orders for battle. He reported the capture of thirty guns and many small arms, and the apparent panic in the enemy ranks. As the Confederate right had had no success in completing the counterclockwise rolling up of the Federal army, Longstreet suggested that they roll up the right in a clockwise manner, such a move being already well under way. Longstreet wondered if some rested or disengaged unit on the right might be added to his troops on the left (how much time would be consumed in this is a debatable but important point) in order to "move swiftly down the Dry Valley road, [and] pursue the retreating forces."

"There is not a man in the right wing who has any fight in him," was Longstreet's recollection of Bragg's amazing reply. Disappointed though he evidently was over the failure of the right, the army commander was not disposed to listen to suggestions. Without expressing approval or disapproval about what Longstreet had done, Bragg turned abruptly and rode to his headquarters from the place where the meeting had been held. Shocked at what he had seen, Longstreet returned to his command. It appeared to him that he could count on little aid from the right wing, and that the left wing must "work along as best it could."

After giving instructions to subordinates for coordinating "our worn battle," Longstreet pushed forward, Federal guns and infantry were compelled to retire, and elevated ground was gained. In due time he came up against George H. Thomas, with his command, on Horseshoe Ridge, where the latter was to wage the fight that gave him his famous nickname—"the Rock of Chickamauga." [30]

What Longstreet wrote in his postwar book, which has been followed so far, must, of course, be laid alongside his official report of October, 1863, in order to see how passing years embellished the old soldier's memory. It was natural that in his report he made no mention of bacon or sweet potatoes, but we are fortunate in finding this detail in his book, for it shows a soldier on the battlefield who was calm and very self-possessed. In his report Longstreet said distinctly that when he talked to Bragg he had only one division that was fresh, and he put at three o'clock the hour at which he requested some rested troops from the right wing to aid the left. Most important of all, however, is the fact that he said nothing whatever about having suggested an advance down the Dry Valley road as a means of getting in the rear of the Federal troops. In his report Longstreet said definitely that at dusk he ordered his advance to stop, believing that pursuit should be postponed until the next day. It might be noted that in his report Longstreet said nothing about having been summoned to confer with Bragg or about that general's abrupt departure, as he does in his memoirs. Horn, perhaps following Longstreet, refers to Bragg's temperamental behavior and his refusal to alter his original strategy or to take suggestions from Longstreet in order to deal with the changed situation. However, even though this may have happened, it is understandable that Longstreet would omit reference to such an episode in an official report written so soon after the actual battle.[31]

According to Thomas's report it was about 2:00 P.M. when loud firing at his right and rear attracted his attention there, as Longstreet renewed his assault. After ascending a hill he encountered a captain who reported inability to deliver a message to Sheridan because of a line of Confederates advancing with skirmishers in front. Getting information from Wood, Reynolds, and others, as well as appraising the situation with his own eyes, Thomas then bent efforts to hold

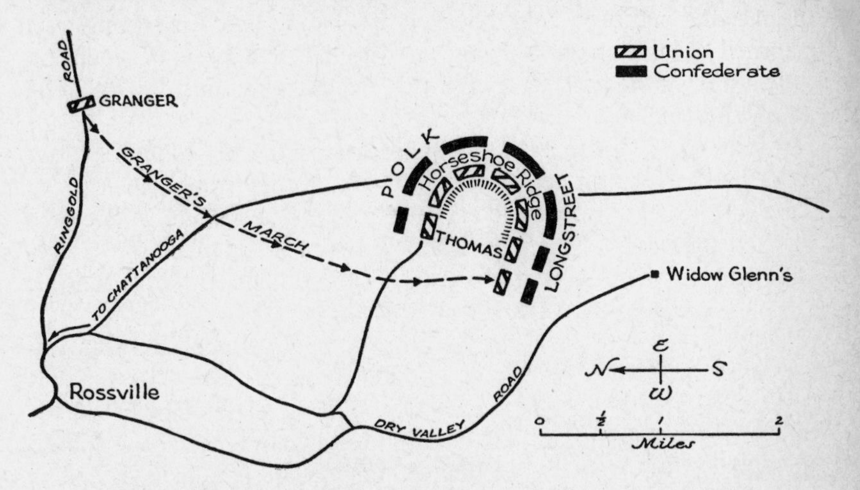

LONGSTREET'S RENEWAL OF THE ATTACK, AFTERNOON, SEPTEMBER 20

the position, which had good defensive features. Fortunately, Gordon Granger had on his own initiative already taken important action.

After having listened to heavy firing from the Federal left, Granger at 11:00 A.M. had marched in that direction with Steedman's division to be on hand to aid Thomas. The keeping of the important Rossville Gap he entrusted to Daniel McCook.

Granger had advanced about two miles when the enemy made his appearance upon the left, and opened briskly upon Granger with skirmishers and artillery. Granger halted his command long enough to convince himself that the Confederates constituted only a force in observation and were not a serious menace. Upon resuming his march toward Thomas's left, now only a mile and a half away, he boldly sent back and had Daniel McCook move forward from the all-important gap he was guarding and take over the role of watching the enemy. Then he continued his advance with Steedman toward the locality where the firing indicated a ferocious contest. Details of the fighting along Horseshoe Ridge will not be given. It was not until late afternoon that it was clear to Thomas that he must abandon the position. So hard had been the fighting and so great the losses that Longstreet on his part thought further action should wait for another day. Thomas was most generous in acknowledging the manner in which a spirited charge by Steedman had relieved great pressure at a critical moment. Ammunition fortunately brought by Steedman was used to replenish by ten rounds or so the all-but-exhausted boxes of Thomas's men, his own ammunition train having been driven away by a mistake of orders. From Garfield, who reached him about four o'clock, Thomas for the first time learned of the magnitude of the catastrophe on the Federal right. Then he received directions sent by Rosecrans to assume command and, in consort with McCook and Crittenden, to take a threatening position at Rossville. One cannot read Thomas's account of the retirement, which began about 5:30 P.M., without feeling that it was magnificently planned and superbly executed. When informed soon after the movement had started that an enemy force was interposing, Thomas changed the direction of Reynolds's line and threw him into a charge which completely routed the enemy. "In this splendid advance more than 200 prisoners were captured and sent to the rear," wrote Thomas.

Leaders and men of brigades revealed their reliable, undaunted, veteran character in one incident after another. Under Thomas's tactically fine eye, troops were placed in the Rossville Gap, on the ridges to its side, in reserve, and in front, with Minty's cavalry on the road to Ringgold a mile and a half in advance of the gap. Unless one is prepared to challenge Thomas's report, he must accept that only a fresh, well knit, and well commanded Confederate force could have dislodged Thomas from his position on the night of September 20.

Within Chattanooga itself, matters were looking more cheerful than they had when Dana wrote the historic dispatch that had begun: "My report today is of deplorable importance. Chickamauga is as fatal a name in our history as Bull Run," and had then used the words, "It was wholesale panic."

Perhaps to explain the tone of his first message, he noted in one written four hours later: "Having been myself swept bodily off the battlefield by the panic-struck rabble into which the divisions of Davis and Sheridan were temporarily converted, my own impressions were naturally colored by the aspect of that part of the field. It appears, however, that only those two divisions were actually routed. . . ."

In estimating the enemy at 70,000 Dana came surprisingly close to Livermore's figure for effectives. Near the end of his dispatch, Dana paid the Federal commander a compliment: "I can testify to the conspicuous and steady gallantry of Rosecrans on the field," adding that the general had done everything possible to rally the broken columns. In closing, however, Dana further blackened McCook. If it had not been for that general's delay of four days, he declared, disaster might have been averted—quite as if Rosecrans would have attacked Bragg and, instead of having his own right "ground up," would have ground up the Confederate right.[32]

The McCook court of inquiry subsequently held paid no attention to McCook's northward march to close up the army, but confined itself entirely to his conduct during the battle. Here its findings were very favorable to the general. On the 19th he had discharged his duty "with activity and intelligence." The court not only held him not responsible for the breaking of his line on the 20th, in view of its length and of his small forces and the fact that he was even told to cover the Dry Valley road, but it added: "Gen. McCook did everything he could to rally and hold his troops after the line was broken, giving the necessary orders to his subordinates." In leaving the field for Chattanooga, the court held McCook guilty of nothing more than lack of judgment; Rosecrans having left, his subordinate could well believe he might want to give instructions on the ground to corps commanders.

It is impossible to say what young Horace Porter thought of the departure from the field not only of Rosecrans but of Dana. For his bravery and gallantry over and above the call of duty at Chickamauga, Porter received in the 1880's the Congressional Medal of Honor, which had been instituted in 1862. To his sister Porter wrote, with regard to fleeing correspondents: "I suppose you have read all sorts of accounts of the battle in the papers, but no true ones, for the first retrograde movement occurred among that lying body of men, called the 'repertorial corps,' and men when scared see things in a very absurd light." [33]

About 10:00 A.M. of the 21st, Thomas received a message from Minty that a strong force of enemy infantry and cavalry was advancing upon him. Minty was ordered to retire and, acting upon reports from citizens as to the vulnerability of his right flank which, if turned, would open his rear to attack, Thomas advised Rosecrans to concentrate his army in Chattanooga. Not until 6:00 P.M., however, did an order come for Thomas to retire. Once more the movement was planned and executed in a masterful manner, and 7:00 A.M. on September 22nd found the troops occupying positions around Chattanooga which had been carefully selected for them. Entrenchments were immediately thrown up and strengthened from day to day, until Thomas could on September 30th pronounce them "strong enough for all defensive purposes."

Thus began the strange siege of Chattanooga, with the enemy looking down from frowning heights upon the Army of the Cumberland which, hemmed to the rear by mountains that cut supplies to a trickle, was expected to be starved into submission.

In an order to his troops Rosecrans termed their campaign a success; their objective had been to take Chattanooga and they had done so. As they eyed their dwindling helpings of food, men in blue, especially those of Crittenden's corps who had once unopposed marched into the city and then set out in pursuit of a supposedly retreating enemy, must have found the general's claim slightly fatuous.[34]

Readers of *Harper's Weekly,* for December 12, 1863, saw a drawing by a famous military artist of a train of pack mules carrying food over Walden Ridge by trails impossible for wagons. From the same pen they could see a sketch of a courier line, and they had the chance to read a description of how posts had been instituted every five miles, so that messages could be carried swiftly. Presumably, those of greatest importance were encoded, though who drew up the codes, how they were distributed, and what units employed them are questions for which there seem to be no answers.

A single telegraph wire out of Chattanooga sufficed for speedy transmittal of Dana's increasing understanding of the battle and of the defects of Rosecrans's character. (There could be leaks, even in sending encoded telegrams, and Dana in fact had to request of Stanton a new code.) "He abounds in friendliness and approbativeness, and is greatly lacking in firmness and steadiness of will," Dana stated in a dispatch on September 27th, and continued: "He is a temporizing man. . . ." Rosecrans's difficulty at present stemmed from the fact that he was much displeased by McCook's and Crittenden's desertion of the field, but was embarrassed by the fact that "if Crittenden and McCook fled to Chattanooga, with the sound of artillery in their ears, from that glorious field where Thomas and Granger were saving their army and their country's honor, he [Rosecrans] fled also. . . ."

While feeling among officers and men against McCook and Crittenden continued, Dana before long reported that the former high esteem of the soldiers for Rosecrans had vanished also, and that they no longer cheered him unless ordered to do so by their officers. Thomas had become the man who held their admiration. Dana said, ". . . should there be a change in the chief command, there is no other man whose appointment would be so welcome to this army." Ultimately Dana modified his harsh attitude toward McCook and Crittenden and said that the latter had "admirable qualities of character." A severe indictment was contained in the statement: "Careful examination of them [reports of officers] seems to prove that the gap in the lines through which the enemy poured, flanking and routing all of three divisions and a part of a fourth, was caused by an order of the commanding general . . . the probability still remains very strong that but for this unfortunate order we should have gained a decisive victory." Apparently Dana did not entirely accept Rosecrans's view as to what Wood should have done upon receipt of the ambiguous order. The Assistant Secretary hazarded the opinion that Rosecrans in his own report would "elaborately show that the blame of his failure in this great battle rests on the Administration; that is, on the Secretary of War and General-in-Chief, who did not foresee Bragg would be re-enforced, and who compelled him to move forward without cavalry enough, and very inadequately prepared in many other respects."

Further and still more devastating analyses of Rosecrans's character continued, until on October 18 we find Dana writing: ". . . the practical incapacity of the general commanding is astonishing, and it often seems difficult to believe him of sound mind. His imbecility appears to be contagious, and it is difficult for anyone to get anything done." [35]

The Federal campaign having been wrecked, the question has often been asked whether the Confederates fully exploited their opportunity. As to any chance on the 20th, surely Longstreet's knowledge of the activity of Mitchell's cavalry in his rear, as well as the terrible fighting he had had to do in order to advance, and his own statement that he thought pursuit ought to wait for the next day, make untenable the contention that Bragg's failure to follow Longstreet's suggestions resulted in Thomas's successful withdrawal from Horseshoe Ridge to Rossville.

In his report, Longstreet spoke of recommending to Bragg, when the latter came to his bivouac on the morning of the 21st and asked for suggestions, that they cross the river above Chattanooga, force Rosecrans from the city, and pursue him all the way to Nashville if possible. If shortage of wagons made this impracticable, he recommended a march against Burnside and the destruction of his force. Here certainly was wishful thinking, for though the abandonment of East Tennessee could have been compelled, Burnside still had a good escape route through Cumberland Gap.

Deducting Bragg's casualties of about 18,000 from the 66,000 effectives that Livermore gave him, Bragg would have had not more than 48,000 men for a forward move, as against some 42,000 remaining to Rosecrans after allowing for his losses. It was Longstreet's feeling that Bragg promised careful consideration of his proposal, if indeed he did not virtually accept it. On the morning of the 22nd, Longstreet, according to his memoirs, started to move, only to halt in disgust because Bragg had decided upon an investment of Chattanooga. With one vacillating general opposing another, both of whom had abandoned a battlefield, it would indeed be folly to predict what would actually have transpired if Bragg had sought to carry out Longstreet's proposal.

Rosecrans certainly had doubtful moments on the 21st as to his ability to hold Chattanooga. In a dispatch at nine o'clock on that morning he indicated that only with maximum assistance from Burnside would he be able to hold his position. Halleck flashed this information to Burnside at 2:45 P.M. Garfield evidently feared a precipitate abandonment of the city, for at 11:00 A.M. the Rossville telegraph operator transmitted to Rosecrans the plea: "General Garfield left here at 10:30; will arrive at Chattanooga about 11:30. He hopes you will not leave before his arrival."

The appearance of Thomas and a large part of the army early on the 22nd evidently allayed Rosecrans's fears, for in a courier message to Burnside he wrote: "Come down on west side Tennessee as rapidly as possible. We shall probably have to hold Chattanooga as a *tête-de-pont* until re-inforcements come up." There is no indication of great or undue precipitancy here.[36]

In a visit that Jefferson Davis made to the army in October, higher commanders were catechized as to their views of Bragg in the latter's presence. After considering the entire matter for a day or so, Davis, accepting a proposal made by Longstreet rather than one put forward by Bragg, ordered an abandonment of the siege of Chattanooga and, using Rome as a base, a movement to Bridgeport following a route west of Lookout Mountain, with the object of intervening between the troops brought from the east by Hooker and the army of Rosecrans. According to Longstreet's book, heavy rains soon after the President's return to Richmond were used as an excuse by Bragg for his failure to carry out Davis's direction.

If a major move were not made against the Federals, the only remaining thing was a cavalry stroke. Though the raid that Wheeler conducted between September 30th and October 17th resulted in the destruction of many wagons filled with supplies, the capture of many points, and the burning of bridges and trestles as far north as Murfreesboro, Wheeler found himself ultimately heavily pursued, and there was no reason to believe that the Federal grip on Tennessee south of Nashville could be essentially weakened, or that it would be possible to prevent the accumulation of supplies at Bridgeport.[37]

Spectacular indeed had been the great columns of smoke rising from burning wagons and supplies in Anderson's Gap, the smaller columns from burning railroad bridges; and ignominious indeed the Federal capitulation at McMinnville. But the real drama of those October days was the logistical miracle in the swift sending of the Eleventh and Twelfth corps from the Army of the Potomac, in contact with the enemy in Virginia, to the vicinity of Bridgeport. People in the North had some of their alarm allayed by the swift and unexpected action. Southern leaders could not contemplate an easy and open road to Kentucky and the banks of the Ohio. An alert and forehanded enemy was prepared to meet them, and they may have thought of other possible concentrations of force of which they did not know.

Writing at Stevenson on October 13th, Major-General Joseph Hooker, who had been replaced as commander of the Army of the Potomac by Meade on the eve of Gettysburg, said that rail communications had been broken for four days by Wheeler's demolitions, adding that in his judgment a much longer time would be required to "repair the reputations of some of the officers to whom the defense of our communications had been intrusted." The general who after a brilliant maneuver had expected Lee to retire from the vicinity of Chancellorsville had, however, a constructive suggestion. Earthworks would be better than stockades for defending bridges. Then, in case the enemy attacked with artillery, defense troops would not be fearful of "splintering and flying timber." [38]

Who was to command the greatly augmented forces in Tennessee? Grant's name had been put on the wire to Washington by Dana, but only with regard to the Army of the Cumberland. Later in the year the big decision was made to unite the departments of the Ohio, the Cumberland, and the Tennessee into the military division of the Mississippi under the command of Grant. The defeat of Rosecrans was certainly a contributing factor. The tone of a telegram Halleck sent to Grant on September 17th, in which he was taken behind the scenes in Washington, suggests a turning to him for something larger. It had been difficult, said the General in Chief, to decide whether the enemy intention had really been to make a concentration in Georgia or to move troops from there to strengthen Lee for a heavy blow against Meade, which their holding of interior lines would have equally facilitated. The *New York Herald* had, indeed—as Freeman has pointed out—carried, on the 9th, a report about the move to Georgia. But this could have been due to deliberate deception, and the high command had done well in making no final decision until it had received Foster's report that trains were running southward.

As he wrote the date of September 17 at the head of his dispatch, Halleck must have thought that Grant would soon be reading his dispatch of September 13 mentioned earlier in this chapter. Fate, however, was to interpose exasperatingly, for it was not until September 25 that Grant began a dispatch to Halleck, "Your dispatches of the 13th are just this moment received. Have been detained between Cairo and Memphis from the 14th to the 22nd." The steamer *Minnehaha* had handled badly a package marked "Important Government dispatches, to be delivered immediately." The entire time had, fortunately, not been lost, for Halleck had sent Hurlbut direct and prompt instructions on the subject of aiding Rosecrans, and Hurlbut, believing that Grant was still in New Orleans, had forwarded them to Sherman. Preparations had been punctually started at Vicksburg to put them into effect.

Grant had immediately directed that the division which McPherson was about to land at Helena should continue up the river to Memphis, to become part of the eastward marching force. Steele, having captured Little Rock on the 10th, would have no need for it. Under the final plan worked out by Grant, McPherson's division was supplemented by two divisions from Sherman's corps, Sherman himself to be in command of the composite force.

To Hurlbut, Sherman expressed the doubt whether troops being sent would arrive in time to be of use, adding, "Still, I have abundant faith in Halleck and will play his game." If Bragg had actually carried out Davis's instructions to give up the siege of Chattanooga, change to Rome as a base, and march toward Bridgeport on the roads to the right of Lookout Mountain so as to interpose between Hooker and Rosecrans, he would have found not only the Eleventh and Twelfth corps on his left but also a composite corps under Sherman. Sherman certainly later saw that the movement eastward was far from being too late to be of important use.

In answer to renewed calls from Banks for help, Grant on September 17 telegraphed to him:

> Inclosed I send you copy of dispatch from the General-in-Chief; also my reply. This will necessarily prevent further re-enforcements going west from here to you until word is heard from the General-in-Chief. We must make no disposition of troops that will endanger the success of Rosecrans.

Then, apparently disturbed lest Halleck think there had been tardiness on his part in sending troops to aid Rosecrans, Grant on September 30 began a dispatch to the General in Chief: "I regret that there should be such apparent tardiness in complying with your orders, but I assure you that as soon as your wishes were known, troops were forwarded as rapidly as transportation could be procured." [39]

Then followed a period of waiting.

APPENDIX

GENERAL HENRY HALLECK

Any argument about the Civil War, no matter how spirited, will end amicably if one of the disputants has enough presence of mind to say, "But wasn't Halleck terrible?" Condemnation ranges all the way from condescending remarks by academic historians with no discernible basic military knowledge to sharp criticisms by soldiers who have not troubled themselves to examine the full record.

A number of reviewers have remarked that I have been kinder than other writers to Halleck. Some have merely noted the fact; others have implied censure. I have wondered whether my critics ever considered whether I had changed my own opinion. The truth is that about no one have I altered my views as much as about Halleck. A dozen years ago I would have made the usual denunciations, pointing to bad orders that Halleck gave, and leveling off with the charge of general unfitness. Had I been asked if I had checked whether Halleck had actually given the alleged orders, or whether his orders had really had the effect claimed, or if I had studied his command problem, I would have had to say I had not. But what of that? I could have stated that everyone said what I was saying, and that therefore it must be true.

In Civil War times, as in these, there were backscratchers. But William Tecumseh Sherman was not one. Sherman, famed for saying that war was hell and could not be refined, almost wept when Halleck was called from Corinth to Washington. The Sherman who poured out his praise and regrets in the letter of July, 1862, was of course not the broadly experienced general of 1865.[1] But he had been through the two days of Shiloh with Grant, and he had been in the advance to Corinth for which Halleck has been ridiculed. While that operation will never be cited as a model, I believe that Sherman even to the end would have called some of Halleck's critics uninformed and unjust.

It is unfortunate that a letter Grant wrote to Elihu Washburne on

July 22, 1862, did not appear in *Grant's Letters to a Friend,* edited by James Grant Wilson. In it Grant said:

> I do not know the object of calling Gen. H. to Washington, but if it is to make him Sec. of War, or Commander-in-Chief, Head Quarters at Washington, a better selection could not be made. He is a man of gigantic intellect and well studied in the profession of arms. He and I have had several little spats but I like and respect him nevertheless.[2]

Grant never wrote a careless word, and I think that when he said "Head Quarters in Washington," he was implying that Halleck's place was not in the field. With that thought there can be no quarrel. But in the words "gigantic intellect and well studied in the profession of arms," there is no hint that Halleck was merely a pedant.

When I began to study military matters seriously, I was surprised and chagrined to find how few, aside from memoirs, were the contributions to military literature by American soldiers. I admired the various drill regulations, field service regulations, and other books, then very few in number, with which a soldier could do business. But I found nothing by American pens to equal Henderson's *The Science of War,* and when I wanted to look at the Civil War from a soldier's discerning viewpoint, it was to Henderson's *Stonewall Jackson,* or Wood and Edmonds's book that I went.

I knew that Halleck had written a book, but with the feeling I then entertained for him I had no desire to examine it. It was only after a change in my estimation that I acquired his *Elements of Military Art and Science.* When I opened it and read, I found not only a mastery of a great subject, but also a well-written and interesting book. Halleck's book is unique, and I give it a place of honor on my bookshelves.

His book proves that as a young officer Halleck had a high interest in his profession. To him, soldiering meant more than drill, and more than keeping office hours. It meant being broadly and thoroughly informed. Sherman bore testimony to this in a remarkable letter he wrote to Halleck on Jan. 29, 1864, while a boat bearing him to Vicksburg was tied up in a fog. Sherman had recently addressed a meeting of Union men in Memphis. To encourage those who saw dark days ahead for Tennessee, he had expressed the faith that men would come forward equal to new needs, citing how they had appeared at the proper moment from the beginning of the war. In that connection he had used Halleck's name, and in his letter he wrote:

> I spoke of your indomitable industry, and called to mind how when Ord, Loeser, Spotts, and I were shut up in our state-room, trying to keep warm with lighted candles, and playing cards on the old Lexington, off Cape Horn, you were lashed to your berth studying, boning harder than you ever did at West Point.

Sherman knew of Halleck's fine book on international law, written in California after he left the Army. He had spoken to the Union men in Memphis of Halleck's "knowledge of law, especially the higher branch of it—the law of war and of nations." He had noticed with concern that newspapers were trying to undermine Halleck's influence, and in his talk he had said he supposed it resulted from Halleck's "abrupt, brusque manner, even to members of Congress." He had told his listeners in Memphis that Halleck knew more about law "than Mr. Lincoln, Mr. Chase, and Mr. Seward combined." [3]

Only four months previously Sherman had received from Halleck a letter that condemned self-servers and that rang with the sentence, "*Duty, Duty, Duty* is the only proper motto now for military men." Too many officers were trying to make reputations for themselves rather than end the war. "Honorable exceptions" there were: Grant and a few others. Halleck's high evaluation of Grant was returned endorsed by Sherman, with the statement that in Grant there was an "utter absence of vainglory and selfish pride." In a few weeks Halleck was to have the chance to prove that he could live up to his eulogy of duty by accepting a subordinate role under Grant.[4]

McClellan probably did not exaggerate when on assigning Halleck to Missouri in November, 1861, he told him that there was no parallel in history to conditions there. Because of the dearth of staff officers, Halleck had to be many men in one. It can be doubted if there has ever been a general in our service better qualified to do that than Halleck. He did not have to consult anyone about sound military organization. He did not have to sit and listen to some judge advocate brief him on difficult constitutional questions. Subordinate officers had to be instructed. Here was a department commander who had a flair for teaching, and officers must have respected the signature at the bottom of the long general order he issued on the laws of war, on courts-martial, and military commissions. It was a wholesome thing for them to learn, as learn they did, that always in the back of Halleck's mind was the Constitution.

Almost simultaneously with Halleck's arrival at St. Louis, Sterling Price entered the state from the Southwest and issued a flamboyant proclamation for 50,000 Missourians to rally to his force. Thus, as Halleck strove to straighten out administrative chaos, he had active operations on his hands. Sherman was one of the few professionally trained officers at his disposal. Halleck sent him to the vicinity of Sedalia. Soon the report reached him that Sherman had panicked and was causing panic in others. He had to be recalled, and Halleck gave him a leave of absence. Busy though he was, he wrote Sherman a fine letter at his home. Then, when Sherman returned to duty, Halleck put him at Benton Barracks to train troops, work which allowed Sherman to find himself. When has a commander in an extremely difficult situation shown greater understanding and wisdom in salvaging an officer of known capacity, who, to put it bluntly, had "washed out" at a critical time? [5]

Halleck has been justly blamed for the lack of cordiality, or actual incivility, that he showed Grant when Grant came to see him in the latter part of January, 1862, to propose an operation up the Tennessee. The abrupt, brusque manner, of which Sherman wrote later, may at times have protected Halleck from self-servers and intriguers when he was in Washington, and also in St. Louis. But it should have been put aside when his Cairo commander came into his office. Grant naturally thought that Halleck believed the entire proposal was preposterous, and that idea is still current. But Halleck had only a few days previously written in a long letter to McClellan that the Tennessee and Cumberland offered the correct entry into the Confederacy. In two or three weeks, after he had more force and could make his bases secure, he expected to use it.

A few days later, after receiving telegrams from Grant and Commodore Foote, Halleck ordered the operation. It was one of the boldest decisions of the entire war. The operation was full of hazard. The Federal line of communications ran within a few miles of the strong enemy position at Columbus, and the Confederate railroads could concentrate superior forces from both Columbus and Bowling Green against the relatively small command with which Grant started. If the operation had failed, the responsibility would have been Halleck's.[6]

Halleck's part did not end with giving the order. He was energy and competence itself in getting reinforcements to Grant. While Grant acknowledged that Halleck had helped by sending new regiments to him, he did not know the full story. To the reluctant Buell at Louisville, Halleck wrote that he was stripping Missouri, and if there were new outbreaks in the state he would put them down later. Buell telegraphed to McClellan that the operation was a proper one, but he accused Halleck of beginning it too soon and without proper preparation. How often, one can ask, has a general *advanced* the time for an operation as Halleck did and with as many uncertain elements as he faced? Halleck is constantly accused of being overcautious. Yet the first great campaign of the war began with a courageous order by Halleck.[7]

Prominent in any list of criticisms of Halleck is the charge that his order for Buell to repair the railroad eastward from Corinth was largely responsible, if not entirely so, for Buell's failure to reach Chattanooga in the early summer of 1862, and thus forestall Bragg. A half-hour's study of the *Official Records* will show that this is false. Three of Buell's divisions crossed the Tennessee River at Florence and marched through Athens without any connection with the railroad. The fourth aided and protected the engineers in railroad work, and the colonel of the engineer regiment reported the repairs complete to Decatur just two days after Buell himself rode through Athens, fifteen miles to the north. From opposite Decatur almost to Stevenson the railroad was already being operated by Mitchel's division. Thus Buell was not delayed by railroad work. And in replying two weeks later to Halleck's dispatch about the President's displeasure with his progress, Buell did not give railroad repairs as an excuse.[8]

Halleck is frequently criticized for breaking up the large army he had at Corinth; and it is asserted that Vicksburg could easily have been taken in the summer of 1862. The beginning of the breakup came when Buell was ordered to Chattanooga. Before the movement had begun, Halleck had informed Lincoln of his intention, and a few days later Stanton told him that the President was "greatly delighted" with his contemplated operation. Thus responsibility really goes back to Washington.[9]

It was particularly the duty of the High Command to issue an order in the case of Vicksburg, if there were to be an objective for Halleck's army. The troops in the operation then in progress against that place had come from Butler's force at New Orleans. Halleck should not be criticized for not aiding an operation about which he knew little. He himself had a very broad front, reaching from eastward toward Chattanooga, across Alabama and Mississippi, and extending into Arkansas. What the Confederates would do to counter Buell he did not know. Nor did he know too much about their strength across the Mississippi and what Curtis's needs there would be. After Halleck had gone to Washington, Buell had to be supported by three divisions from Grant, who had succeeded to command at Corinth. Some troops had also to go to Curtis.

Those who believe that an overland campaign against Vicksburg could have been carried out successfully neglect logistical as well as other factors, all of which are of the greatest importance. The straight-line distance from Corinth was 225 miles, and it was a very hot and dry summer. What happened a year later is certainly relevant. After the surrender of Vicksburg, Grant sent Sherman with most of his army against Joe Johnston, who retired behind the fortifications at Jackson, which had been considerably strengthened since Grant had taken the place in May. Because he saw Sherman could work around to his rear, Johnston evacuated the place in about a week and marched eastward. Why did Sherman not pursue him? It was too hot and dry. He explicitly said so in an order to his three corps commanders, and so reported to Grant. The summer of 1862 was also one of excessive dryness in Mississippi, and Halleck's men were not the seasoned veterans that Sherman had in 1863. And Sherman's supply line was a simple problem compared with the one Halleck would have had.

As to sending a force down the Mississippi to aid Butler's efforts, to do so would have probably meant a Federal defeat in Kentucky, for Grant would not have been able to send the three divisions essential to Buell, without abandoning West Tennessee. It is impossible to send the same troops simultaneously south and north.

As one follows Halleck to Washington, it is well to keep in mind the many and great difficulties of the position he took over. For four months there had been no General in Chief. Lincoln and Stanton had been directing the war with some advice from the elderly Major General Ethan Allen Hitchcock. Thus Halleck did not walk into a well-organized headquarters with plenty of good staff officers of high rank waiting only for a commander, and able to give him a good briefing on the situation. The situation was bad, or soon became bad, on all fronts: on the Peninsula, in northern Virginia, in Tennessee and Kentucky, and ultimately west of the Mississippi. In McClellan, Halleck had a touchy subordinate, who had once been his superior. Nor do I think that Lincoln, in spite of his great patience, was always easy to deal with, especially for one who had trouble seeing life's lighter side. Stanton's tendency toward harshness is well known. Perhaps it was well that Halleck could meet him with the look that photographs reveal. No subsequent General in Chief or Chief of Staff has had to work in an atmosphere as heavily charged politically as that in which Halleck lived.

An indication of the tension is shown in his letter to Banks of April 3, 1863. Halleck had spoken of the disappointed hope of sending reinforcements to Banks from Hunter's command in South Carolina. Then he added:

> It is unfortunate that the Government, yielding to outside pressure and the impatience of the people, has undertaken too many things at the same time. But this has been the result of circumstances which neither you nor I could control. We are only responsible for doing our best with the means at our command.

That he was not unconscious of the problems of the President was shown by the conclusion:

> I hope the weather will soon permit some of our armies to move. A successful operation would greatly relieve the Government.

The order that called Halleck to Washington stated that he was "assigned to command the whole land forces of the United States, as General in Chief." [10] His actual role was, however, very different from what this would lead one to expect. We have Halleck's own description of his position in a reply to the letter from Sherman previously mentioned:

> I am simply a military adviser of the Secretary of War and the President and must obey and carry out what they decide upon, whether I concur in their

decisions or not. As a good soldier I obey the orders of my superiors. If I disagree with them in opinion I say so, but when they decide, it is my duty faithfully to carry out their decision. Moreover, I cannot say to the public I approve this and I disapprove that. I have no right to say this, as it might embarrass the execution of a measure fully decided on. My mouth is closed, except when officially called on to give such opinion.

Lincoln is said to have complained that he could not get Halleck to take greater responsibility. Doubtless this was true on some occasions; doubtless not on others. I find it hard to believe that, after four months of personal command, Lincoln was satisfied to sit back and merely watch attentively, especially in view of crucial situations that existed when Halleck arrived.

It does not seem too important to try to fix responsibility for the way things worked out, for another, more basic thought, arises. At that time ideas about military command had not evolved sufficiently to give anything like proper over-all direction to the entire war, and it seems strange that officers of our army have not emphasized this. The earliest roster of Halleck's staff that I have found is for February, 1863. It shows seven officers and sixteen enlisted men. Only one general officer was on Halleck's staff. I would not try to say how many stars would now be thought necessary for the proper exercise of command over the Federal Army.

The charge that Halleck was habitually overcautious is also applied to his Washington service. I should like to cite what in mathematics we would call a counterexample, a counterexample being a favorite way for one mathematician to wreck a fanciful dream of another mathematician. When Grant in October, 1862, queried Halleck about having Rosecrans continue the pursuit of Van Dorn, the answer he received was: "Why order a return of our troops? Why not re-enforce Rosecrans and pursue the enemy into Mississippi, supporting your army on the country?" [11]

It makes no difference that Grant, who had already made his decision and recalled Rosecrans, replied that in Mississippi there was no support for an army except in forage. What counts is that Halleck proposed a bold, not a timid, course, even in conducting a pursuit which, to be effective, must be pushed. The facts in this case refute the frequent allegation that Halleck was frightened by Grant's calculated risk in cutting loose from his base in the Vicksburg campaign and living on the country.

Up through Vicksburg all of Halleck's communications to Grant were short. His first long letter was dated Oct. 20, 1863, and was occasioned by Grant's assignment to command of the new Military Division of the Mississippi, comprising the Departments of the Ohio, the Cumberland, and the Tennessee. As the command was a new one, there was no file of orders and directives to a predecessor for Grant to consult. Yet knowledge of missions previously assigned was highly important for him. This was what Halleck put on paper three days before Grant arrived at Chattanooga. I quote the first sentence to show how Halleck got down to business with no waste of words:

> In compliance with my promise, I now proceed to give you a brief statement of the objects aimed at by General Rosecrans' and General Burnside's movement into East Tennessee, and of the measures directed to be taken to attain these objects.

When one reads this fine letter, and two others equally long which Halleck wrote to Grant, it is difficult to believe that Halleck was just a clerk, of an elevated sort perhaps, but still a clerk.[12]

In a long letter of January 8, 1864, Grant for the first time was given the full explanation as to why the operation against Mobile that he had recommended after Vicksburg had not been made. I shall note that Halleck introduced the subject, not merely to enlighten Grant on the past, but because the explanation might influence his projected winter operations. Grant was also told that he had not been put in command of an enlarged department merely to consume his time with administrative work. Department commanders were to continue to carry on those heavy duties, and Halleck explicitly indicated that it was desired to have Grant in a position where he could give "full attention to military operations."

A little over a month passed before the next long letter. It carries the date February 17, 1864, and covers three full pages of the *Official Records*. In this letter Halleck described the situation in the East and made appraisals. The objectives in the next campaign must be, he said, the armies of Lee and of Johnston. In view of the fact that he wrote nine days before the passage of the bill re-creating the position of lieutenant general, Halleck made an especially important statement. With reference to the possible line of operations for the Army of the Potomac, he wrote, "The final decision of this question will probably depend, under the President, upon yourself." In order to drive the point home, Halleck returned to this forecast near the end of the letter.[13]

It would certainly have been a satisfaction to Halleck if he could have seen a letter that Rawlins, Grant's adjutant, had written a month previously to Elihu Washburne. The bill creating the position of lieutenant general was still undisposed of, and Rawlins said Grant wanted nothing done "with a view of superseding of General Halleck." Grant had "great confidence and friendship for the General-in-Chief, and would without regard to rank be willing at all times to receive orders through him." While we cannot suppose that Grant had any knowledge of the writing of the letter, it is impossible to challenge its accuracy, and it disposes of the question whether Grant had basically changed his opinion toward Halleck since, eighteen months previously, he had expressed his high regard.[14]

The War Department order that was issued on March 12 disposed of the matter: Grant was made General in Chief. But it should be emphasized that he did not supersede Halleck except in title. His position was an entirely new one, for he could devote the major part of his time to planning, simply because Halleck patriotically took over the role of Chief of Staff in Washington. Grant's proved ability, of course, encouraged Lincoln to all but give up any personal direction of the war. The time was also favorable: Grant, unlike Halleck, did not arrive at a time of crisis.

The War Department order stated that Halleck had asked to be relieved of the position of General in Chief. Personally I do not think that this was mere face saving for Halleck by the Administration, or that he had merely bowed to the inevitable. Halleck had not been happy in the position, and a remark that Lincoln made to John Hay in August, 1862, is relevant. At the time of the Second Bull Run crisis the President expressed to his young secretary his distress over the jealousy and bickering of higher officers. In response to a query about Halleck, Lincoln had replied that that general was wholly and entirely for the good of the service, irrespective of personalities. While that appraisal was based upon only a month's contact with Halleck, Lincoln had every reason to believe that Halleck would continue to give the best that was in him when subordinated to Grant. But of course there were doubters, and Hitchcock states in his diary that in an interview with Lincoln during Early's famous raid he had raised the question whether Halleck was suffering "any painful feeling on account of the appointment over him of General Grant."

One hesitates to reject completely the accuracy of this statement, though the entry in the diary may have been written after the date July 6 under which it appears, just as the next entry was certainly written after July 28. In the entry of July 28 Hitchcock refers to the destruction of Chambersburg which did not take place until July 30 when the town was burned by a detachment of cavalry sent across the river for that specific purpose by Early after he had returned to Virginia from his raid.[15]

From the Union standpoint, the important thing about this campaign is not the appearance of Lincoln in the trenches, though that may have had a stimulating and moral effect. What should be studied is the dispatches between Halleck and Grant, over a telegraph system that was sometimes slow. The question was whether Early, commanding Ewell's old corps, had returned to Petersburg after driving Hunter westward from Lynchburg, or had gone down the Shenandoah Valley.

At 4:00 P.M. on July 3 Halleck telegraphed to Grant that Sigel had reported from Martinsburg that not only Breckinridge but Early were approaching. The dispatch passed one that Grant had sent an hour later, which contained the sentence, "Early's corps is now here." Without delay Grant informed Meade of Halleck's report and queried whether it was certain that Early had returned to his front. Meade replied that no deserters from Early's corps had come in and that the corps had not been reported in his front, but that deserters from other corps had said it had returned from Lynchburg. On the 4th Grant was still unconvinced that Early was not present in the Petersburg lines, but near midnight on the 5th he ended a telegram to Halleck, "I think now there is no doubt but Ewell's corps is away from here." The message also reported that Grant had sent forward one division of the Sixth Corps and all his dismounted cavalry. Those troops, however, were actually sent to Baltimore, and the infantry joined Lew Wallace at Frederick.

On the 9th, Halleck advised Grant to send the balance of the Sixth Corps, but Grant had already made the decision and given an order before Halleck's message arrived. Grant was inaccurate, however, when he said in a dispatch to Meade that Halleck thought that a third of Lee's army was with Early. Halleck had merely stated that that was being reported; he had vouchsafed no evaluation of the report.[16]

It is certainly to Lincoln's credit that he kept much in the background at this time and did not intrude until a dispatch from Grant made an expression by him necessary. Grant had specifically raised the question whether he should come to Washington in a telegram that he sent to Halleck at 6:00 P.M. on the 9th, and had said he could start in an hour if the President thought it advisable. Nineteen hours passed before the dispatch arrived. In replying, Lincoln showed that he was well posted as to the situation, and he said that he thought Grant should leave enough men to keep his hold where he was and bring the balance to Washington. If a vigorous effort were made, he thought the Confederate force could be destroyed. Lincoln stressed the fact that he was not giving an order. But in saying that he was expressing himself because of a suggestion by Grant, he went beyond Grant's query, which had merely been about coming to Washington in person.

Charles Dana had been at City Point, and it was natural that Grant should send him to Washington to forward information, though it looks as if Halleck had been covering essential matters very well. Dana sent a very long and newsy dispatch at 10:00 P.M. on July 11. But the ending of a message he sent at noon on July 12 was inaccurate and highly regrettable: "General Halleck will not give orders except as he receives them; the President will give none, and until you direct positively and explicitly what is to be done, everything will go on in the deplorable and fatal way in which it has gone on for the past week." [17]

Nothing fatal had occurred, and Dana, fresh to the Washington scene, did not know all that had taken place. Certainly he had not read Halleck's file of messages.

From the moment Halleck knew that the balance of the Sixth Corps (two divisions) was coming, he thought not of using them in the trenches, but of preparing them for field service. In reporting Wright's personal arrival on the 11th, Halleck informed Grant that he could furnish transportation to replace the wagons that had been left behind but that he could not furnish light batteries, and he wondered if Grant could not send some quickly. On July 12, the day that Dana sent his dispatch with the colorful ending, Halleck informed Grant that he thought Washington was safe, though Early's lines were still in view. He also sent a reply to General Augur, commanding Washington defenses, that would have pleased Grant. Augur had requested some men from one of Wright's newly arrived artillery regiments; he wanted to put them in Fort Slocum. Halleck asked him if he could not get some "invalid artillerists." He wanted "to keep Wright's corps ready for the field." At 10:25 the next morning Halleck informed Augur that Wright had "orders"—note the word, Dana notwithstanding—to be ready to march the moment it was determined in what direction the retiring enemy had moved.

Early succeeded in recrossing the Potomac safely, though Halleck as well as Grant had hoped he might be cut off. Three hours after Halleck had sent his dispatch to Augur, Halleck was reading an important message from Grant, sent before Grant had read the Dana sentence that has distorted history: Wright should get outside the trenches with all the force possible and "push Early to the last moment, supplying himself from the country." Here was recognition that vigorous pursuit was the most that could be accomplished, and that was exactly what orders already given by Halleck contemplated. The last words of Grant's dispatch, one should note, were almost the same as those used by Halleck in his message about the pursuit of Van Dorn.[18]

The trouble with Early was far from over. In a very vexing way he established himself in the vicinity of Martinsburg, and a well-known dispatch that Lincoln sent Grant on Aug. 3 looks as if the President thought Halleck was lax or indifferent to a telegram Grant had sent him on the 1st. Lincoln asked Grant to check the tenor of dispatches he had received from Washington, when the real question would have been the instructions that Halleck would give to Sheridan whom Grant was sending to take charge of the operations against Early, and Sheridan had not arrived. Actually on the very day that Grant had telegraphed Halleck, Hunter, then at Frederick, Maryland, had wired Halleck that six men in a small brigade had fallen dead from the heat the day before, and that without rest it seemed impossible for the officers of either the Sixth Corps or the Nineteenth Corps (one division of which had arrived) to get much out of their men. A year previously when Sherman had stated that he was not following Johnston because of the heat and lack of water, Grant had at once acquiesced. Perhaps the temperature was partly responsible for the rather uncommon tone in Lincoln's telegram.

The many messages in the thousands upon thousands of pages of the *O.R.* are uniformly serious. Littleness is revealed in some of them; inadequacy to command in some; greatness in some; humor in very, very few. But a dispatch that Halleck wrote in those first two weeks of July, 1864, when many in Washington were frightened, can provoke a smile, a singular fact in view of his stern face.

On July 6, Brigadier General Joseph R. West, of California, whom Halleck may have known in that state, telegraphed to him from Philadelphia, "If there is really a raid can I be of any service in this vicinity?" Perhaps the offer was repeated, for Halleck's reply of July 11 was addressed to the Fifth Avenue Hotel, New York City. Though that was the most crucial day of all, Halleck was certainly not excited, and though the hour was 11:35 P.M. he could still put an estimate of the situation into language which I do not think anyone will say was ambiguous: "We have five times as many generals here as we want, but are greatly in need of privates. Any one volunteering in that capacity will be thankfully received." [19]

A competent study of Halleck is in my judgment a most needed book on the Civil War. It should be undertaken only by a soldier with important command experience, or at least with staff closeness to command. Why should not a general officer of the United States Army set himself the task of putting aright the record of a man who was a devoted student of military art and science and of the laws of war; who had an exalted sense of duty; who straightened out great confusion in Missouri and who courageously made one of the most important decisions of the war and then showed skill in helping make the operation successful; who for many months held a position in Washington harder than any other General in Chief or Chief of Staff has had; and whose telegrams had an enviable clarity? Such a work would be more than a study of Halleck. It would be a study of command at the highest level, and as much a contribution to American military literature as was Halleck's *Elements* a century and a decade ago. Waiting for the title page is the sentence, "He is a man of gigantic intellect and well studied in the profession of arms." What soldier wearing stars, what Chief of Staff, would not be stirred and perhaps a little envious when he read those words and noted below them the name U. S. Grant?

NOTES

References to the *Official Records* are given in such a way as to show the number of dispatches supporting a paragraph, as well as their proper order. Thus, *O.R., 7,* 562–563 indicates a single message running from p. 562 to p. 563, while *O.R., 7,* 562, 562–563, 563, indicates additional dispatches on pp. 562 and 563. The repetition of a page number may also appear, as in *O.R., 8,* 530, 532, 540, 532.

NOTES TO CHAPTER I

1. *O.R., 32,* 407.

2. *O.R., 33,* 815–816. On May 30, Maj. Gen. J. Bankhead Magruder, commanding the District of Texas, New Mexico, and Arizona, complained directly to the Confederate Chief of Ordnance. A vessel bringing 8,000 stand of arms from Havana was long overdue—probably a casualty at sea, Bankhead said, to Federal cruisers. Only a third of his troops were well armed, and some were not armed at all. There would be no weapons whatever for the increased force which he would have to call out in case of invasion. On June 6 Smith wrote to Pemberton, expressing the view that arms might be crossed at Vicksburg; he put his imperative needs at 10,000 small arms and accouterments (*O.R., 42,* 24–25; *33,* 859).

3. *O.R., 33,* 796–797, 789, 851, 873, 871–873 (Smith to Davis, June 16).

On February 7, Hindman asked Holmes that he and the members of his staff who wished to accompany him be ordered to report to Bragg, east of the Mississippi. Holmes promptly refused the request, saying he had no one to take Hindman's place, and stating that he hoped that Hindman would not persist or ask that his request be referred to higher headquarters. Hindman persisted in a letter on the 8th in which he said, "I know my own capacity far better than any one else can. As the positive result of that knowledge, I am convinced that I cannot be useful in your command." Actually, Hindman had been relieved of duty in the department a week previous to this interchange and had been ordered to report at Vicksburg. On Mar. 18, Seddon said in a letter to Kirby Smith that it was "admitted that Hindman had shown energy and ability, but had rendered himself, by alleged acts of violence and tyranny, perfectly odious" (*ibid.*, pp. 784, 785–786, 780, 802–803).

Smith's letter to Jefferson Davis of June 16 gives an over-all analysis of matters in his department. Crops, he said, were unusually abundant, but there was difficulty over laws and arrangements about assessments upon producers. After noting that most of the fighting population was with the armies east of the Mississippi, he said: "The male population remaining are old men, or have furnished substitutes, are lukewarm, or are wrapped up in speculations and money-making. It will be difficult to develop any force from such material." Smith had placed a general officer over the conscript bureau, which had previously been very defective, with indisputable evidences of bribery (Magruder to Smith's chief of staff, May 29, *O.R., 42,* 21–22), and he represented that his own usefulness would be in developing the resources of the department so as to make it self-sustaining, though, if the real occasion arose, he would take the field with troops. The entire "disposable force" in the department was being used in efforts to relieve Port Hudson and Vicksburg.

Because of his efforts to make his department self-sustaining, it has been claimed that Smith sought to develop a little Confederacy of his own, and the name "Kirby-Smithdom" was used derisively at the time, as it still is. Davis saw the necessity of Smith's efforts, and three months before Smith wrote his letter—on Mar. 20—Adj. Gen. Cooper ordered Brig. Gen. Benjamin Huger to go to the Trans-Mississippi Department, to make an inspection not only of artillery but "also of the means and facilities for the manufacture of ordnance and ordnance stores in the department" (*O.R., 33,* 804).

4. *O.R., 33,* 803 (Smith's order of Mar. 18, describing Holmes's command), 794–796 (Steele to Holmes's adjutant, Mar. 5), 796–797 (Holmes to Davis, Mar. 6), 809–810 (Steele to Holmes, Mar. 31), 821–822 (J. A. Scales to Col. W. P. Adair, Apr. 12, a bitter letter that, however, praised Steele).

5. *Ibid.*, pp. 809–810, 843–844 (Steele to Cooper, May 19), 862–863. Steele's letter of Mar. 6 cited in the last note carries the heading, "Hdqrs. Department of the Indian Territory," that of Mar. 31 the heading, "Hdqrs. District of the Indian Territory." In the letter to Cooper, Steele said, "When I reported to General Holmes, in December last, I was assigned to a command in the Indian country after it had been offered to other brigadiers and declined." It is amazing that he should have ever assumed that he was a department commander.

6. *Ibid.*, pp. 337–338.

7. Phillips's and Col. Stephen H. Wattles's reports, *O.R., 32,* 348–350, 350, 350–352; *33,* 883–884, 885. For letters of Phillips to Blunt of May 15 and June 6, see *O.R., 33,* 282–283, 310–311. While Phillips used the heading "Fort Blunt" instead of "Fort Gibson" in his letters to Blunt, Blunt referred to "Fort Gibson" in writing to Schofield.

8. *O.R., 33,* 849, 293.

9. *D.A.B.; O.R., 33,* 856. See also quotation from Smith's dispatch to Holmes of June 4 contained in his letter to Gov. Reynolds of Arkansas of the same date. On June 13 Smith informed Holmes that he was sending Col. Waldo P. Johnson into Missouri with authority to "organize twelve months' volunteers" (*ibid.*, pp. 855–856, 865).

In a letter to Davis on June 9, Smith said, "The movement into Missouri is the *terminus ad quem* of all my hopes; complete success on the Mississippi will, I trust, enable its realization." His *terminus ad quem* on May 20 had been confided to Taylor as the defeat of Grant. Between the two dates considerable had transpired, and Smith himself had had a ten-day struggle against a bilious attack, conquering by "quinine, blue-mass, and quiet," without impairment of his Latin (*O.R., 42,* 41–42, 12–13; *33,* 855–856).

Holmes's bitter feeling against the North was revealed in a letter to Marmaduke on Feb. 27, in which he expressed doubt of the value of any operation in Missouri: "In regard to our friends in Missouri, I think you overestimate their zeal, or rather you underestimate the effect of the iron and diabolical rule of the enemy over there. It is expecting too much of weak human nature to suppose that they will sacrifice all, unless we can give them at least a reasonable show of permanent protection" (*O.R., 33,* 790).

A humorous touch was given the recruiting problem in Missouri by Col. J. Q. Burbridge in a letter of May 10 to Marmaduke's adjutant. Burbridge was sending to Marmaduke under guard a Maj. Scott who he stated had been a private in his old regiment of the Missouri State Guard. He commented: "I do not think he is a spy, but I think he is one of those visionary men who are hardly responsible for what they say. It is all humbug about his having recruited nine companies, but I have no doubt that Scott thinks he has raised them" (*ibid.,* p. 836).

10. *Ibid.,* p. 860.

11. *Ibid.,* p. 861. One of those who had reported adversely about Marmaduke was M. J. Thompson, seen in Vol. III of this work. On May 20 he wrote Price about a speech he had recently made at Bloomfield, Missouri, in which he had told the people—many of them doubtless close acquaintances—that Price would not have approved the actions of Marmaduke's men during their recent raid (*ibid.,* p. 844).

Four days previously a Lee Crandall had sent from Pocahontas by the hand of a Capt. Parker, a very long letter addressed to Price's adjutant. After stating that his officers were succeeding in recruiting in Missouri, he went into particulars about "the last grand raid to Missouri," and put the matter plainly: "The raid injured our cause in Missouri, and a few more such, and saltpeter will not save the State" (*ibid.,* pp. 840–842).

12. *Ibid.,* pp. 846, 851, 845.

13. *Ibid.,* pp. 866–867, 858, 878.

14. *Ibid.,* p. 317. Hurlbut said Price had four brigades of about 1,200 men each, and two 4-gun batteries. He stated that one brigade had been left at Little Rock, where provisions were very scarce, the river being too low for navigation.

15. *Ibid.,* p. 318. The accuracy of the presentation of Union matters in Missouri as given by Monaghan in *Civil War on the Western Border, 1854–1865,* pp. 276–277, is sometimes questionable. He states that Grant called for more trans-Mississippi soldiers, that Curtis, when Halleck levied a second time on him, replied that he could not spare more; that Lincoln without further warning removed Curtis and gave Schofield the department; that Curtis had believed his victory at Pea Ridge had made him invulnerable; but that Lincoln

let him go because his first consideration was to get every man he could for Grant.

It would have been unlike Grant to tell the General in Chief whence reinforcements should come, and his statement in his dispatch to Halleck of May 29 was, "If Banks does not come to my assistance, I must be re-enforced from elsewhere" (*O.R., 36,* 40). As a matter of fact, Schofield had been in command of the Department of the Missouri for a week, and in addition to levying on Schofield, Halleck, it will be recalled, had Burnside send twice as many troops from the Department of the Ohio.

The last call made on Curtis for troops previous to his removal seems to have been for reinforcements to Rosecrans, as shown by the first sentence of a letter he sent Halleck on May 6: "Your telegram and letters, urging me to send troops to General Rosecrans, have been received, and I have responded that I can spare none" (*O.R., 33,* 269–270).

In the previously noted letter to Schofield, Lincoln said, "I did not relieve General Curtis because of any full conviction that he had done wrong by commission or omission." After stating that the Missouri quarrel seemed to grow worse and worse, Lincoln said, "I felt it my duty to break it up somehow, and, as I could not remove Governor Gamble, I had to remove General Curtis."

It is hard to see why Curtis should have been surprised at being removed when he had said in a letter to Gen. Fisk on Apr. 13 that he had "written the President that I will be pleased to have him consummate his effort to relieve me from a very difficult command, but I got no response" (*ibid.,* pp. 215–216). The charge that Curtis felt invulnerable because of his victory at Pea Ridge would have to be well documented before it could be accepted.

Monaghan's statement that immediately upon taking command on May 24 Schofield sent nearly half of the 43,000 men in his department to Grant gives the impression that Schofield found upon Curtis's desk an unfulfilled request to send troops to Vicksburg. Actually, it was on June 2 that Halleck asked Schofield if he could help Grant, and the number of men sent in Herron's division was "about 5,000 men"—not something like 20,000 (*O.R., 38,* 377, 378).

The statement that Schofield, like Curtis, retained hold on Helena is an inaccurate representation of who was responsible for Helena at the time.

16. *O.R., 33, ibid.,* p. 863.

17. *Ibid.,* pp. 857–859.

18. *Ibid.,* pp. 866, 868.

19. *O.R., 32,* 407; Holmes's report, *ibid.,* pp. 408–411 (for date of departure for Jacksonport); *O.R., 33,* 877; Thomas L. Snead, "The Conquest of Arkansas," *B. and L.,* III, 441–459.

20. In the letter to Smith in which he gave a measure of Hindman, Seddon said that Holmes, though esteemed for his virtues, had seemingly "lost the confidence and attachment of all." Smith, in his letter of June 16 to President Davis, described all his three district commanders as "officers of merit and ability." Holmes's defect as a department commander had been, Smith said, in his complete absorption in affairs in Arkansas and Indian Territory, with a consequent neglect of Louisiana and Texas.

On June 30 Hindman, then in Richmond, Va., wrote a confidential letter to

Cooper, asking assignment to a position west of the Mississippi, since he had no chance for a command in the East. But he insisted on being independent of both Price and Holmes. One could not, Hindman stated, serve under Price "without lending himself to factious schemes"; Holmes lacked "system and a fixed policy" (*O.R., 23,* 895–896).

O'Flaherty's efforts to build Shelby into a general of great potentiality is naturally accompanied by criticism of Holmes. He states that Holmes in late 1862 and 1863 had obdurately refused to act against Helena, and adds that at all times Holmes kept a full brigade in Indian Territory "to protect the Indians against only Holmes knew what." That O'Flaherty thought it would have been easy to take Helena is indicated by the assertion that at no times did the Federals there exceed 5,000 men (*General Jo Shelby,* pp. 177–178).

It was seen in Vol. IV that Johnston and Richmond both sought to have Holmes reinforce Vicksburg—not take Helena—and that there was serious misunderstanding on their parts as to Holmes's effective strength. (O'Flaherty says nothing about the shortage of arms and supplies in Arkansas, neither does he give the number of men available after Prairie Grove.) There is no mystery about the Indian question, which has been touched upon in the text, and policy ultimately went back to Richmond. The words quoted seem to indicate that O'Flaherty thought it had been foolish to ally any of the tribes to the Confederacy, but that they should have all been left to the overtures of the North, in spite of the western frontier of Arkansas and the northern boundary of Texas.

As to Federal strength at Helena, a return for Nov. 20, 1862 (*O.R., 19,* 807), shows 20,174 troops, of whom 15,439 were carried as present for duty. Although Frederick Steele took some 10,000 men when he joined Sherman's Vicksburg expedition just before Christmas, there was no time when the Union strength was not well adjusted to Confederate potentialities, if all the proper factors are taken into account.

As if to round out misconceptions about Helena, O'Flaherty states that Prentiss had succeeded Curtis, when in reality there had been three intervening commanders—Frederick Steele, Hovey, and Gorman.

21. *O.R., 33,* 878; *32,* 409.

22. *O.R., 33,* 880–881, 882, 880.

23. *Ibid.,* pp. 884, 886 (Holmes to Price, June 26). Holmes's dispatch was written at Clarendon. On the same day he issued, also at Clarendon, "General Orders, No. 1," which, like the Special Order issued at Jacksonport, was in reality a Field Order with administrative provisions. The Jacksonport order had directed Price and Fagan to supply their commands with "at least twenty days' rations," and had limited wagons to ammunition and supply trains and such vehicles as were necessary to carry cooking utensils (troops were to have no baggage except one blanket). In addition to assigning routes, prescribing march discipline, and giving instructions about trains, the order of the 26th (*ibid.,* p. 887) regulated ambulances.

24. Holmes's report. The attack order is also given in *O.R., 33,* 903—"General Orders, No. 2." In the same volume considerable correspondence will be found about the delays caused by the rains.

25. Porter to Welles, July 9; Lieut. Joshua Bishop to Porter, July 21; *O.R.,*

Navies, Ser. I, XXV, 227–228, 317. On July 7 Porter wrote a sharp letter to Bishop (*ibid.,* pp. 236–237) asking what steps he had taken to find out whether his services were needed at Helena or not. After stating that the river had been held only because the spirit of his instructions had been followed, Porter said, "You are apparently the only exception to the rule, having left your post at a time when the vessel should have been kept there as long as possible." It was a harsh ending for a letter that had begun, "In my instructions to you I ordered you to proceed to Memphis for repairs, if your services were not needed at Helena."

In *Civil War on Western Waters,* Pratt says (p. 182) that Bishop asked "permission" of Prentiss to go to Helena. Prentiss of course could neither give nor withhold permission.

On July 4 Lieut. Commander Thomas O. Selfridge, in the gunboat *Manitou* off White River, wrote to Porter (*O.R., Navies,* Ser. I, XXV, 226) that he had informed Helena and Memphis that convoys would leave the White River on Monday and Thursday, and would be accompanied as far as Lake Providence by two gunboats, one with heavy guns. He wanted Porter to assemble upriver steamers into groups. The enterprising sailor did not confine himself to protecting Grant's supply line. He was sending Porter the fruits of a raid made that day into the interior: a large number of mules, some cows and sheep, and five wagons. A steamer of corn was promised the next week. Selfridge could find no horses, but some of the mules were "very fine." Five wagonloads of shore-leave sailors towed by quality mules would be impressive anywhere. But there was one flaw; plantation harnesses were of "poor material."

26. *O.R., 33,* 335, 339.

27. Reports of Prentiss and Lieut. Col. William H. Heath (33rd Missouri Infantry), *O.R., 32,* 387–390, 400–402.

28. Dyer, *Compendium* (for roster of troops and service records); report of Lieut. Col. Thomas N. Pace (1st Indiana Cavalry), *O.R., 32,* 402–404. The casualty report in *O.R., 32,* 390–391, carries all units except the 2nd Arkansas.

29. *O.R., 33,* 352. Hurlbut had ended his dispatch of June 24 to Prentiss by referring to the possibility of a move northward by Johnston. In that case it might be necessary, he said, to bring Prentiss to Memphis and abandon Helena; but he would not direct such a move without orders from Grant. Hurlbut wanted Prentiss to keep good men east of the Mississippi to give warning of a move by Johnston.

30. Prentiss's report.

31. Porter to Welles, July 9, cited above; Prentiss's report. Prentiss employed the words "My whole force numbered," as a heading for a breakdown of his command into infantry, cavalry, and artillery, with officers and enlisted men shown separately, the total being 4,129. The figure is actually in excess of what he had mentioned to Hurlbut on June 27, when he said, "I have less than 4,000 men here." In *B. and L.,* III, 460, one finds 4,129 given as the Federal "effective strength."

32. Prentiss's report; Rice's report, *O.R., 32,* 395–396.

33. Benton's report, *ibid.,* pp. 396–397.

34. Reports of Walker, Marmaduke, Col. Charles W. Kittredge (36th Iowa),

ibid., pp. 433, 436–437, 398; Pace's report. There is no report for the 5th Kansas Cavalry or one by Col. Powell Clayton, commanding the Federal cavalry brigade. Pace spoke of action by his battery, and Lieut. Melvin C. Wright of the 3rd Iowa Battery spoke in his report (*ibid.*, pp. 404–405) of the section of his battery north of the town being joined by the battery with the Indiana cavalry.

Reports by the commanders of Walker's two regiments (*ibid.*, pp. 434–436) support his statements and show that he was far from being inactive.

35. Reports of Col. W. H. Brooks (34th Arkansas Infantry) and Lieut. O'Connell, *ibid.*, pp. 430–431, 405–406. In addition to his regiment, Brooks had begun his approach march with two companies of cavalry and a section of guns, and was subsequently joined by a battery.

36. Prentiss's, Rice's, and Heath's reports; Salomon's report, *ibid.*, pp. 392–393.

37. Parson's and McRae's reports, *ibid.*, pp. 420–423, 417–420. Parsons indicates that Battery C was carried by what might be called the first real assault against it, but Prentiss explicitly states that the Confederates were twice repulsed, while Salomon says the battery was taken on the third attempt.

38. Prentiss's, Salomon's, McRae's, and Parsons's reports; report by Brig. Gen. J. F. Fagan, *O.R., 32,* 423–427; report by Ensign George L. Smith, *O.R. Navies,* Ser. I, XXV, 229–230.

The *O.R.* uses "Pritchett"; the *O.R. Navies* uses "Prichett"; and the latter is here used. According to Prentiss's commendatory letter to Porter (*O.R., 32,* 391–392), Prichett, upon being informed by Prentiss of the imminence of an attack, had made himself thoroughly acquainted with the topography of the country.

39. Rice's report; Mackey's report, *O.R., 32,* 398–399.

40. Heath's report. It is difficult to reconcile statements in different reports about the captures of various groups of Confederates, but there seems to be little doubt about their numbers. A total of 30 officers and 243 men of Fagan's brigade were reported as "missing," while the figures for the 7th and 10th Missouri were 18 and 251, respectively (*ibid.*, p. 412).

41. Pace's report. Pace spoke of "splendid English rifles" that were taken from captured enemy sharpshooters. They may have been Whitworth rifles of hexagonal bore with which Confederate sharpshooters were frequently armed, and which had great accuracy and range.

Heath states that upon returning to Battery C, his men found "both guns of the battery turned upon Fort Curtis and loaded with shell, but not discharged, for want of friction primers." This suggests that the four batteries may have had only two guns each.

42. Holmes stated that he issued his order for withdrawal at 10:30. Col. Brooks, commanding the distracting force on the south, said he received it at 12 noon, and that, at his direction, the torch was applied to Negro quarters. With them were destroyed 5,000 pounds of bacon, 1,500 bushels of corn, "and a quantity of commissary stores and clothing."

Holmes's statement that the operation should have succeeded must be given little weight. It was easier to indict subordinates for failure in execution than to criticize his own decision to proceed with the operation after learning that the approaches to Helena were more difficult than he had supposed. Conforming to a pattern set by some of his subordinates, he meted out blame generously.

The halt of Price's column, of which Holmes as well as Fagan complained, was made, Price claimed in his report (*O.R., 32,* 413–417), in order not to arrive prematurely upon the ground, and occurred a mile and a half from his objective. If it was true, as Price states, that Holmes joined him soon after the halt and remained "till the dawn of day," Holmes's criticism is hardly just. Fagan's colorful and dramatic writing makes one a little distrustful of him.

Holmes said that no satisfactory explanation had been given by Walker for failure to make the attack that Marmaduke requested, and he sought to excuse himself by saying that his own remoteness from that part of the field made it impossible for him to give specific orders. Walker had no reason to know that Holmes would not be in a position to give new orders, and Marmaduke should have made some appeal to Holmes.

Holmes stated that when he rode into Battery C everything was in confusion, regiments and brigades being mixed up indiscriminately. He complained because men were not restrained from prematurely advancing into the town after the capture of Graveyard Hill. Parsons, on the other hand, blamed Holmes for the fact that parts of some regiments had rushed "into the town and even to the river bank." Holmes, he said, had given a personal order to one regimental commander, and other commanders had drawn an inference from it.

Although Holmes's conduct of the battle is open to criticism, it goes too far to say that the Confederates failed merely because of lack of coordination. Holmes did not have even a two-to-one superiority in numbers, and the Federal works greatly multiplied their strength.

The defense seems to have left little to be desired, though it is not clear how command was distributed between Prentiss and Salomon. Apparently the 28th Wisconsin, of the brigade of Col. W. E. McLean (from whom there is no report), was from the start in support of Battery B, against which no attack was made. Salomon said that at an early hour he moved two of its companies to the valley west of Fort Curtis. More of the regiment could doubtless have been withdrawn if needed.

It is better merely to speak, as Henry does (*The Story of the Confederecy,* pp. 294–295), of an unsuccessful attack on Helena, or, at most to include, like Eaton (*A History of the Southern Confederacy,* pp. 207–208), the information that it was made by Holmes, than to suggest, as Parks seems to do (*General Edmund Kirby Smith,* pp. 279–280), that the operation could have succeeded if there had been an attainable coordination. Parks's statement that the combined forces were "before Helena by July 3" overlooks a very questionable part of the plan—the difficult night approach march. From his statement that Marmaduke and Fagan had been repulsed before Price "began moving," a reader is hardly likely to suspect that Price had begun his march at midnight. In his *The Confederate States of America,* Coulter makes no reference whatever to the Helena defeat.

43. *O.R., 32,* 385, 386, 384. Hurlbut stated that Prentiss had already sent

860 prisoners, but Prentiss's report of July 9 put the number of unwounded prisoners sent North at 727, with 47 more to be sent.

44. *Ibid.,* pp. 384–385. O'Flaherty quotes at length (*op. cit.,* pp. 185–186) from the very flowery postwar eulogy of Shelby by his former adjutant, Maj. John N. Edwards. Edwards pictures the lifting fog on July 4 revealing an iron-clad escorting a large steamer, whose roof and decks were blue with uniforms. Apparently O'Flaherty not only accepted this as true, though it could not have been, but he added the statement that after the defeat of the Confederates on the other two sides of the Helena triangle, the Federals in front of Shelby were reinforced. The authority for this is not clear, but may have been the unreliable Edwards. Federal accounts make no mention of such a shift, and Marmaduke said he received the order to retire at 11:00 A.M.

O'Flaherty states (p. 187) that half of the 67,000 men in the Trans-Mississippi Department were on furlough or on sick leave on July 4, 1863. A large number of them were simply absent without leave, and there was, as previously noted, also a shortage of arms. O'Flaherty's statement about the Trans-Mississippi army never having been used would seem to have come from the belief that out of the total on the rolls, a large, well equipped, and adequately supplied field force could have been formed. To arrive at the actual potential would require a difficult and discerning military analysis.

45. *O.R., 32,* 386–387, 386, 391–392 (Prentiss to Grant, July 5; to Hurlbut, July 6; to Porter, July 9); *O.R. Navies,* Ser. I, XXV, 229 (Prichett to Porter, July 6), 228 (Porter to Welles, July 11). See also Porter to Welles, July 9 (*ibid.,* pp. 228–229), in which he is more restrained, merely giving Prichett "great credit for the share he took in the fight. . . ."

Horace Greeley evidently thought Porter was not always too eager to put credit where it was due. In his splendid editorial about the capture of Vicksburg, which appeared in the *Tribune* on July 8, Greeley said, "Admiral Porter's official dispatch announces the surrender of Vicksburg to 'the United States forces'—under Gen. Grant, he might have gracefully added."

46. *O.R. Navies,* Ser. I, XXV, 232–233.

47. *O.R., 32,* 390–391, 412. The 772 given as "missing" in the Confederate report is in extremely close agreement with the 774 that Prentiss gave in his report for the unwounded prisoners (727 already sent North and 47 still at Helena). But the 173 given as killed is completely out of harmony with the "at least" 400 of the enemy that Prentiss stated had been buried, though it may have been much nearer the truth.

Pratt states (*loc. cit.*) that 600 dead were found in the ravine where the *Tyler*'s shells had fallen so heavily. This seems to have been a poor rendering of the report to Prichett by Ensign Smith, who said he had visited the ground and had found about 600 "killed and wounded."

48. *O.R., 32,* 440–442. Prentiss must have sanctioned his medical director's visit and offer of the 7th, and McPheeters would certainly have been surprised to know that when Prentiss was a prisoner at Madison, Ga., a Confederate captain had described him as one of the most violent enemies of the South and an unprincipled scoundrel, whose conduct was so base and treacherous that he deserved "no humane treatment" (*O.R., 117,* 912).

NOTES TO CHAPTER II

1. *N.Y. Herald,* July 8, 1863; *National Intelligencer,* July 7; *N.Y. Tribune,* July 8. In introducing Halleck, according to the *Herald*'s account, Stanton, when referring to Grant, said that Halleck had "from the first stood by him, with firm and unfaltering faith and trust." Several senators and congressmen spoke briefly, and the crowd afterward went to the house of Secretary Seward, whose rather general speech on the war was longer—as given in the *Herald*—than that of Lincoln. Lincoln's speech is in *Collected Works of Abraham Lincoln,* VI, 319–320.

2. *N.Y. Tribune,* July 11. This account ended: "The prisoners are a very sorry looking set. Only two or three were reading; these were privates. The officers were playing cards. When I went aboard they were eating their breakfast, and the way some of them gnawed bones made me conclude they were hungry still. It is not in the nature of things that such ignorant, poverty-stricken beings, can stand up against the intelligent and wealthy Northern soldiers. Their doom is as sure as that, in common life, honesty and industry bring their just rewards."

3. In his *The Military Telegraph During the Civil War,* Plum goes out of the way to reflect upon the naval officer who brought to Cairo Porter's dispatch to Welles about the surrender of Vicksburg, and makes statements some of which seem inaccurate. Though not claiming to have been present, Plum says, "The pompous naval officer strutted into the telegraph office and demanded possession of the wire to send the news of the surrender of Vicksburg to the Secretary of the Navy. . . ." Then Plum asserts that while the receiving clerk was counting the long message, A. J. Howell, the manager of the office, wired Col. Stager in Washington, "Pemberton surrendered July 4." He goes on to make the claim that Howell's laconic message enabled Stanton to spread the news over the land "by the time Sec. Gideon Welles had adjusted his spectacles" to read Porter's message (I, 320–321).

Porter's message (*supra,* IV, 420) consisted of a single sentence and was not long. Whether such a dispatch as the one Plum ascribed to Howell was sent or not, one can be sure that Stanton would have been slow to accept it without confirmation, and it is a historic fact that it was Welles who took to Lincoln the news of the surrender, and Porter's dispatch that was circulated.

But Howell—if he indeed was the manager of the Cairo office—could have done a real service by sending to Stager the word of the arrival of the *Silver Moon* with the Helena prisoners.

4. *O.R., 41,* 617–618 (Farragut to Emory, July 5, a dispatch that will be referred to later); *O.R. Navies,* Ser. I, XXV, 105; *O.R., 41,* 53. In his article "The Capture of Port Hudson," *B. and L.,* III, 586–598, Richard B. Irwin states that he as adjutant general sent to the "general-of-the-trenches" duplicate notes announcing the surrender of Vicksburg, with instructions that one of them be thrown into the enemy lines. This he says was done, and that its receipt was acknowledged with the call, "That's another damned Yankee lie." Later, reference is made to a dispatch to Gardner from the Confederate com-

mander on the left that speaks of Federals shouting that Vicksburg had surrendered.

5. *O.R., 41,* 52–54. If a note such as Irwin mentioned had been thrown over, it would seem that it would have carried his signature, and that some responsible officer would have seen that it reached Gardner, and that he would have expressly mentioned it in writing to Banks. But his note began, "Having received information from your troops that Vicksburg has been surrendered. . . ."

6. *Ibid.,* p. 4.

7. *O.R., 41,* 9; *38,* 647, 702. In his report Banks said that after garrisoning necessary points the number of men he could have employed for "permanent operations against Port Hudson" did not exceed those mentioned (*O.R., 41,* 8).

8. *O.R., 38,* 714, 810, 828, 845, 842. Rust's brigade was sent to Bragg (*ibid.,* 739).

9. *O.R., 38,* 871; Brown, *Grierson's Raid,* 174; Grierson's report, *O.R., 36,* 527. Grierson spoke of having made a strong demonstration in the direction of Fayette (twenty-five miles northeast of Natchez), with the view of creating the impression that he was going to Port Gibson or Natchez, while he quietly took the road in the opposite direction leading southeast to Brookhaven.

10. *O.R., 38,* 881.

11. *O.R., 41,* 492–493. The order for the movement toward the Mississippi (*ibid.,* pp. 486–487), dated Alexandria, May 14, stated that the 3rd Division (Paine's) would march the next morning at 4:00 A.M. In his letter to Halleck, Banks said Grover's division had left on the 14th.

12. *O.R., 21,* 1116.

13. *D.A.B.*

14. *O.R., 41,* 497. It is difficult to tell just what troops were left with Emory. Rosters indicate something like a brigade, which, it will be seen, is confirmed by a later dispatch by Emory.

15. *Ibid.,* pp. 489, 12.

16. *Ibid.,* pp. 489–490. Andrews gave the strength of the two divisions then at Simmesport as 6,200, and put at 3,800 the number of men still on the way from Alexandria under Weitzel. He also indicated that the force "with Chickering and below Opelousas" amounted to 2,840. He apparently expected Banks to order the Chickering force to Morgan City, though it actually was used to guard the trains in the move to Port Hudson (*ibid.,* p. 441, Banks to Halleck).

17. *Ibid.,* pp. 496–497. Throughout the *O.R.* and in the *O.R. Atlas* the name is spelled "Simsport," and the plantation is that of Sims. The Navy records have "Simmesport"—in accord with modern atlases.

18. *Ibid.,* pp. 488–489 (Irwin to Banks, a longer letter than that referred to in n. 15, also headed 9:00 P.M., May 17).

19. *D.A.B.; supra,* I, 266.

20. *O.R., 41,* 498–499; *21,* 309–311. In the letter Banks reported he had sent to Morgan City (to him, Brashear City) something like 20,000 beeves, mules, and horses, 5,000 bales of cotton, and many hogsheads of sugar. He stated that he had given the people to understand that those who were well disposed and entitled to receive the favor of the government would receive compensation for this property according to its value at the time of his arrival,

bearing in mind its restricted markets and liability to destruction by guerrillas or confiscation by the Confederate government. Some protests had been received from British and French subjects; he had put the protests on file without any response except a verbal explanation to all parties. He made a general recommendation on the subject of trade which was, he admitted, in conflict with the Confiscation Act, but which he thought would be beneficial. He also enclosed a dispatch to the Secretary of State, with the request that it be put in his hands.

He spoke of a wide and unqualified desire by many people for the restoration of the Union; said thousands would renew their obligations of support if he encouraged them; stated that 400 prisoners had voluntarily taken the oath of allegiance; and added, "There is an excellent opportunity, by a wise and conciliatory policy, to realize, in this quarter at least, the most sanguine expectations of the President."

21. *O.R., 21,* 43 (in Banks's report); 499–500 (order for movement); 519–520 (Banks to Grant, May 28); 493–494 (Andrews to Banks). Banks's letter to Grant began, "Upon the receipt of the report of General Dwight, who visited you recently, my command moved from Simsport for Port Hudson, landing at Bayou Sara at 2 o'clock on the morning of the 22d."—a statement that incorrectly gives the impression that the entire command arrived then.

Andrews's letter—written at 10:00 P.M.—reported the arrival of two boats loaded with ammunition and subsistence stores. One boat towed a schooner "loaded with coal for the fleet, which is much needed."

22. *Ibid.,* pp. 35–36, 38, 39, 501–502 (Weitzel to Irwin). Weitzel had arrived in the morning and was engaged in crossing the trains and spare horses. Worried over the nonarrival of a boat from below, he had sent another with a guard to seek it; a postscript reported both boats safe.

23. *Ibid.,* p. 12 (Banks's report), 137–138 (Grierson's report). The complete lack of general reports by division commanders makes it impossible to give exactitude to the movement from Simmesport.

24. Grierson's report.

25. *O.R., 41,* 39, 167–168, 137–138, 67, 179.

26. A return for May 19 (*O.R., 42,* 10) gives Beal and Miles a present strength of 5,327, while the personnel for the heavy batteries numbered 388. Augur's two brigades, including 167 cavalry—but not Grierson—had a strength of 6,657 on May 31 (*O.R., 41,* 527).

27. *O.R., 41,* 501.

28. *O.R., 41,* 503; *O.R. Navies,* Ser. I, XX, 206 (Farragut to Welles, from New Orleans, May 20); *O.R., 41,* 43–45 (Banks to Halleck, May 30).

Farragut said: "I have just returned from a visit to Captain Alden's command, below Port Hudson, but reached this city too late to see General Banks. I, however, met General Augur, who was on his way to Baton Rouge, to make the necessary preparations for the attack." Banks said that Chickering's train guard of about 3,000 would arrive "to-morrow."

A War Department order of Jan. 5, 1863, had stated that the troops in the Department of the Gulf would constitute the Nineteenth Corps—as from Dec. 14, 1862—and it named Banks as commander (*O.R., 21,* 636).

29. *O.R., 41,* 92.

30. *O.R., 41,* 506–507; Irwin's *B. and L.* article; *O.R., 41,* 507, 508–509. The attack order is discussed in n. 32.

At 1:00 P.M. of the 25th Sherman reported that he had not been able to draw out artillery fire from the enemy at night, but had while reconnoitering in the morning; he spoke of the complexity of roads, and of the great extent of his line; he wondered if he could get artillery ammunition from Springfield Landing, but said he was "finely off for subsistence supplies" (*O.R., 41,* 505).

At the same hour Banks was writing to Palmer that he feared the enemy might try to escape across the Mississippi from some place between Thompson's Creek and "Fancy Point." He requested some shelling and sent a sketch to help navy gunners. On the 24th Col. Lew Benedict, commanding a detachment across the river from Port Hudson, wrote that he was confident the enemy could not cross and escape by roads that had been pointed out to him as a possibility; but he would close all such roads. Benedict had captured an enemy signal detachment and a lieutenant who had just crossed over; but he had obtained from them no information of consequence (*O.R. Navies,* Ser. I, XX, 210; *O.R., 41,* 502).

31. *O.R., 41,* 507.

32. Irwin's *B. and L.* article; *O.R., 41,* 43–45 (Banks to Halleck, May 30), 511. In his letter to Halleck, Banks said the assault on the left and left of center by Sherman and Augur was made at 2 o'clock, and that fighting continued until 4. In his 1865 report he stated that the plan of attack contemplated "simultaneous movements upon the right and left," and that if the "movement" on the left had been made simultaneously with the "attack" upon the right, there probably would have been success—presumably because Weitzel would not then have halted, as Irwin indicated.

The order said: "General Weitzel will, according to verbal directions already given him, take advantage of the attacks on other parts of the line to endeavor to force his way into the enemy works on the right." Grover was to hold himself in readiness to reinforce troops on the right or left, if necessary, "or to force his own way into the enemy's works." It was specified that behind the skirmishers on the left there should be assaulting columns ready to take advantage of openings.

Except for the ending, one might call it a halfhearted attack order. The fact that Banks personally ordered Sherman and Augur to attack seems to indicate that he had thought that his division commanders should be guided by the concluding injunction.

The First Louisiana Native Guards was composed of "free Negroes of means and intelligence" with colored line officers, but with a white lieutenant colonel in command. The Third was composed largely of ex-slaves and had white company officers. The two regiments were handled as a brigade by the commander of the Third, and they had made a hard night march from Baton Rouge to be present in the attack (Williams, *Negro Troops in the Rebellion,* 215–217).

For the attack of May 27 see also Irwin, *The 19th Army Corps,* Chap. XVI.

33. *O.R., 41,* 511, 519–520.

34. Livermore, *Numbers and Losses,* p. 101; *O.R., 41,* 505; Irwin's *B. and L.* article.

Livermore puts Banks's effectives at 13,000 and Gardner's at 4,326. This gives 141 Federals hit in every 1,000, while each 1,000 Confederates hit 436 men.

In his report of 1865 Banks said that nothing but the assault would have convinced his men of the numbers of the enemy or the strength of his works; Irwin stated that the men, elated by their successes in the Teche country, "were in the best of spirits for an immediate attack." But it would seem that soldierly ardor could have been restrained until the arrival of the additional 5,000 men of which Banks spoke.

The notes between Banks and Gardner about stopping hostilities show how difficult such an act is even by men of good will without each thinking the other is taking unfair advantage of the truce.

35. *O.R., 41,* 513–517 *passim,* 519.

36. *O.R., 42,* 26.

37. *O.R., 41,* 180. A citizen who returned to Jackson on June 2 after two ineffectual attempts to get into Port Hudson gave a different picture: cavalry commanders, he thought, were inefficient; and he had seen too much drunkenness among officers and men (*O.R., 38,* 943).

38. *O.R., 41,* 181, 138, 126–127 (Paine's report), 181; *42,* 39.

39. *O.R., 41,* 109, 79, 100. On May 28 Banks asked Farragut for 500 hand grenades and an officer who could instruct his men in their use. In reply Farragut said that he had none, that they were not in use in the navy, though he did not know why, for they had been highly esteemed in the War of 1812, and he still thought well of them. The next day he wrote that he had learned Porter had plenty in his fleet, and he was sending for some (*ibid.,* pp. 511–512, 520–521).

Banks's gentlemanly and appreciative nature was at no time more clearly revealed than by a letter he wrote Halleck on May 31 devoted exclusively to high praise of Grierson (*ibid.,* p. 524).

40. *O.R., 41,* 536–537; *O.R. Navies,* Ser. I, 219; *O.R., 41,* 525–526 (Grant to Banks, May 31), 14 (Banks's statement in his 1865 report concerning the effort on the morning of the 11th), 525, 551, 550.

Along with the three deserters, Dwight sent to corps headquarters a long digest of what they had told him, and said they wished to be sent to New York.

On May 31 Farragut informed Banks as to what five deserters had said of the situation in Port Hudson. In acknowledging "the cheering report," Banks said, "We are closing in upon the enemy, and will have him in a day or two." Banks was buoyant to the end of his letter; replying to what Farragut had reported about Grant, he said, "General Grant's success is glorious" (*O.R., 41,* 524–525, 525).

In his dispatch Grant described Johnston's position at Canton with a reported 40,000 men and 20,000 to a certainty, said he himself would "be crippled beyond redemption" if he detached 5,000 men, and ended, "All I want now is men."

41. *O.R., 41,* 552–553 (Banks's note to Gardner), 553 (Gardner's reply), 554–555 (order for attack); 45 (Banks to Halleck); Irwin's *B. and L.* article. See also Irwin, *The 19th Army Corps,* Chap. XVII.

Different paragraphs of the order—not all of which is given—have different times of writing. Paragraph XV is a page long and shows that much attention was given to details, though the hour of writing—11:30 P.M., June 13—was late. It stated: "Generals Augur, Grover, and Dwight will not wait for signals, but act at the times specified herein without further orders. The standard is the telegraph time at these headquarters. General Arnold [corps chief of artillery] will have charge of all artillery in position excepting such as may have been placed under the direction of division commanders. . . . Either of the three commanders of a point of attack is authorized to order the fire of artillery near him to cease if he finds it inconveniencing his troops or movements. He will report his act to these headquarters." Although the paragraph began with the statement, "A general assault upon the works of the enemy will be made tomorrow morning," Dwight—with two regiments lent by Augur—was told merely to "make an attempt to gain an entrance to the enemy's works on the extreme left."

The map of Port Hudson made by Banks's engineer that appears in the *O.R. Atlas* as Plate XXXVIII, 3, shows the Confederate line as virtually continuous, with many batteries. The Federal works had several large gaps and in only a few positions was close to the Confederate works. No commanders of sectors appear, but as reproduced in *B. and L.*, III, 597, division commanders are shown and Weitzel is indicated as such, though he does not so appear in the roster of troops or the casualty report in *O.R.*, *41*, 67–70, and Irwin speaks of him as merely commanding the brigade on the extreme right. An editorial note says that Weitzel's status gave difficulty.

42. *O.R.*, *41*, 57–66, 128–129, 129, 130, 45.

43. Livermore, *op. cit.*, pp. 105, 101. Livermore estimated Banks's attacking columns at 6,000, and accepted Banks's figures (*O.R.*, *41*, 47) for the losses—203 killed, 1,401 wounded, and 188 missing. The Confederate loss was small indeed—22 killed and 25 wounded. For the Federals the number of men hit per thousand, both on May 26 and June 14—141 and 267, respectively—was high, though there were comparable relative casualties in other engagements of the war. For example, the Murfreesboro figures are 223 for the Federals and 266 for the Confederates. Although uncertainty surrounds all such statistics, which are given an exactness that is not justified, the figures do have considerable significance when very small or very large.

44. *O.R.*, *41*, 557.

45. *Ibid.*, pp. 564–565. Banks said that two companies of the 4th Wisconsin "went over the works and were captured for the reason I have stated"—the defection of other men. He likewise said, "I do not hesitate to say that the opinion was universal among our troops and those of the enemy that the work must fall." While the first part of this sentence accords with the "determined purpose" which he had told Gardner his men had when he demanded surrender, there still seems something to explain.

Col. Thomas S. Clark, of the 6th Michigan, who commanded a brigade (26th Connecticut, 15th New Hampshire, 128th New York, 6th Michigan, 14th Maine—the first two nine-month regiments), wrote in a report two days after the assault, "The nine-months' troops have demonstrated by their gallant conduct that they can be relied on in any emergency." He gave his losses as

1 killed, 115 wounded, 10 missing. The number of killed and wounded is suspiciously out of balance, and Clark himself noted the smallness of his casualties, considering the advantages of the enemy and the many and difficult obstacles his men encountered. One cannot but wonder a little about his attack. On May 27 the original brigade commander was wounded and his successor killed. Was Clark preyed upon by this fact and did he make his report with unusual haste to get his statement before Banks? The brigade casualties for the entire siege were quite high—surely for the most part incurred on May 27—with the killed and wounded in normal balance (*ibid.*, pp. 122–123, 68).

In reporting his repulse to Farragut, Banks said he *believed* his men were "in tolerable good spirits," a guarded appraisal hard to interpret. While no charge of defection on June 14 was made in his final report, he said that subsequently a great deal of embarrassment and trouble was caused by the nine-month men, the 4th Massachusetts "being in open mutiny." (There was a question as to dates of expiration of enlistment. Was it the same for an entire regiment, or different for different companies, depending upon when they entered Federal service? In answer to Banks's query, the assistant adjutant general of the Army wrote him on June 29 that for an entire regiment the enlistment period would expire "nine months from the date the last company of the regiment was mustered into the service of the United States"—a rule that had been applied in all cases [*ibid.*, p. 608]). For the sake of commanders and adjutants one trusts that there had not been much transferring between regiments.

While Irwin said nothing about disaffection during or after the assault (there must have been some afterward), one cannot but wonder about his statement that Dwight's column was "misdirected."

The editors of *B. and L.* noted (III, 599) that there is a great discrepancy between strengths given by Banks for his "effectives" and the figure shown on his returns. The one for May 21 gives not less than 30,000 "present for duty" at Port Hudson, not including the Corps d'Afrique. While including the "Corps," the return for the end of June gives 23,962 as "present for duty" (*O.R.*, *41*, 526–528, 611). The editors state that Col. Irwin, who as adjutant had made out the returns, had informed them that the figures "for May 31st and June 30th were totals of former months carried forward, whereas the actual strength was as given by him"—at no time in excess of 13,000 effectives. What is meant by "totals of former months carried forward, whereas the actual strength was as given by him," is somewhat mysterious.

Perhaps the best statement of strength was that which Andrews gave Banks in his letter of May 17, previously noted, which he prefaced with a remark about the difficulty of giving precise figures because of numerous details of men that had been made and the large number of sick. He said, however, that the figures for various units could not be far from those he gave—which totaled 12,840, including the command of Chickering then at and below Opelousas. The increase caused by Augur and Sherman was offset by the some 4,000 casualties in the two assaults. In his article Irwin said, "The illness and mortality were enormous."

46. *O.R.*, *41*, 561 (Palmer to Banks, June 16, saying he could "no longer signalize to the admiral"); 96, 558 (Farragut to Stone, June 15), 537–538;

O.R. Navies, Ser. I, XX, 221. After speaking of a trip by the gunboats to Simmesport and the destruction of flats and boats there, Farragut said the water was so low, or soon would be, that the Confederates could occupy the place with impunity. Boats had already been compelled to come out of Red River "for want of water to pass the bar."

47. *O.R., 42,* 53.

48. *O.R., 41,* 559, 562. In a message to Farragut on the 17th, which the admiral forwarded the next day to Banks, Palmer said that there was no doubt that Kirby Smith was in the vicinity, and from reliable sources in Bayou Sara he had learned of the intention to capture Donaldsonville and keep Banks from obtaining supplies out of New Orleans. He had dropped down the river a little so as to shell a hostile party of which he had heard, but on sending a scout ashore so as to get their location, he found that they had disappeared. He added that he did not know whether they were mustering in force "to drive our friend Colonel Sage into the Mississippi," and then run supplies into Port Hudson, or to go to Donaldsonville—but one or the other must be their purpose (*ibid.,* pp. 566–567).

49. *Ibid.,* pp. 571–572.

50. *Ibid.,* pp. 574, 574–575, 576.

51. *Ibid.,* pp. 575, 192–197 (report of Col. Albert Stickney), 216–220 (report of Col. J. P. Major, Confederate), 585. Col. Major described the circumstances that kept him from attacking with his entire force, and stated that if he had done so he would have carried the position.

52. *Ibid.,* pp. 210, 595 (Stouder to Emory), 189 (Emory's report). The Confederate reports are well supplemented by Taylor's account in *op. cit.,* pp. 140–142.

Stouder was Emory's telegraph operator, and he sent the general a copy of a telegram that had been received on the 24th by Col. S. B. Holabird, New Orleans quartermaster (after whom the present-day Quartermaster School is named), from W. H. Talbot, commander of the transport *Saint Mary's.* It had been sent from Southwest Pass (one of the mouths of the Mississippi), and stated that on arrival at Atchafalaya Bay, the gunboats *Hollyhock* and the transport *Kepper* had been met, and they had reported the surprise and capture of Brashear City (Morgan City) at 5:00 A.M. of the 23rd. Talbot described the manner in which the enemy had crossed Berwick Bay, and said, "Nothing was saved"—except the provost marshal and a few others who were already aboard one or another of the vessels.

The *Hollyhock* was a 300-ton 3-gun side-wheeler. In his report, Emory, in addition to describing the vulnerability of the works from the rear, said the gunboat appeared to be "too frail" to be of any service, which compensated for his having said in a dispatch to Irwin that he did not see how the enemy had crossed Berwick Bay "in the face of the gunboat" (*ibid.,* p. 597).

53. *Ibid.,* pp. 227, 211–212.

54. *O.R., 41,* 190, 226; Taylor, *op. cit.,* p. 12. Taylor gives Mouton the first name Alexander instead of Alfred—an error easily made: the convention had met in Alexandria.

55. *O.R., 41,* 227–229 (Green's report); *O.R. Navies,* Ser. I, XX, 354 (log of *Princess Royal*). There were three casualties on the *Princess* from grape

thrown by enemy guns and the bullets of sharpshooters. A gun-server was shot through the head, a seaman through each leg.

56. Green's report. Green spoke of no small-arms fire but named a captain and a lieutenant who were wounded in the head "with bricks thrown by the enemy, which had first been thrown by our men," and said there were other officers and men similarly wounded. He stated candidly that he had expected that the permission to pick up wounded and bury dead would be refused, and said he sent it as early as he did—at daylight—so as to get a great number of wounded away by having instructions taken to them under the flag of truce.

In an indorsement to Green's report, Taylor ascribed the defeat not to the returnable quality of brickbats but to the failure of a guide to get one of the Confederate regiments to the fort. Had it not been for that, there would have been success, he claimed. He conceded that in some respects the attack might have been unwise; yet he would not censure Green, because he had a disposition "to attack the enemy wherever he finds him" (*O.R.*, *41*, 229).

57. *O.R.*, *41*, 605, 188 (Emory to Banks); *O.R. Navies,* Ser. I, XX, 348 (log of *Kineo,* speaking of a transport with reinforcements still on board); *O.R.*, *41;* Dyer, *Compendium,* p. 749 (Federal casualties, also force involved). Bullen signed his dispatch to Banks "Commanding Post." So also did Maj. H. M. Porter, the provost marshal, sign a dispatch announcing the victory, as well as a long report of July 1. Banks called Bullen the commander (*O.R.*, *41*, 202, 202–203, 15).

58. *O.R. Navies,* Ser. I, XX, 337 (log of *Winona*), log of *Kineo.*

59. *O.R.*, *21,* 166–167 (Weitzel's report, Donaldsonville, Oct. 25, 1862); Weitzel said, "I entered the place without opposition at about 10 A.M." He gave high praise to the navy, saying his transports had not been fired upon because so well covered by gunboats. In a long letter to Weitzel on Nov. 2, George C. Strong, Butler's adjutant, said it was under advisement to build a fort at Donaldsonville (*ibid.,* pp. 162–163).

Farragut had shelled the town on August 9, 1862, and had landed a party that burned part of it. Two days later a group of citizens sent him a protest, to which he replied the same day: "Every time my boats are fired upon I will burn a portion of the town" (*ibid.,* pp. 795–796, 696).

60. *O.R.*, *41,* 603, 606, 613, 609, 608–609. After learning that some companies of Confederates had crossed to the east bank of the Mississippi and that there were plans for more to follow, Emory asked Farragut to have all craft of any kind removed from the west bank all the way from a point eighteen miles below New Orleans to Donaldsonville. He also clamped down on steamers, allowing none to depart from New Orleans without written permission (*ibid.,* pp. 606–607, 607, 604, 612).

61. *O.R.*, *41,* 398; *O.R. Navies,* Ser. I, XX, 240–241; *O.R.*, *41,* 599–600.

62. *O.R.*, *41,* 102.

63. *O.R.*, *41,* 494, 534, 564–565, 603. June 27 was a very critical day in Washington. At 1:00 P.M. Hooker telegraphed Halleck from near Harpers Ferry a request to be relieved from command of the Army of the Potomac, and Meade was promptly appointed to the position. Halleck had already—shortly after noon—received a dispatch from the commander at Baltimore saying that outside the forts he had only 800 men to defend the city—all

raw. The message also reported that a column of 5,000 Confederates had gone through Gettysburg (*supra,* II, 654; *O.R., 45,* 360).

Unfortunately the lack of the hour on his letter to Banks prevents one from knowing whether Halleck wrote before or after the reception of Hooker's somewhat dramatic telegram, but something of his reaction to the crisis in the East was revealed by the ending of his letter:

> I regret exceedingly that we can get no more troops to send you. The discharge of nine-months' and two-years' men has so reduced our forces that we can hardly defend Washington and Baltimore. The effect of the Copperhead disaffection at the north has prevented enlistments, and the drafting has not yet been attempted. We have been forced to resort to State militia, most of whom refuse to be mustered into the service of the United States. Notwithstanding that Pennsylvania is invaded by a large army, the militia of that State positively refuses to be mustered. This is the work of the politicians.

It was pointed out *supra,* II, 747, that Pittsburgh militia refused to cross the state line when some efforts were being made to intercept Lee's retreat.

64. *O.R., 41,* 46–48 (Banks to Halleck, June 29).

65. *Ibid.,* pp. 97, 98.

66. *Ibid.,* pp. 128, 72–74. Irwin's description of the attack shows that it had been carefully planned, the enemy force splitting into three columns, with a special objective for each. After describing the stampede which he had himself witnessed, he said, "This affords a pretty fair idea, I think, of the alarm of yesterday."

67. *Ibid.,* pp. 216, 212–214. The letter previously described, that Taylor sent Logan on June 15 ended by saying that Logan could communicate with him or the officer in command of the region by way of Morganza, and he (Taylor) would, "if practical," communicate with Gardner "to-night," sending Logan's "dispatch to him at the same time." It was an amazing disregard of time and space. It would be interesting to know when Taylor's message reached Logan.

68. *Ibid.,* pp. 617–618 (Farragut to Emory, referring to a long letter from Porter), 74–75 (John C. Palfrey, captain of engineers, to Irwin), 48–49 (Banks to Halleck). The beginning of Banks's letter shows that he had not written to Halleck since June 29, but he made no reference to the attempt that he had said Dwight would make that night. A cavalier was a raised work designed to command enemy lines.

69. *Ibid.,* pp. 176–177, 177.

70. Irwin, *B. and L.* article; *N.Y. Times,* as quoted in *Harper's Weekly,* VII, 497–498 (Aug. 8, 1863).

71. *O.R., 36,* 199; *41,* 182 (Johnston to Cooper, July 3, quoting Logan's dispatch in full), *Harper's Weekly, loc. cit.* Johnston's dispatch indicates that it was sent via Montgomery on the 6th and received in Richmond on the 9th. *H.W.* illustrates both the surrender and the firing of the salute.

On Jan. 28, 1864, Congress passed a resolution thanking Banks and his officers and men for the capture of Port Hudson, a resolution that declared the capture "removed the last obstruction to the free navigation of the Mississippi River" (*O.R., 41,* 911).

Inasmuch as it was stated in the text that Port Hudson is too often treated as a sideshow to Vicksburg, a sketch will be given of the manner in which the operation is set forth in the literature.

Greene's treatment in *The Mississippi* is adequate and discerning, though it must be said that it fails to note the important part the navy played during the siege. It is to be particularly observed that he gives good coverage to Banks's move up the Teche and points out fully how the investment of Port Hudson was accomplished. Although Mahan, quite as one would expect, stresses the activities of the navy in his *The Gulf and Inland Waters,* he also makes it clear that portions of Banks's corps came from different directions and joined at the objective point (p. 167).

It is hard to understand why soldiers such as Wood and Edmonds, who drew heavily on Greene and quoted from Irwin's article—which covered the entire campaign—should have said nothing in their *The Civil War in the United States* about Banks's operations up the Teche, and the manner in which he completed the investment of Port Hudson, which obviously had elements of distinction. In the book in question, Banks arrives, as it were, from nowhere and invests the 7,000 Confederates with 30,000 men, the present-for-duty figure to which reference has previously been made. The distinguished British writers did not fail to state that two assaults were repulsed with heavy loss, but they say nothing about Federal soldiers shouting the news of the Vicksburg surrender to the besieged Confederates. The statement about Gardner "being informed of the fact" would probably cause a reader correctly to believe that there had been an official communication of the news, which, of course, was the really important thing. Anyone familiar with soldiers would know that the Federal troops broke out into shouts upon hearing of the Vicksburg surrender, and, if limited for space, would pass over that fact for something of significance.

Steele's cursory treatment of Port Hudson in *American Campaigns* is little less than shocking. But it is not less amazing than the fact that many officers of our army should have been nurtured on a work in which the treatment of the Civil War was not in the least built upon the *Official Records.* But Steele's failure to describe the method of Banks's concentration and the formidable difficulties that confronted him cannot be excused, for the union of his forces was clearly set forth in Irwin's article, and the *B. and L.* was used by Steele. Only a sentence or two would have been needed. Because Steele was writing for soldiers, it was not merely a question of doing Banks justice, but of setting before military readers an operation militarily instructive.

As one comes to recent works the records grow worse and worse—with one notable exception. It is not surprising that Pratt in his chatty *Civil War on Western Waters* should devote three pages (pp. 157–159) to Farragut's failure to pass the Port Hudson batteries in March with more than two ships; the action merited good coverage. But not a word is said of naval operations during the siege (pp. 161, 157–159, 161). Banks's entire force is made to arrive from Alexandria because Banks "decided there was nothing doing there." Strangest of all, Pratt states that Port Hudson "was not a very active siege." The naval facts were readily available in Mahan's fine book. Mahan states (p. 168) that the half dozen mortar-schooners maintained a constant bombardment and succession of artillery fights with the river batteries of the Confederates, and were exposed to the fire of fourteen 8- and 10-inch smoothbores, and 7½-inch rifles. The commander of the mortars estimated that between May 23 and June 26 a thousand shot and shell were fired at him by the weapons mentioned. The ironclad *Essex* was "hulled" 23 times besides being hit frequently above decks; her injuries were severe. The mortar-schooners received so many "hard knocks" that their captains were specially commended by both their immediate commander and Admiral Farragut. Banks's report makes it clear how continuously active operations were on land. There was, he said, incessant fighting night and day for a period of 21 days, in addition to the assaults. While this statement may be a little discounted, the 565 casualties during the siege, in addition to the 3,798 suffered on May 27 and June 14, speak with considerable eloquence (*O.R., 41,* 70, 47).

While Pratt has Banks's entire army reach Port Hudson via the Red River, Catton apparently has it all come up directly from New Orleans, and there is a note of disparagement in his statement (*This Hallowed Ground,* p. 264) that Banks had *at last brought up* the army that did not come in time to meet Grant. Instead of being informed of the quite bold and skillful way in which Banks's forces were united behind the target, the reader is told that Banks was not a "very skillful strategist anyway." The assaults of May 27 and June 14 are not mentioned, but it is said that the capture of the place by assault was impossible. This assertion is at variance with Irwin's judgment about the first attempt, and it clearly implies that the well-prepared effort that Banks had prepared for July 9 would have failed. Gardner is not even mentioned; thus the important query he addressed to Banks is not made a part of the story. A reader could in fact believe that the Confederate troops, their will to resist shattered by the shouting of the Federals, the playing of their bands, and the "broadside" about the surrender of Vicksburg that had been thrown to them, merely walked over to the Federal lines and gave up.

In books about the Confederacy one naturally does not expect to find much about Banks's campaign prior to the siege, though an explanation of how it happened that Port Hudson had not been abandoned would be in order, and the noting of the two Federal assaults that had been repulsed would seem almost called for. Neither, however, is mentioned by Coulter in his *The Confederate States of America,* or by Eaton in his *A History of the Southern Confederacy.* Coulter does not give the name of either commander; Eaton does not name the Confederate general, though he observes that in some ways Port Hudson was more important to the logistics of the South than Vicksburg, because of its location near the mouth of the Red River. These two works, it should be said, are not primarily military.

One must praise what is given in Henry's *The Story of the Confederacy* (pp. 261, 264–265), a book that is not only entertainingly written but reveals a refreshing grasp of matters militarily significant. Henry states that Banks was as pugnacious as Grant, and he does not overlook the aid given by the Federal fleet. Furthermore, he states that Banks "largely stripped" New Orleans of troops and says that Taylor caused "the level-headed Emory" to warn Banks of the danger to the city. The Federal effort on the night of June 10 is mentioned quite as well as the two major assaults, and it is said that Banks planned another for July 9. Finally, Henry has Port Hudson surrender because Banks had a copy of Grant's dispatch about the capitulation of Vicksburg tossed into the Confederate lines. While this is not exactly what Banks said in his report, or what Irwin wrote in his article, a reader should feel that inside Port Hudson there was a disciplined military force under a commander, and that it was the commander who made the decision to surrender. That was not only the truth; it is a truth that every American can cherish.

NOTES TO CHAPTER III

1. *O.R., 41,* 626–627, 626, 230–232 (Green's report), 627–628. Capt. F. A. Faries of a Louisiana battery gave a rather detailed report (*ibid.,* pp. 220–222) of the firing his battery did. He found the *Essex,* which was doing convoy duty, quite immune to the metal he could throw, but pronounced the 12-foot Mississippi levee in which his guns were embrasured "the best of earthworks" against her 11- and 15-inch guns. The *Essex*'s heaviest guns had a caliber of 9 inches. Lighter gunboats shielded frailer boats with their hulls.

Emory said that the 3,000 enemy who were coming in to occupy the river below New Orleans were, so far as he knew, quite distinct from Taylor's force, estimated at 13,000, and that they consisted of watermen, fishermen, and irregular forces from the lagoons and bayous of southern Texas and Louisiana.

2. Green's report. At the time the name of the bayou was written "La Fourche" and it is found in reports both with and without the redundant article "the." The name today is "Lafourche," the French article having disappeared as such. The Rand McNally pocket map of Louisiana gives both in the index, and on the map itself not only the Bayou Lafourche that was prominent in the operations of 1863, but Bayou La Fourche, a little east of Monroe.

3. Grover's and Dudley's reports, court-martial record, *O.R., 41,* 204, 209, 205–206. Green put his killed and wounded at 9 (one died of wounds), and 24, respectively, and the Federal casualties at little less than 1,000. Grover said he thought the Confederate loss about equal to "ours," adding that a Confederate officer, who came under a flag of truce to collect the killed and wounded, would not give their loss, though he said it was less than that of the Federals. As compiled from nominal lists, the *O.R.* (*ibid.,* p. 205) gives the Federal loss in ten infantry regiments and two batteries as 50 killed, 223 wounded and 186 missing.

The date July 14 that appears on Green's report is certainly in error by several days; it conflicts with what is said about remaining for two or three days.

4. It may be recalled that Parke's two divisions were part of the force that had been watching Johnston—and had from their arrival been in the vicinity of Haynes Bluff. Some divisions from the other corps were also part of the "Army of Observation," located either at Haynes Bluff or at crossings of the Big Black. See *supra,* IV, p. 408.

5. *O.R., 38,* 474, 552–553, 471, 472.

6. *Ibid.*, pp. 476–477, 476, 472.

7. *Ibid.*, pp. 480, 478. On the 7th McPherson issued an order that said battle flags, guidons, and colors that had been surrendered had been taken by unauthorized persons. A search and report on the search were given high priority (*ibid.*, p. 485).

8. *O.R., 37,* 520–521; *38,* 474–475.

9. *O.R., 38,* 481–482; *37,* 521. Sherman's dispatch from Bolton ended, "To-morrow I will feel toward Clinton with cavalry, but await Parke's arrival before moving farther." The troops, Sherman said, were suffering excessively from the heat and dust. When Parke did not arrive, Sherman sent him an order to stop work on the bridge that was to have led him to Brownsville before swinging down to Clinton; instead he was to cross at Messinger's Ford.

10. *O.R., 37,* 521; *38,* 496 (order of July 10, headed "near Jackson"), 522–523.

11. *O.R., 37,* 521 (Sherman to Grant, July 11).

12. *O.R., 38,* 502–503; *37,* 522–523, 522.

13. *O.R., 37,* 525–527 (Sherman to Grant, July 14), 523; *38,* 503 and 503–504 (Ord's instructions to Lauman, July 11); *37,* 540–541 (undated report of the scout C. Spencer), 524 (Sherman to Grant, July 14), 574–576 (Ord's report). Spencer's report was very detailed, with names of division and brigade commanders, and regiments by states, so far as he had been able to learn them, with a sketch showing location of units. He said the cavalry was camped about a mile behind the town, to give protection to the trains, which were immense. He stated that supplies were meager and all were received by way of Meridian. He reported on the number of locomotives and cars available to Johnston. Spencer had traversed nearly the entire state of Mississippi, and besides the command of Johnston, the only other forces of consequence in the central and northern parts of the state were those of Chalmers, Gholson, and Ruggles. Almost the entire population was in arms, with but few men at home.

14. *O.R., 37,* 527 (Sherman to Grant, 8:30 P.M., July 15).

15. *O.R., 38,* 520; Sherman's and Parke's reports, *37,* 532–537, 555–557; Ord's report.

16. *O.R., 38,* 522.

17. Sherman's report.

18. *O.R., 38,* 531–532 (Sherman to Porter); Sherman's report; *O.R., 37,* 526. In his letter to Porter, Sherman spoke of the statehouse, the governor's mansion, and "some fine dwellings" being untouched by fires.

19. *O.R., 37,* 540. The nine persons on the Jackson committee—appointed by the mayor—signed a pledge to distribute the supplies equitably among the needy inhabitants. The statement about supplying hospitals is in Sherman's report.

20. *O.R., 37,* 550.

21. Parke's report; *O.R., 38,* 506; *37,* 523.

22. Sherman's report; *O.R., 38,* 493–494 (Pemberton to McPherson, July 10), 495–496 (McPerson's reply, s.d.); *37,* 523 (Sherman to Grant, July 13). Pemberton said that he proposed to start his movement the next morning at

4 o'clock, or as soon thereafter as possible; he gave the order of march and the routes. McPherson stated that Brig. Gen. John D. Stevenson of his command would see that all arrangements were carried out in the proper manner, adding that Grant had told him that Pemberton would detail officers to act in conjunction with the Federal provost marshals.

23. *O.R.*, *38*, 481, 1000. Pemberton's dispatch looks like a reply to a message that Davis had sent on the 14th and that had been received on the 15th, when Pemberton was at Brandon. On that day and from that place Pemberton wrote Grant, enclosing an open letter to Smith, asking for copies of the rolls, if completed, and "the number of each grade who marched out of Vicksburg as effective"—the information to be furnished with the least possible delay (*ibid.*, pp. 1002, 1005–1006).

24. *Ibid.*, pp. 478, 484.

25. *Ibid.*, p. 502. Pemberton was not exactly an easy person to deal with, and seemed almost at times to feel that Grant had done the surrendering. He does not seem, however, to have again challenged by implication Grant's truthfulness, as he had the previous fall, to receive from Grant an uncommonly sharp reply (*supra*, IV, 185).

A number of questions arose on which Grant had to make rulings.

On the 7th John Logan "solemnly" protested to Grant against the manner in which Confederate officers were being permitted to intimidate servants in the presence of Federal officers appointed to examine whether the former slaves wanted to accompany their old masters. Grant ruled at once that if a suspicious number of blacks were going out with the Confederate troops, *all* should be turned back except such as were voluntarily accompanying *families;* and even then there should not be more than *one* per family. Pemberton made something of a remonstrance to the note he received on the subject from McPherson (*ibid.*, pp. 483, 484, 487).

In addition to the desire to take out servants, Pemberton informed McPherson on the 6th that his generals would like to take mounted couriers with them. The early reply that he requested was forthcoming, but it was in the negative. Certain allowances of wagons for various headquarters were, however, provided. But there was one request that Pemberton declined to make of Grant. He would not ask whether men who preferred prison to parole would be allowed to go North as prisoners. No matter what Grant might rule—he ruled they could—Pemberton would not put the question, he informed Martin Smith in reply to a "private" note (*ibid.*, pp. 481, 993).

Maj. N. G. Watts, who had been Confederate agent for exchange at Vicksburg, declined to sign rolls that carried men who had escaped (on the 8th Pemberton protested to Grant that men of a Louisiana regiment were crossing the Mississippi in skiffs, in violation of the terms of capitulation). It was not necessary for Watts to sign anything, Grant informed McPherson in a communication that ended, "Major Watts, with the balance, is at present a prisoner of war."

The terms of surrender, Grant said, were unambiguous and had been accepted by Pemberton "in unmistakable language." All men in the garrison at the time of the agreement were bound by Pemberton's word, Grant ruled. The rolls were merely to serve as a means "to negotiate for the exchange of prisoners hereafter." Obviously Pemberton would not have objected to the escape of his men in skiffs—in fact he would have been delighted when he saw them—if he thought they were hastening away to join some other Confederate unit; but he did not want a Federal prisoner given up for a man who had deserted (*ibid.*, p. 488).

It was otherwise with the men who declined to be paroled and who were sent North, and also with the sick and wounded. For them—if the Confederates had enough Federals on hand—the Washington government might get two men for one. To avoid this, Grant directed that special rolls be made; then their names could be dropped from the rolls that regimental and other commanders submitted for their commands as of the time of surrender. (*Ibid.*, p. 495, Grant to McPherson, July 10, with instructions about checking men against rolls as they marched out.)

When Pemberton marched away, Grant's annoyances with his captured men were not over. On the 16th he wrote to Banks: "The wounded and sick rebels in hospitals here have proven themselves so troublesome that I acceded with great promptness to the proposition from General M. L. Smith to move all who may be unable for land carriage to Mobile, Ala., and Monroe, La. I send Colonel Lagow, of my staff, with the first batch." From Port Hudson they were promptly passed to New Orleans (*O.R.*, *38,* 518–519; *41,* 644–645).

26. *O.R.*, *38,* 1001, 1002. Davis's dispatch to Pemberton was dated the 14th, but stated that Johnston had telegraphed him the day before that Pemberton was recommending a 30-day furlough.

27. *Ibid.*, pp. 994–995.

28. *Ibid.*, pp. 1006–1007, 1010, 1015 (Pemberton's circular order on the subject of furloughs, dated July 18, "On the march"). Davis's telegram of the 17th giving discretion to Pemberton ended, "Twelve thousand arms were sent to General Johnston for militia; they could not have been issued. Five thousand are at Selma, and more will be sent."

29. *Ibid.*, p. 1014.

30. *O.R.*, *119,* 117, 204.

31. *Ibid.*, pp. 147, 184–185, 233. The 405 officers captured at Port Hudson were not paroled, but were sent to New Orleans; a large number of them, including Brig. Gen. Beal, being then sent back up the river to Grant, with the request that he send them to a proper place in the North (*O.R.*, *41,* 642, 641, 643, 644–645).

32. *O.R.*, *52,* 693–694 (Halleck to Grant, Sept. 17); *119,* 611, 599.

33. Herron's report, *O.R.*, *37,* 667–669; *38,* 490–491 (Grant to Banks, July 9); *41,* 624–625 (Banks to Grant, July 8); *38,* 500 (Grant to Herron, July 11, 499 (Grant to Porter, July 11).

In the letter to Banks, Grant said that he expected that Port Hudson would have fallen before the arrival of Herron, but having heard of the position of Taylor's force, he thought Herron (who was going without baggage, hospitals, or artillery), could replace troops that Banks would want to send southward. (It was a fine example of Grant's constant readiness to assist another commander, even before he was asked.) Grant requested Grierson's return as soon as possible, as he needed cavalry. He also gave information about Sherman's move, and about the victories at Helena and Vicksburg (the news from Helena had been sent to him on the 5th by the superintendent of telegraphs). Pemberton's men had certainly learned about Gettysburg and Helena, and the tail of his column should have had the Port Hudson news before leaving, and it would not have taken long for the leading men to have it. The beginning of the letter, "I send Maj. Gen. F. J. Herron to Port Hudson . . ." looks as if Herron was carrying the communication. If so, one wonders whether Banks received the budget of important news.

In the dispatch to Porter, mentioning the reports about Yazoo City, Grant queried: "Will it not be well to send up a fleet of gunboats and some troops, and nip in the bud any attempt to concentrate a force there? I will order troops at once to go aboard of transports." Obviously a force other than Herron's was in his mind. Probably as a response to Grant's note, Porter wrote: "Port Hudson surrendered unconditionally on the 9th inst. The steamer has just brought the dispatches. As General Herron is all ready, allow me to suggest that he move up the Yazoo to-morrow morning, when I shall be ready" (*O.R. Navies,* Ser. I, XXV, 281).

34. Herron's report; Walker's report, *O.R. Navies,* Ser. I, XXV, 284; Brown's and Creasman's report, *O.R., 37,* 671, 671–673. Herron stated that there were two tinclads, but Walker listed the *Kenwood,* the *Signal,* and the *New National,* the second, like the first, having six guns, while the *New National* had but one. Though Herron spoke of giving orders to Walker, he could have done no more than request or recommend action. No order from Porter to Walker is in the naval records, but Walker said he went "to cooperate with the force under General Herron," and the cooperation appears to have been perfect.

While it would seem that Brown was not under Creasman, the latter wrote, "I ordered Captain Brown, C. S. Navy, to destroy or render useless the heavy artillery, which he failed to do, informing me afterward that he did not have time, and to destroy them by blowing them up would have given the enemy notice of our intention to evacuate and thereby endanger our retreat." Brown telegraphed Johnston from Meridian that his few men had gone to Mobile (*O.R., 37,* 670).

35. Herron's report; Porter's reports of July 14, 22, and Aug. 23 (with enclosures), and log of the *Kenwood, O.R. Navies,* Ser. I, XXV, 282–286.

In the report of July 22, Porter put the value of the steamers destroyed at $800,000. In his first report he spoke of getting the *De Kalb* up as soon as possible, and the next day he wrote to Capt. Pennock at Cairo to "make all arrangements at once for sending me a bell boat with people to raise the *Cincinnati,* which is an easy job, and the *De Kalb,* which I am afraid is much hurt, and the *Cairo,* which lies 10 or 20 feet under water. I will have them all in commission again if I can, and better vessels made of them." In his final report he said the *De Kalb* was too much damaged to save her hull, "two torpedoes having exploded under her, tearing her bow and stern all to pieces." (Walker's report mentioned a single "torpedo.") In his letter to Welles of July 15 Porter said of the *De Kalb*'s crew, "Their labors in recovering their guns and stores will not be surpassed by anyone on any other occasion."

36. Herron's report; Brown to Brig. Gen. James R. Chalmers, from Lexington, Miss., *O.R. Navies,* Ser. I, XXV, 290. Chalmers would soon be in com-

mand of part of the Confederate troops in northern Mississippi, and Brown wrote him that he had no one to execute Johnston's order to destroy public property along the Yazoo, and asked if Chalmers could detail companies of local cavalry to burn the cotton in Holmes and Carroll counties. In his report of July 22, Porter had put the value of the cotton seized by Herron at $550,000. He also stated that Herron had seized the cotton—which he put at 3,000 bales—because of the treachery of citizens of Yazoo City. They had failed to give warning about the "torpedoes," though they had had opportunity to do so. This sounds like typical Porter embellishment.

The order for Herron to move eastward arrived as he was about to execute an earlier order to leave two regiments to carry on demolitions at Yazoo City and return with the balance of his command to Vicksburg, as he might "be needed below" (*O.R.*, *38*, 509, 513, 520).

37. *O.R. Navies,* Ser. I, XVIII, 472–475 (Farragut's report about the surrender of Baton Rouge, with enclosures); 489–491 (Palmer's report about Natchez, including correspondence with the mayor).

38. Beauregard to Brig. Gen. C. G. Dahlgren, *O.R.*, *21,* 744–745. Dahlgren had been in command of the very small detachment at Natchez, and wrote (*ibid.*, pp. 736–738) Beauregard on May 17 from Washington (a few miles east of Natchez). He stated that after his adjutant had refused to accept Palmer's letter, the Federal officer had called for someone in the crowd to take it. The man who "rushed forth" to accept it was promptly arrested, and was at the moment in jail at Fayette awaiting trial. Beauregard approved and commended the arrest.

39. *O.R. Navies,* Ser. I, XIX, 181. In connection with the Vicksburg situation, Farragut made a statement that could well have been noted previously. In a letter from Baton Rouge on May 10 to Commander S. P. Lee of the *Oneida,* who commanded the first ships sent up the river, the admiral said (*O.R. Navies,* Ser. I, XVIII, 478–479): "I had a man on board last night who is just from Memphis and Vicksburg, and he states that they are beginning to fortify Vicksburg; that they have only a small battery of six guns on the slope of the hill, and are commencing another just below the town, but there are no guns there yet.

"If it is possible for you to get a gunboat into the Yazoo River a few miles they will be able to capture or compel the enemy to destroy the ram now building there, which is a thing of the first importance, as they say it will be finished in three weeks."

The ram referred to was the *Arkansas.*

40. *O.R.*, *7,* 199; *10,* 137–138; *36,* 53, 149, 112–113.

41. *O.R.*, *37,* 680–682 (Ransom to Lieut. Col. W. T. Clark, McPherson's adjutant, July 16).

42. *O.R.*, *38,* 511; *41,* 643 (Stone to Grant).

43. *O.R.*, *38,* 521 (McPherson to Ransom, 536–537, 549–550). McPherson said: "With regard to the contrabands [concerning whom, as well as the great quantity of lumber at Natchez, Ransom had requested instructions], you can say to them that they are free, and that it will be better for them, especially the women and children, old and infirm, to remain quietly where they are, as we

have no means of providing for them at present." Strong, able-bodied men who would make good soldiers could be brought back, if they were "willing to come and will leave their families behind them."

44. *O.R., 36,* 47.

45. *O.R., 38,* 540–542, 498; Phisterer, *Statistical Record,* pp. 263, 262.

46. Grant's Headquarters Papers, XXIV, 148; *O.R., 109,* 442 (Halleck to Grant, Aug. 28). Halleck said that immediately upon receipt of Grant's letter of July 27 he had approved all of Grant's recommendations and submitted them to the Secretary of War. Though he had tried, he had failed to keep open any major generalcies, and only part of those Grant had recommended for brigadiers could be made at present. Without waiting for Grant's official letter, he had obtained some suggestions from Rawlins so that Grant's army could have a chance at getting vacancies.

47. *O.R., 38,* 537, 487.

48. *O.R., 37,* 663–666, 666.

49. *O.R., 24,* 593.

50. *O.R., 37,* 673–676. Col. J. K. Mizner, Dodge's chief of cavalry, endorsed on Hatch's report: "The taking of the bridges and forcing a crossing by the Third Michigan Cavalry, the storming and carrying the earthworks by the Ninth Illinois Infantry, and the charge of the Second Iowa Cavalry, gives evidence of the firmness and reliable character of these troops."

51. *O.R., 34,* 822 (report about capture of Union City); *supra,* IV, 411; *O.R., 38,* 512.

52. *O.R., 38,* 550, 1034–1035. In an order issued at Panola on May 30, Chalmers divided his command—all cavalry—into three brigades. The first two included units not called Partisan Rangers, but regular Confederate organizations; the third brigade, under Brig. Gen. J. Z. George, consisted of three Mississippi Ranger units—one regiment and two battalions (*ibid.,* pp. 934–935).

On July 9 George wrote Chalmers (*ibid.,* pp. 995–997) urging that state forces in the northern and western part of Mississippi be organized "in the future as guerrillas." In an endorsement, Chalmers indicated that guerrilla companies were not only in existence, but were costing the Confederate government more than they were worth, and he commented, "Their ranks are very thin until a muster for pay is ordered, and then they are quite full." He stated further that the freedom of guerrillas from military restraint had an injurious effect on men in the regular service, and caused many desertions from both the infantry and cavalry. Nonetheless, Chalmers thought that guerrilla companies, under proper officers, could be of use, and he recommended "that all guerrilla companies be composed of non-conscripts, and organized under the act of Congress authorizing companies of 20 or more for home defense, without compensation."

One must surely believe that Chalmers—who had commanded the first Mississippi regiment mustered into Confederate service, and who had commanded a brigade of Mississippians at Stones River—spoke advisedly when he referred to "guerrilla companies," and one must strongly suspect that Richmond authorities knew that Confederate money was being used to support units for which the label "Partisan Rangers" was a deceptive mask.

Brigaded with the 2nd Missouri Cavalry and a battalion of Waul's Texas Legion was the 1st Mississippi Partisan Rangers, the regiment of Col. W. C. Falkner, who for a while had commanded the brigade. An admirable account of the entire record, which, in addition to the *O.R.*, uses much material in the National Archives, has been given by Andrew Brown ("The First Mississippi Partisan Rangers, C.S.A.," in *Civil War History,* I, 371–399, already cited *supra,* IV, 506 n. 29). Brown states that Falkner's regiment differed essentially from other Mississippi Ranger organizations; it was the only one that was initially organized as a regiment, and, "despite its name, it was not designed primarily for guerrilla warfare, but to operate within and as a part of the regular Confederate cavalry forces." That the men were nonetheless hard to distinguish from civilians is seen from the statement that in the summer of 1862 uniforms were of such a nondescript character that ten civilians may have been included in eleven prisoners that Sheridan reported. After having been once disbanded in deference to the Confederate Conscription Bureau, the regiment was re-formed by Falkner with some difficulty, and Brown states that on July 20, 1863, Falkner wrote Chalmers requesting "that the regiment be detached for guerrilla service"—in itself a sharp and most revealing reversal of his former attitude (pp. 372, 378, 386).

Upon learning of the evacuation of Jackson, Ruggles assumed that Chalmers would be compelled to fall back from Panola, where he had been for some time, and wrote to him about cooperation. He commented, "The period is critical, and requires our utmost vigilance" (*O.R., 38,* 1016).

53. *O.R., 38,* 570–571. The order called upon citizens of Mississippi within the region described (the Mississippi Central extended from Jackson, through Grenada, to Grand Junction, but, inasmuch as Grant had troops at Natchez, he may have also had in mind the railroad south of Jackson, which was the New Orleans, Galveston, and Great Northern) to go about their usual business; urged that the freedom of Negroes be acknowledged and that contracts be made for their labor as free men; stated the conditions upon which private property would be taken, and said that otherwise it would be respected; and prescribed how cotton was to be handled. Once more Grant condemned the behavior of some of his men, saying that conduct disgraceful of the American name had frequently been reported to him, "particularly on the part of portions of the cavalry." It is unlikely, however, that the summary punishment he prescribed for officers and men "apprehended in acts of violence or lawlessness" stopped the evil.

Anticipating the capture of Vicksburg, Secretary Salmon Chase had written to Grant on July 4 about the subject of trade, and enclosed a copy of a letter just written to a supervising agent of the Treasury Department in Cincinnati. Grant's acknowledgment of the communication on July 21 ended: "No theory of my own will ever stand in the way of my executing in good faith any order I may receive from those in authority over me, but my position here has given me an opportunity of seeing what could not be known by persons away from the scene of war, and I suggest, therefore, great caution in opening trade with rebels" (*ibid.,* pp. 570–571, 538).

54. *Ibid.,* pp. 454–456 (roster of the 16th Corps for June 30), 538.

55. *Ibid.,* pp. 555–556, 563. In his report Sherman said that the tendency

to plunder and pillage, even though it was confined to a few, was a discredit "on all of us." A few days later, in transmitting the record of a court martial for Grant's action, he stated that the behavior of the army made him ashamed of it. His outburst was caused by the burning of a cotton gin during the return from Jackson, and Sherman would have executed the guilty man on the spot —he had himself caught him in the act—but the culprit had pleaded the order of a superior, and a court had absolved the officer. Sherman would have felt a little better if he had known that a day or so before he had seen the wanton act, Johnston was denouncing his division commanders for apparently doing nothing to check Confederate soldiers from engaging in robbery and plunder. They must, he said, in the future always post guards around property near where they were camped, with orders to shoot down men indulging in depredations (*ibid.*, pp. 574–575, 1023–1024).

56. *Ibid.*, pp. 565–566.

NOTES TO CHAPTER IV

1. *O.R.*, *41*, 624–625; *38*, 499–500, 498–499.

2. *O.R.*, *41*, 648 (Stone to Banks, Port Hudson, July 20); *38*, 527–528 (Banks to Grant); *21*, 590–591 (Halleck's instructions of Nov. 9, 1862). Grant's letter had not reached Banks at New Orleans, but its contents had been telegraphed from Port Hudson.

3. *O.R.*, *38*, 513. Along with this dispatch Grant probably received one sent by Halleck at 10:30 A.M. of the same day to both him and Prentiss, about a reported move of Price into Missouri, which had come from Schofield, and which is considered in the next chapter.

4. *Supra*, II, 750; *O.R.*, *38*, 497–498. A copy of Halleck's letter was sent to Banks on the 13th with a covering message that said: "General Emory's last dispatch was not encouraging. But long ere this you will have been so reenforced as to be able to recover whatever you may have lost" (*O.R.*, *41*, 636). Without question the reinforcements to which he referred were those that Grant had said in his message of July 4 he would send to Banks. It was not until the receipt on the 15th of Grant's telegram of the 11th that Halleck knew all of Grant's "spare troops" were with Sherman, and that none had gone to Banks.

5. *O.R.*, *37*, 523; *38*, 529–530; *32*, 18–19 (Schofield to Grant). Schofield's letter and Grant's reply are referred to in the next chapter.

6. *O.R.*, *38*, 542.

7. *O.R.*, *41*, 652–653. A copy of Halleck's dispatch of the 22nd was enclosed in the letter to Banks.

8. *O.R.*, *38*, 546–547. Grant said that either Sherman or McPherson would be a good man to whom to entrust a Mobile operation; he had no choice between them, both being unexcelled, in his estimation, by any officer in the army.

Two days later Grant wrote a letter to Brig. Gen. J. D. Webster, his superintendent of railroads, in which he made a very interesting comment. Webster had written him two letters, presumably from Memphis, on the 20th, which the editors of the *O.R.* indicate as "not found." That Webster had raised the point of repairing the Memphis and Charleston Railroad east of Corinth was shown by Grant's indicating that he was not yet prepared to say whether any move would be required in that direction. After stating that, with the force then present in West Tennessee, it would not be possible to give adequate protection to an extension of the rail line, he remarked: "I am anxiously waiting for some general plan of operations from Washington. It is important that the troops of different departments should act in concert; hence the necessity of general instructions from one head" (*O.R.*, *38*, 552–553).

It is to be observed that Grant limited himself to the necessity of "general instructions," and that two days before writing to Webster he had read Halleck's letter that showed the difficulty of full decision in Washington because of slow communications, and the lack of full knowledge about both Federal and enemy forces. Only a few days previously Grant had called Sherman back from pursuit of Johnston because of the heat and dryness, at a time when he also feared that illness in his command might reach a serious state. Halleck's letter left Grant free for cooperation with Banks and Schofield, officers whose temperaments made cooperation possible. The extension of the railroad east could only have been for cooperation with Rosecrans, and Grant's experience with him had not been satisfactory. What was needed was, of course, actual *unity of command,* and the "one head" who could have brought about full coordination of the Army of the Tennessee and that of the Cumberland would have had to be in the theater of operations, and eventually would be Grant himself. But it is going too far casually to say that the administration should have done in July what it did in October after disaster had overtaken Rosecrans. This theme will, however, be touched upon in the appendix dealing with Halleck, where the general inadequacy of higher-command conceptions that then existed will also be briefly discussed.

9. *O.R.*, *41*, 661–662, 651–652.

10. *Ibid.*, p. 666. Banks's letter began, "I have the honor to acknowledge receipt of your telegram of 27th July, transmitted to me by General Grant." Although a telegram from Washington could have reached Vicksburg by way of Cairo in four days, there seems to be an error in the date set down by Banks, or in transcribing or printing. On July 27 Grant began a letter to Banks (*O.R.*, *38*, 553), "Herewith I send you dispatch just received from Washington." In a footnote the editors of the *O.R.* identify Halleck's message as that of July 22, which is given in full in the text.

Grant's letter to Banks, written the day after the one to Webster, is of considerable importance. He had been called upon, he said, to send troops to Helena because of Price's movement (thus cooperating with Schofield, some of whose troops were still under Grant's command); and he had also been "compelled" to return the 9th Corps to Kentucky (a surprising way to put the matter after he had told Halleck over three weeks before that he would return it to Burnside). Because of shortage of transportation, it might be a week before all troops were off. But, as was his habit, Grant was ready to do what he could to aid others; if the troops he had sent were insufficient—presumably those dispatched to Helena—he would also send the freshest division he had, though all were much in need of rest. He remarked, "Sickness is showing itself to a very extent in this command, though there is but little fatal disease."

Grant inclined to the belief that Kirby Smith had withdrawn his forces from Monroe and vicinity to Shreveport, though he had taken no pains to find out, *"not being prepared to make any move against them just now."* (Emphasis supplied.) By the time transportation was secured, he could, if necessary, co-operate with an army corps "for the extinction of Smith's forces," provided no Washington order required his troops elsewhere. If his troops were to rest for a while, he would send an army corps to Natchez; in that case there would always be a disposable force to give Banks any required aid.

11. *Supra,* IV, 324.

12. *O.R., 38,* 569, 584. After expressing some views about Negro troops, and saying that he had been very glad to learn from Dana that Grant believed the Emancipation Proclamation had been of some help in his military operations, Lincoln, in his dispatch to Grant, queried, "Did you receive a short letter from me dated the 13th of July?" The letter in question was the "you were right, and I was wrong" masterpiece used as an end paper in Vol. IV of this work. One can do nothing but speculate as to the reason for Lincoln's question; but so far as the *O.R.* indicates, he received no answer.

13. That both Grant and Banks fully recognized at the time that there might be government policy that would rule out a Mobile operation is clear from the quotation made from Banks's dispatch from Vicksburg.

In his *Strategy, The Indirect Approach,* pp. 333–334, Liddell Hart gives an interesting discussion of areas where decision belongs to the government. He points out, as others have, that Clausewitz's definition of strategy intrudes on governmental policy prerogatives, while that of Moltke fixes the responsibility of a military commander to those who employ him.

14. *Ibid.,* pp. 578 (Halleck to Grant, Aug. 6), 580 (Grant to Banks, Aug. 7). Indianola, destroyed by cyclones in 1885 and 1886, was on Lavaca Bay, ten miles southwest of Port Lavaca, and about 110 miles west southwest of Galveston (*O.R. Atlas,* Plate CLVII).

Halleck's telegram of July 30 directing Grant to send troops reads: "You will send Major-General Banks a corps of 10,000 to 12,000 men, to report at such point as he may designate; probably at New Orleans" (*O.R., 38,* 562).

The letter to Banks in which Grant explained that one division of Ord's corps, which he was sending, was being replaced by that of Herron, which was then at Port Hudson, contained a note of surprise: "General Halleck's dispatch does not seem to be in response to any dispatch received from you or myself." While Halleck's telegram of July 15 had disposed of a Texas expedition "for the present," the number of men that Grant was directed to send to Banks was—suggestively, one might think—precisely the number that Grant had told Halleck that Banks had requested for a Texas operation.

In replying to Grant on Aug. 10, Banks did not call attention to his letter to Grant of July 8, which he knew had gone on to Washington. Instead, he wagered the thought that the troop movement, "not having reference to your dispatch or my own" (apparently those of Aug. 1, which could hardly have been expected to explain a message Halleck had sent two days previously), might have been caused by information that Washington had of the sailing of the "iron-clads from Liverpool" then under construction. Southerners, he said, had been overheard saying that their destination would be the Southwest, for a possible attack on New Orleans.

15. *O.R., 41,* 673. In a letter to Lincoln on Aug. 17, dealing with raising Negro troops, Banks spoke as if Mobile and Texas were equally desirable in that regard, adding the wise comment: "It is impossible to raise Negro regiments except we get possession of the country where negroes are. This is a fact overlooked by many persons who are greatly interested in the success of these organizations" (*ibid.,* pp. 688–689).

16. Halleck to Banks, Aug. 12, *ibid.,* p. 675.

17. *O.R., 41,* 18; Grant, *Memoirs,* I, 578–579. After saying, "Halleck disapproved of my proposition to go against Mobile . . . ," Grant states on the next page, "The General-in-chief having decided against me, the depletion of an army, which had won a succession of victories, commenced, as had been the case the year before after the fall of Corinth when the army was sent where it would do the least good"—a statement that probably has contributed to the unfavorable, if not contemptuous, view that many have about Halleck.

One cannot read Grant's criticism without recalling that he himself called back the powerful army under Sherman from pursuing Johnston. While no one seems to have seriously questioned this act, a comparable degree of understanding has not been given to decisions made in Washington.

The reference to Corinth was not a happy one. As noted *supra,* IV, 25–26, Halleck had informed Stanton of his plan to send Buell toward Chattanooga, and had received the reply that the President was "greatly delighted" over his proposals; thus it was Lincoln whom Grant was really criticizing. That it would be necessary to support Buell by divisions from Grant's army in West Tennessee was, of course, not foreseen. But Halleck was just as prompt in ordering Burnside and Schofield to send troops to Vicksburg when he received Grant's telegram that he should be strengthened.

Unfortunately, the Mobile-Texas question is not easily handled briefly and accurately, and one must never forget the physical condition under which Grant wrote his *Memoirs.* The writer, however, cannot but believe that Grant's postwar change of feeling toward Halleck, that was explained *supra,* III, 514, n. 45, regrettably manifests itself at places in his *Memoirs.* If Halleck, when he sent Grant the letter from Adj. Gen. Thomas and his reply, which were there described, had merely stated that he regretted that the entire incident had arisen from a telegram that he had sent to McClellan because of failure to receive reports from Grant, the latter would certainly have accepted the explanation without any ill-feeling or resentment. (In a letter to Washburne, Grant actually defended Halleck's suspending him from command—Wilson, *Grant's Letters to a Friend,* pp. 8–9.) Whether Halleck had engaged in deliberate deception must be a matter of individual opinion (just as must be the thought that Grant held too tenaciously to his new feeling). But whether the misconception that he put in Grant's mind was intentional or unintentional, he paid heavily for it.

Grant's statement that the danger of foreign intervention could have been removed by the prompt occupation of Brownsville will be commented upon in connection with Banks's Texas operation.

18. Nicolay and Hay, *Abraham Lincoln, A History,* VIII, 285–286. Halleck's

proposal of the Red River route is described, and it is stated that Banks rejected it "on account of low water and other reasons that were afterwards proved to be sound"—a judgment that anticipates the Red River campaign of the next spring.

Some choleric pages in Welles's diary dated July 31, 1863, do not give so much light as one would wish on the Texas matter, though it is indicated that Secretary Seward knew something of the schemes of Louis Napoleon. Seward is denounced for not getting the matter before the entire Cabinet; at the meeting that day he had taken "Stanton aside and had ten minutes' private conversation with him in low tone." At 2 in the afternoon, Welles, at Seward's request, had gone to the War Department, and he commented, "Why a special meeting of only three with General Halleck?" Welles could not say how much Halleck knew about matters withheld from a majority of the Cabinet; but he had no doubt that Halleck was better posted than himself. In spite of the fact that the General in Chief had "some scholastic attainments," Welles's view of him was clearly unfavorable, and he seemed annoyed because Seward was "profoundly deferential" to him. As Welles and Seward left the conference, "General Halleck lighted another cigar."

Welles stated that Halleck had not decided between Mobile and Texas; he was waiting to hear from Banks. His placing with Halleck the decision between the two targets is of no weight whatever, in view of Lincoln's telegram to Grant of Aug. 9, as well as what the President's secretaries later wrote. Actually at 5 of the afternoon of the meeting that was rather painful to Welles, Halleck telegraphed Banks: "General Grant has been ordered to send you a corps of 10,000 to 12,000 men for operations west. Get everything ready. We are only waiting for your answer to my dispatch of the 24th" (*Diary of Gideon Welles,* I, 388–392; *O.R., 41,* 664).

19. *O.R., 38,* 587–588. There is a marked similarity between parts of this letter and parts of the one to Banks on July 27, discussed in n. 10.

20. Halleck to Grant, Aug. 22, *O.R., 52,* 108–109; Banks to Halleck, *41,* 697–698. There is no reason for believing that Grant discounted the statement in Halleck's letter, "The Government is exceedingly anxious that our troops should occupy some points in Texas, with the least possible delay." And, although his expressed concern about his movements having appeared slow may have applied solely to such matters as the return of Parke's corps, he probably was gratified by the General in Chief's remark: "I have heard of no complaints whatever about the movements of your army since the fall of Vicksburg; on the contrary, everyone supposed that it would require some rest before undertaking new operations."

Banks spoke of the intense conscription efforts in Louisiana and Texas, with the indication that they would yield "a pretty formidable army if concentrated against us in Texas, or if thrown against New Orleans." As usual, however, there were discordant elements in the situation. The severe conscription, as well as Federal successes, had produced demoralization. Deserters arriving the day he wrote had reported a collision between disaffected Texans and other troops.

21. *O.R., 38,* 1016; *110,* 508; *38,* 1017, 1019.

22. *O.R., 38,* 1048, 1049, 1051, 1028, 1036.

23. *Ibid.*, pp. 1036, 1037, 1042–1043 (Johnston to Cooper, Aug. 2). The information in the dispatch of Aug. 2 was based upon what was told to Johnston by the brother of one of his cavalry scouts, just arrived from Vicksburg.

24. *O.R.*, *42*, 128, 152, 152–153. Banks, as his letter to Grant on Aug. 10 shows, had been entertaining hopes that Mobile might be evacuated. But since Johnston's visit, he had found Mobile papers evasive, though Johnston was made to say that "the post was one of the strongest on the rebel seaboard." This, Banks added, was "undoubtedly true." On July 25 Hurlbut sent Halleck a comprehensive intelligence summary based upon the report of a man who had left Mobile on the 21st and had picked up information along his route. On the 29th Dodge sent Hurlbut a long report about Mobile. Maury's work certainly soon rendered information about protection against land attack quite out of date. Intelligence, however, continued to reach Banks, partly at least from deserters, who, though welcome, were not always reliable, even when it appeared that there was no question but that they had eagerly slipped away and had not been sent out from the hostile lines with stories to deceive. On Aug. 28 Banks wrote Grant that "a deserter just in from Mobile" reported the greatest confusion among the ill-fed and greatly discontented troops (*O.R.*, *41*, 673–674; *38*, 551, 561; *41*, 701).

That sailors were relieving the boredom of blockade duty by cogitating about the austerity of life within the Confederacy, which their vigilance helped produce, is proved by a message that Capt. W. M. Walker of the U.S.S. *De Soto* wrote on Aug. 22 to the commander of the naval forces off New Orleans. Within a few days he had captured a steamer trying to make Mobile from Havana loaded with, of all things, salted beef and pork for the Confederate Government. When a vessel, at great cost and risk, had such a cargo, it looked to Walker as if supplies in the Gulf States were getting low. He suggested that the commanding general be informed, and in a note the editors of the *O.R.* commented that the original Walker dispatch was found in the files of the Department of the Gulf. It is safe to assume that the information reached Washington through normal naval channels. In view of what Maury had said about accumulating supplies, here again is information hard to evaluate. Always, however, there are the troublesome paradoxes. Soon after Grant had found it easy to live on the country after his supplies at Holly Springs had been destroyed, and only a few months before he found meat abundant in the Vicksburg region, Secretary Seddon, it may be recalled, had written to Pemberton that he might find it necessary to continue to make contracts for meat that he knew would come from the North (*O.R.*, *41*, 693–694; *supra*, IV, xxx; *O.R.*, *25*, 839–840).

25. Grant, *op. cit.*, I, 578.

26. *O.R.*, *38*, 578, 1049, 1050, 1051.

27. *O.R.*, *128*, 687–688. On Aug. 5 Johnston issued an order that officers on conscript service would not be interfered with. (Brig. Gen. Gideon J. Pillow was chief of conscription in Tennessee, Alabama, and Mississippi.) In a letter to Johnston on the 10th from Columbus, Miss., Brig. Gen. Ruggles discounted the amount of actual disaffection among citizens, though he admitted that there was much discouragement; he also thought the sheltering in state organizations

of men subject to conscription had resulted from overextending a provision that Davis had intended should be only temporary (*O.R., 38,* 1045–1046, 1053–1054).

For an interchange of dispatches between the adjutant general and the governor of Mississippi on the one hand, and Davis on the other, over the question of exempting from conscription some men for special organizations "to render the navigation of the Mississippi River impossible, or at least perilous," see *O.R., 128,* 697, 701, 707, 712–713. On the general subject of conscription at the time under consideration, see Brown, *Conscription and Conflict in the Confederacy,* pp. 204–225.

28. *O.R., 38,* 588–589; *109,* 398–399.

29. *O.R., 38,* 563–564, 566–567, 583–584. Hurlbut said in his letter to Lincoln that he would write the Mississippi men unofficially, and he sketched what he would say, among other things: "As aliens by your own act, you cannot appeal to the Constitution. The Confederacy, the embodiment of treason, cannot be treated with. The States can. The terms must be prescribed by Congress. I think that if you continue in armed resistance six months longer, you will have no slave property to quarrel about."

30. *O.R., 50,* 5–24 (reports on the operation with annexed pertinent communications); *38,* 574 (Grant to Sherman, Aug. 4, a warning order), 578 (same, Aug. 6, final directions and Sherman's reply), 575 (Grant to Hurlbut, Aug. 4), 1036–1037 (E. D. Frost and T. S. Williams to Johnston's adjutant, July 29), 1046 (Gilmer to Johnston, Aug. 6), 1024–1025 (Chalmers to Johnston, July 22), 1029 (Chalmers to Johnston's adjutant, July 25, about value of the rolling stock), 1034–1035 (same, July 28, about Chalmers's health), 1044–1045 (Chalmers's circular); *53,* 513 (Chalmers to Johnston).

In his letter to Halleck of Aug. 11 Grant went somewhat into detail about the Grenada operation, and said it was reported that there were about 80 locomotives and 600 to 800 cars at the place; in the message to Hurlbut he put the number of locomotives at from 40 to 70, and the cars at several hundred. Mizner, in his dispatch to Hurlbut, said that Phillips had captured "about 50 railroad men and a number of prisoners." Phillips stated that he had taken 58 prisoners, of whom 18 were paroled, the others being brought in, without making clear whether the latter included civilian railroaders or not. In some of the reports the number of cars destroyed is put at about 500.

Frost's and Williams's statement about taking rolling stock to the Alabama River virtually proves—ferrying, even if possible, would have been slow and difficult—that by this time there was a bridge over the Tombigbee at Demopolis, as shown on the end map in this volume, which is virtually the same as a pocket map included in Vol. II of Badeau's *Military History of Ulysses S. Grant.* The line appears continuous in *O.R. Atlas,* Plate CLVIII, but the folding map in Black's *The Railroads of the Confederacy* shows a break at the river.

Concerning the completion of the line from Meridian to Selma, see Bragg to Cooper, June 26, 1862; Griffin to Bragg, June 26; Cooper to Bragg, July 10; *O.R., 17,* 624–625, 625, 644. Finishing the road would seem to imply building a bridge.

In his letter to Johnston of July 22, Chalmers suggested that the regular

Missouri, Arkansas, Tennessee, and Texas cavalry units in his command, then reduced to about 800 effectives, should be sent across the Mississippi, to be recruited from deserters, stragglers, and new conscripts. That accomplished, he suggested a return by a grand tour north as described in the text.

31. *O.R., 50,* 12 (Hurlbut to Rawlins, Sept. 13).

32. Dana, *Recollections of the Civil War,* pp. 63–77. The originals of the Dana letters of July 12 and 13 are not in the Stanton Papers; his retained copies are not with the copies of his other letters to the Secretary of War, which, like the Stanton Papers, are in the Manuscripts Division of the Library of Congress.

33. Nicolay and Hay, *op. cit.,* VII, 280–281 (Lincoln's unsent letter to Meade), Grant to Dana, Aug. 5, 1863, from a copy in the possession of U. S. Grant, 3rd, who has no knowledge of the Dana letter to his grandfather. Grant was grateful to Halleck (see his letter of Aug. 11, quoted in the text) for Halleck's having associated himself with Dana to protest calling Grant to the command of the Army of the Potomac.

In a letter to Washburne at the end of the month—Aug. 30—Grant expressed sentiments similar to those in his letter to Dana. Washburne had written him on the 8th, enclosing a letter from Sen. Henry Wilson, of Massachusetts, a member of the powerful Senate Military Committee, who became Vice President in 1873 when Grant became President. This letter unfortunately does not seem to have survived. In replying to Dana, Grant said:

"I fully appreciate all Senator Wilson says. Had it not been for General Halleck and Dana, I think it altogether likely I would have been ordered to the Potomac. My going could do no possible good. They have there able officers who have been brought up with that army, and to import a commander to place over them certainly could produce no good. . . . I believe I know the exact capacity of every general in my command to lead troops, and just where to place them to get from them their best services. This is a matter of no small importance."

By this time, Grant's ideas on slavery had taken a decided turn, and they are worth quoting in full:

"The people of the North need not quarrel over the institution of slavery. What Vice-President Stephens acknowledges the cornerstone of the Confederacy is already knocked out. Slavery is dead, and cannot be resurrected. It would take a standing army to maintain slavery in the South if we were to make peace to-day, guaranteeing to the South all their former constitutional privileges. I never was an abolitionist, not even what could be called anti-slavery, but I try to judge fairly and honestly, and it became patent to my mind early in the rebellion that the North and South could never live at peace with each other except as one nation, and that without slavery. As anxious as I am to see peace re-established, I would not, therefore, be willing to see any settlement until this question is forever settled."

The inconsistency between Grant's closing statement and his earlier one that slavery was already dead is certainly not worth dwelling upon. Grant included in his letter high praise of Rawlins, close friend of Washburne, pronouncing him "no ordinary man" (James Grant Wilson, *Grant's Letters to a Friend,* pp. 27–29).

Asst. Sec. of the Navy Fox described the feeling in Washington over Lee's escape, and at the same time revealed that he was of a mind with Hurlbut about the war being near its end, when he said in a letter to Porter on July 16: "Lee has finally got off into Virginia, much to the disgust of everybody, but he has left 40,000 [an exaggeration] of his army of invasion behind. The rebellion is going overboard fast." More of the Fox letter is worth quoting. (Fox, it may be recalled, had resigned from the Navy only in 1856, after 19 years of important service.)

"It would be a great blessing if you and Farragut could hitch teams and capture Mobile, thus finishing the Mississippi and the Gulf now, whilst all rebeldom is in an infernal panic. This is my own idea without taking into consideration army movements in the great work still resting on your hands. I only know the people are struck with rapid deeds like this and will appreciate the disregard of self, which would be implied in your serving for the public good under that noble old chief, Farragut."

While by this time, Halleck was doing well in his expressions of appreciation of Grant, there was more of flattery in Fox's dealing with Porter: "If the Mississippi had been opened when we determined upon continuing work upon Charleston, we should have sent for you as one that knows no failure and that loves fighting" (*O.R. Navies,* Ser. I, XXV, 306–307).

34. For the intricate question of the Marine Brigade, see *O.R. Navies,* Ser. I, XXV, 293–301, particularly Halleck to Grant, Aug. 27, 1863; Stanton to Grant, Aug. 29; Porter to Welles, Sept. 20; Welles to Porter, Oct. 21; Porter to Ellet, Oct. 30.

The transfer was not at first approved by the War Department, though Welles had concurred in Porter's recommendation that it be done. Then a letter which Grant had written on Aug. 14 to Adj. Gen. Thomas, who was at Vicksburg, saying that he would be glad to have the change made, was received in Washington, and straightway Halleck telegraphed Grant that the Secretary of War directed that he assume command of the brigade and reduce it to discipline, Stanton sending confirmation as to the transfer two days later. In his Oct. 21 dispatch Welles said that the transaction had been effected without his knowledge, but he did not complain, merely telling Porter that his connection with the organization had ceased. In his letter to Ellet, Porter said, "As our official relations are at an end, permit me to express my appreciation of the zeal you have always manifested in regard to the public service, and with best wishes remain. . . ." Any expression of grief or even regret at losing Ellet would have been hypocritical, for on the preceding day Porter had said in a letter to Sherman (*ibid.,* pp. 520–524), "Moreover, the Ellets have been guilty of very dirty, underhand work toward myself in publishing contemptible articles in the papers. . . ."

35. *O.R., 38,* 550 (Grant to Gen. Smith, Confederate paroling officer, July 24).

36. In his letter to Halleck of July 24 Grant said: "The negro troops are easier to preserve discipline among than our white troops, and I doubt not will perform equally well for garrison duty. All that have been tried have fought bravely." In informing Grant on Aug. 3 that his views with regard

to Negro troops were approved, that Thomas was on his way to Vicksburg, and that Grant could raise regiments from Confederate deserters and Mississippi citizens, Halleck's mind reverted at the end to a very different but important subject: "It will be well to keep up the impression in your army that Mobile will be the next point of attack" (*O.R., 38,* 571).

NOTES TO CHAPTER V

1. *O.R., 33,* 789.

2. *O.R., 32,* 32; *33,* 61–62. Phillips had been in correspondence with several of the Texas Unionists.

3. *O.R., 33,* 356–357. Phillips said: "An excellent crop of wheat and corn has been raised. The wheat [is] harvested south of the river in Arkansas. There never was a crop so abundant. It will be two months before the corn is fair for bread, but it is tasseling, clean, and plenty of rain. The rebels have allowed the 'Mountain Feds' to harvest their wheat, but are now conscripting everything. Some have to submit; others are fleeing to the mountains." He spoke of a man who had raised a company of Unionists, but had been "enrolled by Holmes, and offered the pleasant alternative of hanging or going back to the rebels." The man had gone back, "biding his time."

4. *O.R., 32,* 447–449 (Blunt's report on Honey Springs, with casualty figures); *33,* 921–922 (Steele to Brig. Gen. S. P. Bankhead, July 11), 940–941 (Steele to Maj. W. B. Blair, Holmes's adjutant, July 22).

Blunt put the enemy killed and buried on the field at 150, the wounded at 400, and the prisoners taken at 77. He also captured one gun, 200 stand of arms, and 15 wagons. His own losses, tabulated by units, amounted to 13 killed and 62 wounded.

Steele was expecting Bankhead, who commanded the northern subdistrict of Texas, to furnish reinforcements, and outlined a plan for him to cross the Arkansas above Fort Gibson and strike at Fort Scott.

5. *O.R., 33,* 398–399; *111,* 565–567, 567.

6. *O.R., 33,* 395 (Blunt's illness), 950–951 (Steele to Blair, July 29), 411 (Blunt to Schofield, July 30), 956 (Steele to Blair, Aug. 7, about Arkansas troops), 958 (same, Aug. 3, about powder), 956–957 (same, Aug. 7, about Texas troops), 961 (same, Aug. 9), 467 (Blunt to Cloud, Aug. 14).

Steele referred to the powder in several letters. In that of July 22 he said, "The *morale* of the troops is considerably affected by the bad quality of the powder which we have, which is so easily injured by the least dampness as to be worthless. This powder came from San Antonio. It is supposed by the men to have been sent to Mexico by the Yankees purposely to sell to us." He also spoke of desertions in several letters. In that of Aug. 9 he said, "I have captured some of these deserters, and, if a court can be had that will do its duty, will have them shot."

In the postscript to his letter of July 30, Blunt said, "Guerrilla bands are numerous in Southwestern Arkansas, hunting Union men who have fled to the mountains. Many of them have been compelled by starvation to come in, when they have been shot or hung. About 200 have been murdered recently in this way in Washington, Crawford, and Sebastian Counties."

In reading of the harshness with which Unionists in Arkansas were treated, one can well recall that—like Louisiana and Missouri—it had never had any existence as a state outside the United States. All three were formed from territory *purchased* by the United States. While Louisiana and Arkansas had adopted ordinances of secession, no word truthfully describes their action except "rebellion." Rebellion is, of course, a right that people possess, but it is sophistry to argue that states formed out of the Louisiana Purchase could rightfully "secede." The question of the "right of secession," which is particularly involved in the case of states that had had separate existence as colonies, has been entirely passed over in this work. But the author finds it refreshing to see a writer of Richmond, Virginia, using for a book the title *Experiment in Rebellion.* The fact might well be pondered by Northern writers who have eschewed the name "Civil War" and employed the ponderous circumlocution "War Between the States."

7. Blunt to Maj. H. Z. Curtis, *O.R., 33,* 462–463.

8. *O.R., 32,* 598–599.

9. *O.R., 33,* 468–469.

10. Davidson's report of Sept. 1, Steele's report of Sept. 12, *O.R., 32,* 483–486, 474–477; *38,* 577 (Hurlbut's order about bitters), 583–584 (Hurlbut to Grant, Aug. 8).

On Aug. 4 Davidson detached and sent his supply train to Helena to fill up. Hurlbut gave the composition of the bitters, and took pains to see that no one would escape.

11. *O.R., 32,* 18–19 (Schofield to Grant, July 8), 19–20 (Grant to Schofield, July 15; also in *38,* 516–517); *33,* 367, 374, 376, 513, 518; *38,* 513, 518; *33,* 376.

12. *O.R., 38,* 539 (also in *33,* 384). In a dispatch informing Schofield that he was sending a division to Helena "to go after Price," Grant said, "I have no more troops here not worn out," but added that he would send other troops to relieve those at Helena (*O.R., 33,* 385).

13. *O.R., 33,* 407, 414–415. Davidson had begun his dispatch of the 13th to Schofield about Price, "Information obtained by one of Glenn's men from a captured lieutenant of Kitchen's regiment to-day. Price crossed from Jacksonport to Crowley's Ridge, by a good road, 40 miles. . . ." (Crowley's Ridge runs from near Bloomfield southeasterly into Arkansas. After the St. Francis cuts through it near the Missouri-Arkansas line, the ridge is the watershed between that river and the Black.) Then Davidson said that if he did not advance, Price meant to attack him at Bloomfield. The source of the information hardly justified Schofield's telegraphing Halleck categorically, "Price is moving up Crowley's Ridge, to attack General Davidson at Bloomfield."

At 8:30 A.M. of the 15th Davidson telegraphed Schofield from Cape Girardeau, where he had gone to fill his train, that he thought Price was on the ridge, and he would be glad to go down either on the ridge or to Batesville, if Schofield could give him some infantry; Schofield replied that he could furnish no infantry, and that all that Davidson could do would be to wait for cooperation of troops from Vicksburg. Without saying what he intended doing, Davidson answered the same day, "The division will leave Bloomfield on the 17th, and I will make good time" (*O.R., 33,* 376, 377).

That Davidson was acting largely on his own judgment is indicated by Hurlbut's statement in a letter to Grant on Aug. 4: "So far as I can ascertain, Davidson has committed a very serious blunder in coming down Crowley's Ridge, leaving Marmaduke with some regiments at Jacksonport. He should have struck them. By his proposed movements to Des Arc or Clarendon, he opens Missouri to a raid. I had already sent him my views, and to-day sent him Schofield's order to strike at Jacksonport" (*O.R., 38,* 575–576).

In a long letter to Hurlbut on Aug. 6, Schofield said Davidson's "movement to Wittsburg, leaving Marmaduke so far in his rear, exposed my advanced posts to attack and capture, and compelled me to withdraw some of them, which was done in time to prevent any loss beyond the capture of a considerable train and its escort." But he also said, "General Davidson is a most excellent and energetic officer, and has a splendid division of cavalry." In the letter he also made a statement that shows why Vicksburg telegrams to Washington were going by way of Cairo. After saying that he wanted to have telegraphic communications set up with Little Rock as quickly as possible, he added, "Presuming the line from Cairo to Memphis will soon be repaired and kept in order, the best line for my purpose will be directly from Little Rock to Memphis" (*O.R., 32,* 22–24).

14. *O.R., 33,* 464–465 (endorsement on a note from Hurlbut to Grant dated Aug. 21, when Grant was in Memphis).

It will be recalled that, in order to facilitate his Vicksburg operations, Grant had been given command over western Arkansas early in 1863. In telegraphing Halleck at 10:30 P.M. July 15, that Davidson would move forward immediately and assist the forces from Helena, Schofield said: "Please inform me if Eastern Arkansas is to be restored to this department. With your approval, I wish to go myself soon." The query does not seem to have been answered, but on the 30th Halleck telegraphed Schofield that troops he sent would unite with those from Hurlbut's corps and be temporarily under Hurlbut's command. This contradicted a telegram to Grant on the 27th in which Halleck said that troops sent into Arkansas would be under Schofield (*O.R., 33,* 376, 409, 402).

It is not particularly strange that Snead in his article "The Conquest of Arkansas" (*B. and L.,* III, 441–459) did not make it clear that Steele was actually sent to Helena as a result of the belief that Price was headed for Missouri, and states instead that he was "sent with a force to Helena, and instructed to form a junction with Brigadier-General Davidson, who was moving south from Missouri, by Crowley's Ridge, and to 'break up Price and occupy Little Rock'." The words Snead quotes are from a telegram that Halleck sent to Hurlbut on July 30 saying that Davidson was moving south to cooperate with the Helena force, and which ended with the sentence, "The main object is to break up Price and occupy Little Rock" (*O.R., 33,* 408).

By the 30th Halleck evidently recognized that Price was not going to invade Missouri. As a result of his direction for Hurlbut to get in touch with Schofield about plans for the campaign, Hurlbut went to Cairo to confer with Schofield, and was there on Aug. 6. Schofield, however, did not think a meeting was necessary and did not go to see Hurlbut (*O.R.*, *38*, 575–576; *33*, 431, 435).

15. Steele's report to Schofield of Sept. 12; Steele to Schofield, Sept. 1; to Schofield or Hurlbut, Aug. 26; to Hurlbut, Aug. 23; Davidson's report of Sept. 1; Davidson to Steele, Aug. 15; *O.R.*, *32*, 474–477, 474, 473, 472, 483–486, 483.

16. Davidson's report of Sept. 1; Price's report, *O.R.*, *32*, 520–522; Federal casualty report, *ibid.*, p. 482; Steele's report of Sept. 12. The reported Confederate casualties on Aug. 27 amounted to only 14 (*ibid.*, p. 523).

17. *O.R.*, *32*, 474. Without counting the newly arrived brigade of Col. James M. True, Steele's force on Aug. 31 numbered 9,435 officers and men present for duty out of an aggregate present of 13,207 (*O.R.*, *33*, 505).

18. *O.R.*, *33*, 465, 380, 512, 513.

19. Steele's report of Sept. 12; addendum by Price, dated Nov. 25, 1863, to report by Col. A. S. Dobbin, *O.R.*, *32*, 523–525 (*re* Walker-Marmaduke duel).

Price said, "Having been informed toward midnight of September 5, that a duel was pending between Brig. Gen. L. M. Walker and Marmaduke, I sent to each of them an order to remain closely at his headquarters for twenty-four hours. This order did not reach General Walker, but did reach General Marmaduke. The duel took place, nevertheless, the next morning, and General Walker was mortally wounded." Unfortunately, Price did not give the date of Walker's death. In the roster of West Point graduates it is stated that Walker died at "Little Rock (in duel) 19 Sept. 63." Had he been found in a hospital in Little Rock, it seems strange that Steele did not mention it either in his report of Sept. 12, or in that directly to Halleck of the 23rd.

Without giving the date of the duel, O'Flaherty says (*General Jo Shelby*, p. 181), "Marmaduke shot Walker dead in a duel afterward as a result of their quarrel as to who was at fault at Helena."

While Marmaduke's criticism of Walker after Helena must have resulted in bad feeling between the two officers, the duel was certainly brought about by incidents not long preceding it. The article on Marmaduke in the *National Cyclopaedia of American Biography* says, after referring to Marmaduke's activities in the defense of Little Rock, "At this time he fought a duel with Gen. Lucien [Lucius, according to the West Point register] Walker—the outcome of the latter's refusal to be responsible for a certain order, when he was called a coward by Marmaduke. It was agreed that they were to advance at ten paces and continue firing until their revolvers were emptied. Walker fell mortally wounded at the second fire."

In the article on Marmaduke in *D.A.B.* there is no reference to the duel, nor is there any in the article cited in the bibliography to the *D.A.B.* sketch: "John Sappington Marmaduke" (by J. F. Lee), in *Mo. Hist. Soc. Colls.*, July, 1906. As Marmaduke was a governor of Missouri after the war, the circumstances of the duel must have been well publicized, though probably not without dispute as to responsibility. But it is not a subject that the author felt any zest in pursuing. It will be added, however, that in a report to Cooper on Nov. 22, 1862, about absent general officers, Bragg said that Walker was not a safe man to entrust with any command. There were imputations against him that would cause his case to go before an examining board, and Bragg approved Walker's application for transfer to Arkansas (*O.R.*, *30*, 417, 508).

20. Lieut. Col. F. A. Dick to Col. William Hoffman (Federal Commissary General of Prisoners), Mar. 5, 1863, *O.R.*, *118*, 319–321; Price's report.

21. Steele's and Davidson's reports; Merrill's, Glover's, Ritter's, Hadley's, Clarkson's, and Dobbin's reports, *O.R.*, *32*, 483–486, 491–496, 501–503, 510, 488–490, 523–525.

22. Steele's and Davidson's reports of Sept. 12, reports of Glover, Merrill, Dobbin, and Ritter; report of Capt. Thomas E. Vaughn, report of Steele to Halleck of Sept. 23, Davidson's congratulatory order of Sept. 13, *O.R.*, *32*, 519, 479–482, 488.

The reports of Glover and Merrill are quite detailed as to the action at the Bayou Fourche. Merrill said, "The negro guide whom I had with me disappeared with the first shell that exploded near me, and was not to be found again during the action." Merrill was initially under the impression that the bayou below a dam was perfectly dry, and not having been able to connect with Glover's right, he had been slow in advancing his line, fearing his right might be turned. In a personal effort to locate Glover's left, he found to his surprise that the bayou was full of water and seemingly impassable except near its mouth. Having made this discovery, he pushed forward, with the result that the right of his line received some of Glover's fire.

Steele's statement that he marched on the morning of the 10th with not over 7,000 men is quite consistent with a strength return for the day. The return gives him 10,477 present for duty out of a total present of 14,362. Davidson showed only 3,537 present for duty out of 5,372 present. The strength present and absent of the units composing the expedition was 23,620 (*O.R.*, *33*, 523). In his report to Halleck, Steele spoke of the ambiguity of command, and mentioned, though not especially complainingly, that he had always considered Schofield his junior. He also recorded that a clerk at Price's headquarters had informed him that the Confederate paper strength was 20,000, and that they had had 10,000 men fit for duty on the 10th.

The nominal casualties for Sept. 10, which in the Confederate case are also marked "incomplete," were: Federal, 7 killed, 64 wounded, 1 missing; Confederate, 6 killed, 19 wounded, 13 missing.

23. Steele's report of Sept. 12; Merrill's report on the pursuit, *O.R.*, *32*, 496–500.

24. Steele's report to Halleck (about McPherson's division and alarm of the Unionists); Hurlbut to Steele, Sept. 9, *O.R.*, *33*, 519–520; Grant to Halleck, Aug. 11, *O.R.*, *38*, 587–588.

Hurlbut told Steele that he had had two engines and ten cars seized on the Little Rock Railroad. He noted that the line had a gauge of 5 feet, 6 inches, while all cars he had at Memphis were of 5-foot gauge. But the gauge of roads in Missouri being 5 feet, 6 inches, he would order 20 cars down from St. Louis.

25. *O.R.*, *33*, 522–523.

26. *Ibid.*, p. 522.

27. *Ibid.*, p. 355. The letter was in answer to one from Schofield of July 2 that seems not to be in the records.

28. *Ibid.*, pp. 355, 361–362.

29. *Ibid.*, pp. 330, 331–332.

30. *O.R., 33,* 373–374, 366 (Blow to Lincoln, July 13), 375; *119,* 110 (Blow to Stanton, July 13). On July 20 Lincoln acknowledged receipt of Schofield's letter of the 14th, stated he thought Schofield's suggestion of discontinuing proceedings against McKee a very proper one, then said, "While I admit that there is an apparent impropriety in the publication of the letter mentioned, without my consent or yours, it is still a case where no evil could result, and which I am entirely willing to overlook" (*ibid.*, p. 383). This completely passed over the question that had aroused Schofield: How did McKee come by the letter?

31. *Ibid.*, pp. 355 (dispatch of Schofield to Halleck, July 7, previously cited), 357; *supra,* II, 754. For the New York riots, see Werstein, July, 1863.

32. *Supra,* IV, index, for previous references to Davies and Fisk; for Brown see *O.R., 33,* 383, 315.

The "active industry" of Fisk was mentioned by Gen. Ross in his report on the Yazoo Pass operation (*O.R., 398; supra,* IV, 328). Although Fisk was relieved by a War Department order of Apr. 22 from further duty in the Department of the Tennessee, and was directed to report to Curtis, his name appears on the roster of Ross's division at Helena for May 31 (*O.R., 33,* 236, 301).

33. *Supra,* IV, 19–20; *Palmyra Courier,* Aug. 15, 1862, quoted in *O.R., 117,* 886–887.

Earlier in the summer Porter had captured Palmyra and carried away an elderly and distinguished citizen named Allsman, who had acted as a guide in hunting disloyal persons. On Oct. 8 McNeil caused the provost marshal of northeastern Missouri to address a letter (*O.R., 19,* 719) to Porter—sending it through his wife, who lived in the county just to the north, and who was known to be in communication with him—stating that if Allsman were not returned to his family, unharmed, within ten days, ten men of Porter's band, unlawfully sworn by him to carry arms against the Government of the United States, and who were in custody, would be executed. It was already believed that Allsman, like some other Union men, had been killed, and nothing having been heard from Porter, ten of his men were publicly shot on the Palmyra fairgrounds on the 18th. (One of them was known to have shot and killed a Union neighbor the previous year.)

In commenting, the *Courier* said, "It seems hard that ten men should die for one. Under ordinary circumstances it would hardly be justified; but severe diseases demand severe remedies. The safety of the people is the supreme law. It overrides all other considerations. The madness of rebellion has become so deep seated that ordinary methods of cure are inadequate."

On Nov. 17 Jefferson Davis sent to Gen. Holmes a slip from the *Memphis Appeal* of the 3rd that had a long quotation from the *Palmyra Courier* giving a full account of the Palmyra affair (which was used above). The headline "Horrible Federal Outrage—Ten Confederates Murdered—The Full Particulars of the Scene" is alone sufficient to suggest that the *Memphis Appeal* had migrated, for Sherman would hardly have permitted such screaming, even though strong Secessionists were allowed to remain in the town. The paper had indeed departed on the eve of the great naval battle that preceded the

Federal occupation, to carry on its hardy condemnation of Yankees from different towns, as the fortunes of war forced it from one location to another. (Information kindly supplied by Paul Flowers, of the *Memphis Commercial Appeal.*)

Davis referred to the execution as "the murder of ten Confederate citizens of Missouri by order of General McNeil, of the U.S. Army," and directed Holmes to make demand through a flag of truce for the surrender of McNeil to the Confederate authorities, with the warning that if this were not done, he, Holmes, was "ordered to execute the first ten U.S. officers who may be captured and [or?] fall into your hands." On Dec. 7 Holmes transmitted the demand to Curtis, enclosing the slip from the Memphis paper. In view of the fact that Missouri had never seceded either through a vote by a special convention or a legal legislature, it was stretching things to say that the unfortunate men were "Confederate citizens"; but probably the man who is sometimes described as a great Constitutionalist believed that the mere fiat of the Richmond Congress had changed the citizenship of the men. In his reply to Holmes on Dec. 27, Curtis said, "You have no military power in Missouri and have had none in North Missouri for a year past, much less a civil organization which would induce any man to call himself a 'Confederate citizen' " (*O.R.*, *117,* 946; *32,* 816–819; *118,* 146–147).

On Dec. 1 the *N.Y. Times* published some extracts from British papers, condemning the Palmyra shootings, along with an editorial that spoke of "butchery." On the 10th McNeil's provost marshal, W. R. Strachan, wrote an enlightening letter to the editor in McNeil's vindication. It set forth the history of what had occurred, and said that it was unfortunate that the bridge burners convicted months before had not been shot in accordance with the sentences Halleck had approved. (Halleck at first suspended the sentences, saying they would be carried out if there were other instances. Then, after the capture of Fort Donelson, he had commuted the sentences in the belief that mildness would foster a return of Missourians to loyalty [*supra,* III, 168–169, 270].) Some of the bridge burners had actually been released, and Strachan stated that leniency had caused an increase in attacks upon the property and lives of Unionists, and he described circumstantially the murders of seven loyal men. (It may be recalled that East Tennessee Unionists who had burned bridges were hanged at the direction of Richmond [*supra,* III, 147].) The provost marshal also said that the nine men shot at Palmyra who had not been connected with the murder of the Unionist, had once been pardoned upon signing an oath that said "death would be the penalty for a violation of this their solemn oath and parole of honor," but that they had violated their oaths.

With much emphasis Strachan said it ill became British papers to condemn McNeil, seeing that British officers had recently caused Sepoys to be tied to the mouths of cannons and blown to pieces. In his mind there was just as much rebellion in Missouri as there had been in India, and with less reason: Missourians who were attempting to overthrow the Government of the United States had never been an oppressed people; they had enjoyed the same privileges and opportunities as those who were still adhering to the government they had all once supported. The marshal may not have been able to write with the finesse of Henry Raymond, but he could make himself clear, and he could thrust deeply, as he did when, in closing, he said that if the editor condemned McNeil, then he should also throw some anathemas at "General Schofield, who issued Order No. 18, or General Halleck, whose orders touching bridge-burners and guerrillas I had supposed until now that even the editor of the *Times* approved of" (*O.R., 32,* 861–866).

34. *O.R., 33,* 378–379. Just before he was relieved, Curtis had issued an order "to warn the public of the severe penalties which will follow new transgressions in this department, and for the convenience of district commanders, judge-advocates, and military courts." It had sections dealing with the spy, correspondence with the enemy, mail carrying, etc., the partisan, the brigand, the guerrilla proper, relieving the enemy, disloyal persons, and transgressions of the laws of war. (Such an enumeration alone shows how involved the whole matter was.) The order quoted at length from Halleck's work on international law, special instructions from him, and from Acts of Congress. All newspapers within the department were directed to give one insertion of the order, and send a copy to department headquarters with a reasonable bill (*ibid,* pp. 237–244).

35. *Ibid.,* pp. 365–366. Strachan stated that since the Palmyra executions there had not been a murder of or a single outrage on a Union man in northeast Missouri, and it is notable that the District of Northeastern Missouri, which had existed through June, had been eliminated. It had recently been under the command of Guitar, who had been a colonel in the Missouri militia, and the garrisons in the district on June 30 were all militia units (*ibid.,* pp. 343, 348).

36. *Ibid.,* p. 315.

37. Ewing's report, *O.R., 32,* 579–585. For an account of the attack on Lawrence, see Nevins, *Ordeal of the Union,* II, 434–437. Nevins comments: "The moral position of the Free-State men was perfect; that of the overwhelming force gathered to raid this little town of several hundred people, smashing, burning, and looting was beyond redemption."

38. Connelley, *Quantrill and the Border Wars,* pp. 42, 48, 49, 53, 83, Chaps. VI–XI; *O.R., 8,* 57, 335–336. The Connelley book is documented largely by extensive primary-source material that was in his possession.

39. *O.R., 19,* 225–226; Connelley, *op. cit.,* pp. 269, 275, 278–281. Connelley states, though without giving authority, that after Aug. 15 Quantrill and his men were regular Confederate soldiers, properly enrolled. He also suggests that Price may have given Quantrill a colonel's commission.

40. *O.R., 33,* 63; Connelley, *op. cit.,* pp. 282–283.

41. Connelley, *op. cit.,* pp. 311–334. Connelley's statement about one of the efforts to warn Lawrence differs from that of Ewing. Connelley has the fine Kentucky horse that a Jerry Reel was riding stumble in the darkness and fall upon him. His companion got Reel to the roadside and then sought aid, but by the time it had been secured Quantrill had entered Lawrence. Ewing gives the name as J. Reed, says nothing of a companion, and has the horse killed by the fall. Both Connelley and Ewing state that the rider died the next day.

42. Connelley, *op. cit.,* pp. 335–395. Connelley puts the number of dead at about 150, adding that, as many bodies were consumed in burning buildings,

the exact number can never be known. The figure in the text is taken from Monaghan (*Civil War on the Western Border,* p. 286); Alice Nichols gives the same number for the men and boys who met "sudden death" (*Bleeding Kansas,* p. 257). Connelley makes it clear that wanton killing was by no means congenial to all of Quantrill's band. Col. Holt seems to have devoted himself to saving lives, and Quantrill himself intervened to spare some.

Efforts have been made to justify, or at least to explain, the Lawrence massacre, as retaliation for raids and outrages by Kansas troops in western Missouri. There had indeed been excesses during raids by Lane and Col. C. R. Jennison, and, in Halleck's view, they had alienated many Missourians with Unionist sentiments. But, as previously noted, Lane, when forced to make a choice, gave up a brigadiership and returned to the Senate, and Jennison, a one-time fellow raider of Quantrill's during the latter's Lawrence days, raided no more into Missouri after 1861, though he made threats aplenty, and Curtis spoke with some approval of the Jennison brand of terrorism. By Dec. 31, 1862, not a single Kansas company was stationed in the central border region of Missouri, the garrisons being mostly Missouri militia units. After the creation of the District of the Border, Ewing considerably strengthened garrisons and, regular Missouri regiments having largely been sent south, 11 Missouri towns in his district received companies of volunteers (four in the new headquarters town of Kansas City). But in those towns there still were 16 companies of Missouri militia (*supra,* III, 477, 388; Connelley, *op. cit.,* p. 149; *O.R., 19,* 618–619, 688–689, 714; *32,* 891; *33,* 343, 419–420).

After noting that Lane's burning of Osceola, Mo., on Sept. 22, 1861, had been cited by Missouri writers as justification for the Lawrence massacre, Connelley (a native of Kentucky, and a four-year resident of Springfield, Mo., before moving to Kansas City, Kan.) quotes George W. Martin, Sec. of the Kansas State Hist. Soc., as follows: "Lane went to Osceola on a legitimate errand of warfare—to destroy certain supplies of the enemy—Sterling Price having captured Colonel Mulligan at Lexington. Lane was fired on from ambush, and in returning the fire killed one man. Lane's men helped the women get their personal effects from their houses. Lane took the records from the court-house before applying the torch, and returned them at the close of the war." Though not an admirer of Lane, Connelley insists that his action "was not of the vicious predatory nature practiced later by guerrillas in Kansas," adding that "non-combatants were not killed." Connelley seems to accept a later-told story that Jennison directed the hanging of a perfectly harmless man, and states that Jennison no doubt should have been hanged for his crimes in Missouri, though he does not seem to impute to him personal killings (Connelley, *op. cit.,* pp. 295, 208, 303–304n.).

Martin stated that there had been six raids from Missouri into Kansas before John Brown made the first raid from Kansas into Missouri in December, 1858, on which occasion he brought out 11 Negroes. Connelley put into the record (*op. cit.,* p. 288) the views ultimately held by Jo Shelby of the early expeditions of Missourians into Kansas, as given to him in frequent conversations with Shelby after Shelby had become a U.S. marshal during Cleveland's second administration. Shelby had been prominent in the early invasions of Kansas; he had gone there to kill Free-State men; and he did kill them. Of his actions he had grown to be ashamed, declaring that neither he nor any other Missourian had any business in Kansas with arms in their hands, and stating that the trouble thus started on the border bore fruit for ten years. He should have been shot in Kansas, Shelby told Connelley, adding that John Brown was the only man who knew it and would have done it.

After paying high tribute to Shelby as a soldier, Connelley states that it took a brave man and a great man to make such a confession as he made. O'Flaherty makes no reference to Connelley in his *General Jo Shelby*. But Shelby's final views, quite as well as his discharge of his last duties as an officer of the United States, are certainly of importance; and it is difficult to challenge the testimony of the man who wrote a 5-volume history of Kansas and a 5-volume history of Kentucky, who had a prominent part in the fight that led to the dissolution of the Standard Oil Co., and who in addition was a distinguished student of Indian languages (Connelley, *op. cit.*, pp. 295, 208, 304, 388–389; *Who Was Who,* Vol. I).

43. Ewing's report; *O.R., 33,* 479–480. Plumb (the subject of a biography by Connelley) wrote no report, but Capt. C. F. Coleman, of the 9th Kansas Cavalry, spoke of being relieved of command by the arrival of Plumb with about 30 men when six miles south of Lawrence. He described the pursuit, spoke of intercepting the raiders on the Fort Scott road, and stated that in the clash "their rear gave way and joined their main command" (*O.R., 32,* 589–590). See also Monaghan, *op. cit.*, pp. 287–288.

In *Bleeding Kansas,* Alice Nichols says (p. 258) that according to some reports Lane assembled a fighting crew and rode after Quantrill but could not overtake him, while according to others Lane did not start until Quantrill was safely out of reach. Even though Ewing was not in the original pursuing group, he certainly received an oral report from Plumb, and it is difficult to see why there should be any question over his official statement about Plumb's being joined by or joining near Palmyra a party of citizens "who had been hastily assembled and led in pursuit by General Lane," and that the junction took place when Plumb caught up with the raiders.

44. *O.R., 33,* 475, 479. In his reply to Lincoln on Aug. 28 (*ibid.,* pp. 482–484), Schofield said that he had modified his former severe mode of dealing with guerrillas, robbers, and murderers, and was treating with severity—though more mildly—lawbreakers who professed to be Union men but who were "loud-mouthed radicals." On Aug. 25 he had issued a general order about men returning "from the broken rebel armies" (*ibid.,* pp. 474–475).

45. *Ibid.,* pp. 484–488, 490. On Aug. 28 Schofield forwarded to the Adjutant General of the Army a copy of the letter Gov. Carney had written him on the 24th demanding a court of inquiry into the cause of the success of Quantrill's raid. The next day he wrote the governor of his action (*O.R., 32,* 577–578) and said that he had no doubt but that the court, which he had strongly urged, would be appointed. No such inquiry was held, reports showing clearly the reasons for Quantrill's success. Ewing blamed a Capt. Pike for not following promptly when he heard that Quantrill had crossed the border, saying, "Quantrill would never have gone as far as Lawrence, or attacked it, with 100 men close in his rear." (Connelley is very hard on Pike, and calls his actions especially strange in view of the fact that his home was in Lawrence.) On his

part, Schofield in his report (*O.R., 32,* 572–575) said that it was possible that Ewing might have done more than he had to guard against such a calamity as had taken place, but he thought Ewing was "entitled to great credit for the energy, wisdom, and zeal displayed" in command of his district.

In his letter to Carney, Schofield left no doubt as to his action in case of an invasion of Missouri from Kansas.

46. Ewing's and Schofield's reports; *O.R., 33,* 473 (G.O. 11). Ewing put at not over 20 the number of families affected by the order who had not willingly or through fear cooperated with the guerrillas in some way.

It was a strange coincidence that Ewing's expulsion order, and Grant's order expelling Jews from his department, should have both been headed "General Orders, No. 11."

For George Caleb Bingham's picture "Order No. 11," which shows a pleading family being harshly evicted from an impressive mansion, see Garwood, *Crossroads of America,* opposite p. 97. Bingham owned a cheaply constructed building in Kansas City in which a number of girls, including three sisters of Bloody Bill Anderson, were confined for having been engaged in furnishing information to guerrillas. When the building collapsed on Aug. 13 preceding the Lawrence raid, one of the Anderson girls was killed. Garwood (p. 54) has Quantrill tell Anderson that he could get more revenge in Lawrence than anyplace else, with Anderson replying, "Lawrence it is." Connelley makes it quite clear that the raid had been planned before the accident, but it is probable that Anderson killed in Lawrence with uncommon zest because of his recent bereavement.

47. Schofield's report; *O.R., 33,* 508 (Schofield to Halleck, Sept. 3), 521 (Halleck to Schofield, Sept. 10).

For entries that Schofield made in his journal during his visit in Lawrence and western Missouri, see his *Forty-six Years in the Army,* pp. 80–84. Whether a three-cornered quarrel was increasing or lessening Schofield's difficulty it is hard to say, but on Sept. 2 he recorded that Carney meant to run for the Senate against Lane, and he wanted to kill off Ewing, whom he considered a formidable rival, or at least a supporter of Lane.

Even in Missouri—notably in the German press—Schofield received abuse for interfering with Lane's projected invasion. He was denounced as a Copperhead, and the *Westliche Post* said his order made him "the accomplice and protector of the bushwhackers." His efforts and those of Gamble to get "peace on the blood-drenched border of Kansas, stemmed," the paper said, from the wish "to protect the rebels from a just revenge" (*O.R., 33,* 547–565; newspaper extracts sent to Halleck by Schofield).

48. Schofield's report.

49. *O.R., 33,* 523; Schofield's report. O'Flaherty speaks (*op. cit.,* p. 330) of the "atrocities committed, on the one side, by Quantrill, Anderson, and Todd, and by Lane, Jennison, Ewing, and McNeil on the other." This is a very strange grouping indeed. Even Lane and Jennison stood far above Quantrill, Bloody Bill, and Todd, and other killers who could have been mentioned with them, such as the Younger brothers, and Frank James, who, according to Connelley, "was as ferocious and merciless as a hyena" at Lawrence. Shelby, who never had much use for Quantrill, would, in his later days, surely have remonstrated

at grouping Ewing with guerrillas. McNeil's approval of the sentence against the 15 men of Porter's band and his execution of the 10 at Palmyra were no more atrocities than were the Confederate executions of some of the Union soldiers who had been in the Andrews raid into Georgia. Though the Federal soldiers had not gone as spies, they were captured behind the enemy's line in civilian clothes and according to military usage could be presumed to be spies. Strachan stated that all the men shot at Palmyra had once given paroles, and historic "G.O. 100" of the U.S. War Department stated, "Breaking the parole is punished with death when the person breaking the parole is captured again" (*O.R., 124,* 160). Though this order was not issued until after the Palmyra shootings, it in general set forth established military usage.

50. *O.R., 33,* 533, 534–535; *124,* 817–818. Nicolay and Hay devote Chap. II, Vol. VIII, of their *Lincoln* to the subject of habeas corpus, and discuss the passage of the congressional Act and the events of the summer of 1863 that led to the issuance of Lincoln's proclamation.

51. *O.R., 33,* 546–547, 563, 539, 534, 538, 547, 537, 541.

52. *O.R., 111,* 573–577 (letter of Oct. 3 to Lincoln from Chas. D. Drake, criticizing Gamble's militia organization); Schofield, *op. cit.,* pp. 84–86; *O.R., 33,* 542–543.

53. *O.R., 33,* 539–541.

54. *Ibid.,* pp. 477 (capture of Thompson), 542, 541, 567–568.

55. *Ibid.,* pp. 574–575.

56. *Ibid.,* pp. 472–473.

57. *Ibid.,* pp. 587, 590, 591. On Sept. 30 Gamble wired Lincoln, "Dispatch from Leavenworth published to-day about my arming rebels is utterly false, and is intended to prejudice your action. Truth by mail" (*ibid.,* p. 584).

58. *O.R., 33,* 588, 591–592.

59. *O.R., 33,* 586, 588; *111,* 571–573 (Blunt to Lincoln, Sept. 24, replying to Lincoln's letter of Aug. 18, received Sept. 23).

60. Nicolay and Hay, *op. cit.,* VIII, 214–217; *O.R., 111,* 573–583 (supplementary addresses to the President by members of the delegation).

61. *O.R., 33,* 604–606, 601.

62. *O.R., 33,* 607 (Allen to Halleck); *111,* 584 (Halleck to Schofield). Allen reported that 14 first-class boats had been burned, and said, "I apprehend that there are disloyal men in disguise in the employ of every steamer." In his letter to Schofield, Halleck said, "I know that the President was very much embarrassed by General Burnside's [action] against the newspaper press."

63. Nicolay and Hay, *op. cit.,* VIII, p. 213; Schofield, *op. cit.,* pp. 86–87. When the Missouri State Convention, which had been expected to vote for secession but which failed to do so, adjourned in March of 1861 to meet in December, it wisely appointed a committee with power to call it together in case of necessity. A meeting was called for July 22, and many state officers, including Gov. Jackson, as well as some convention members, having gone over to the South, the convention, with a quorum present, declared state offices vacant and appointed Gamble as provisional governor. On June 15, 1863, Gamble called the old convention back into session and offered his resignation. It was declined, and he was requested to exercise the duties of governor until

the first Monday in November, 1864, and until his successor was elected and qualified (Nicolay and Hay, *op. cit.*, IV, 225; VIII, 207).

64. *N.Y. Tribune,* Sept. 10, 1863.

65. *Ibid.*, Sept. 4. The Memphis banquet and the trip down the river with Grant from Cairo to Vicksburg are described in Eaton, *Grant, Lincoln, and the Freedmen,* Chap. VIII.

On returning from his visit at Washington to present Grant's letter to Lincoln (*supra,* IV, 406–407), Eaton was surprised to find the general and his staff aboard the headquarters boat at Cairo, about to leave for Memphis and the banquet at the Gayoso House. Eaton was invited to go along, and was able to give some eagerly desired news that he had picked up in Washington about Gettysburg and other matters. Both on the way to Memphis and from there to Vicksburg, Grant talked freely to Eaton about his entire career, explaining, in particular, how the story of his drinking at Cairo was started. Although Eaton states that it was more than probable that Grant had followed the example of other officers while he was in the Far West, he says that he felt impelled to state as plainly as he could that in his judgment "Grant's temperance was unimpeachable after he had re-entered the service and started upon his great career."

Eaton observes that Grant makes no mention of the Cairo visit in his *Memoirs;* as he was in Memphis on Aug. 21 (*supra,* n. 14), his visit there was short.

66. *O.R., 52,* 197.

67. *O.R., 38,* 569, 584. Halleck's telegram had a second sentence: "The orders sent through you to General Banks will indicate what operation is next to be undertaken."

68. Grant, *Memoirs,* I, 579 (Long, ed., p. 303); Badeau, *Military History of Ulysses S. Grant,* I, 413.

To the writer, the change in Grant's high regard for Halleck is one of the most regrettable occurrences of the early postwar years, as far as the record of the great conflict is concerned. That an act by Halleck was responsible was made clear in n. 17, Chap. IV. The belated discovery of the act should have had no influence, however, on Grant's opinion of Halleck's military understanding or capacity; but it seems to have. To what extent Grant was influenced by such men as Badeau is a moot question, but it is known that Grant was ill used by some of his friends.

In view of what Grant said in his *Memoirs,* it is ironical that on Aug. 11—while Halleck's permission to visit New Orleans was on its way to him—Grant expressed in his long letter to Halleck his obligation for Halleck's continued interest in his welfare and that of his army.

69. *O.R., 52,* 224–225. Grant's letter does not look like an answer to Halleck's. It contained considerable interesting information. Signs of Negro insurrection were beginning to appear, several white men having been murdered. Mobile was not mentioned as a possible objective, though Grant said the enemy in his front, except cavalry, had apparently gone there, adding the comment, "Movements in Banks's department evidently indicate to them an early attack on that city." Another important statement will be noted in connection with Rosecrans's operations.

70. *Ibid.*, pp. 694, 694–700, 732, 735. Sherman's letter was in reply to one Halleck had written on Aug. 29, which is not in the *O.R.* but which is in Sherman, *Memoirs,* I, 335, where it is marked "private" and is followed by Sherman's reply.

Halleck had said that the difficult problem of Reconstruction in Louisiana, Mississippi, and Arkansas would soon be before the Administration, and he believed the President would be disposed to receive advice from generals who had been in those states, and who knew more about conditions "than gassy politicians in Congress." He had received a letter from Banks on the subject, but nothing from Grant in reply to a letter he said he had written him immediately after the fall of Vicksburg. (No such letter by Halleck seems to be in the *O.R.,* and it may have been "private," like the one to Sherman. The sentence in his letter to Grant of July 11 about Arkansas, Louisiana, and Texas certainly did not call for views such as Halleck asked for.)

Halleck wished Sherman to consult with Grant, McPherson, and others of cool good judgment, and write his views fully, so that he would be in a position to use them with the President. Accepting Halleck's suggestion that he write unofficially so that his letter would not have to be on file—and thus possibly be used against him "hereafter"—Sherman marked his answer, "private and confidential."

In his letter to Halleck, Grant touched briefly on the situation in Louisiana and Mississippi, where he said there was much fine feeling toward the Union, and said he would write again if he recovered sufficiently in a short time to do so. He enclosed two papers which had recently been received and which gave resolutions that had been adopted at meetings.

NOTES TO CHAPTER VI

1. *Supra,* I, 106, 107, 108–110; Dyer, *Compendium,* p. 970 (units at Rich Mountain); *O.R., 2,* 214–218 (Rosecrans's report); Henderson, *Stonewall Jackson,* p. 91.

As the commander who had to authorize the movement that Rosecrans had suggested to him, and who would have had to accept the responsibility for failure, McClellan deserves credit, as Halleck does for Grant's move up the Tennessee, and as Lee does for Jackson's march to Pope's rear and his final march to Hooker's flank at Chancellorsville. But the doubt that McClellan revealed while in front of the regiments that were not engaged in the turning movement was described by John Beatty, who was also critical of McClellan's failure fully to exploit the chance of following up the enemy (*supra,* I, 109, 111). (Rather strangely, Col. Samuel Beatty, seen in a prominent role at Stones River, commanded one of the regiments in Rosecrans's column.) From McClellan's sentence in a dispatch of July 12 to Col. Townsend (*O.R., 2,* 203), "I turned the enemy's very strong intrenchments on Rich Mountain yesterday with General Rosecrans' brigade of four regiments and one company of cavalry," one would not surmise that Rosecrans had come to his headquarters at night to suggest the operation. See also comment on McClellan's failure to give Morris credit for a pursuit conducted by one of Morris's subordinates (*supra,* I, 110–111).

2. *Supra,* III, 419, 440.

3. *Supra,* II, 551–552; *O.R., 25,* 251 (Halleck to Rosecrans, Oct. 1, 1862); *supra,* IV, 145.

4. *Supra,* IV, 79–80, 105, 94–95, 88, 89, 276.

5. *O.R., 25,* 239 (Rosecrans to Halleck, Sept. 26, 1862); *30,* 318 (Stanton to Rosecrans, Jan. 11, 1863).

After stating in his letter to Halleck that a feeling of shame and indignation had come over him as he wrote his acceptance of the just-received commission as major general of volunteers "for 'meritorious services in Western Virginia,' to date from September 17, 1862," Rosecrans said, "If fighting successful battles having important results; if successfully defending a mountainous country against an active and powerful foe; if pacifying and restoring law and order to a vast region with 300 miles of mountain frontier, and the successful administration of a department deserved anything from the hands of the Government it deserved my promotion from the date of the close of those services crowned with success." After asking, "But what do I find?" he gave the answer: He had been ordered from the command of an army whose confidence he possessed to an army where he found himself subordinate to seven officers, whom he named—Grant was not one of them, it should be mentioned. It was said, *supra,* IV, 81, that Rosecrans's promotion was "long overdue," and in the part of the appendix to Vol. III dealing with the question whether George H. Thomas had been unfairly treated because of his Virginian birth, as is frequently charged, it was stated (p. 447) that Rosecrans was really the general who had the right to feel that he had suffered from discrimination.

In his letter Rosecrans said that he would resign if it were not for the crisis facing the country, to which he added, "As it is a crisis I beg you to intercede for me, that some measure of justice may be done me." After stating that he knew that the country was aware of the strength of his "demand," he did a little lecturing: "I trust it may seem to the administration, as to me, that no statesman or government ever gains by partiality and injustice." Then, expressing awareness that it was a tax on Halleck to read a personal letter because of the "great cares and anxiety" of his position, Rosecrans gave the assurance that he would "not fail to appreciate and repay, sooner or later, any care or intervention" Halleck might make.

In replying (*O.R., 25,* 251), Halleck stated that as soon as he had arrived in Washington he had tried to get Rosecrans "appointed" [promoted], but had "found that there were objections," which, however, he had "finally succeeded in removing." He also said, "It would have given me the greatest pleasure if your commission could have been dated back, but the War Department has decided that only in case of reappointments can commissions be dated back of the adjournment of Congress. Whether this is right or wrong I cannot say, but so it is."

Rosecrans was not on the list with Buell, Pope, Curtis, and others that Lincoln proposed for major generalships on March 3, 1862, and who were appointed as of March 21. His name was first submitted, along with others, for confirmation by the Senate on Feb. 25, 1863. While there was favorable action on some of the nominees on March 3, it required a second recommendation on March 9 to bring confirmation on the 10th to Rosecrans and some others, the vote being 19 to 17. In accordance with a notation on the second recommendation, Rosecrans's appointment dated from March 21, 1862.

6. *O.R., 30,* 306 (Stanton to Rosecrans and Rosecrans to Stanton, Jan. 7, 1863); *29,* 185–186 (Rosecrans to Stanton, Jan. 5). It was greatly to Rosecrans's credit that he promptly urged deserved promotions of subordinates. His request for Morton was in his victory message that began, "God has crowned our arms with victory. The enemy are badly beaten, and in full retreat." The dispatch of the 7th began, "The grand divisions of this army are as justly entitled to be corps as those of the Potomac."

Stanton's dispatch of the 11th saying that the date of Rosecrans's commission would be attended to suggests that Rosecrans had telegraphed about his own case, but nothing appears to be in the *O.R.* to that effect, and it may have been merely delayed action on Rosecrans's September letter to Halleck.

7. *O.R., 30,* 308.

8. *O.R., 29,* 185; *30,* 298 (order to Thomas as well as directions for a reconnaissance on the Murfreesboro Pike by two brigades).

9. *O.R., 30,* 297. See also Boyle to Rosecrans, Jan. 3, *ibid.,* p. 296.

10. *Ibid.,* p. 299.

11. *Ibid.,* pp. 299, 302, 300–301.

12. *O.R., 29,* 185–186; *30,* 303.

13. *O.R., 30,* 301–302.

14. *Ibid.,* pp. 310, 312, 312–313.

15. *Ibid.,* p. 318.

16. *Ibid.,* p. 495.

17. *Ibid.,* p. 318.

18. *Ibid.,* p. 319.

19. *Ibid.,* pp. 322, 323, 322.

20. *Ibid.,* p. 323.

21. *Ibid.,* pp. 323, 324.

22. *O.R., 29,* 982, 983; *30,* 324 and 326 (orders from Rosecrans directly to Harlan).

23. *O.R., 29,* 983; *O.R. Navies,* Ser. I, XXIV, 19.

24. *O.R., 29,* 661 (identification of Wade's command); 980–981 (Gaddis's report); *30,* 311–312 (Rosecrans's order). The statement that the *Hastings* was flying a hospital flag when fired upon is from the report of Surg. Luther D. Waterman (*O.R., 29,* 981–982).

When the *Hastings* arrived at Louisville, Boyle refused to burn the cotton or to let Gaddis go back to captivity. In this action Wright at first concurred. Then on Jan. 24 Gaddis appealed to Wright in a letter in which he asked for his case to be disposed of as quickly as possible, and said, "I am of the opinion that nothing short of an understanding between Secretary Stanton or General Halleck with the rebel Secretary will insure my safety either in the Army or out of it. I know them too well." Wright referred the strange matter to Washington, and on Jan. 31, Maj. Gen. W. A. Hitchcock, Federal Commissioner for Exchanges, wrote at length to Stanton about the case. He stated that Gaddis's pledge was invalid—the Confederate commander "might with as much propriety have required from Chaplain Gaddis a pledge to fire the city of Louisville as a condition for allowing the *Hastings* to pass." He may or may not have been correct when he wrote, "Under such circumstances it might be assumed that the Confederate commander had no expectation of a compliance with such a pledge and only accepted it as a matter of form under cover of which to allow the wounded men to proceed undisturbed." According to Hitchcock, Gaddis's return to captivity was a matter for him to decide freely without intereference by outside authority. The chaplain's conscience had to struggle with a peculiar problem, and the *Official Records* give no indication of his decision (*O.R., 118,* 200, 209, 228–229).

25. Waterman's report.

26. *O.R., 29,* 983 (Bragg to Cooper); *35,* 614 (order by Bragg of Jan. 22, referring to Wheeler as a major general); *30,* 504 (thanks of Confederate Congress, referring to Wheeler as a brigadier general, the rank he held at the time of his river attack); Dyer, *"Fightin' Joe" Wheeler,* pp. 87–90; *O.R., 29,* 979–980 (Rosecrans to Thomas).

Using a book published in 1912 that he himself says lacks objectivity—and which appears to consist of fifty-years-after-the-event recollections of one of Wheeler's men—Dyer says that Wheeler divided his force, sending Wade up the south bank of the Cumberland, while he with the balance crossed at Clarksville and ascended the other bank. The *Charter* then appears as destroyed not far above Clarksville, in flat contradictions to Mitchell's telegram that she was burned near Ashland five miles above the shoals. Dyer gives the name of the destroyed gunboat as the *Slidell,* which looks as though liberal-minded Northerners wanted to honor and do penance for having captured and incarcerated the distinguished Confederate Commissioner to Europe. However, the actual name of the steamer was the *W. H. Sidell,* which was, suggestively, the name of the major to whom Gaddis said he telegraphed upon reaching Clarksville.

Dyer calls Mitchell "petulant," adding that he was "testy" and should have "damned" Bragg's cavalry rather than the railroad, asserting that "the locomotives were entirely ready to pull troop trains if the tracks would stay intact for a few hours." This not only neglects the fact that Mitchell had said two locomotives had broken down but also suggests that Dyer believed the railroad between Nashville and Gallatin had recently been damaged. This, of course, would require authentication. In his dispatch to Cooper on Jan. 17 (*O.R., 29,* 983), Bragg said, "General Wheeler, with a portion of his cavalry brigade, after burning the railroad bridges in the enemy's rear, pushed for the Cumberland River. . . ." Bridges over Mill Creek, between Murfreesboro and Nashville, were probably meant, a view supported by a heading in *O.R., 29,* 979: "January 8–14, 1863.—Wheeler's raid, including affairs at Mill Creek, Harpeth Shoals, and Ashland, Tenn."

Dyer speaks of steamboats unloading supplies from Louisville and Paducah at Ashland for hauling to Nashville. It is difficult to understand why supplies would have been unloaded *above the shoals.* In a message to Cooper on Jan. 21 (*O.R., 29,* 983–984), Bragg spoke of the Confederate cavalry crossing to the north side of the Cumberland "by swimming their horses through the angry torrent, much swollen by recent rains," after which they destroyed much subsistence "just loaded for transportation to Nashville by wagons." This not only says nothing about the origin of the supplies (could they have been locally collected?) but seems to challenge the allegation of a crossing by any part of Wheeler's force at Clarksville.

For communications from Rosecrans to Johnston, and Gaddis to Rosecrans, about the treatment of men on the *Hastings,* see *O.R., 118,* 282–285. Wheeler returned the papers because he thought the language reflected upon Bragg, but Rosecrans reforwarded the dispatches with the statement, "The inclosures mentioned within have been abstracted. Duplicates are reinclosed." From this it looks as though Wheeler had kept the copy of Gaddis's report that Rosecrans had intended for Joe Johnston. Whether Johnston received the second copy is not clear.

27. Wagner's report, *O.R., 29,* 984–985.

28. *O.R., 30,* 492. Bragg denounced wanton waste as unworthy the character of a Confederate soldier, injurious to the cause he was defending, and alike disastrous to personal honor and military discipline. The growing evil must be checked; inspectors were to make reports; and citizens were invited to bring in their accounts for losses to "be audited and paid, and the amount charged against the responsible commander."

Five days after the issuance of Bragg's order, Gen. Patton Anderson, commanding Withers's division of Polk's corps, gave an order beginning, "The brigadier-general commanding has noticed, with surprise and regret, the continued disregard of existing orders relative to the protection of private property manifested by the troops." Fence rails were throughout the war an item that soldiers especially liked—they were admirably adapted to camp and cooking fires. Anderson's order ended, "The burning of rails is strictly forbidden" (*ibid.,* pp. 496–497).

Federal Brigadier General John Palmer, commanding a division in Crittenden's old "Left Wing," soon to become Wood's corps, beat Bragg by one day in issuing an order criticizing officers for allowing men to kill stock, burn rails, and seize forage (*ibid.,* p. 309). Though Palmer said nothing about charges against the pay of officers, he stated that he would habitually be with his command on the march or in camp, and would give his attention to its comfort. He would always, he said, be ready to take responsibility for necessary seizures of property, allowing "none to be taken under other circumstances." In connection with Palmer's fine service at Stones River, it was noted (*supra,* IV, 269) that he was a lawyer friend of Lincoln and a future governor of Illinois. It might be added that he too was born in Kentucky and moved to Illinois in 1832, two years after Lincoln, who moved there shortly after his 21st birthday, following fourteen important formative years in southern Indiana.

29. *O.R., 30,* 492–493. The letter, of much general interest, shows the peculiar way Bragg repaid Davis for the confidence the President had placed in him; "The unfortunate withdrawal of my troops, when they were not absolutely necessary elsewhere, has saved Rosecrans from destruction. Five thousand fresh troops, as a reserve on the first day's battle, would have finished the glorious work. I told the President Grant's campaign would be broken up by our cavalry expeditions in his rear before Stevenson's command could meet

him in front, but he was inexorable, and reduced me to the defensive, or, as he expressed it, 'Fight if you can, and fall back beyond the Tennessee'." A comment on the point raised by Bragg was made *supra,* IV, 285. In addition, it should be noted that Grant's campaign had not been "broken up." On the day that Bragg wrote, Grant was at Memphis, preparing to throw his full strength down the Mississippi, and before January had ended he was personally in front of Vicksburg, where Pemberton gave Stevenson an important defensive role on the 21st (*O.R., 38,* 592). Just how much Bragg knew on Jan. 11 about the blow that Sherman had struck against Vicksburg at the end of December cannot be said. He should have known of Sherman's repulse and withdrawal, but he was hasty if he assumed that the campaign for that place was over.

Bragg told Johnston that, it being known that Rosecrans was being largely reinforced from Kentucky, for him to have remained longer at Murfreesboro would have been suicidal.

30. *O.R., 30,* 328.

31. *Ibid., 30,* 315, 503. The roster of Rosecrans's command for Dec. 26, 1862, to Jan. 5, 1863, in *O.R., 29,* 174–182, shows cavalry with some divisions and lists Otis's 4th U.S. Cavalry as unattached. Wagner, in reporting on his expedition, spoke of Otis's *brigade* of 700 (and such a strength would indicate two—possibly three—regiments). Unfortunately, Rosecrans's return for Jan. 10, 1863, does not give separately the strengths of infantry, cavalry, and artillery, as that of Bragg for the 20th does. Although Johnston had on Jan. 9 directed that Col. Roddey, commanding cavalry in northern Alabama, should henceforth take orders from Bragg (*ibid., 30,* p. 491), Roddey is not included in Bragg's return for the 20th. A figure for Roddey's strength on May 10 will be given later.

32. *O.R., 30,* 331. It would appear that Rosecrans had not been influenced by a report telegraphed him on the 14th by the Nashville Chief of Police, quoting a report made the night before by a scout, just back from the vicinity of Chattanooga. It gave Morgan 5,000 men, twice his actual strength. The 4,000 men the scout said were at Cumberland Gap were also about double the 2,113 vouched for as "accurate" in a report telegraphed on the 21st to Johnston by his adjutant in Chattanooga (*ibid.,* pp. 330, 503).

33. Gen. Ballard's statement that Lincoln would have been justified in recalling McClellan for disobedience to the order that had been given him about leaving sufficient troops for the protection of Washington when he moved to the "peninsula" has been mentioned earlier in this work. Involved also was the *truthfulness* of a report that McClellan had made to Lincoln (*supra,* I, 159–160).

Halleck had temporarily suspended Grant from command soon after his capture of Fort Donelson had given the North its first great victory because he had not been receiving reports that Grant had been dutifully sending, and, as noted previously (*supra,* III, p. 333), Grant in a letter to Washburne had defended Halleck's action. Buell was sent to the sidelines not long after Kentucky had been freed of Bragg and Kirby Smith; he seemed reluctant about advancing toward East Tennessee, a difficult operation, undoubtedly, in the season just ahead. McClellan was disposed of seven weeks after he had turned Lee back at Antietam; Lincoln thought he had the "slows." It has been seen that the replacement of Meade by Grant might have been made in July, 1863, because Meade had allowed Lee to get back into Virginia after Gettysburg, had it not been for the intervention of Halleck and Dana, who knew Grant would not desire command of the Army of the Potomac. In World War I Joffre removed Lanrezac from command of the French Fifth Army, although in the retreat to the Marne Lanrezac had heartened the people of France by dealing the Germans a good solid blow; Joffre did not like the quibbling and complaining that Lanrezac had engaged in upon receiving an order difficult to execute (Joffre, *Memoirs*).

34. *O.R., 30,* 307, 326, 326–327, 331, 332, 338–339, 341. Hard to reconcile with Meigs's *inference* that Rosecrans would want 5,000 horses is Halleck's note to Meigs on the 14th: "Major-General Rosecrans complains that his requisitions for horses to mount infantry regiments are not properly filled. . . ." This seems unjustified by any dispatch from Rosecrans in the *O.R.* But Meigs's telegram to Rosecrans of the 14th (*ibid.,* p. 328): "General Halleck informs me that you complain that your requisitions for horses for mounting infantry are not filled, and desires the evil removed. Upon whom have you made requisitions? . . ." did not bring from Rosecrans a denial of having actually made requisitions. Instead, his dispatch of the 15th, previously partly quoted, began, "Captain Jenkins [Louisville quartermaster] was our dependence, but lately we have also telegraphed General Allen [then still a colonel], at Saint Louis."

For Halleck to Ripley, Ripley to Rosecrans, and Halleck to Rosecrans about saddles, and Stanton to Rosecrans (Jan. 15), saying, "The Quartermaster-General is doing all he can to procure horses. You may buy horses and saddles if you can procure them," see *ibid.,* pp. 329, 331.

In speaking of the quartermaster being the sufferer, it looks as though Rosecrans meant that quartermaster corrals or picket lines had been visited, though he may have meant that horses which freelancers had taken from the country had depleted a source for quartermasters.

35. *O.R., 30,* 331, 338–339. Meigs's reply to Rosecrans's request for 8,000 horses ended, "Why do you not send your infantry in wagons for forced marches to intercept cavalry?" While there was a certain intrusion in this, it was an honest, dignifiedly phrased question; and considering the frequent intrusions that Rosecrans made on the roles of superiors, his answer was not becoming: "Your dispatch received; thanks. Have no wagons to spare, and these are cumbersome. In these narrow roads can't travel across the country. Would do well on Pennsylvania avenue." If the last sentence was spiteful, the one before it shows confused thinking. It is entirely possible that Rosecrans had plenty of unused wagons, although wagon trains were operating between Nashville and Murfreesboro. It may be recalled that in the late fall of 1861 Pope had effectively hauled infantry in wagons on intercepting missions in Missouri (*supra,* III, 117).

36. *O.R. Navies,* Ser. I, XXIV, 8–14, *passim.* Goddard's dispatch of the 17th was not sent as a result of Welles's telegram of the 13th as the Secretary not unnaturally supposed, but it began and ended by referring to information received by Rosecrans from Halleck, which Pennock pronounced not true. It would seem probable that Welles's telegram of the 19th to Pennock was received after Pennock had replied that day to Goddard.

On the 23rd Welles telegraphed Pennock that it was imperative to have more gunboats in the Cumberland and Tennessee to protect transports, and directed him to send a steamer "immediately with this telegram to Admiral Porter." He added that 200 men for the gunboat squadron would be sent from the East in three or four days (Rosecrans had offered some to Pennock). In his dispatch to Rosecrans about the *Silver Lake* and *Lexington,* Pennock said, "Have sent a telegram from Navy Department to Admiral Porter by dispatch boat."

37. *Ibid.,* pp. 15–16, 17. In his telegram, Fitch said he had been unable to communicate with the *Robb.* A telegram received that day by Pennock from the *Robb*'s commander, Lieut. Jason Goudy, explained why. He was at Hamburg, having convoyed a steamer and a barge loaded with supplies for Dodge at Corinth. As Confederate batteries had been emplaced behind him, Goudy wanted some gunboat help, if available, but said he intended to fight his way up the river, with his transports. Pennock replied that it would be hazardous to move without aid; he himself had none to give, but he had telegraphed Fitch at Smithland (at the mouth of the Cumberland), and he directed Goudy to apply to the army for cooperation.

38. *O.R., 30,* 330, 330–331.

39. *O.R., 30,* 328 (Halleck to Rosecrans, Jan. 14), 332; *supra,* IV, 294. Halleck's dispatch of the 14th appears also in *O.R., 30,* 320, under date of Jan. 12.

40. *O.R., 30,* 333, 334, 337, 337–338. In a telegram of the 16th (*ibid.,* p. 333) Rosecrans listed nine cavalry regiments that were still in Kentucky and which he said belonged to his command. Wright, in his dispatch of the 17th, said he knew nothing of some of the specified regiments, and stated that if Rosecrans called all of them forward, he would nearly strip the railroad. Nonetheless, Wright said he was ordering all forward, except the 8th Kentucky, which he stated did not belong to Rosecrans. This regiment was, Wright added, with Bruce, and could not in his judgment be spared at the moment.

41. *Ibid.,* pp. 312, 317.

42. *Ibid.,* pp. 313, 319–320. Maynard began his letter with the provocative sentence, "I have attempted long and in vain to call the attention of the military gentlemen to the vital importance of occupying East Tennessee." To emphasize his views he enclosed a clipping from the *Richmond Dispatch,* which said that if the Federals got possession of the region they could not be dislodged by 200,000 men, and which then commented, "And East Tennessee is precisely the very portion of the Confederacy which it is most inconvenient for us to lose, since it cuts it completely in two."

Halleck's statement that Carter's operation "was both known and approved at headquarters here before it was undertaken" was certainly well justified, even though there appears to be no dispatch giving his endorsement. In a very long letter of Dec. 18 to Halleck's chief of staff, Wright had described the proposed operation at length and explained why something of the sort had not been attempted earlier. As it was not until the 25th that Carter's force was assembled, at some distance from the mountains, a disapproving telegram could have stopped it. Wright telegraphed Halleck about the success of the expedition on Jan. 7, and on the 9th—the day before Maynard wrote—Halleck had replied with a highly complimentary telegram (*O.R., 30,* 197–198; *29,* 88–89, 86, 87).

It might be mentioned that the war continued for a year and a half after East Tennessee was occupied; but it is not likely that Maynard ever felt that he had been unjust in his accusations.

43. *O.R., 34,* 16; *30,* 492–493, 495, 490. In a dispatch to Stanton at 11:15 P.M. of Jan. 11, Rosecrans had mentioned Savannah as one point from which he was "well satisfied" that troops were coming to reinforce Bragg (*O.R., 30,* 317). On Jan. 7 Johnston had telegraphed Davis that Bragg wanted 20,000 men to secure East Tennessee. Even at this date Johnston apparently thought that a big loss of territory to the Confederacy was unavoidable, and he sought to force a decision by the President with the question, "Which is the most valuable, Tennessee or the Mississippi?" (*ibid.,* pp. 487–488).

44. *O.R., 30,* 333, 302–303, 334–335. Halleck to Burnside, *ibid., 31,* 979.

45. *O.R., 34,* 15–16 (report of forage-master Edward Potter about the capture of the wagon train), Bragg, Bragg's dispatch to Cooper; Rosecrans to Halleck, *ibid.,* p. 31.

Potter was captured but escaped when near McMinnville. He said, "About 80 rods from where our capture was made we passed 2 men, who said they were patrols, and that everything was all right in front."

46. *O.R., 34,* 39; Guderian, *Panzer Leader,* p. 94. For details of the attack on Fort Donelson and interesting comments on a resulting dispute between Wheeler and Forrest, see Henry, *"First with the Most" Forrest,* pp. 124–126.

47. *O.R., 34,* 31; *35,* 630.

48. *O.R., 34,* for various reconnaissances, expeditions, and skirmishes; *35,* 57, 58, 59.

49. *O.R., 34,* 50–58, 64.

50. Mende, *An American Soldier and Diplomat,* Chap. II.

51. Porter Papers. In Mende no mention is made of the high opinion that Porter had, initially at least, of Rosecrans.

For reference to Morgan's wedding, see *supra,* IV, 250. As stated *supra,* III, 469, n. 73, all Confederate general officers wore the same number of stars on their collars; but in this work, one-star, two-star, three-star, and four-star are used for a Confederate officer as they are, or would be (in the case of four stars), for a Federal officer. The errors in Vols. I and II and the facts about the insignia of Confederate generals were called to my attention by Erdman Brandt, close student of the Civil War, in whose veins there is good Rebel blood, but who has proudly worn with distinction in hard combat the uniform of the United States.

52. *O.R., 35,* 92; *supra,* III, 251–252, 285–286, 387–388.

53. Beatty, *Memoirs of a Volunteer,* pp. 169–239.

NOTES TO CHAPTER VII

1. *O.R., 34,* 77.

2. Coburn's and Baird's reports, *ibid.,* pp. 85–93, 83–85.

3. Coburn's report, and Coburn to Gilbert, three messages, *O.R., 34,* 78, 78–79. There is disagreement between Coburn's report and his messages to Gilbert as to the enemy force.

4. Henry, *"First with the Most" Forrest,* pp. 129–131; Gilbert's report, and Capt. Thomas W. Johnston to Gilbert, *O.R., 34,* 76–77, 79. Gilbert said, "I had discussed the movement so fully with Colonel Coburn that I had but little occasion to correspond with him after he set out." He had not, he said, kept a copy of the note he sent Coburn, nor did he state when the note was dispatched; but it must have been on the 4th, for he said that he had no correspondence with him on the 5th and heard nothing from him until his defeat. But see n. 11.

5. Van Dorn to Johnston, *O.R., 110,* 425; Coburn's report; reports of Col. Thomas J. Jordan (9th Penn. Cav.) and Van Dorn, *O.R., 34,* 79–83, 116–118. Coburn put his killed at 60 and his wounded at 232, 28 of the latter being mortally wounded. The Confederate killed, wounded, and missing were, respectively, 56, 289, and 12.

That Coburn could keep a cool head was shown by an unusual incident. After he had ordered his battery to fire more slowly and carefully, it ceased entirely, and when the infantry was retiring, it made ready to leave its position. To his order for it to remain where it was and continue firing, he received the reply that ammunition might be exhausted. Being skeptical, he had his adjutant and quartermaster check ammunition chests, and received the report that there were 70 rounds per gun of shell, grape, and canister. Though Coburn deemed this ample for a retreat, he ordered that it be used economically. Nevertheless, the battery disappeared, and upon the report of its commander Coburn wrote the indorsement: "The statement that the artillery held the ground till the infantry retired, is unfounded in fact. On the right, the infantry held the very spot covered by the battery two hours after it had left the field" (*O.R., 34,* 115).

Coburn stated that when he remonstrated with Confederate officers because overcoats, leggings, knapsacks, and extra clothing were taken from his men, he was told that it was "by order of General Bragg, in retaliation for an order by General Rosecrans, stripping Federal uniforms from our soldiers." His request to see Bragg was refused. He recorded that at Lynchburg there was a snow of 18 inches. If he was outspoken about treatment received on the journey to Richmond and in Libby Prison, he was also critical of the initial treatment received from the Federals: "Exchanged at City Point, we were ordered on the steamboat State of Maine (lousy from stem to stern) by Colonel Ludlow [Federal agent of exchange], and fed, like dogs in a kennel with bread and meat cut up and cast into two large boxes, until our arrival at Annapolis." No excuse would seem possible for the unsavory method of feeding. But it would have been impossible to keep an exchange boat from becoming infected with lice unless, immediately upon exchange, men had been bathed, fumigated, and given new clothing, which could hardly have been done with City Point in the hands of the Confederates (*ibid.,* pp. 92–93).

6. *O.R., 34,* 74. Rosecrans ended his dispatch to Halleck by saying that he knew from Confederate general orders that they claimed 65,000 men at the Battle of Stones River. In the account of the battle in this work, reference was made (*supra,* IV, 276–277) to a message sent Rosecrans on the first day, which gave the report brought to the Nashville chief of police by two agents who had just come from Murfreesboro: while Bragg was claiming 60,000 men, a major in private conversation had put his strength at only 40,000. The last figure is

very close to the present-for-duty strength of 37,712 for Dec. 31, which is given in *O.R., 29,* 674.

If Rosecrans actually believed the 65,000 figure, his recent denunciation of McCook becomes still more worthy of condemnation.

7. *O.R., 34,* 115.

8. *O.R., 35,* 93, 654. Rosecrans's aggregate present and absent was 142,606, up 15,226 from his last return, due largely without doubt to troops received from Kentucky. Bragg's comparable figure was 83,801, down 3,969 from his last return. (As a rule, returns were made on the 10th, the 20th, and the last day of the month.)

Stanley's cavalry division had a present-for-duty strength of 5,040, out of an aggregate present of 6,611. As Rosecrans's return again did not give figures for the different arms, it is impossible to tell exactly how many cavalry and infantry he had. In addition to the men composing it, what was called his field army in the text had 6 heavy guns (in the predominantly largest corps of Thomas) and 201 fieldpieces.

The aggregate present in Rosecrans's detachments were: at Nashville, 1,642, with 25 heavy and 17 field guns; at Gallatin, 3,458, with 9 field guns; at Clarksville, 2,877, with 4 field guns. Listed in forts under Col. Lowe were 2,817 men, with 4 heavy and 8 light guns. Col. Innes's Michigan Engineers had a strength of 678 men; Morton's Pioneer Brigade had 1,468. At Nashville there were 3,233 convalescents, and at Gallatin 520.

In the Department of the Ohio (uncertain western Virginia, the troublesome part of Kentucky east of the Tennessee River, and Copperhead-ridden Ohio, Indiana, and Illinois), Wright had an aggregate present of 37,182. Boyle's District of Western Kentucky had 14,446 men, with 8 heavy and 13 light guns; central Kentucky had 8,621 men and 18 field pieces; eastern Kentucky had only 1,800 men and 4 guns; western Virginia had 8,471 men and 4 guns (*ibid.,* p. 94).

That Forrest's brigade had been transferred to Van Dorn is shown by a note on the return cited. At this time Bragg did not show on his return a "cavalry corps." In the return proper Wheeler's "command" is listed; in the note there is reference to his "division" and to his "command," and in such a way as to preclude the word "division" from meaning the troops Wheeler had led before he was given a larger body. Whatever may have been the status of Van Dorn and Wheeler, Bragg seems to have been personally directing them separately. See also n. 19.

9. *O.R., 34,* 134–135.

10. Minty's report, *ibid.,* pp. 129–131. Henry states (*loc. cit.*) that Coburn had expected to rendezvous with Sheridan at Spring Hill. Had this been so, Coburn would probably have so stated in his detailed report; but he made no reference whatever to Sheridan. The claim is also hard to reconcile with the dispatch that Sheridan sent to Goddard (still Rosecrans's adjutant) from Eagleville on the 5th (the day of Coburn's battle; and his actions on the 4th, as described in a dispatch to McCook, do not appear like the beginning of a move to Spring Hill (*ibid.,* pp. 128–129, 127–128).

11. Smith's report, and Granger to Rosecrans, *O.R., 34,* 142–144, 142. The report by Capt. W. M. Flanagan (*ibid.,* pp. 132–133), commanding the 3rd

Ohio Cav., which was attached to Minty when he moved from Franklin on the 9th, speaks of "a junction at Columbia pike with a heavy column of troops under command of General Granger." Flanagan also mentions a union "with the remounted cavalry under General Granger's command, numbering about 3,500." Granger's statement in his dispatch to Rosecrans that Rutherford Creek was "still too high to cross either infantry or artillery," shows the mixed nature of his command; but the unfortunate absence of a report by him leaves uncertainty as to its size.

In Henry's account of this operation (*op. cit.*, pp. 131–132) there is neither a confirmation nor a denial of Minty's claim that Forrest was personally present when Minty forded Rutherford Creek. It would seem difficult, however, to challenge Minty's statement that as he "formed on the south bank, the enemy appeared in line in the distance, and, dismounting, advanced on foot, with their battle-flag flying," or the additional claim that the Confederates remounted and fell back when they saw that one of Minty's regiments was moving to their left, and one of Smith's to their right. Some discounting must be done of Henry's statement that the withdrawal eastward of Forrest's "rear guard" resulted in something of a mystification of the Federal cavalry commanders. Minty said he pursued them five miles, quite far enough to ensure that no immediate trouble was to be expected from them, and then returned to the Columbia Pike.

Smith was evidently at Brentwood during Coburn's defeat at Spring Hill, but he seems to have been under Gilbert's call, for Gilbert on Mar. 5 telegraphed him of his apprehension for Coburn, and directed him to be ready to sustain him. Then he wired: "There is a considerable fight going on at Spring Hill. I am taking my whole force out, and you will crowd all the force you can." The next day Granger was at Franklin and informed Smith that the infantry would be left at Brentwood but that he was to come forward with all his cavalry, bringing his camp and garrison equipage. (*O.R., 109,* 338).

12. *O.R., 35,* 684; *supra,* p. 343, n. 5, *re* loss of overcoats by Coburn's men.

13. *O.R., 34,* 127.

14. *Supra,* IV, 198–199 (repulse of Van Dorn at Davis's Mill); see *supra,* n. 11, about infantry and artillery not being able to cross Rutherford Creek.

15. *Supra,* IV, 221 (engagement at Red Mound) (*re* Kirby Smith).

16. Flanagan's report. Flanagan said, "We found the enemy had withdrawn his whole force across Duck River, taking the ferryboats and his pontoons with him, and had planted his artillery on the opposite side of the stream."

Henry (p. 132) speaks as if the Federals had arrived at the Duck in daylight and does not have them make the decision to return to Franklin until they had "gazed across the bottoms and booming current of the Duck to Columbia on its hills beyond," which does not harmonize well with what Granger wrote from Rutherford Creek. One should not say, as Henry does, that the Federals returned to Franklin "by a forced march," unless one can support the claim by a Union document. Minty wrote laconically: "March 12, returned to Franklin"; Flanagan said the march was resumed at dawn, that Franklin was reached at 2:00 P.M., and rations prepared for the move on to Camp Stanley. Never was a column in enemy territory in much less danger of even petty annoyance than Granger's was on Mar. 12; and the march was probably merely a normal one for road-experienced troops who wanted some hot food instead of cold cooked rations. It was less than 20 miles from Rutherford Creek to Franklin.

17. Hall's and Minty's reports, *O.R., 34,* 155–158, 159–160. Duke states (*Morgan's Cavalry,* p. 259) that sometime in February, after Morgan had been reinforced by two fine Kentucky regiments, his command was divided into two brigades, each containing four Kentucky regiments. Although the *O.R.* contains only a brief report (*O.R., 34,* 160) by Morgan about the battle at Vaught's Hill, Duke quotes at considerable length from what he calls an official report, without indication of where he found it. One of the quoted extracts ends, "Two more rounds would have made our victory complete and two thousand Federals would have been the result of the day's fighting." This, of course, was mere bragging in the grand style, though the overestimation of the force confronting him is not so great as that sometimes made both by Federal and Confederate commanders. Holland, in *John Morgan,* p. 197, has Morgan put the number of necessary rounds at five. Duke states that, upon running out of ammunition, Morgan fell back and was met at Milton by an ordnance train and four guns, which caused him to renew the attack.

According to Duke, Morgan had no need of the services of a surgeon, but only of a tailor, for, without mentioning so much as a scratch to his person, he states that Morgan's "clothing was torn with balls." In a way this is more picturesque than the slight arm wound of which Hall spoke in words that indicate he had his information directly from a Confederate surgeon, without the interposition of a third party, who can always distort. No writer of contemporary telegrams could possibly equal what an "old soldier" can do after practicing with a story for years.

Duke claims that "perhaps" not over 1,000 Confederates were actually engaged, and he makes a remark that indicates the arrival of an era of good feeling: "All who have given any account of this battle concur in praising the conduct of the combatants. It was fought with the utmost determination and with no flinching on either side" (*op. cit.,* pp. 272–274, 276, 275).

18. *O.R., 34,* 160. Morgan said, "The Federals are reported advancing upon us again to-day. If they should, will fight them at this point." This statement does not harmonize with the report of Col. H. A. Hambright, commanding the fresh infantry brigade that reached Hall on the evening of the 20th. He said, "On the morning of the 21st, a cavalry reconnaissance was ordered. They scoured the country around as far as Liberty, and reported no enemy in sight.

"From information received from citizens and others, I was convinced that the enemy had been warned of our approach, and, not wishing to renew the fight, had fallen back" (*ibid.,* pp. 158–159).

Hambright apparently ranked Hall, for it was he who made the decision to return to Murfreesboro—Hall leading, then Hambright, then the cavalry.

19. Smith's, Forrest's, and Lewis's reports, *O.R., 34,* 179–181, 187–189, 191. For Henry's treatment, see *op. cit.,* pp. 133–136. While Smith said he had between 560 and 700 men, Henry states that he had "about 700." He gives no figures for Forrest's strength, nor does the latter, though he speaks of having two brigades in the operation. Smith's figure of 5,000 for the enemy is undoubtedly a considerable exaggeration.

Henry's statement that Forrest in his counterattack retook the wagons that

Smith had recaptured gives the idea that *all* were retaken. Smith, on his part, said he had recaptured all the wagons and does not speak for Forrest getting back any of them. Forrest has Smith succeed in getting possession of "several of the wagons captured at the stockade," but does not specifically say that he retook any of them. Yet there is the implication that he did. But why should one not accept that Forrest had retaken some that had been recaptured by Smith, and at the same time believe Smith's statement that, except for the three he ordered burned, he did bring back the others? Henry implies that Forrest had been unable to march away with any of those retaken. But Forrest says only that "several" of the wagons in question were burned—for want of harness and mules—and states that he got back to Columbia with 11 wagons taken at Brentwood.

In Forrest's report there are references to Hillsborough. This is a town which no longer exists under that name and is probably the place now known as Lieper's Fork, six miles west of Franklin, rather than the Hillsboro of today, ten miles southeast of Manchester. The Hillsborough Pike referred to in several reports led to the town in question.

While the number of men Forrest had in the Brentwood operation was not revealed by him in his report, he said in a dispatch to Wheeler on Feb. 18 that—provided nine expected companies were "anything like full"—he would have "about 3,000 troops." The confusing situation with regard to Bragg's cavalry that was commented about in n. 8 had disappeared by the end of March, and his return for the 31st refers to both "Van Dorn's cavalry corps" and to "Wheeler's cavalry corps." Yet an annexed table gives "Forrest's cavalry brigade" an effective strength on Apr. 1 of 2,535, and the figure precludes its referring to a brigade once commanded by him and still going by his name (*O.R., 35,* 638, 733).

The puzzling question is disposed of by Forrest's report on the Brentwood operation. Written Apr. 1, it is headed, "Hdqrs. First Division, First Cavalry Corps."

20. *O.R., 34,* 118. The telegram reporting the operation that Bragg sent to Cooper on the 27th (*ibid.*, p. 187) spoke as if all of Forrest's division were involved.

21. *Ibid.*, pp. 176–177.

22. Reports of Granger, Capt. Charles G. Matchett (commanding 40th Ohio), Stanley, and Capt. James B. McIntyre (commanding 4th U.S. Cavalry), *O.R., 34,* 222–233; *O.R., 35,* 236 (Granger to Rosecrans). As Granger gave it, his statement about his force being composed principally of raw men would apply to both Smith's and Stanley's cavalry, to which, however, it was quite inapplicable.

Matchett's explanation of how he got back from a position in a wood and across an open field, with the Confederates charging him, is very interesting, as are also his actions after reaching the town. Strangely, he was left quite on his own resources, never receiving any instructions from Granger. Being probably uninformed about the cavalry action, he attributed the departure of the enemy from his vicinity entirely to artillery fire, and he states that at a little after 5 he moved from the pontoon bridge to his old guard line. He made no reference to Baird's crossing.

It was McIntyre's regiment that captured the battery and the sizable number of prisoners—400 to 500 being abandoned by him, according to his report. His statement that his command had inflicted a loss of at least 100 in killed and wounded does not accord with the total casualties of 70 given for the Confederates, which were, however, compiled from "nominal lists" (*ibid.*, p. 239).

23. *O.R., 35,* 219.

24. Various reports, *O.R., 34,* 215–227.

25. *O.R., 30,* 337.

26. *O.R., 35,* 213–214 (Wood to Garfield, Apr. 6); *supra,* III, 400–404. Wood said that he had on more than one occasion had some brief conversation with the commanding general "in regard to the enterprise proposed" by Col. Streight "for cutting the enemy's communications in his rear." His letter was devoted to how—if the proposal were carried out—it should be timed with the advance of the army. A postscript stated that since writing the letter, Wood had learned that it had been decided to make the expedition.

A narrative of the Andrews raid by two of his men, which was sent to Stanton on Apr. 3, 1863, and which was not cited in connection with the effort, is in *O.R., 109,* 347–348.

27. *Supra,* IV, 32–33; *O.R., 29,* 503.

28. Wagner's report on his reconnaissance, *O.R., 29,* 984–985; Streight's report on his raid, *O.R., 34,* 285–293; *29,* 509–510.

There is confusion about Federal Tennessee regiments because some bore the label "Tennessee," while others were described as "West Tennessee," "Middle Tennessee," or "East Tennessee." Without saying that they were from Alabama, Dyer states (*Compendium,* p. 1639) that two companies of the 5th Regiment of Tennessee Cavalry (1st Middle Tennessee) were in Streight's raid.

29. Beatty, *Memoirs of a Volunteer,* pp. 184, 185. Beatty stated that another man was to be shot on the 14th for having deserted in the previous fall. A man in his own division who had been sentenced to death had escaped. On Jan. 11 Rosecrans had telegraphed Stanton (*O.R., 30,* 318):

"The crimes of spying, murder, arson, rape, and others, as well as desertion, are increasing, and the power to check them by inflicting the penalty of death is nullity, for [with] the delays necessary to get them before a regular trial by general court-martial, and then holding them until the matter is reviewed and approved by the President, such a time elapses that the troops are relieved and the culprit escapes. This ought to be remedied."

On the other side of the line, there must have been a conflict between Polk's humanitarian feelings as a former clergyman and his sense of the requisites of military service when he read the almost callous ending to a dispatch from Wharton to him of Dec. 24, "Please direct me where I shall send deserters for trial; some one must be shot from this command, and that speedily" (*O.R., 30,* 461).

30. Streight's report; Garfield to Streight, *O.R., 34,* 281–283. Garfield said, "A copy of the general order [G.O., *49,* 1863] from the War Department in regard to paroling prisoners, together with necessary blanks are herewith furnished you." In the absence of an agreement between Rosecrans and Bragg, paroling of any Confederates that Streight might capture would have been

quite as much out of harmony with the Dix-Hill cartel as that by Wheeler at Harpeth Shoals was. Both sides were at this time, however, doing "battlefield paroling," in spite of the terms of the cartel.

31. Streight's report; Streight to Garfield, *O.R., 34,* 283. Dodge's report will be cited later.

32. How many men were in the defending line of heavy sleepers, and how many in the attacking force that encompassed them? Forrest, after giving his men some rest and fording the river near where Streight had burned the bridge, had divided his command, sending—according to Henry—one regiment to the left and one to the right, while he himself with a small part of his command moved down between them. Simple arithmetic gives the answer for the Federals. Subtracting from the 1,500 with which Streight had left Tuscumbia 130 for the killed and wounded, 200 for those who Streight said had given up from exhaustion and were captured, and another 200 for the party sent ahead, we have 970 as the number that still should have been with him. While this figure could not have been exactly correct, no other that differs from it much can be accepted without good substantiation.

For Forrest there are interesting official figures that happily make up for the absence of a report by him (he submitted one on the Brentwood operation). Bragg's return for May 10 gives Forrest an effective total of 1,577 out of an aggregate present of 1,742. These numbers must have been sent in by Forrest himself, though they would in themselves not necessarily imply that all these men were close at hand on May 3. To Bragg's chief of staff, Col. W. W. Mackall, a high-ranking West Pointer of the class of 1837 (and thus a classmate of Bragg, John Sedgwick, and Joe Hooker), the *smallness* of the figure looked suspicious, and he wrote upon the return: "There is evidently error in Forrest's command. He crossed 2,500 effectives over the Tennessee, and Roddey (not reported) had not less than 2,000." Anyone who does not accept Mackall's figures should challenge them explicitly and give a good reason for their rejection. There is no doubt that the pursuit had been exhausting to the Southern horsemen, but after a good rest from the Brentwood operation, Forrest's command had left Spring Hill only three days before Streight had marched from Eastport; and the miles between these two places and the historic position east of the Chattanooga were about the same. His men were seasoned cavalry who knew their horses, and who were known by the animals which had often borne them upon their backs. Unlike Streight, Forrest had moved with equipment to keep his horses shod—though after the rest at Spring Hill he should have started with mounts well ironed.

To claim that Forrest had "at hand" fewer than 600 men, while Streight had 1,466 (as Henry does), is not a compliment to Forrest or to the endurance of his men. Forrest had a great amount of natural military acumen, as well as enterprise and energy that communicated itself to subordinates and men. He should have realized that to conduct a proper pursuit he ought not to have too large a force in Streight's rear, but should have a major part of his command straining every nerve to get in front of the Federal column. Streight spoke of scouts reporting enemy forces moving to head him off, and two or three times he urged weary men forward to prevent encirclement. If only two regiments or so were present, and no others were athwart Streight's path when

Forrest sent the Federal commander a demand for surrender, what had become of the balance of 2,500 effectives that Mackall said had crossed the Tennessee, and where were the 1,742 effectives that Forrest himself soon reported? Henry has the Eleventh Tennessee of James H. Edmondson sent from Hog Mountain to move parallel to Streight and intercept him should he attempt to get back to the Tennessee. Here is a touch of good command—much better than the "raging" up and down his line that Forrest had previously done. But the Eleventh Tennessee and its commander disappear; they are not even mentioned again in Henry's book. Scarce indeed were good roads in the mountainous country; but roads there were, and after Streight had turned eastward, his objective should have been clear to Forrest.

Of course, Forrest should have reported to Van Dorn, or directly to Bragg, as soon as he learned of the Federal column moving southward from Tuscumbia; and no time should have been lost in getting on the wires the fact that the column had turned eastward at Russellville. Streight could hardly identify the commands to which the small Confederate squads belonged with which he had had occasional skirmishes before he reached Moulton on the evening of the 28th, but they must have belonged to the combined forces under Forrest's overall command. The records, however, seem to contain nothing like the alerting message that was called for, and there are dispatches that indicate it never was sent. On April 28, Johnston telegraphed Cooper, "General Forrest, at Cortland, near Decatur, reports enemy 10,000 strong in his front [Dodge, of course], with a heavy column threatening his left and pressing him back." A dispatch that Mackall sent Van Dorn two days later—the day when Streight ambushed Forrest, captured two of his guns, and wounded his brother—reveals no awareness of the Federal stroke eastward; the instructions it transmits for Roddey suggest, in fact, complete ignorance. Not until May 4—the day after Streight's capture—is there evidence of information that should have been at hand several days previously. Forrest, the Knoxville adjutant informed General Pegram, was pursuing a force estimated at 1,000, which had destroyed the supply depot at Gadsden, and which was threatening Rome and the railroad, and which might attempt to return through East Tennessee; in this case, it was hoped that Pegram might be able to intercept them. Not until Forrest rode into Gadsden after Streight's brief stop on May 2 does it look as if Tullahoma and Chattanooga knew what was taking place.

Bragg, in a telegram to Cooper on May 5, indicates that it was not until April 28 that Forrest discovered Streight's move, and he states he pursued with two regiments—which leaves out of account those of Roddey that Forrest sent to the rear after the first engagement. Two days later Johnston raised to three the number of regiments with which Forrest was "led to Rome." Though it was an achievement to catch up with Streight and encompass his weary, poorly mounted infantry with trained cavalry, the military student, searching for operations that can be cited as models, could give higher praise to Forrest's pursuit if he were told of other units of that general's division that were in the vicinity of Rome on May 3. In appraising Forrest's pursuit, one can well think of the Army of the James, which, after a forced all-night march, stood athwart Lee's path of retreat at Appomattox on April 9, 1865, and compelled surrender.

Puzzling as are the questions which have been raised, the losses suffered by the regiments which Forrest led in the pursuit are still more perplexing. Streight insisted that because the Confederates did the assaulting in the various engagements, their casualties must have been much greater than his own. The serious student must regret any figure by the Confederate commander for the casualties inflicted by Streight's rifles, and the number of Forrest's men who found the pace too hard, in spite of short periods for recuperation that he wisely gave them. In the absence of anything else, one can with reason, by using Mackall's figure of 2,500 for the strength of Forrest's division at the outset, and Forrest's return for May 10, put his combined casualties at 758—a large figure indeed.

33. Streight's report; Henry, *op. cit.*, Chap. X; *O.R., 35,* 829, 799, 803, 814; *34,* 294, 293.

Henry's chapter, entitled "The Pursuit and Capture of Streight," is a skillful blending of Streight's and Forrest's actions. In addition to Streight's report—the only official account—Henry used for the Federals *The Prisoner of War,* by Lieut. A. C. Roach, Streight's aide, which was published in 1865. Streight's ability and great determination are recognized and well praised by Henry, but the reason for the Federal commander's leaving the two captured guns at Hog Mountain is not given, and a reader might think that Forrest recovered them in usable condition.

As Henry seems to accept (p. 144) Streight's statement about leaving Tuscumbia with 1,500 men—and a basis for rejecting it would seem called for—and definitely states that Streight sent forward a detachment of 200 men, the assertion that 1,466 Federals were surrendered at noon on May 3 is hard to comprehend—unless one is to believe that Streight picked up more Unionists in Alabama than he lost as battle and march casualties.

Streight said that he "yielded to the unanimous voice" of his regimental commanders and that he entered into "negotiations with Forrest to obtain the best possible terms." But not a word in his report supports the claim that after a conference with Forrest—while guns and men were disappearing and reappearing, and Forrest was sending off orders to nonexistent units, so as to give the impression of an overwhelming force—Streight went back for a second consultation with his officers, and only then yielded to their desire. The words that Forrest—according to Henry—put into Streight's mouth are highly suspect, though they make a good story. After all, the well-educated and experienced Streight was far from being naïve.

While some of the other unofficial Confederate material with which Henry gives color to the story seems beyond question, one cannot but feel that local accounts were much embellished with the passing of years. The highly dramatic pursuit and capture is precisely the sort of thing that lends itself to myth, and it gave a great opportunity for persons previously of no particular consequence in the community to make themselves heroes.

34. *O.R., 118,* 737, 745–746; Streight's report. Streight spoke in his report of the very bad treatment given his wounded men, charging even that medical stores and instruments were taken from surgeons left with them. He said, "Many thanks to the Union ladies of that country, for they saved many a brave

soldier from a horrible death." As he wrote his report at Chattanooga on Aug. 22, 1864, he could well have received information from men who had survived.

A letter that Forrest wrote on Oct. 22, 1863, to Brig. Gen. John Winder, in Richmond, reduces damage done by Streight's men to what one would expect. After speaking of an agreement he had made to respect the private property of Streight's men and officers, Forrest said: "Colonel Streight's command had done but little damage to property, having destroyed only one furnace and one stable. Many of the residences by the roadside had been pillaged before I began to press them."

35. *O.R., 119,* 241–242.

36. Streight's report; Dodge's report, *O.R., 34,* 246–260. It was on Apr. 5 that Rosecrans first informed Hurlbut that he proposed to send an expedition of about 1,700 under an able officer, *properly fitted,* to carry out the railroad raid, and after describing the cooperation he would like, he concluded, "Will you carry this out?" He had previously informed Dodge of his plan, as a dispatch from Dodge to Hurlbut on the 4th shows. Dodge said that he hoped Hurlbut would give his approval and stated that he would take sufficient force to ensure the expedition's success. In sending forward the dispatches to Grant, Hurlbut indicated pleasure by saying the operation would draw enemy forces into Alabama and make easier the cavalry operation he was planning—Grierson's raid. On Tuesday, Apr. 7, Rosecrans informed Dodge that the expedition was preparing rapidly, and would probably leave on Thursday; on the 16th Hurlbut wired Rosecrans: "Dodge is now on Bear Creek. Nothing heard of your expedition" (*O.R., 35,* 215, 214–215, 214, 218, 243).

37. *O.R., 34,* 283; *35,* 306. While Davis, after his visit to Murfreesboro in December, had linked North Alabama with East Tennessee as a region where sentiment was "far from what we desire," opposition to the Confederacy was by no means general except in the mountain region. From Florence, sixteen "citizens of North Alabama" sent to Seddon on Jan. 6, 1863, a petition for troops to give protection, and they strongly condemned excesses by the Federals (*O.R., 30,* 449–450, 442–443).

38. *O.R., 35,* 295–296, 306–307; *34,* 328; *35,* 309, 309–312, 308–309.

The setting up of military governments and the efforts to bring seceded states back into the Union through newly elected state governments while the war was in process were the beginning of Reconstruction. Whatever one may think of the postwar policy, it must be conceded that the problem was extremely difficult and that many considerations were involved—arising perhaps from personal feelings whether leniency and appeasement were to be followed rather than harshness. Buell's opposition in early March, 1862, to the establishment of a government in Tennessee, and his warning to Johnson that he would be received with hostility rather than enthusiasm, were previously noted (*supra,* III, 518–519).

As a strong Union man from East Tennessee, Johnson was certainly hardly a person to win strong Secessionists or even tepid ones to the Federal cause except by actual performance; and since Buell had uttered his warning the Confederates had retaken much of once-abandoned Middle Tennessee. While one can understand Rosecrans's fear of dual authority, Tennessee being the first seceded state in which Reconstruction was attempted, and Rosecrans having his time well occupied with purely military operations, one can also have much sympathy with the Administration's wanting a war governor directly responsible to the Secretary of War and through him to the President. (We have seen that not long after the Battle of Stones River, Lincoln telegraphed directly to Johnson about the political effect of the victory.)

It might be remarked that as a brigadier general Johnson actually ranked Mitchell, Rosecrans's commander in Nashville, and thus in the case of emergency could have given orders of a purely military nature to Mitchell, although it is doubtful if he would have done so. In general, it looks as though Rosecrans and Johnson worked harmoniously. On Apr. 4 Rosecrans sent a dispatch to Stanton and Johnson jointly in Washington, saying that from War Department letters there seemed to be an impression of conflict of authority. After alluding to his efforts to support the civil power, the general said, "Please communicate to me fully and freely all matters of conflict and complaint, and be assured I will rectify, or show you decisive public reasons for not doing so." In an acknowledgment of the 8th Johnson suggested a conference. Then in a dispatch of the 11th, after asking whether a reported purpose to brigade the four East Tennessee cavalry regiments under Col. Robert Johnson (commander of one of them) would promote the public interest, Andrew Johnson said: "If so, it would be gratifying to me as well as others. I shall proceed at once to raise 25,000 troops, cavalry and infantry."

The authority to raise troops which had been given Johnson on Mar. 28 provided that he could include not over a brigade as "a Governor's Guard," over which he would have sole authority. As a mere personal guard, the number looks impressive, but certainly Governor Johnson had need of more troops than a small bodyguard to execute some of the nine formidable duties that Stanton assigned him on Apr. 18—for instance, protection of public buildings and vacant and abandoned structures of all kinds. (On Apr. 2 Asst. Sec. of War Watson had assigned him four duties.) As Johnson was charged with the responsibility cited, not only in Nashville but throughout the state, that part of the order would seem to have been impractical; as new towns or regions were taken over, it would seem that troop commanders would have to give property protection unless too great a drain was put on their combat strength. Actually, in spite of the great assurance in Johnson's telegram of Apr. 11, no new Federal regiments were raised in the state, and the single regiment assigned to Johnson's undivided control in early May was probably no more than he needed for Nashville; also, he should have been able to work harmoniously with Mitchell, and relieve the latter of what would otherwise have been a troublesome aspect of the occupation of the Tennessee capital (*O.R., 35,* 207, 220, 228; *124,* 105–106, 122–123, 115; Dyer, *Compendium,* service records of Tennessee troops with dates of formation).

39. Senate Executive Journal, Vol. 13; *supra,* IV, 556, 238; *O.R., 35,* 172; *109,* 345, 345–346; *35,* 196.

40. *O.R., 34,* 152 (brief itinerary of 9th Corps); *110,* 430–431 (Davis to Johnston). Both divisions of the 9th Corps went by water from Newport News

to Baltimore; the 1st division then evidently took the B.&O. for Parkersburg, to be ferried up the Ohio to Marietta, where it again got a rail line; the 2nd division went from Baltimore via Harrisburg, Pittsburgh, and Columbus.

41. *O.R., 35,* 277, 217, 220, 283, 305, 111, 326; *5,* 129–132.

On Apr. 4 Halleck wired Burnside that the Secretary's order to relieve Boyle was peremptory, and the same day Burnside issued an order for Boyle's relief, with the now one-star general, Wright, taking his place as commander of the District of Western Kentucky, with headquarters at Louisville. In a dispatch on the 6th Asst. Sec. of War Watson explained to Burnside the Department's feelings about Boyle—there had been charges and countercharges between him and an ordnance officer. Perhaps it was before the receipt of this dispatch the same day that Burnside said in a dispatch to Stanton, "I sincerely hope you will leave General Boyle with me in this department." In another message on the 6th he told Halleck that Boyle, who had not been well, would report in Washington as soon as possible, adding the hope that Boyle would be allowed to retain his command. While there seems to be no new order on the subject in the *O.R.,* Boyle was back in Louisville at least by Apr. 24. A War Department order of May 18 relieved Wright of duty in the Department of the Ohio and directed him to report to the commanding general of the Army of the Potomac (*O.R., 35,* 210; *109,* 349; *35,* 216, 217, 273–274, 341).

On Mar. 23 Wright had made the State of Indiana into the District of Indiana, with Brig. Gen. H. B. Carrington in command (headquarters in Indianapolis); on Apr. 6 Burnside made the State of Ohio into the District of Ohio, with Brig. Gen. John S. Mason in command (headquarters in Cincinnati); on Apr. 7 he made the State of Illinois into the District of Illinois, with Brig. Gen. Jacob Ammen in command (headquarters in Springfield). Western Virginia ceased to be included in the Department of the Ohio on Mar. 16—West Virginia became a state on June 20, 1863. On Apr. 11 Burnside issued an order stating that the troops in the Department of the Ohio would thereafter be known as the Army of the Ohio (a designation, it will be recalled, that the Army of the Cumberland had once carried), and that army headquarters would be at once removed to the field (*O.R., 35,* 168, 218, 220; Phisterer, *Statistical Record,* p. 35; *O.R., 35,* 231–232).

For the troops, their stations and commanders, in the six districts of Burnside's department on Apr. 30, see *O.R., 35,* 297–298.

42. *O.R., 35,* 313, 312, 313. In a dispatch on the 3rd (*O.R., 35,* 312) Hartsuff informed Burnside that he had talked with Rosecrans after his arrival at 10 o'clock the preceding night, but that the general could not decide immediately upon the point submitted to him. There would be another conference that day and a final one at night at which the corps commanders would be present. There was still another meeting the next day that lasted until about noon.

43. *O.R., 34,* 328; *35,* 315, 314.

44. In *The Army of Tennessee,* p. 453, Horn gives not only the name of the owner of the private residence where Van Dorn was killed, but identifies the assassin, and mentions the two reasons advanced. *D.A.B.* ignores these matters, saying only that Van Dorn was shot while sitting at his desk in his headquarters. Johnston's message to Richmond could well have given the impression that

death had been due to natural causes, and Brig. Gen. W. H. Jackson in an order of May 7 assuming command of Van Dorn's corps spoke only of Van Dorn's "having just died" (*O.R.*, *110*, 467).

45. *Supra,* IV, 364–365.

46. *O.R.*, *35,* 833–834 (Buckner to Seddon, May 12). Buckner stated that he had arrived in Knoxville the previous day.

47. *Ibid.*, pp. 823–824.

48. *Ibid.*, p. 824.

In one place Duke (*op. cit.*, p. 229) speaks of Morgan's intense aversion to subordinate roles. Duke's treatment of Wheeler and of Morgan's reaction to being made subordinate to him seems fair and sound, and not colored by regard for Wheeler's distinguished postwar career. It is especially notable that Duke said that, while Wheeler did not possess the instinctive strategical astuteness characteristic of Morgan and Forrest, he was nonetheless skillful and was better suited than either of the others for the duties demanded of the commander of a large cavalry force permanently attached to an army (*op. cit.*, pp. 248–249).

49. *Ibid.*, p. 316. In spite of the fact that Burnside had told him that there was heavy pressure in favor of a move on Knoxville—probably meaning by the Administration—Rosecrans seemingly did not approve a move in that direction, for he said, "To go to Jamestown is to go to East Tennessee."

50. *O.R.*, *35,* 315–316; *supra,* II, 611–612; *O.R.*, *35,* 316. The proceedings of the commission that considered the Vallandigham case are in *O.R*, *118,* 633–646, and the Albany resolutions denouncing his arrest are in *ibid.*, pp. 654–656.

On May 20 Halleck wrote Burnside that he had just come from an interview with the President and the Secretary of War where the case was mentioned. While there had been no objection to Burnside's action, there was embarrassment as to the disposition of the prisoner. (Close confinement during the remainder of the war had been specified but, as previously noted, this was changed by Lincoln, and Vallandigham was sent south.) At the meeting, Stanton had expressed the view that military jurisdiction in Illinois, Indiana, and Ohio should be avoided as much as possible. It was hard to find military commanders with sufficient judgment and discretion to avoid conflict with civil authorities, and most of their duties could be carried out by provost marshals under law. In many cases officers had been entirely in the wrong, having assumed powers that did not belong to them (*ibid*, pp. 664–665).

51. *O.R.*, *35,* 827, 835; *supra,* IV, 361; Chap. II of this volume.

52. *O.R.*, *35,* 827–828.

53. *Ibid.*, pp. 828, 825–826. The order relieving Marshall directed him to report to Johnston for assignment to a brigade. The Kentucky-born Marshall, who had been graduated from West Point in 1832, had, after resigning from the Army, served as a volunteer lieutenant colonel in the War with Mexico, after which he had been sent by his state to the House of Representatives. Though opposed to Secession, he had quickly received an appointment as brigadier general, and he was seen in an earlier volume leading his command into mountainous East Kentucky to cooperate with Kirby Smith during the Smith-Bragg

invasion of 1862. Because of Smith's vacillation Marshall did nothing but march and countermarch, and several horses would probably have approved sending the overweight general to a less hilly region.

Marshall reported himself back at Abingdon, Va., from his Kentucky venture on Nov. 3, 1862. His infantry did not exceed 2,500, and he wanted advice from the Sec. of War (Randolph at the time) as to what to do with his twelve-month mounted men who, having served their time, desired to be "disorganized." A letter two days later that went into details complained of Kentuckians in the vicinity of Abingdon who would not enlist at home, and who were not only eating Virginia food but were a positive nuisance; Marshall wanted authority to conscript them. In an endorsement Randolph directed Marshall to keep his promise to the twelve-month men, and queried, "Can you not employ your cavalry in driving hogs out of Eastern Kentucky?" Probably prior to raising this point, the Secretary had on Nov. 8 telegraphed Marshall about numerous complaints of serious marauding by his men, and directed him to use force if need be to protect the people near Abingdon. In a lengthy reply on the 12th Marshall questioned the fairness of the charge that he was indifferent to discipline, and asserted that prices in the region were so excessively high that he could not procure forage at what he regarded as a fair price. Another Marshall letter of the 18th opened with the statement that he did not think soldiers would make willing or good hog drivers; the letter then gave more of the Kentucky story. He had marched and countermarched without complaint over orders; companies of Kentuckians who had started for the state with ardor had subsequently deserted; attempts to bring infantry recruits from the state had been a signal failure. The war in the border counties, according to Marshall, was being waged in a deadly and fierce manner, though the number of participants—all mountaineers—was small. Farther on in Kentucky the people had not regarded the arrival of the Confederate army "above the pageant of an agricultural fair or a good cattle show" (*O.R., 30,* 386, 389–391, 392, 394, 400–401, 407–409).

On Jan. 17, 1863, Marshall, previously quite independent, was put under the commander of the Department of East Tennessee, then Brig. Gen. D. S. Donelson, who had just succeeded Brigadier Henry Heth, who on his part had taken over a second time from Kirby Smith after the latter had returned for a few days to Knoxville on Dec. 23 (*ibid.,* pp. 499, 461).

When Pegram made his so-called raid into Kentucky from East Tennessee he passed through Marshall's domain, and on Mar. 11, 1863, Davis wrote Marshall about complaints Marshall had made because of what Davis called wounds to his "soldierly sensibility." While Davis said there had apparently been reason for Marshall's remonstrances, he was sure that Donelson had meant no disrespect or intrusion. On the 16th Davis informed Johnston that Marshall was proposing to go into Kentucky, and he inquired whether the move would be a diversion. In replying two days later, Johnston stated that the cavalry from East Tennessee had been ordered to Kentucky, not as a diversion, "but to observe the enemy, subsist, and drive out cattle." The Department of East Tennessee, he said, was too weak to do more than control the disloyal (*O.R., 110,* 433; *35,* 713).

54. *Supra,* IV, index (references to Grierson's raid); *O.R., 35,* 826; *supra,* IV, 370.

55. *O.R., 34,* 281. It was not until May 13 that Cooper ordered Bragg to send Streight along with his officers and men to Richmond without delay (*ibid.,* p. 295).

56. In the dispatch of Apr. 5 in which he informed Hurlbut of his planned expedition, Rosecrans gave the objective as the cutting of the Georgia Railroad, and in a message to Stanton May 10 he said Streight's object had been "to cut the railroad connections effectually between Atlanta and Chattanooga" (*O.R., 35,* 215, 322). On the other hand, Garfield, in the actual instructions given to Streight spoke of cutting "the railroad*s* [emphasis added] which supply the rebel army by way of Chattanooga." While this clearly means more than one road, it is difficult to see how it could have even been hoped that Streight might make his way far enough north to damage the line from Chattanooga to Knoxville; and when he began to press hard to reach Rome he clearly had in mind only demolition on the road from Dalton.

One naturally raises the question whether it was expected that Streight's command would be sacrificed, even if it carried out its object. In his dispatch to Hurlbut, Rosecrans said that the expedition would return southward and westward by way of the Sand Mountains and Corinth. Garfield's instructions, on the other hand, said: "You may return by way of Northern Alabama or Northern Georgia. Should you be surrounded by rebel forces and your retreat cut off, defend yourself as long as possible, and make the surrender of your command cost the enemy as many times your number as possible." Streight, as proposer of the attempt, must have given thought to the question, and being resourceful as well as determined, may have believed he could extricate himself. There may have been a touch of pure Garfield in the last part of the quotation, but Rosecrans *should have* read and considered carefully the final written instructions given to Streight, and responsibility for everything in them lay upon him.

NOTES TO CHAPTER VIII

1. *O.R., 40,* 437–438. A footnote to the message—addressed to Burnside—says: "Similar letters to. . . ." That it went to Rosecrans by telegraph is proved by the fact that his reply (*O.R., 35,* 316) was dated 8:30 A.M. the next day—May 8—and began, "Thanks for your dispatch. It relieves our great suspense. . . ."

2. *Supra,* IV, 239; *O.R., 110,* 427–428.

3. *O.R., 36,* 238; *supra,* IV, 557, n. 9. For the relations between Davis and Johnston while Johnston was commanding at Manassas, and then in general command on the Peninsula before the Battle of Fair Oaks, see Govan and Livengood, *A Different Valor.* For Johnston's own comment upon the interrupted trip to Mississippi and his reason for not carrying out the order that sent him back to Tullahoma, see Johnston, *Narrative of Military Operations,* p. 163.

4. Beatty, *Memoirs of a Volunteer,* pp. 177–188, 173, 186, 182. For a diagram of the Murfreesboro fort, see *O.R. Atlas,* Plate 112.

Under date of Mar. 16 (*op. cit.,* p. 172) Beatty wrote: "The army, under

Rosecrans' administration, looks better than it ever did before. He certainly enters into his work with his whole soul, and unless some unlucky mishap knocks his feet from under him, he will soon be recognized as the first general of the Union. I account for his success thus far, in part at least, by the fact that he has been long enough away from West Point, mixing with the people, to get a little common sense rubbed into him." Not having seen the correspondence between Rosecrans and his superiors, Beatty was unfamiliar with some of the revealing things about the officer he was praising so strongly. Nor was he aware of many telltale facts about the battles of Iuka and Corinth. It would be interesting to know what Beatty would have thought had he known that at Corinth, Hamilton returned an order to Rosecrans after writing upon the back, "Respectfully returned. I cannot understand it" (*supra,* IV, 89).

On April 11 Burnside telegraphed Halleck about the near completion of fortifications for the protection of Cincinnati that had been begun by Wright, and asked authority for turning an infantry regiment into one of artillery, which he said could easily be filled up to the maximum number. He also asked permission to have constructed at once by hired labor eight small works for the protection of Louisville, which he said could be done in two or three weeks. He stated that the fortification of the two cities would render the forces in the department not less, but more, mobile. Halleck's answering telegram, dated the following day, stated that armaments for the forts contemplated were not available, and commented that, in general, such construction was done by troops and contrabands (*O.R., 35,* 230–234).

5. *O.R., 35,* 750–751.

6. *O.R., 25,* 773, 749 (return of Apr. 10, 750; *supra,* IV, 337–338).

The return of Apr. 10 gives 35,931 present for duty out of an effective total for the army of 49,401, and an aggregate present of 65,077. A note on the return states that the army had stopped increasing since the enforcement of the conscript law had been taken out of the army's hands. It also says: "Previous to the 1st of April, the recruits and stragglers returning to the army overbalanced the men sent to the rear." There had been an increase of 514 in the effective total since the first of the month.

While the meaning of "effective total" would seem in general clear, there was evidently some misunderstanding of it among Confederate officers, for Bragg issued a circular on Jan. 29 in which he stated that in the future the designation would show "only the fighting field force—those who are carried onto the field of battle with fire-arms in their hands." Thus the Confederate "effective total" would seem comparable to the Federal "present for duty equipped," which, however, did not appear on the returns of Western forces (*O.R., 35,* 619; *supra,* II, 781).

A letter that Davis wrote Johnston on Mar. 20 reveals the continual difficulty the Confederates were having with ciphers, and in connection with the question of reinforcements it speaks of the desire to send troops westward from the Army of Northern Virginia. While Lee had hoped that this could be done, and the wish still continued, the prospect had diminished (*ibid.,* p. 712).

7. *O.R., 35,* 751. The advantage in mobility that went with the possession of water routes was forcefully indicated by the closing sentence of a long and important dispatch that Johnston sent Cooper on Apr. 6 (*ibid.,* p. 740). Grant

could, he said, transfer a large body of troops to aid Rosecrans in a fourth of the time required for returning Stevenson's division to Bragg, or sending an equal force. This must, of course, be regarded as a mere guess, made without consideration of logistical problems facing the Federals. Mississippi River steamers could not all use the Cumberland, and if troops were debarked at Louisville, there would be a long rail movement or march ahead of them. It may be recalled that Bragg had in 1862 moved 35,000 infantry from the Corinth region to Chattanooga in about a month. A move of a large part of Grant's army from the vicinity of Vicksburg to central Tennessee in a week would have been quite out of the question.

8. Beatty, *op. cit.*, p. 186.

9. *O.R.*, *35,* 761–762 (Davis to W. P. Johnston, Mar. 12); 757–761 (W. P. Johnston to Davis, Apr. 15); 762–773 (exhibits from supply officers).

The exhibits are of much interest. The ordnance officer said 140 rounds of ammunition were supplied each man—40 in his cartridge box, 100 in regimental wagons, under charge of ordnance sergeants acting under the direction of the brigade ordnance officer. In some cases the bullets for the Enfields were a little too large, but new supplies were coming from the Richmond Ordnance Bureau. Arms, accouterments, and ammunition were carelessly wasted by troops on the march, 4,000 rifles having been lost in the retreat from Murfreesboro to the Tullahoma lines. Stoppage of pay on muster rolls would not correct the evil; nothing but holding commanders directly responsible would be effective. The 6-pounder and 12-pounder howitzers were too heavy for the cavalry. Light rifled guns were being supplied as far as practicable. Shortage of leather was precluding a full supply of infantry accouterments and artillery harness; harness, because of poor quality and poor care, did not last long.

The army quartermaster reported the command fully supplied with clothing except shoes, with 6,000 suits in depots at Chattanooga. If 10,000 pairs of shoes requisitioned from Columbus and Atlanta, Ga., were obtained, all wants for a month would be supplied. There was a full supply of horse and mule shoes, and arrangements had been made for the manufacture of 150,000 per month in the future.

An Atlanta quartermaster reported enough leather for the manufacture of 40,000 pairs of shoes, all obtained by purchase at fair prices in Middle Tennessee, the people selling freely at a price not exceeding half the market price in the region. The development of machines that would split leather had reduced the shortage of leather for uppers. But machines were idle at times, and output of shoes could be increased if shoemakers were detailed from the Army—incompetent mechanics were sometimes sent. During March, 3,285 pairs of shoes had been made at a cost of $4.23 per pair.

No part of the clothing was being made by contract; woolen goods were made from wool furnished by factories operated by the quartermaster. About 20 tailors were doing the cutting and trimming, while about 3,000 women—whose male supporters were mostly absent with the army—did the sewing. If authorized to use his own agents to buy wool in Texas during the coming spring and summer, the quartermaster thought he could pledge himself to increase production of clothing by at least 33 per cent. (The capture of Vicksburg and Port Hudson would interfere with such plans.)

10. *O.R.*, *35*, 799.

11. *O.R.*, *35*, 300–304; Sheridan, *Memoirs*, I, 353–356. Meigs stated that the sudden demand for 12,000 horses and pressure on officers to forward them promptly had resulted in lowering of inspection requirements. In analyzing Rosecrans's statement that he should have 22,000 or 32,000 mounted men instead of 12,000, so that he could completely dominate the country, Meigs spoke of the added animals that would be needed to transport forage, and said that he doubted "the wisdom of building up such masses, which crumble of their own weight." Horse owners, he said, would not bring animals from a distance because of the chance that they would be rejected; he himself had not enough agents to cover the country, and from field commanders he had been unable to obtain even sufficient competent officers to supervise inspections at depots.

Meigs's letter, though probably the result of many requests, may have been finally prompted by a telegram Rosecrans had sent Halleck on Apr. 17. After asking whether two regiments of Michigan cavalry would be sent him, he said that his true objective being the hostile army and not a locality, his fundamental need was mounted forces *sufficient to control the country,* and to follow and destroy the enemy, *in case he beat them.* (Emphasis supplied.) So long as Rosecrans doubted whether he could win in battle, Washington could not but question his ability at exploitation, even if given the means. Three days after Rosecrans's dispatch, Burnside informed Halleck that Rosecrans's requirements in animals were so large that he was finding it very difficult to organize supply and ammunition trains for his department. On May 7 a quartermaster captain at Louisville wrote Meigs that he had never sent a single horse to St. Louis and could not imagine how Rosecrans had heard that he had—which suggests some accusations on the latter's part (*O.R.*, *35*, 245, 259, 315).

12. *Ibid.*, 320–321 (Rosecrans's reply to Meigs); 95 (Halleck to Rosecrans, Mar. 1); 111 (Rosecrans's reply).

A strong denunciation of Halleck's dispatch of Mar. 1 is contained in Cist, *The Army of the Cumberland*, pp. 149–151. Cist, who was one of the many officers made a brevet brigadier general near the end of the war, joined the Army of the Cumberland in July, 1863, as a first lieutenant and was made an assistant adjutant (*O.R.*, *35*, 531). As little of the *O.R.* had appeared at the time of the publication of his volume, he was not too familiar with the earlier history of the Army of the Cumberland or its predecessor (Buell's Army of the Ohio). Bitterly anti-Halleck, he ascribed (p. 41) Buell's failure to reach Chattanooga to Halleck's order to repair the Memphis and Charleston Railroad and use it for obtaining supplies—a persistent myth examined *supra*, IV, Chap. II. Cist was a strong defender of Rosecrans and descended to personalities when, in discussing Halleck's telegram, he said, "The mistake that Halleck made was in thinking that what would prove a tempting offer to a man like himself, would be so to Rosecrans." It seems strange that Cist—or anyone—could not see that the reading of Halleck's message implied that what he said had the approval of Lincoln or Stanton, and that he should forget Lincoln would have the responsibility for recommending to the Senate the appointment of which Halleck spoke. Cist's statement that from the time of Rosecrans's answer all his requests for the improvement of the efficiency of his army were treated with great coolness is a broad statement that overlooks much and cannot be accepted.

13. *O.R., 35,* 326, 335, 338.

14. *Ibid.,* 365, 366, 369.

15. *Supra,* IV, 399. For some time after its arrival in Kentucky, the 9th Corps was under Brig-Gen. Orlando B. Willcox. Parke, its former commander, upon reporting in Cincinnati, was assigned to duty in that city on May 22, but on June 5 resumed his place as corps commander. Willcox remained in the West and by June 10 was in command of the District of Indiana (*O.R., 34,* 3; *35,* 149–150; *109,* 359; *34,* 4; *35,* 419).

16. *O.R., 34,* 10; *supra,* IV, 364; *O.R., 35,* 854.

17. *O.R., 34,* 8; *supra,* IV, 405–406.

18. *O.R., 34,* 8.

19. *O.R., 35,* 420–424. Garfield's letter must be read in its entirety to obtain an adequate appreciation. On June 17 Gen. Wood wrote Garfield that he had meditated thoughtfully on the able and well-considered paper Garfield had done him the honor of reading to him "yesterday afternoon." Wood advised delay in moving until there was a solution of the complications on the Potomac and the Mississippi (*ibid.,* 433–434).

Mr. Richard Schuster of Laconia, N.H., has put into my hands a penetrating analysis of Garfield's campaign in East Kentucky. By way of summary of Garfield's traits he says:

"1. He was fundamentally bold and aggressive, undaunted by responsibilities or tales of enemy prowess, and fond of moving rapidly.

"2. He was capable of making the most of situations confronting him. He could utilize to the fullest the resources at his disposal (unorthodox transport facilities, the marching powers of green troops, the most useful qualities of the best subordinates), a good administrator and inspiring leader, and a competent and resourceful logistical planner and executor.

"3. After the East Kentucky campaign, he was probably overconfident.

"4. He was overly fond of too complex combinations."

How much Garfield influenced Rosecrans in what lay ahead, and to what extent details of movements reflected his experience, cannot, of course, be stated with certainty. But some of Mr. Schuster's views will be noted in their proper places.

20. *O.R., 34,* 10.

21. *Ibid.,* 9. As telegrams had passed rapidly, it is here assumed that Rosecrans's dispatch was received on the day it was written.

In *Memoirs,* I, 259–260, Sheridan states that when called on in June for his views (he says that Rosecrans called upon most of his corps and division commanders for their opinions on certain propositions), he opposed a forward movement on the grounds that it was better to hold Bragg in Middle Tennessee than force him back into Georgia, from whence a part of his force could be sent to oppose Grant. Leaving aside the question of accuracy of statements made twenty-five years after the event, it is to be noted that the reason stated was not given by either Rosecrans or Garfield. Furthermore, the Confederates had already reinforced Johnston, and a train movement from the general Tullahoma area would have required less time than one from Chattanooga, if Bragg's army had been forced back.

22. *Supra,* II, 623 (Beverly Ford and Brandy Station); IV, 411–412. In Vol. II the Beverly Ford and Brandy Station actions were put on June 10, though the correct date, as stated in Dyer's *Compendium,* was June 9.

23. *O.R., 34,* 10.

24. Rosecrans's report and roster of troops, *O.R., 34,* 402–409, 411–418; *supra,* IV, 264; reports of McCook, Crittenden, Thomas, Brannan, Stanley, Granger, *O.R., 34,* 465–469; 521–522; 430–433; 451–452; 538–541; 535–537. All the reports cited are general; that is, they covered the entire operation, except that of Brannan, which is dated June 28 and covers operations up to that time, a second report (*ibid.,* 453) dealing with later days.

For charges made by Buell in July, 1862, against Turchin, and for his court-martial, see *supra,* III, 540, and Beatty, *op. cit.,* 116–117, 118 (editorial note), 124. Turchin was promoted from colonel to brigadier-general during the course of his trial. Though Buell approved the sentence that he be dismissed, higher authority apparently set aside the action, probably influenced by the fact that six members of the court had recommended clemency.

On March 28, 1863, Army Headquarters assigned Turchin to Rosecrans, who on Apr. 17 placed him in command of a brigade in Thomas's corps. A directive to Turchin from Stanley on June 1 indicates that by that time Turchin had been changed to a cavalry command (*O.R., 35,* 183, 246, 386).

The use of the word "was" in Rosecrans's description of the orders he states were given to corps commanders at the meeting shows that they were not exact copies of anything actually handed out on the evening of the 23rd. It is interesting to note that Cist in giving the same material (*op. cit.,* 157) omits the word "was" wherever it occurred, and thus produces the effect of an actual order. But in giving the order to Thomas, Cist neglected to change "could" to "can" or "will" in the clause, "so that McCook and himself could be within supporting distance of each other."

25. Rosecrans's report; Cleburne's report, *O.R., 34,* 586–587; Rosecrans to Stanton, *O.R., 30,* 317.

26. Rosecrans's report; Mitchell to Granger, June 24, *O.R., 34,* 532; Palmer's report, *O.R., 34,* 528–530. Both Rosecrans's and Granger's reports make it clear that Mitchell was to move on the 23rd, and that of Stanley states definitely that Mitchell was engaged that day. The reference being to the 23rd, Rosecrans's statement, "On the same day, Palmer's division and a brigade of cavalry were ordered to move . . ." taken in connection with the preceding paragraph of the report, cannot but make the reader believe that Palmer was to move on June 23, and not merely that an order to move was sent to him that day. Cist actually states that Palmer with a brigade of cavalry moved to the vicinity of Bradyville on the 23rd (*op. cit.,* p. 157).

27. Brannan's report of June 28; Stanley's report; Rousseau's report, *O.R., 34,* 434–436; Crittenden's report.

On Mar. 18 Beatty recorded that shelter tents had been issued that day to the division that included his brigade, and went on to give unfavorable comments that had been made about the "dog tents" when used for a time the preceding fall by the Pioneer Brigade (*op. cit.,* 173–174).

In his report (*O.R., 34,* 509–510) of the operation now being considered, the commander of the 1st Ohio wrote, "From Murfreesborough to Beech Grove the men carried knapsacks, in addition to blankets, shelter-tents, and haversacks, and, constantly seeing other troops more lightly equipped, uttered no word of complaint" (a comment that indicates a lack of definiteness in army orders on the subject of equipment).

28. Wilder's report, *O.R., 34,* 457–461; *supra,* III, 63–64; Beatty, *op. cit.,* 177. Wilder's statement had been made the day of Beatty's diary entry, for Beatty said that Wilder and Col. Harker had called on him and Col. Funkhouser just after the two of them had disposed of a bottle of wine, whereupon they "entered forthwith upon another."

29. Shields, *From Flintlock to M 1,* 119; Logan, *Cartridges,* 68; 1949 catalogue of Francis Bannerman Sons, 265, 259 (references covering what is said about the Henry and the Springfield); Shields, *op. cit.,* 121 (*re* the Spencer); Bannerman catalogue, 265 (1857 order for Colts); *supra,* IV, 239, 244; Wilkerson, *General John T. Wilder,* 13–14 (Wilder's obtaining of Spencers); Buckeridge, *Lincoln's Choice,* 34–35.

The Bannerman catalogue is a mine of information and has many pages of drawings of U.S. military arms, with brief descriptions. It seems to have high rating among careful students of weapons, and its statements can probably be relied upon. (The valuable material has appeared in different editions of the Bannerman catalogue.) The Henry had a caliber of .44, and its 200-grain bullet was propelled by 26 grains of black powder according to Logan, and by 28 grains according to Shields. The Spencer had a caliber of .56 and its 350-grain bullet (Logan, *op. cit.,* 72, describes the carbine; see *ibid.,* 71, for discussion of the rifle) was driven by 45 grains of black powder, according to both Logan and Shields. The 500-grain Minié ball for the 58-caliber Springfield was propelled by 60 grains of black powder (Logan, *op. cit.,* 15–16; on p. 185 he gives the weight of the bullet when cast on an Ideal Mould as 494 grains).

The small book on Wilder by Samuel C. Williams, a former justice of the Tennessee Supreme Court, is an amplification of his article in *D.A.B.* The great-grandfather of Wilder, a native of New York State, had lost a leg at Bunker Hill; his grandfather at age 16 entered the Revolutionary War, fought in several engagements, and was wounded by a bayonet thrust. The future general's father raised a company of lighthorse for the War of 1812, was in two engagements, and lived to see the achievements of his son in the Civil War. After several years at Columbus, Ohio, Wilder removed to Greensburg, Ind., in 1857, and was soon the builder of mills and hydraulic works in Indiana and neighboring states. In 1866 he moved to Chattanooga and started several industries. Later he moved to Johnston City, the home of Judge Williams, who gained a rather close acquaintance with the subject of his biography.

Williams states that it was a representative of the Spencer Company who demonstrated the merits of that weapon at Murfreesboro; Buckeridge says it was Spencer himself. Unfortunately neither gives the day, but Beatty's diary entry would indicate it was after Mar. 23. The Buckeridge book is an over-enthusiastic extoller of the Spencer, and contains many statements subject to challenge and some that indicate a lack of military background. For instance, Wilder is described as being on Rosecrans's staff. The staff of a general is definite and known, and the word should be used correctly by anyone writing on a military subject. Confidence in his book is not increased by Buckeridge's reference to the modest building in Cairo where Grant had his headquarters during the Vicksburg campaign. Nor is the error mitigated by the statement that when Spencer arrived in Cairo, Grant was at Vicksburg.

The Spencer was made as a rifle and as a carbine. Both Williams and Buckeridge have Wilder's brigade armed with the rifle, as does Wilder himself in a postwar paper cited in n. 30. But Dyer has the 17th Indiana (Wilder's old regiment) receive Spencer *carbines* on May 18, with the 98th Illinois and the 123rd Illinois receiving them on May 31 and June 5, respectively, while he says nothing about the rearming of the 72nd Indiana, though he states the regiment was mounted on Mar. 17 (*Compendium,* 1125, 1088, 1098, 1145).

30. Wilder's report. In Appendix C of his book, Judge Williams gives Wilder's official report on the Battle of Hoover's Gap, and in Appendix D a paper Wilder read before the Ohio Commandery of the Military Order of the Loyal Legion in 1907. In the address Wilder states that Reynolds's adjutant had appeared while the fight was in progress with an order for him to fall back, as the division had stopped to repair a bridge. Wilder refused to obey, and told the officer to inform Reynolds that he could not be driven from his position. Just when the enemy had fallen back after the second attack, Rosecrans, Thomas, and Garfield appeared, and after them Reynolds who, when the situation was explained to him, told Wilder he had acted properly. From his statement that he was recommended for promotion the next morning, one might think Wilder soon was a brigadier-general, but he did not attain that rank until Aug. 7, 1864, and then only by brevet. In the paper he has Lilly's battery consist of six 10-pounder Rodmans and four mountain howitzers, which would make it an unusual battery indeed. How much of the 1907 paper is embellishment occasioned by 44 intervening years one cannot say.

31. *O.R., 35,* 317 (Halleck's order of May 8 *re* Willich); McCook's report; reports of Johnson and Davis, *O.R., 34,* 483–485, 469–472; McCook to Garfield, 462.

32. Johnson's report; Sheridan's report, *O.R., 34,* 514–517.

33. Crittenden's, Stanley's, and Granger's reports. Col. Eli Long, commanding the second brigade of Turchin's division, states in his report (*O.R., 34,* 567–569) that he camped for the night near Bradyville in close proximity to Palmer's division. Stanley having departed with Minty's brigade, it was natural that the original purpose of a march by way of McMinnville should be given up.

Wood's report (*O.R., 34,* 523–528) began with a discussion of the conflicting rumors that had been circulating as to Bragg's strength, which concluded, "However, the weight of probability favored the conclusion that the rebel army had been considerably, if not very materially, weakened." Then he said it was doubtless this consideration that resulted in the army commander's issuing an order for an immediate advance on June 23. Perhaps Wood felt the letter he had previously given Garfield (*supra,* n. 19) called for such an unusual beginning. But Wood proceeded to make some valuable remarks. Rosecrans's order, he said, had directed that the army move as light as possible, leaving behind all unnecessary baggage, but taking 12 days' rations for men and 6 days' forage for animals. Three days' subsistence was to be carried in haversacks, the balance, less 6 days' supply of meat which was to be driven, was to be transported on wheels, with not only officers' baggage cut down, but cooking utensils for officers and men. A close and accurate computation by staff officers that Wood directed indicated that 6 wagons for the weaker regiments and 7 for the stronger would suffice.

Horn states (*The Army of Tennessee,* 235), but without giving the date, that Stanley's cavalry advanced on Shelbyville is an ostentatious manner that would indicate an advance in force, adding that at night they built campfires in the region from Polk's left to the Shelbyville pike, so as to create the impression of a strong infantry advance. It has been seen that Mitchell's advance on the 23rd did not come up to expectations, and in a message to Rosecrans on the 25th (*O.R., 34,* 542) he spoke of having slept on the ground that night—a common place for soldiers to sleep—but said nothing about campfires. Nor did Stanley, who, it has been seen, joined Mitchell with Minty's brigade late on the 24th. And how fires could have been built in the torrents of rain that he said fell that night is not easy to see. Neither Rosecrans nor Granger spoke of any such effort to deceive. Nor does W. N. Polk speak of any such ruse in *Leonidas Polk,* II, 215ff. (It may be recalled that W. N. Polk, dean of the medical school of Cornell University at the time of the writing of his book, had been a lieutenant and assistant chief of artillery in his father's corps.)

Perhaps Horn's uncited authority was the article "Manoeuvering Bragg Out of Tennessee," by Gilbert C. Kniffin, in *B. and L.,* III, 635–637. Kniffin exchanges the positions of Hardee and Polk, having the former at Shelbyville. He states that Stanley was ordered to advance in bold array from Eagleville on Shelbyville on June 24, which is quite an inaccurate description of the intended cavalry moves as set forth in the text of this work. Could it be that Kniffin transported to the Shelbyville country the campfires that McCook was ordered to build, and did build, beyond his right flank the night before the Battle of Stones River (*supra,* IV, 265)?

34. *Supra,* IV, 510; *O.R., 35,* 448, 453–454, 883, 884, 885. Garfield addressed the telegrapher as "Van Duser," and the name is so spelled in the index to *35.* But in *O.R., 24,* the name appears as "Van Duzer," as it does in the General Index to the *O.R.*

As engines unfit, or nearly unfit, for service, McGowan reported 12 of the 19 between Chattanooga and Knoxville, 9 of the 12 between Knoxville and Lynchburg, two-thirds of the 34 between Chattanooga and Atlanta, three-fourths of the 53 between Atlanta and Savannah. Twenty-six engines were being used between Chattanooga and Tullahoma, and the doctor said the bridge over Chattanooga Creek, near Chattanooga, ought to be destroyed if possible, for that would not only cut off supplies from Bragg but curtail the supply of coal for nearly all the furnaces of the South. At the time he had passed over the road from Atlanta to Mobile there were 70 engines, but only 6 were suitable for the 70-mile stretch of 6-foot track, and there were only a few cars that could be used there.

McGowan told of the work being done to complete a line from Talladega,

Ala., to Rome, Ga., which would shorten the route to Mississippi by 500 miles. It was scheduled for completion in a month, but would be useless if the Confederates lost Mississippi, unless they should make a stand at Selma. He also indicated that this new line was the only way to get the stock of locomotives accumulated in Mississippi (which Grant destroyed in the raid on Grenada) into the heart of the Confederacy. He stated that Johnston had 40,000 troops in the rear of Grant, and that they had been sent from every part of the South and every point where they could be spared.

35. Reports of Wilder, Johnson, and McCook.

36. Granger to Rosecrans, *O.R., 34,* 532–533; Granger's report.

37. Long's report, *O.R., 34,* 567–569; *35,* 882.

38. Reports of Thomas, Wilder, and McCook; McCook to Garfield, *O.R., 34,* 463–464; Granger's report. McCook said that everything had been very quiet in the gap all night, but that Davis was then attacking, as had been directed, and that he was finding some opposition. Two brigades of Sheridan's division were on the march to Beech Grove, via Hoover's Gap, the third to follow. Johnson's division was to be withdrawn from the gap during the day and would march for the Manchester pike. Davis would follow, leaving a brigade and mounted infantry to observe the gap.

McCook's postscript may have been the result of a dispatch (*O.R., 35,* 457) that an aide of Rosecrans had written him at 9:30 P.M. of June 25. After saying that the commanding general hoped McCook's demonstration would "result in convincing the enemy that the main attack will be by your force," the aide added, "Please give your opinion on this." This suggests that the idea of trying to give the impression that the main effort was being made against Shelbyville had been given up.

39. *O.R., 35,* 760. In addition to Liddell's brigade at Wartrace, Johnston said Hardee had one at Manchester.

40. *Ibid.,* 886, 885, 887. That Joe Johnston had a good deal of faith in Bragg seems indicated by a dispatch he sent Cooper on May 9 (probably after the telegram informing Seddon that he was leaving for Mississippi though unfit for field service): "I earnestly recommend to the War Department that General Bragg's command be extended over Tennessee. It is of great importance" (*ibid.,* 826).

Leaving Mt. Vernon, Ky., on June 14 with 700 men of the 1st Tennessee Mounted Infantry, detachments from five other regiments, a section of guns, and a wagon train that he dropped after sixty miles, Sanders struck southward toward Tennessee. Learning upon arrival at Montgomery on the 17th that a small party of Confederates were a mile away at Wartburg, Sanders sent 400 men of the 1st Tennessee ahead of his main column to surprise and capture them. No fewer than 102 unsuspecting men and two officers (including an aide to Gen. Pegram) were gathered in, together with artillery ammunition, subsistence stores, and tools, as well as six wagons with mule teams. Prisoners were paroled and property destroyed—except, one may be sure, the mules. Thus auspiciously the expedition was launched by this first accomplishment by eager East Tennesseans, eager for so long to strike into their native region.

Then Sanders marched upon Kingston with full knowledge that the alarm had been spread by some escaping Confederates camped at a little distance from the main group. Bypassing Kingston, where the brigade of John S. Scott (seen in the last volume in Kirby Smith's victory at Richmond, Ky.) and a battery were guarding the ford over the Cinch River, and avoiding Loudon, where he learned that three regiments and eight guns were guarding the bridge, Sanders struck the railroad at Lenoir City, 25 miles southwest of Knoxville. Although some Confederates had marched out only 30 minutes previously, the Federal raider captured an artillery detachment of eight officers and 57 men, who seemingly felt they must not desert their three 6-pounders. The large brick depot, stocked with five guns, 2,500 small arms, ammunition, cavalry, and artillery equipment, and a car filled with saddles and artillery harness, were burned. But some 75 C.S. mules and horses went along with Sanders as he moved toward Knoxville, destroying the telegraph and railroad at intervals of about a mile. Unfriendly pickets were encountered about a mile from Knoxville at 7:00 P.M. on June 19. Leaving a portion of the 1st Ky. Cavalry as a decoy, Sanders, as soon as it was dark, skirted the town with the balance of his force, and after driving in pickets northeast of Knoxville, cut the railroad so that troops could not be sent to protect the bridges above.

At daylight Sanders moved up toward the city on the Cumberland Gap road, and found the enemy well placed on heights, with 8 or 10 guns protected by cotton bales, streets barricaded with the same material, and a defending force he estimated at 3,000, including impressed citizens. After skirmishing for a while he withdrew, but not until he had captured 2 more guns, 31 prisoners, about 80 C.S. horses, and the camp of a regiment of conscripts with its tents and equipage. Then Sanders headed northeast toward Strawberry Plains, 15 miles away, tarrying, however, to destroy bridges and depots. When the enemy defending the great bridge near the Plains had opened on his advance with 4 guns, Sanders dismounted his infantry, and moved them so as to get in the Confederate rear. There was skirmishing for about an hour, when some of the enemy escaped on a train, while Sanders gathered in 5 more guns, additional prisoners, and a vast amount of stores and equipment. In the booty were 600 sacks of salt, an item badly needed in the South. The night was spent in the destruction of the 1,600-foot railroad bridge that spanned the Holston on 11 piers, which with trestle work made a structure 2,100 feet long.

Still not satisfied, Sanders continued up the railroad at daylight on the 21st, and at New Market, 7 miles beyond Strawberry Plains, destroyed a 300-foot bridge, a large quantity of varied stores, a saltpeter factory, and all the machinery in a gun factory. Then he turned toward home. When not far from Rodgers's Gap, he found it was blocked by fallen timber and guarded by infantry and artillery, and learned that the same was true of other normally used gaps. After destroying all his guns and artillery ammunition, with the enemy in front and rear, he started for Smith's Gap, through which ran a rough bridle pass, from which a cavalry regiment had to be driven away. On June 24 he reached Boston, Ky., with a loss of 2 killed, 4 wounded, and 13 missing, the 170 or so officers and men who had taken the wrong road having successfully rejoined him.

Although he gave generous praise to subordinate officers, Sanders said, "To Sergeant Reynolds, First East Tennessee Volunteers, and his guides, I am chiefly indebted for the main success." A short preliminary report from Boston,

Ky., brought from Burnside a telegram on the 25th: "Please accept my best thanks and hearty congratulations for the brilliant success of your expedition" (*O.R., 34,* 384–389; includes Burnside's reports to Halleck and Sanders's preliminary reports and final report of July 26).

On the 19th the Knoxville adjutant telegraphed Cooper that an enemy force of 2,000 had appeared at Loudon at 5 in the morning. He said bridges on the railroad and mountain gaps had garrisons deemed strong enough to prevent surprise. Buckner, he said, had left that morning to concentrate his forces at Clinton; he pronounced a raid on Knoxville as not improbable, but said measures for its protection were being taken. Burnside reported to Halleck that intelligent men from the neighborhood said it would take months to repair the Strawberry Plains bridge, but in a dispatch to Cooper on the 24th Buckner said cars would be able to cross a trestle-bridge he was building within 2 weeks, while small bridges would be repaired in 4 days. Apparently dubious, Seddon wrote in an endorsement to the Engineer Bureau: "Do you understand how General Buckner can so speedily renew the bridges?" (*Ibid.,* 390; the report of the officer who assumed command in Knoxville in Buckner's absence is on pp. 391–393.)

41. Reports of Wilder and Rosecrans; *O.R., 35,* 471 (Garfield to McCook, 1:00 P.M., June 27); 470 (Garfield to Crittenden).

42. *Ibid.,* 474 (Garfield to Turchin); Rosecrans's report, *34,* 402ff.

43. *O.R., 35,* 479–480 (Granger to Rosecrans); 479 (Garfield to Granger); 478–479 (Rosecrans to Thomas, McCook, and Crittenden); Rosecrans's report.

44. Rosecrans's report; Wilder's report, *O.R., 34,* 457ff.; Beatty, *op. cit.; O.R., 35,* 485–486 (Rosecrans to Burnside); 486 (Rosecrans to Pennock, and Granger to Rosecrans).

45. Rosecrans's report; Thomas's report, *O.R., 34,* 428ff.

46. Horn, *op. cit.,* 235; Beatty, *op. cit.,* 212.

47. Rosecrans's return, *O.R., 34,* 419ff.

48. Horn, *op. cit.,* 237.

49. *O.R., 34,* 583, 584 (Bragg to Cooper).

50. *O.R., 35,* 889 (Buckner to Cooper, and Pegram to Cooper).

51. *Ibid.,* 514 (Stanton to Burnside, and Halleck to Burnside).

52. *O.R., 34,* 584 (Bragg to Cooper).

NOTES TO CHAPTER IX

1. Halleck's report, *O.R., 34,* 7.

2. Innes's report, *ibid.,* 582–583.

3. *O.R., 35,* 552; 552; 554; 555; 555–556.

4. *Ibid.,* 585; 592; 594.

5. *O.R., 109* (supplementary), 433–434.

6. Reports of Rosecrans, Thomas, Crittenden, and McCook, *O.R., 50,* 51; 245; 601; 485. See also Henry Cist, *The Army of the Cumberland* (Chap. IX).

7. Wilder's report, *O.R., 50,* 445.

8. *Supra,* III, 426; Cist, *op. cit.,* Chap. XI.

9. Burnside's report, *O.R., 51,* 547; *35,* 593.

10. Letter of Rudolph Williams, 111th Ohio, in the possession of the writer. *Harper's Weekly,* Vol. VII, No. 315, pp. 741–742.

11. *Supra,* IV, 110.

For a vivid account of the capture in July, 1862, of Cumberland Gap by troops of George Morgan's division, see "The Journal of Stephen Keyes Fletcher" (contributed by Maxwell Keyes Fletcher, III, edited by Perry McCandless), in *Indiana Magazine of History,* June, 1958, pp. 141–190. Fletcher was ordnance sergeant in the 33rd Indiana, commanded by Col. Charles Coburn, the officer previously seen in the hard battle at Spring Hill and captured there by Van Dorn and sent to Libby Prison, where he complained of poor accommodations and bad food before he was exchanged. The regiment was in Albin Schoepf's brigade of George Thomas's division. Some of its operations were described previously (*supra,* II, 150), in connection with the operations of the Confederate commander Felix Zollicoffer. The suffering and deaths of ill-conditioned men stand out in Fletcher's pages. He records a brief conversation he had with Sherman when he once went back to replenish ammunition. Great skill and daring were shown by the column of Federal troops that worked through a gap to the south of Cumberland Gap and captured that strategic gateway from the rear. In the "Journal" there is also an account of George Morgan's abandonment of Cumberland Gap the following September and his famous and skillful march to the Ohio River when Kirby Smith and John H. Morgan sought to capture and destroy him.

On the whole, the "Journal" seems to the present writer to be about the best soldier's journal he has ever read, because of its literary qualities, the sketches that embellish it, and the way it reveals the transformation of soft, untrained regiments into seasoned soldiers, able to provide for themselves with some degree of comfort under hard field conditions.

12. Burnside's report, *O.R., 51,* 548.

13. *Ibid.,* 21.

14. Atkins's and Wilder's reports, *O.R., 50,* 453–455; 445–449. Garfield to Crittenden, *52,* 491–492.

15. Burnside's report; Frazer to Burnside, and endorsement, *O.R., 51,* 621–622; Burnside's report.

16. *O.R., 52,* 488, 489.

17. Charles Dana, *Recollections of the Civil War,* p. 107.

18. Cist, *op. cit.,* pp. 176–177.

19. Dana dispatches, in *O.R., 50,* 182ff., *passim.*

20. Wood to Crittenden, *O.R., 52,* 634; Negley to Thomas, 645 and 645–646; 644.

21. *Ibid.,* 602; 647; McCook's report; Dana dispatches.

22. *Supra,* II, 761ff.; Halleck to Grant or Sherman, *O.R., 52,* 592; 643; 617, 638, 655; 642, 655.

23. *Ibid.,* 691; Burnside's report; Dana dispatches.

24. Dana dispatches.

25. Dana, *op. cit.*

26. Dana dispatches; Thomas L. Livermore, *Numbers and Losses in the Civil War in America,* pp. 105–106; Stanley Horn, *The Army of Tennessee,* Chap. XIV.

27. Thomas's report.

28. James Longstreet, *From Manassas to Appomattox, passim.;* Longstreet's report, *O.R., 51,* 287; Johnson's report, 451.

The reasons for the disposition as given in the text, namely, Hood's division to the right of Bushrod Johnson, are the following clear statements on p. 288 of Longstreet's report: "I set to work to have the line adjusted . . . to make room for Hood in the front line"; ". . . thus making his division [Hood's] the main column of attack"; "Hood's column broke the enemy's line . . ."; and "Johnson's division followed [in time of striking, not physically behind Hood] the movement."

29. Dana dispatches; McCook's report; Wood's report, *O.R., 50,* 625.

30. Longstreet, *op. cit.*

31. Longstreet's, report. For a fuller discussion of the actions taken after the breakthrough than was thought necessary for the purposes of the text, see reports by Brannan, Wood, Davis, and Sheridan in *O.R., 50,* 400, 405; 625; 496; and 578. That the resistance of these officers against Longstreet was sufficient to make him glad to give up his attacks is abundantly clear from his own report, previously cited, as well as from his memoirs. Sheridan's interesting account in his memoirs is quite in line with his official report.

As one would expect, Col. Sanger (Sanger and Hay, *James Longstreet*) analyzes Longstreet's actions from a military point of view more fully than other writers merely because he possessed a basis for doing so. Although he is capable of criticizing him, Sanger is a great admirer of Longstreet and praises him for having had the courage to act independently when the occasion demanded. At Chickamauga, by altering Bragg's battle plan, by which he would have waited his turn to move by echelon from the right, Longstreet seized the opportunity presented to crush the weakened Federal right. Sanger comments, "There was no time to consult Bragg, even had Longstreet wished to do so," and goes on to compare this exercise of initiative at Chickamauga with his earlier action at the second battle of Manassas. Both were, he said, the work of a "master tactician."

Col. J. B. Mitchell's *The Decisive Battles of the Civil War* admirably fills a longfelt need. Leaving out detail, it concentrates on the purposes of commanders, the schemes of maneuver, and the blows that were effective. Because of his understanding of the problems that face a field commander, Mitchell is less severe on Bragg than most writers have been. He makes it clear that Rosecrans's shifting of Thomas to the left resulted in Bragg's finding the Federal army differently situated on the 19th than it had been on the evening of the 18th. From Mitchell's account it would look as if Longstreet was perfectly aware that a gap existed in the Federal right at the time he struck. Longstreet's own account, however, makes this doubtful. From what Mitchell says one might also think that it was Hood's division that went through the gap, when in reality it was that of Bushrod Johnson.

Mitchell's maps add greatly to his account and aid the reader in understanding what took place.

Deaderick's *Strategy in the Civil War* supplements in many particulars Mitchell's book. Of necessity it deals with tactics quite as much as with strategy. Like Sanger and Mitchell, he does not point out that Hood's division had been removed from behind Bushrod Johnson's before Longstreet attacked. That such was the case is, however, implied when he speaks of Hood breaking the Federal line. He has Wood receive an order to support Reynolds, without referring to the words "close up on," which caused ambiguity and led to the acrimonious dispute.

A defense of General Polk is to be found in the work of his son (*Leonidas Polk,* by W. M. Polk). The son's statement that his father on the night of Sept. 20th recommended to Bragg that the Confederates assume the offensive is accepted without question by Freeman (Douglas S. Freeman, *Lee's Lieutenants*) in his detailed two-chapter discussion of Longstreet at Chickamauga. Other writers, including Horn, seem to have passed over the Polk claim.

Archibald Gracie, basing his study *The Truth About Chickamauga* upon a minute examination of the *O.R.,* analyzed Federal actions in a rather unsystematic manner. Gracie, himself a nongraduating member of the West Point class of 1881, and whose father commanded a Confederate brigade in Preston's division of Buckner's corps, believed that the Chickamauga Battlefield Commission was not entirely truthful in its portrayal of Confederate actions. He took special pains to point out the confusion that has resulted from the error of equating Snodgrass Hill with Horseshoe Ridge, of which it was only the southern extremity. He seemed to believe that the single division of his corps that Buckner had on the left could, had it not been held in check, have won a crushing victory. This is an extravagant position indeed that ignores the natural feeling that Longstreet, commander on the left, had about the adequacy of his unengaged forces when he talked to Bragg.

Like the account in the present work, Sandburg's brief but interesting treatment in *Lincoln—The War Years* (pp. 420–425) draws upon Dana's dispatches to Stanton. He is in error, however, in saying that Longstreet brought 20,000 men from Virginia. Using October returns and allowing for casualties, 17,000 would be the maximum figure, though of course not all of these arrived in time to participate in the crucial battle. Of the two divisions and a brigade that Longstreet brought, only Hood's division was present on the 19th, with McLaws's on the 20th, the artillery and the rest of the infantry not even having arrived at Atlanta.

32. Thomas's report; Granger's report, *O.R., 50,* 854–855; Thomas's report; Dana dispatches.

33. Crittenden and Negley court of inquiry, *O.R., 50,* 961; Porter Papers (unpublished), letter from Chattanooga, Oct. 3, 1863, to his sister.

34. *O.R., 50,* 78.

35. Dana dispatches.

36. Longstreet's report; Longstreet, *op. cit.* Halleck to Burnside, *O.R., 52,* 769; 760; *50,* 149.

37. Longstreet, *op. cit.*

When Brig-Gen. George Crook, in command of cavalry and mounted infantry that was observing the right bank of the Tennessee above Chattanooga, reported Wheeler's crossing to Rosecrans, the Federal commander, to his credit, directed Crook "to gather all the cavalry and mounted men and pursue the enemy." Crook's report (*O.R., 51,* 684) seems careful in the extreme, and gives confidence in the reliability of his account. It was not until Wheeler had destroyed many wagons at Anderson's Cross-Roads and had combined two columns and captured McMinnville that Crook closed upon his rear. It is notable that Wheeler does not record the strength of his command, though he says it was larger than Crook's. Crook, on the other hand, put his own strength at 3,500 effectives after he gained contact. He gives various reasons for his estimate of 5,000 or perhaps 6,000 men under Wheeler. There are discrepancies between Crook's and Wheeler's accounts of the clashes from the time the pursuit began and the time when Wheeler crossed the Tennessee near Muscle Shoals. Crook states explicitly that at Farmington his infantry charge broke through the enemy's line, "capturing four guns, some wagons, and several prisoners."

In the report that he wrote after superseding Rosecrans, Thomas states that a copy of Wheeler's report had been found, "in which he forgets to mention the loss of four of his guns at Farmington. His report is probably equally truthful in other respects"—a judgment that may be a little too severe (Thomas's report, *O.R., 51,* 664).

Other important Federal reports that can be laid alongside that of Wheeler are those by Mitchell, Col. E. M. McCook, and Col. Oscar H. La Grange (*ibid.,* 669; 675; 682).

Wheeler admits a heavy attack on his rear while engaged in destroying wagons in Anderson's Gap. From Colonel McCook's account it is clear that Wheeler was assailed briefly and skillfully by only two regiments, McCook's account being supported by a vivid story written by the artist-correspondent Theodore R. Davis, who claimed to have been present and who said that Wheeler narrowly escaped being sabered (*Harper's Weekly,* Vol. VII, No. 315, 1863, p. 690).

When Roddey crossed to the north bank of the Tennessee and sought to renew operations in the vicinity of Winchester, he too was assiduously pursued, despite his hit-and-run tactics, until he reached the area near Pulaski. Crook's statement as to what followed is particularly detailed and seems convincing. Wheeler's failure to recommend a repetition of a raid such as he had just completed is certainly full of significance.

In a rather frank preliminary report (*O.R., 51,* 666) written on Oct. 12th, Wheeler said that while most of his men had "fought nobly," others had "acted shamefully." He went on, "Many men were allowed by their officers to throw away their arms to enable them to bring out private plunder." Yet even in this report Wheeler said nothing about the four guns that one must believe Crook captured in his charge at Farmington. He spoke only of being compelled to abandon two guns because of his inability to haul them, as well as because of their poor condition, stating at the same time that he supposed the enemy would boast that he had captured them.

Wheeler strongly recommended the promotion of John T. Morgan and some other officers, stating that they were the type needed in such an operation as he had conducted.

An interesting and readable account of Wheeler's operations is given in Chap. V of John P. Dyer's *"Fightin' Joe" Wheeler.*

38. Hooker's report, *O.R., 51,* 712–713.

39. *O.R., 52,* 772; 944. In this letter Grant also reverted to his desire to strike some sort of blow at Mobile. The 16,500 men he had left to guard the river from Vicksburg to Bayou Sara were enough only for defense. Commenting upon his inability to exploit the Mobile situation, Grant concluded: "I do not say this complainingly, but simply regret that advantage cannot be taken of so fine an opportunity of dealing the enemy a heavy blow."

NOTES TO THE APPENDIX

1. *O.R., 25,* 100.

2. Unpublished letter from U. S. Grant to E. B. Washburne in the Illinois Historical Library, Springfield, Ill.:

"CORINTH, MISSISSIPPI
"July 22d, 1862

"HON. E. B. WASHBURNE,
"GALENA, ILL.

"DEAR SIR:

"Your letter of the 15th enclosing copy of a statement of the character and standing of Capt. Henry S. Fitch, Assistant Quartermaster, is just received. It seems to be supposed that I made or had something to do with the appointment of Capt. F.

"Such is not the case. Capt. Fitch was among the first appointments made by the President, in his Dept. after the breaking out of the War.

"On my taking command at Memphis I found him on duty there. If disposed I could not have removed him without charges and I knew of none against him.

"I am not responsible for the acts of Capt. Fitch further than the accounts of his that I may be called on to approve and the general duty to guard the public interest, in every particular, devolving upon me as commander.

"I am glad you called my attention to this matter. I never knew Capt. F. either personally or by reputation until I met him in Memphis.

"You will see by this letter that I am back again to this place. I was in hopes of another field, probably the taking of Vicksburg, but the call of Gen. Halleck to Washington made my recall necessary.

"I do not know the object of calling Gen. H. to Washington but if it is to make him Sec. of War, or Commander-in-Chief, Head Quarters at Washington, a better selection could not be made. He is a man of gigantic intellect and well studied in the profession of arms. He and I have had several little spats but I like and respect him nevertheless.

"I would have written you from Memphis but was kept very busy and know you are so, and besides I had nothing special to write about.

"All my staff are well. Hoping to hear from you frequently I remain

"Truly your friend
"U. S. GRANT"

3. *O.R., 58,* 259–261 (Sherman to Halleck).

4. *O.R., 109* (supplementary), 717 (Halleck to Sherman).

5. General Order No. 1, in *O.R., 8,* 476–478; *ibid.,* 695–697 (Proclamation to the People of Central and North Missouri); *109* (supplementary), 198 (Halleck to McClellan), and Sherman's *Memoirs,* I, 216; *O.R., 8,* 514 (Halleck to McClellan).

6. *Ibid.,* 508–509 (Halleck to McClellan); *7,* 120ff. (Halleck's report).

7. *O.R., 109* (supplementary), 211 (Halleck to Sherman); *ibid.,* 211ff. (Special Orders No. 140, to Steele, is typical); *7,* 593 (Halleck to Buell); *ibid.,* 585 (Buell to McClellan).

8. *O.R., 11,* 233 (Halleck to Buell), *et passim; 10,* 672ff. (Buell's report); *23,* 76–77 (Buell to Halleck); *11,* 275; *23,* 104 (Halleck to Buell); *ibid.,* 122–123 (Buell to Halleck). For further discussion of this matter, see *supra,* IV, Chap. II.

9. *O.R., 11,* 288; *22,* 9 (Halleck to Buell).

10. General Order 101, Aug. 11, 1862, in *War Department General Orders.*

11. *O.R., 24,* 156 (Halleck to Grant).

12. *O.R., 54,* 667 (Halleck to Grant).

13. *O.R., 58,* 40–42 (Halleck to Grant, marked "Confidential"); *ibid.,* 411–413 (Halleck to Grant).

14. Letter from Rawlins to Washburne:

"HEAD QU. MIL. DIV. OF THE MISS.
"NASHVILLE, TENN. Jany 20th 1864

"DEAR WASHBURNE

"On my return from the North I was pleased to find your very welcome and interesting letter of the 20th ult. and I hasten to assure you, your friendship for the General, your devotion to our common country and heroic manifestation of interest in the welfare and success of our army here, through evil as well as good report, in the dark hour of the Nation's despondency, as well as in the light of its victories, are truly and honestly appreciated, and to you, more than any one in Congress, the great heart of this Army warms with gratitude as its true representative and bold and uncompromising defender. So give yourself no concern in the matter of the Cavalry regiment you speak of, for the General fully understands your motives and knows them to be prompted solely by a desire for the public service and in friendship to him.

"I see by the papers the bill creating a Lieutenant General is still undisposed of. So far as General Grant may be regarded in connection with it, I can only say that if the confering of the distinguished honor upon him would be the taking him out of the field, or with a view to the superceding of General Halleck, he would not desire it, for he feels that if he can be of service to the Government in any place it is in command of the army in the field, and there is where he would remain if made a Lieut. General, besides he has great confidence and friendship for the General-in-Chief, and would without regard to rank be willing at all times to receive orders through him.

"The advocacy of the New York Herald and other papers of the General for the Presidency gives him little concern; he is unambitious for the honor and will voluntarily put himself in no position nor permit himself to be placed in one he can prevent that will in the slightest manner embarrass the friends of the Government in their present grand effort to enforce the rightful authority and restore the Union of the States. Of his views in this matter I suppose he has fully acquainted you.

"The presence of Longstreet in East Tennessee is much to be regretted. Had General Grant's orders been energetically, and with a broader judgement, executed by General Burnside, Longstreet would have been forced to have continued his retreat from Knoxville to beyond the Tennessee line. The General's official report will show the facts and orders and be satisfactory I have no doubt to the Government.

"Our forces in the Holsten Valley, east of Knoxville, have been compelled by Longstreet to fall back toward Knoxville. Whether he intends to again undertake the capture of that place, or simply to extend his forage ground, is not as yet known. In either design he must be foiled. Gen. Grant, Gen. W. F. Smith and myself go forward tomorrow to Chattanooga, that the General may be enabled to give his personal attention to affairs in the direction of Knoxville. Fred, the General's oldest son, is lying very sick at St. Louis with "typhoid Pneumonia" and he was intending to start to see him this morning but dispatches from Knoxville detained him and he turns in the direction of duty to his country, leaving his afflicted family to the care of friends. I am sorry I did not see you when in New York—there is much that I would have been pleased to tell you that one cannot write. When North, on the 23d day of December, 1863, at Danbury, Conn., I was married to Miss Mary E. Hurlbut, a native of that place and daughter of S. A. Hurlbut Esq. I first met her in Vicksburg, in the family at whose house we made Headquarters after the fall of the place. She was in the City during the entire Seige, having gone South with friends previous to the breaking out of the rebellion. From my acquaintance with her she was in favor of the Union and will instruct and educate my children in the spirit and sentiments of true patriotism that I hope will ever actuate them in the support and maintainance of the princely inheritance bequeathed us by our revolutionary fathers, and now being daily enhanced in value and increased in endearment by the sacrifices we are making for its preservation. She is now with my three little ones at the home of my parents near Galena. I saw few of my friends in Galena during my limited stay, having been there only about six hours of daylight. I had hoped to spend a week but detention East from snow prevented it. Galena was really lively and all seemed well. General Grant is in excellent health and is "himself" in all things. Col. Bowen, Maj. Rowley, & all send their regards to you. General Wilson has been ordered to Washington to take charge of the Cavalry Bureau. He is a brave and accomplished young officer and has rendered valuable service in the field. I hope he may be successful in his new duties and bespeak for him your kind offices of friendship. I met Russell Jones in Chicago and he had me go to see the Antrobus [Horn?] paintings of the General. They are both very fine and the full size one I regard as the finest likeness I ever saw. I am no judge of paintings but I examined this one closely and compared it in my own mind with the General & pronounced it like him and since my return I have looked at and watched the General with interest and compared him with the picture and am sure he is like it.

"Hoping to hear from you soon, I remain

"Your Friend

"JNA A RAWLINS"

"To.
"Hon. E. B. Washburne, M.C.
"Washington, D.C."

15. General Order No. 98, March 12, 1864, in *War Department General Orders;* Hitchcock, *Fifty Years in Camp and Field,* p. 464.

16. *O.R., 71,* 15 (two dispatches); 16 (Grant to Meade, and Meade to Grant); 33, 60 (Grant to Halleck); 135 (Halleck to Grant, Grant to Meade, Meade to Grant).

17. *Ibid.,* 192; 223.

18. *Ibid.,* 192; 221–222; 225–226; 226; 264; 222 (Grant to Halleck).

19. *Ibid.,* 81 (West to Halleck); 196 (Halleck to West).

BIBLIOGRAPHY

(Only works quoted or cited as authority)

Agassiz, George R., ed., *Meade's Headquarters, 1863–1865: Letters of Colonel Theodore Lyman*. Boston, Atlantic Monthly, 1922.

Badeau, Adam, *Military History of Ulysses S. Grant, from April, 1861, to April, 1865* (3 vols.). New York, Appleton, 1881.

Bannerman, Francis, and Sons, Catalogue of (1949).

B. and L. See next entry.

Battles and Leaders of the Civil War, Robert V. Johnson and C. C. Buel, eds. New York, Century, 1884–1888.

Beatty, John, *Memoirs of a Volunteer,* Harvey S. Ford, ed. New York, Norton, 1946.

Black, Robert C., III, *The Railroads of the Confederacy.* Chapel Hill, University of North Carolina Press, 1952.

Brown, Dee Alexander, *Grierson's Raid.* Urbana, University of Illinois Press, 1954.

Buckeridge, Justin O., *Lincoln's Choice.* Harrisburg, Pa., Stackpole, 1956.

Catton, Bruce, *This Hallowed Ground.* Garden City, N.Y., Doubleday, 1956.

Chicago Tribune.

Cist, Henry M., *The Army of the Cumberland* (Vol. VII of *Campaigns of the Civil War*). New York, Scribner, 1883.

———, "Comments on General Grant's 'Chattanooga,'" in *B. and L.,* III, 717–718.

Civil War History. Iowa City, State University of Iowa, 1955—.

C.C.W. Report of the Committee on the Conduct of the War, Senate Document, 37th Congress, 3rd Session, 1862–1863, Vol. IV.

Connelley, William Elsey, *Quantrill and the Border Wars.* Cedar Rapids, Iowa, The Torch Press, 1910.

Coulter, E. Merton, *The Confederate States of America, 1861–1865* (Vol. VII of *A History of the South,* W. H. Stevenson and E. M. Coulter, eds.). Baton Rouge, Louisiana State University Press, 1950.

Cramer, Jesse Grant, ed., *Letters of Ulysses S. Grant to His Father and His Youngest Sister, 1857–1878.* New York, Putnam, 1912.

D.A.B. See Dictionary.

Dana, Charles A., *Recollections of the Civil War.* New York, Appleton, 1899.

———, and James H. Wilson, *The Life of Ulysses S. Grant, General of the Armies of the United States.* Springfield, Mass., Bill, 1868.

Deaderick, Barron, *Strategy in the Civil War.* Harrisburg, Pa., The Military Service Publishing Company, 1946.

Dictionary of American Biography. New York, Scribner, 1928–1936, 1948.

Dowdey, Clifford, *Experiment in Rebellion.* Garden City, N.Y., Doubleday, 1946.

Duke, Basil W., *Morgan's Cavalry.* New York and Washington, Neale, 1909.

Dyer, Frederick H., *A Compendium of the War of the Rebellion.* Des Moines, Dyer, 1908.

Dyer, John P., *"Fightin' Joe" Wheeler.* Baton Rouge, Louisiana State University Press, 1941.

Eaton, Clement, *A History of the Southern Confederacy.* New York, Macmillan, 1954.

Eaton, John, *Grant, Lincoln and the Freedmen: Reminiscences of the Civil War.* New York, Longmans, Green, 1907.

Encyclopaedia Britannica.

Eskew, Garnett L., *Willard's of Washington.* New York, Coward, 1954.

F(ield) M(anual) 100–5: Field Service Regulations—Operations. Washington, Government Printing Office, 1944.

Freeman, Douglas Southall, *Lee's Lieutenants* (3 vols.). New York, Scribner, 1942–1944.

Fuller, J. F. C., *The Generalship of Ulysses S. Grant.* Bloomington, Indiana University Press, 1958.

Fullerton, Joseph S., "The Army of the Cumberland at Chattanooga," in *B. and L.,* III, 719–726.

Garwood, Darrell, *Crossroads of America.* New York, Norton, 1948.

Govan, Gilbert E, and James W. Livingood, *A Different Valor, the Story of General Joseph E. Johnston, C.S.A.* Indianapolis, Bobbs-Merrill, 1956.

Gracie, Archibald, *The Truth About Chickamauga.* Boston, Houghton Mifflin, 1911.

Grant, Jesse R., *In the Days of My Father General Grant.* New York, Harper, 1925.

Grant, Ulysses S., *Personal Memoirs of U. S. Grant* (2 vols.). New York, Webster, 1885.

———, Headquarters Papers of (63 vols.). MS. Collection, Library of Congress (received in 1953 from Maj. Gen. U. S. Grant 3rd).

———, "Chattanooga," in *B. and L.*, III, 679–711.

Greene, Francis V., *The Mississippi* (Vol. VIII of *The Campaigns of the Civil War*). New York, Scribner, 1884.

Guderian, Heinz, *Panzer Leader* (abridged edition). New York, Ballantine, *n.d.*

Halleck, Henry W., *Elements of Military Art and Science, etc.* New York, Appleton, 1846.

Harper's Weekly.

Harrington, Fred Harvey, *Fighting Politician: Major General N. P. Banks.* Philadelphia, University of Pennsylvania Press; and London, Oxford University Press, 1948.

Henderson, (Col.) George Francis Robert, *Stonewall Jackson and the American Civil War.* London and New York, Longmans, Green, 1936.

Henry, Robert Selph, *"First with the Most" Forrest.* Indianapolis, Bobbs-Merrill, 1944.

———, *The Story of the Confederacy.* New York, Grosset & Dunlap, 1931; and Indianapolis, Bobbs-Merrill, 1936.

Hitchcock, (Maj. Gen.) Ethan Allen, *Fifty Years in Camp and Field, Diary of Major General Ethan Allen Hitchcock.* New York and London, Putnam, 1909.

Holland, Cecil F., *Morgan and His Raiders: A Biography of the Confederate General.* New York, Macmillan, 1942.

Horn, Stanley F., *The Army of Tennessee.* Indianapolis, Bobbs-Merrill, 1941; Norman, University of Oklahoma Press, 1953.

Humphreys, Andrew A., *The Virginia Campaign of '64 and '65.* New York, Scribner, 1883.

Indiana Magazine of History.

Irwin, Richard B., *History of the Nineteenth Army Corps.* New York, Putnam, 1892.

———, "The Capture of Port Hudson," in *B. and L.*, III, 586–598.

Joffre, Marshal, *Memoirs.*

Johnston, Joseph E., *Narrative of Military Operations.* New York, Appleton, 1874.

King, Charles, *The True Ulysses S. Grant.* Philadelphia, Lippincott, 1914.

Lewis, Charles L., *David Glasgow Farragut: Our First Admiral.* Annapolis, United States Naval Institute, 1943.

Lewis, Lloyd, *Sherman, Fighting Prophet.* New York, Harcourt, Brace, 1932.

Liddell Hart, B. H., *Strategy, the Indirect Approach.* New York, Praeger, 1954.

Lincoln, Abraham, *Collected Works of Abraham Lincoln* (8 vols. and index), Roy P. Basler, ed. New Brunswick, Rutgers University Press, 1953–1955.

Lincoln, Robert Todd, MS. Collection in Library of Congress.

Livermore, Thomas L., *Numbers and Losses in the Civil War in America, 1861–65*. Bloomington, Indiana University Press, 1957.

Logan, Herschel C., *Cartridges*. Harrisburg, Pa., Stackpole (*n.d.*, but in print).

Longstreet, James, *From Manassas to Appomattox: Memoirs of the Civil War in America*. Philadelphia, Lippincott, 1896.

Lyman, Theodore. See Agassiz, George R., ed.

Mahan, Alfred T., *The Gulf and Inland Waters* (Vol. III of *The Navy in the Civil War*). New York, Scribner, 1883.

Mende, Elsie Porter, in collaboration with Henry Greenleaf Pearson, *An American Soldier and Diplomat: Horace Porter*. New York, Stokes, 1927.

Meredith, Roy, *Mr. Lincoln's Camera Man, Mathew B. Brady*. New York, Scribner, 1946.

Missouri Historical Society Collections

Mitchell, (Lt. Col.) Joseph B., *Decisive Battles of the Civil War*. New York, Putnam, 1955.

Monaghan, Jay, *Civil War on the Western Border, 1854–1865*. Boston, Little, Brown, 1955.

Moore, Albert Burton, *Conscription and Conflict in the Confederacy*. New York, Macmillan, 1924.

National Cyclopaedia of American Biography. New York, J. T. White, 1893–1956.

Nevins, Allan, *The Ordeal of the Union* (2 vols.). New York, Scribner, 1947.

New Orleans Daily True Delta.

New Orleans Louisiana Deutsch Zeitung.

New York Herald.

New York Times.

New York Tribune.

New York World.

Nichols, Alice, *Bleeding Kansas*. New York, Oxford University Press, 1954.

Nicolay, John G., and John Hay, *Abraham Lincoln: A History* (10 vols.). New York, Century, 1890.

O'Flaherty, Daniel, *General Jo Shelby, Undefeated Rebel*. Chapel Hill, University of North Carolina Press, 1954.

O.R. See *War of the Rebellion.*

O.R. Navies. See next entry.

Official Records of the Union and Confederate Navies in the War of the Rebellion. Washington, Government Printing Office, 1894–1927.

Parks, Joseph H., *General Edmund Kirby Smith, C.S.A.* Baton Rouge, Louisiana State University Press, 1954.

Phisterer, Frederick, *Statistical Record of the Armies of the United States* (supplementary volume of *Campaigns of the Civil War*). New York, Scribner, 1883.

Plum, William R., *The Military Telegraph During the Civil War in the United States, with an Exposition of Ancient and Modern Means of Communication, and of the Federal and Confederate Cypher Systems; also a Running Account of the War Between the States.* Chicago, Jansen, McClurg, 1882.

Polk, William M., *Leonidas Polk, Bishop and General* (2 vols.), new edition. New York, Longmans, Green, 1915.

Porter, Horace, Papers of. MS. Collection in the Library of Congress.

———, *Campaigning with Grant.* New York, Century, 1897.

Pratt, Fletcher, *Civil War on Western Waters.* New York, Holt, 1956.

Register of Graduates and Former Cadets. West Point, U.S. Military Academy, 1948.

Richardson, Albert D., *The Secret Service, the Field, the Dungeon, and the Escape.* Hartford, Conn., American Publishing Co., 1865.

———, *Personal History of Ulysses S. Grant.* Hartford, Conn., American Publishing Co., 1868.

Richmond Examiner.

Roach, Alva C., *The Prisoner of War.* Indianapolis, Railroad City Publishing House, 1865.

Sandburg, Carl, *Abraham Lincoln: The War Years* (4 vols.). New York, Harcourt, Brace, 1939.

Sanger, Donald Bridgman, and Thomas Robson Hay, *James Longstreet.* Baton Rouge, Louisiana State University Press, 1952.

Schofield, John M., *Forty-six Years in the Army.* New York, Century, 1897.

Senate Executive Journal.

Sheridan, Philip H., *Personal Memoirs of P. H. Sheridan, General United States Army* (2 vols.). New York, Webster, 1888.

Sherman, William T., *Memoirs of William T. Sherman.* Two vols. in one. New edition, with Foreword by B. H. Liddell Hart. Bloomington, Indiana University Press, 1957.

Shields, Joseph W., *From Flintlock to M 1.* New York, Coward, 1954.

Smith, W. F., "Comments on General Grant's 'Chattanooga,' " and "Postscript," in *B. and L.*, III, 714–717, and 718.

Snead, Thomas L., "The Conquest of Arkansas," in *B. and L.*, III, 441–459.

Steele, Matthew F., *American Campaigns.* Washington, Combat Forces Press, 1951.

War Department General Orders.

War of the Rebellion: Official Records of the Union and Confederate Armies. Washington, Government Printing Office, 1882–1900.

Washburne, Elihu B., Papers of. MS. Collection in the Library of Congress.

Washington Evening Star.

Washington National Intelligencer.

Washington National Republican.

Welles, Gideon, *Diary of Gideon Welles* (3 vols.). Boston, Houghton Mifflin, 1911.

Werstein, Irving, *July, 1863.* New York, Julian Messner, Inc., 1957.

Who Was Who in America, Vol. I. Chicago, A. N. Marquis, 1943.

Williams, George Washington, *A History of the Negro Troops in the Rebellion, 1861–1865.* New York, Harper, 1888.

Williams, Samuel C., *General John Wilder, Commander of the Lightning Brigade.* Bloomington, Indiana University Press, 1936.

Wilson, James Grant, *General Grant.* New York, Appleton, 1900.

———, *General Grant's Letters to a Friend, 1861–1880.* New York, Crowell, 1897.

———, *The Life and Public Services of Ulysses Simpson Grant.* New York, DeWitt, 1885.

Wilson, James Harrison, *The Life of John A. Rawlins.* New York, Neale, 1916.

Wood, W. Birkbeck, and J. E. Edmonds, *A History of the Civil War in the United States, 1861–5.* New York, Putnam, 1905.

INDEX

Ranks shown are the highest held in connection with mention in this volume. The abbreviation C.S. denotes civil as well as military officers of the Confederate States. A hyphen is used between nonconsecutive page numbers to indicate scattered references to the subject as well as continuous treatment. No references are made to the notes.

March 9, 1864

General Grant

The nation's appreciation of what you have done, and its reliance upon you for what remains to do, in the existing great struggle, are now presented with this commission, constituting you Lieutenant General in the Army of the United States. With this high honor devolves upon you also, a corresponding responsibility. As the country herein trusts you, so, under God, it will sustain you. I scarcely need to add that with what I here speak for the nation goes my own hearty personal concurrence.

The original of the speech made by President Lincoln at the White House on March 9, 1864,